D1569196

Following the Wrong God Home

LITERATURE OF THE AMERICAN WEST
WILLIAM KITTREDGE, GENERAL EDITOR

Following the Wrong God Home

Footloose in an American Dream

CLIVE SCOTT CHISHOLM

UNIVERSITY OF OKLAHOMA PRESS • NORMAN

Flagstaff Public Library
Flagstaff. Arizona

This book is published with the generous assistance of The Kerr Foundation, Inc.

Library of Congress Cataloging-in-Publication Data

Chisholm, Clive Scott, 1936–
Following the wrong god home: footloose in an American dream / Clive Scott Chisholm.
p.   cm. — (Literature of the American West; v. 12)
Includes bibliographical references and index.
ISBN 0-8061-3488-7 (alk. paper)
1. West (U.S.)—Description and travel.   2. Mormon Pioneer National Historic
Trail—Description and travel.   3. West (U.S.)—History, Local.   4. Frontier
and pioneer life—West (U.S.).   5. Mormon pioneers—West (U.S.)—History.
6. West (U.S.)—Biography.   7. Chisholm, Clive Scott, 1936—Journeys—West (U.S.).
8. Canadians—West (U.S.) Biography.   9. Walking—West (U.S.).   I. Title.   II. Series.
F595.3 .C48 2003
978—dc21
2002067524

Following the Wrong God Home: Footloose in an American Dream is
Volume 12 in the Literature of the American West series.

The paper in this book meets the guidelines for permanence and durability of the
Committee on Production Guidelines for Book Longeivty of the Council on Library
Resources, Inc. ∞

Copyright © 2003 by the University of Oklahoma Press, Norman, Publishing Division of
the University. All rights reserved. Manufactured in the U.S.A.

1   2   3   4   5   6   7   8   9   10

PS
178
C542f

For

Sean Mitchell Chisholm

1963–1988

"Short life, hard trail"

and for

Linda, Caitlin, Christopher, and Finn

The dream is a lie, but the dreaming is true.

ROBERT PENN WARREN

If you don't know the kind of person I am,

and I don't know the kind of person you are,

a pattern that others made may prevail in the world,

and following the wrong god home we may miss our star.

WILLIAM STAFFORD, "A RITUAL

TO READ TO EACH OTHER"

Contents

Acknowledgments

Following the Wrong God Home belongs to the American Dreamers I met on the road to Salt Lake City whose stories and generosity to a displaced Canadian made the writing of this book possible. I was moved daily by the kindnesses of extraordinary Americans, many of whom invited me to dinner, offered a spare bedroom, and shared their stories while putting up with the bent edges of mine. I'm indebted to my wife, Linda, and my family for patience and perseverance over the long haul it took to finish what came to be called, in Chisholm family lore, "The Book Everlasting."

Others who encouraged my writing and read parts of or all the manuscript with bare-knuckle criticism were Martin Naparsteck and Chris Chester. Chris Chester's blinders-free reading of the first draft and his tactful comments improved a style that owed less to narrative than long-winded commentary, and, as with Martin Naparsteck, the candor of a long-term friendship led to constant conversation about writing and its demands.

Dawn Marano, acquisitions editor at the University of Utah Press, believed enough in the book to offer a contract and to devote three years of insightful editorial support and encouragement. On the eve of the book's production, a director at the press found *Following the Wrong God Home* too hot to handle in a state where both the legislature and university funding are controlled, disproportionately, by the state's dominant religion. "I'm not going to fall on my sword for this one," he said. But Dawn Marano's elegant suggestions and track marks are all over the book.

I'm also grateful to the editors of gutsy Signature Books in Salt Lake City for offering the book another contract and a second chance to be published in the Beehive State. But *Following the Wrong God Home* needed a home outside Utah's borders and finally found one, thanks to Daniel Simon and the staff of the University of Oklahoma Press. Copyediting as an art form was supplied by John Mulvihill, for which I'm in his debt.

Also, I salute the Osage for putting me on a good red road, for his infectious talent, his comradeship over the years, and the pleasure of his company on many journeys together. His sage advice, "Proceed as the way opens," became a mantra for me. During the writing of the book we fell out for a while, but we got over the rough spots.

Lastly, I acknowledge the Mormon people for their version of the American Dream. Although we may not share the same Dream, be it Dream at all, I trust we share humor and compassion for our differences. Whatever God I followed across their trail to Promised Land, it was the wrong God for me. The God they follow seems right for them.

Following the Wrong God Home

Prologue

"What have we here?" he asked the woman.
   "Ah," she said, "he comes from somewhere away. A poor devil who is walking the world."

   LAURIE LEE, *AS I WALKED OUT*
   ONE MIDSUMMER MORNING

I have had my health tolerable well so far and am in no ways discouraged but no man knows anything of the trip until he tryes it it is attended with so much phatigue and danger that a man knows not of until he has had some experience.

   G. W. CRANE, FIVE HUNDRED MILES
   FROM NO PLACE, JUNE 17, 1849

One night in early July 1985, in what seemed the exact middle of no place, I gave up the American Dream. I was lying with my head out of a small mountain tent, looking up at a scrim of stars, when it drifted away. Forty-nine, I was pressing the edge of a walker's luck, averaging twelve miles a day while seeking an accommodation with American land, its people, its memories, and, especially, its Dream. Alone on a remote section of Wyoming's Sweetwater River, I'd arrived at a high point in the geography of out-of-touch.

   To tell the truth, I hadn't been doing much American Dreaming. For seventy-two days I'd followed a nineteenth-century emigrant trail from the Missouri River, pondering Dream's possibilities, tracing an exodus that took 143 men and boys, 3 women, and 2 children beyond the boundaries of the United States in search of a homeland. As their leader said, "If there is a place on this earth that nobody else wants, that's the place I'm hunting for." I was certain they weren't

WYOMING

SOUTH DAKOTA

NEBRASKA

Dr. Steven Combs
Steve Senteny

Elfriede and "Pepper" Martin
Opal Lambhere

Pauline Cunningham
"The Osage"

The Dunns

Buddy and Babe Brisco
Ellis Countryman

Jim Amos

Lake McConaughy

Nellie Snyder Yost
"Buffalo Bill"
The Sillasens

Betty Menke

Barbara Yoder
Dallas Coder

Mitchell
Scottsbluff

Chimney Rock

Broadwater

Ash Hollow

North Platte

Gothenburg

100th meridian

Cozad

Hendee Hotel

South Platte R.

COLORADO

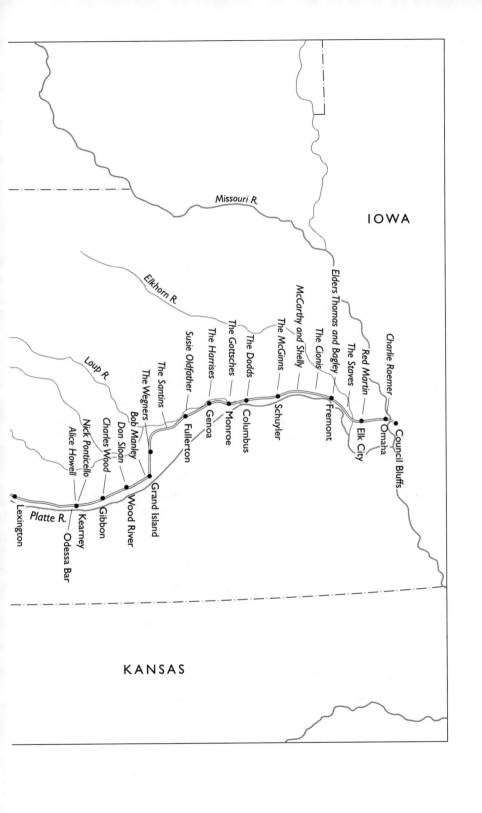

IOWA

KANSAS

Missouri R.

Elkhorn R.

Loup R.

Platte R.

Council Bluffs
Omaha
Charlie Roemer
Elk City
Red Martin
The Staves
Elders Thomas and Bagley
The Cionis
McCarthy and Shelly
Fremont
The McGinns
Schuyler
The Dodds
Columbus
The Gottsches
Monroe
The Harrises
Genoa
Susie Oldfather
Fullerton
The Santins
The Wegners
Bob Manley
Don Sloan
Grand Island
Charles Wood
Wood River
Nick Ponticello
Gibbon
Alice Howell
Kearney
Lexington
Odessa Bar

dreaming at the time. They were awake and struggling for survival: the United States had shown them the door. On June 24, 1847, they halted for the night close to my camp, forming a semicircle of wagons. Then, as now, the river was "three rods wide . . . and very cool" with "plenty of willow bushes for fuel."

That day, I'd walked over twenty miles through sand, sagebrush, and furnace heat toting a thirty-pound backpack. In a landscape to swell the eye and stagger the heart, I doused myself in one of the most generous streams of American history. I stumbled into camp dragging the Dream behind me and walked out next morning dreamless and alert.

• • •

By eastern standards, the Sweetwater River is little more than a gravel-bottomed stream, desolate but for a fringe of scrub willow lining its banks. By western standards, it was a miracle. Without it, the flood of nineteenth-century emigrants would have hobbled or choked on sand or poisoned water before reaching South Pass and the Continental Divide in the shadow of the Wind River Mountains. Beyond that lay a vast track of semiexplored Mexican territory known to them only as "Oregon."

Oregon was an ignis fatuus advertised as America's "Manifest Destiny"—the equivalent of Promised Land or the American Dream-of-the-Month. The term appeared first in the *Democratic Review* in 1845, riding a braying ass of snake-oil journalism—a slogan dreamed up by a reporter named John L. O'Sullivan. To the Yankee journalist, it was "our manifest destiny to overspread the continent allotted by Providence for the free development of our yearly multiplying millions." If *God* was on O'Sullivan's side, *free* punched the national hot button.

Over 650,000 Americans headed west to "Oregon" over the next three decades. In 1848, when gold was discovered in California, thousands hit the Yellow Brick Road. (The average "strike" by any "argonaut" in 1849 was two hundred and fifty dollars.) By 1850, O'Sullivan's manifesto had become de facto national policy, if not a quasi-religious mandate. Blowhard senators like Missouri's Thomas Hart Benton pumped Manifest Destiny to fever pitch. People left farms, homes, and families for a stake in the West; American and European emigrants hauled their baggage—political, cultural, religious—overland to a Brave New World.

The continent was crossed for trade with China. For beaver. For God. For gold. For buffalo. For buffalo bones and, finally, to fill its spaces, lay it out and own it. Mile by mile, it was carved to fit a fear of anything not ordered, platted, or drawn in straight lines on a map, and as when we butcher the proverbial pig, we seem unable to rest until even its squeal is used up. But in 1847, the humorist Josh

Billings saw through the false advertising: "Thar is such a thing as manifest destiny," he wrote, "but like the number of rings on a rakoon's tail, ov no great consequence only for ornament." The American Dream is one of its recent gimcrack decorations.

Robert Louis Stevenson described the dark side of American Dreaming in 1879. As he rattled out of Omaha on the Union Pacific Railroad, bound for San Francisco, his fellow passengers hailed from Virginia, Pennsylvania, Iowa, Kansas, Maine, and New York. Talk "ran upon hard times, short commons, and the hope that moves ever Westward." As the train steamed across the plains, Stevenson noted: "We were continually passing other emigrant trains upon the journey east . . . as crowded as our own. Passengers ran on the platform and cried to us through the windows, in a kind of wailing chorus, to 'Come back!'" In their wailing, Stevenson isolated the American fever: "We are a race of gypsies, and love change and travel for themselves."

• • •

Like the rings on the raccoon's tail, my lot in life had grown ornamental—an insinuation of acquisitiveness and consumption. Something had gone badly wrong. My kids were walking billboards for Nike, Coca-Cola, Pepsi, or whatever rock band was the rage of the week—metamorphosing into a near mindless conformity. American Dreams were sold in air-conditioned temples called "malls." My professional life was a roller-coaster ride of frustration. Worse, I'd lost my Canadian identity, living as an interloper in a borrowed country. I wanted out. So I borrowed a journey from one people's search for "homeland" and went to see for myself if something was out there that could jump-start my life again—some older, more functional engine of imagination, hope, and community.

In January, I bought a backpack. For three months it shone iridescent blue from the cave of my closet. All winter I filled it with fear. Late in March, I spread its contents over the floor of my cabin in the New York woods and counted coup on my old enemy, indecision. I would leave in April, I said, as they had done when the plains were free of snow and the grasses green enough to feed horses, oxen, and cattle. An airline ticket, snug in its envelope, glared at me from my desk. My wife looked warily at my on-the-road stuff. Dream gear.

"Enough is never enough," she said. "Hit the road."

Two weeks later, I did.

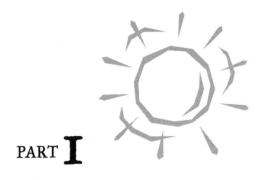

PART **I**

Sailing the Coast of Nebraska

I

Solvitur ambulando *(The problem is solved by walking around.)*

This city . . . we called 'Winter Quarters.' . . . Many hundreds
were laid in the silent grave, to rest from their sufferings and toil.
ORSON PRATT

I stood in front of the Mormon Trail Auto Parts store (now gone) with Charlie
Roemer (now dead) a few miles north of Omaha, watching three red-tailed hawks
riding updrafts over the Missouri River half a block away—a day muggy as a
sauna. April 14, 1985. Charlie was somnolent after a three-egg omelet, five cups of
coffee, and a grab-yo-ass smile from a green-eyed, red-headed waitress at Joe's
Diner on Thirtieth Street. Jerry Feagins, owner of the auto parts emporium, eased
onto the street and joined us, eyes following the hawks' lazy circles, face skewed to
curious as if we knew something he didn't. It was a day of new beginnings, sun-
crushed and mysterious as the glaze on a Hopi pot.

"Some power called 'em up," Charlie said, watching the whirling raptors.
"Maybe the Osage done it."

The Osage was a mutual friend, a man trying to fit into a recently resurrected
Native American heritage like a government- school Indian squirming in a too-
tight white man's suit, a man of abundant words and even more abundant
notions, a journey-ridden road warrior, a man of magical possibilities and short
temper. He'd talked Charlie into driving me to Omaha.

"Just like him to put on a show," I said.

Two days before, the Osage had led the way on a ten-mile walk along the Atchi-
son, Topeka, and Santa Fe Railroad below the Missouri River bluffs—a day of
high clouds and pale sun. Deep in the Show Me State, we headed upriver to look

at fading pictographs first noted by Lewis and Clark in 1802, including "a naming sign," he said, a rising summer moon. All afternoon, his eyes flashed like sunlight on mica. On the walk, he'd summoned up an owl that stared at us from a perfect oval in a limestone cliff, a bird of prophecy.

Now the owl's shadow was on Charlie; three cigarette butts, one for each hawk, lay on the sidewalk, and we'd been there less than twenty minutes. Charlie's face had already begun to take on skeletal essentials, and when he laughed, which he did frequently, it was hollow, like an echo inside bone. When he smiled, it was the grin of skulls. He saw me frowning at the butts.

"Just nervous," he said, fumbling for a fourth unfiltered cigarette. "If you want, I can get a note from my mother."

Feagins, who started his Mormon Trail Auto Parts business because its name came to him in a dream in 1982, handed me an orange Day-Glo baseball cap with the store's logo emblazoned on it—a hat to startle a blind bat at midnight. "Doesn't hurt to advertise," he said.

Day-Glo orange contrasted alarmingly with my shimmering royal blue backpack. It had already been a day of unexpected contrasts (heat was rising too fast for mid-April, and my fast break from New York was turning into a slow start). Charlie was flaking and peeling from heat, jacket and sweater draped over one arm, a look of no-cold-beer-since-yesterday tattooed on his face. As I looked toward the corner of 30th and State, my feet began sweating inside their leather casings—Frankensteinian footwear that the Osage had dubbed "the Karloffs."

"If you make Salt Lake City in those things," he said in his best grouser's voice, dancing around me like a rooster in a pit, hooting with native glee, "I'll buy you the best dinner in the city."

At worst, the Osage is cocksure and infuriating, a word-spurred bantam ready for any dustup. At best, he has an uncanny eye for detail, so, without taking a step, I knew he was right about the boots. Pissed me off. Metamorphosing himself into a new name, he'd managed to turn himself into a shaman in the bargain. I could see him sniggering through his smoky beard, living dead center in Missouri's heartland, with his native third eye sizing up the startup scene as I began a thousand-mile journey on what I hoped was the good red road.

"Game time," Charlie said, glancing at his watch and snuffing another smoke under his shoe.

I hefted the pack. Seventy pounds. I struggled to cinch the waist belt, sucking gut until its metal buckle bit and the pack settled its weight on my hips. Next door, where Zesto's was doing unexpected April business, folks who'd bellied up for root beer, sundaes, cones, and shakes, tongues slurpy, gawked at a middle-aged man festooned in yuppie sporting goods. With solemnity and a half-assed embarrassed grin, Charlie handed me a 4 foot 7 inch cottonwood walking stick handmade by the Osage for my journey, its haft decorated with the sacred circle and the four roads of the Plains Indians, each painted red for good luck. He'd cut the stick on a trip we'd taken to the Black Hills the year before. "Power wood," he called it.

Crafty is closer to the mark.

Born a trickster, he knows that a walking stick leads the way. Like an uninvited leg, something of his Osage making would reach the end of the journey ahead of me. To spite him, I named it "Roadmaker" after an *Omaha* chief. When I fisted it too tightly, it sent a spasm up my arm. Spooked, I put on the Day-Glo hat to cover my encroaching baldness and shook hands with Jerry Feagins.

"Y'look like a refrigerator on stumps," he opined too loudly. "Kind of in technicolor."

Some rube at Zesto's laughed. I thought about staring him down, but couldn't; pivoting was painful. When I glanced footward, the pack's waist belt was out of sight, overhung with belly. At that moment, I expected Charlie to genuflect or say something bordering on scriptural, maybe "Go with God," since he'd once flipped a light plane, crashed in a Milan, Missouri, cow pasture, and walked away so smitten by his unexpected salvation that, for a time, he became a stump preacher.

"Curiosity is the essence of walking," John Hillaby says. "If you don't know what's around the corner, then for God's sake, no matter what the weather is, get around the corner and get a new view on life." Scripture enough for me. I walked to get a handle on the illusions that seemed to make up American Dreaming. To do it, I planned to follow in old footsteps, taking the journey of a self-styled "peculiar people" to their Dream's end. I was thinking of this when all three hawks disappeared beyond the trees, tailing east toward Council Bluffs.

"Good day for beginnings," I lied.

"Took the words out'a my mouth," Charlie replied, focusing my camera, looking at me through its tiny lens, the way I imagined God saw creation since any larger view would only be discouraging. Then, as if to reassure me, a lone hawk returned, circling directly overhead.

That was the Osage's doing. I swear it. After all, he'd talked me into it. I'd tried to give the journey to him, more grist for his talent to grind. He refused. "It's yours to do," he said. "That is, if there's enough Canadian left in you." I wasn't sure, but given to omens, I stepped down hard on the Cornhusker State, power underfoot.

Click. I began at shutterspeed.

Click. What can I say about that first step?

Click. 2,177,141 to go?

Done with photography, Charlie called after me. "You got it wrong, Bud. The count begins with *left* . . . then *right*."

• • •

It was a journey born in pain. In June 1846, after a bruising winter trek from the Mississippi River across "the big mud hole" of Iowa, they settled along the west bank of the Missouri River in rough-hewn log hovels and "sod caves," making do with short rations and trying to keep downwind of a stinking, mosquito-infested slough that festered at river's edge. By July, when malaria set in, they began burying the dead on a ridge above the camp in a makeshift cemetery hugging a lip of prairie. By early fall, thirty-five hundred refugees had swarmed into the encampment, give or take a handful. Squatted illegally on Indian land, they played a bad hand straight, making quick treaties for water and timber with the Otoe and with Big Elk, chief of the Omaha. They wanted no trouble and got none.

In August, they began dying in earnest, keeping it up all summer and fall. A visitor to the camp, Thomas Kane, remembered women "in the open tents keeping the flies off their dead children." As cold weather set in, malaria eased, but it was soon followed by "bilious fevers," "the shaking ague," and a "strange scorbutic" called "Black Canker." The last began with pain in the toes and ankles, spread upward, swelling tissue as it climbed, addling the blood until the limbs turned black; the flesh softened and fell away. Gums and fingers were eaten by it. Scurvy.

Throughout the winter, the scourge ravaged on. Tuberculosis, measles, pneumonia, and "dropsy" were added to the list of deadly illnesses. In December, when the ground froze a foot deep, diggers and pallbearers made several climbs daily to the icy prairie above the town. If you had cash, a burial cost $1.50, a coffin $3.50. Nobody knows for sure how many died, but in April, when they pulled up stakes and moved on, an estimated five hundred and fifty were under the sod—Nebraska's first permanent white residents. Half were children under the age of nine. With Yankee matter-of-factness, their leader named the place "Winter Quarters," but it was commonly known in grief as "Misery Bottoms." Thomas Bullock said it best: "I wod rather die chewg a root, than lie bleaching on the banks of this river."

• • •

At the corner of 30th and State, when I began climbing toward the old burying ground, my pocket compass came to its true point and promise: *West.*

FOLLOWING THE WRONG GOD HOME

Halfway up the hill, I stopped and looked back, trying to imagine Thomas Kane's August "ooze by the water's edge . . . which stank in the sun like a naked mussel shoal," or James Linn's "choking crowd of . . . sedgy grasses" with curtains of mosquitoes rising from "half-buried carrion and yellow pools of what the children called frog's spawn." But hell wouldn't come clear. I closed my eyes and inhaled, hoping studied memories of 1847 might conjure a trace of smoke from the eight hundred daub-and-wattle chimneys that cast a gray, choking pall over ruts frozen two feet deep in the mud of that wet, fatal fall. Then I tried conjuring death's remnants, like shard, being hauled up this track to last rest. No such luck.

That afternoon, sun lay on the Florence city park where mothers once brushed flies from their children's corpses and where ague-ridden Barnes Pratt "shook till it appeared my very bones were pulverized. I wept, I prayed, I besought the Lord to have mercy on me." A triangle of boys tossed a ball in loopy arcs over cropped, green grass, each toss cutting through Pratt's invisible history. A car labored up the asphalt, crept slowly past, Charlie's skeletal face leering, one hand raised in a high five. I read his lips: "Left, right. Left, right."

• • •

"Birdseed," Bob Harpster said the night before while guarding the Weber Mill and Elevator Company against strangers. Although you wouldn't guess it driving by, the Weber Mill and Elevator is a shrine. Bob and his father, Ernie, who own the business, would like to forget it. In the middle of a working day, occasional tours are "a pain in the ass."

Standing on the loading dock, Bob had the look of an aggrieved owner's son, unaware that our encounter hung on a ghost story and I wanted to summon the dead to the evening shift. In yellow, mote-filled light from a 100-watt bulb, Harpster and his skeleton crew hefted fat, grain-plumped sacks through the shadows, past phantoms in the adze-gnawed beams and the spaces between. The last rope-drive grain shaker in America rackety-racked in the background, grading cracked corn into "fines and cobs" for the state's poultry. Like a sagging rural patriarch, the oldest working gristmill west of the Mississippi grumbled on in a nineteenth-century voice. Of the eight hundred cabins and dugouts at Winter Quarters in 1846–47, only parts of this mill remain.

"They come out in buses," Bob complained. "The original scam was they wanted my Dad to give it to 'em. Now they say they haven't any money. I got no time for 'em."

"I'm a writer," I said, as if that counted for anything.

"Don't beg," Charlie whispered. "It's pitiful."

Bob was coated in dust, a smear of plaster-white belly showing between T-shirt and jeans, a red seed-company baseball hat pulled down tight against the tops of his ears. Above a T-square jaw, his mustache bristled with a fluff of chaff.

"I don't let 'em in," he said. "I tell 'em it's the insurance." He waved Charlie and me inside. "There isn't much to see. It's just a mill. Always has been."

Just a mill or not, Harpster laid an admiring hand on a dark beam, smiling sheepishly, his arm sinking in shadow like a wand into dark oil. "One thing . . . they did good work. Built her to last. You can tell from the adze marks when they were drunk."

"Or hungry," I volunteered.

"That too."

"What happened to the original millstones?"

"Dunno. Maybe you could ask Lyman Weber."

. . .

"Heaped over in the old sub-basement," Lyman Weber told me when I finally looked him up two years later. "Diversion dam, gearing and wheel . . . that and a whole lot more got buried the year of the big shift. Flash flood. Took fourteen feet of Missouri River in thirty minutes. Hail the size of a man's fist. Washed the place off the foundation . . . so I moved the mill eighty yards to the west."

Weber talked from a rocker, frail from a recent illness, his voice hollow. The living room was filled with collectibles—ceramic owls, dolls, miniature glass pianos, and a wall of family photographs, all smiles and teeth. The whites of his eyes looked cracked as old china. In the mid-1800s, Lyman's grandfather, a yeasty man from Wurms, Germany, headed west in a prairie schooner with a hand-painted sign advertising "Pike's Peak or Bust." When he stumbled back to Florence and bought the mill in 1879, it advertised "Busted B' God." In 1964, Lyman sold out.

"I dug up them millstones in nineteen-and-thirty or so and put 'em in Mother's rock garden," he went on. "I was diggin' for a steam pipe when I struck 'em. Broke one. Pretty soon they come to me and wanted 'em for a museum. So I shipped 'em west in thirty-six."

"Where are they now?"

"Damned if I know. Never heard from 'em. Never got so much as a receipt. Never."

. . .

Neither Lyman Weber nor Bob Harpster mentioned "them" by name—nor did the Major Isaac Sadler Chapter of the Daughters of the American Revolution when it finally went public with the mill's history in 1924. Ernie Harpster keeps

FOLLOWING THE WRONG GOD HOME

the mill's now-retired original black-on-gray painted sign well out of sight under a pile of feed sacks. Outside, a new bronze marker corrects the DAR's error of deliberate omission.

"They don't like this old sign much," Bob said, propping the original under a naked bulb so I could photograph its niggardly praise. "If I didn't keep it covered up, it'd most likely get stole."

Site of the Old Grist Mill

Built in 1846

by

Omaha's First White Settlers

"Parsimonious sons-of-bitches," I carped, in the heat of the moment ignoring the DAR's gender.

Charlie saw anger building in me and eased toward the door. "Don't blow a fuse, Bud. The war's over."

He was right, of course. It wasn't my business. But I've never liked a gaggle of feminine-proper up to some half-good: it was the DAR's grudging legitimacy on the retired sign that caused me to short-circuit—the way they avoided the name. Mormons.

• • •

Day-Glo and royal blue, I shimmered into the Mormon Pioneer Cemetery at 4:30 P.M. and sat on the fieldstone base of Avard Fairbanks's larger-than-life memorial to the Mormon dead—big, bronze, baloney. I stripped off the backpack and stretched out on the warm grass, eyes at ground level. Gravestones were going under at crazy angles, like crooked eyeteeth in a gumline. Some had sunk almost out of sight; dates and names flaked into illegibility by weathers. Others had fallen, sod lapping their edges, until all that was left was an oval of gray alone in the grass with an occasional letter—an "O" or "T," say—staring at you like a rune.

Fairbanks's memorial to the Mormon dead is tediously sentimental—an angst-ridden representation of a father and mother huddled over the open grave of a dead child, a bitter wind tangling the woman's skirts. Stoic and Teutonic, the rugged Mormon father towers above his pretty wife, sheltering her in his billowing cloak, both fixated on the tiny, swaddled corpse. It's art of a sort, but *fabula*—not exactly legend, more like myth, but in no way reality. Only weepy background music and free tissues were missing. The six hundred names on bronze tablets, laid row on row below the statue in a "memorial plaza," struck me as tone deaf, as if the Mormon Tabernacle Choir were singing off-key. The true melody—

haunting, ageless, voiceless—was scored under the grass; nature alone could read its notes.

. . .

"Napping?"

"Something like that," I answered.

It was Charlie come round to save me from an overdose of maudlin. From my vantage point at ground level, Charlie looked as if he was hanging by a wire attached to his skull, so narrow and bony he seemed to dangle. His eyes were large and dark-rimmed as a hardboiled egg refrigerated past prime, crosscut and folded open on a pale china plate. When he opened his mouth, I could see the outline of his upper denture.

The Osage told me that Charlie once sneezed both his upper and lower out of his mouth like small pink boomerangs, whonking them off a board he was sawing and into the grass. "Aw, damn," he said, "there they go again." He mimed a Popeye look, gummed a laugh, picked up his choppers, and stuck them back. If he was vain, I never knew it.

I pointed to Fairbanks's rendering of Mormon grief. "Are there bronzes in heaven, Charlie?"

Charlie's eyes narrowed to slits, and a thin stream of smoke seeped out between his teeth. "Dunno," he said. "But the Book says with God, all things are possible."

"So you don't rule out statuary in the hereafter?"

"Hell, I don't rule out nothin', Bud. Even dead artists got to have *somethin'* to do. Maybe they paint the clouds."

Now that he's dead and the University of Missouri Medical School has finished dissecting him, I'd like to call down into the Show Me soil and bring him back to that moment in the Mormon Pioneer Cemetery. I'd like to see his middle-distance stare, eyes seeing but not, already going beyond, although it took eight years before cancer gave him a ticket. Near the end, he took to handcrafting oak crosses of simple beauty. I think of mine as a postcard.

Charlie's whereabouts are uncertain to me, but I let him go too easily, and I've let others go that way too—not missing enough the unasked questions or the lost words between us. I'd like to think that dead artists, dead writers, and dead Charlies have something yet to do in another life, but I can't imagine statues there. Charlie could. Sadly, only the living among us are recoverable—something I keep meaning to mention to the Osage.

. . .

Next morning, Charlie produced a box of twenty-five maduro double coronas, *hecho a mano* in Honduras—my favorites. Round as a buffalo nickel and six inches long, each contained enough nicotine to sedate a village. "Portable campfires," he quipped.

To honor gift and giver, I lit up across from the Vickers plant on Seventy-second Street near Crown Point Road while he snapped a final photo. Then he scrambled into his Pontiac, cranked it over, and shaking hands through the window, said, "Goph'er it!"

"Regards to the Osage."

"Hell, he bet against you, Bud! I'm the only friend you got who stands to make money!" Easing into Omaha's morning traffic, he racketed away, fading, disappearing. Gone.

"Goph'er it!" in Charlie's drawl settled an odd metaphor on me that day. From my background reading, I knew there were gophers aplenty on the prairies and plains of America, each with an eccentric capacity for burrowing beneath the surface. The problem is, gophers have no sense of direction when burrowing into things, tunneling endlessly with no rhyme or reason.

I worried about that. A lot.

2

E ultreia, E sus eia, Deus aid nos. *(Above our head, Below our feet, God be our hope.)*   LANGUEDOCIAN TRIPLET

Their desire was to establish themselves in some lonely valley of the mountains . . . in some sequestered spot, where they and their children could worship God, and obey his voice, and prepare themselves.   ORSON PRATT

Untangling myself from the suburbs was like a snake shedding its skin—a slow process. I couldn't slough its tangle fast enough. By ten o'clock, under a disk of white sun, sweat was already pooling in the small of my back. A snarl of roads came together near Northwest High School ("No Horses or Motor

Vehicles Permitted on the School Grounds"), all converging on a bridge across Little Papillion Creek. I rested on the bleachers of the baseball diamond ("Home of the Huskies") and shed the Karloffs, calling down curses on the Osage who obviously understood boots made to scale the east face of the Eiger.

Traffic streamed through the intersection and over the bridge, most of it headed for the Plaza North Shopping Center where parked cars already looked blurry in heat sumping from the asphalt. On the other side of the creek a grade rose steeply to a crest of prairie. The clouds of butterflies for which French trappers named the creek—probably swallowtails—were still three weeks away from their brief season in the sun. A kid with a basketball ambled past, stopped to gawk. He had a pointy face with tight-set ears and hair that looked like it was combed in a blender. He was shirtless, and his Nikes looked three sizes too large, his head one size too small, his eyes all-seeing and fixed on the backpack.

"Wat'cha up to?" the kid asked.

"Five eight," I answered. "And shrinking."

• • •

On April 5, 1847, after a journey of five miles from Winter Quarters, a New York potter named Heber Kimball set up a base camp "a short distance East of Little Papillion Creek . . . forming a nucleus for others of the pioneer company to gather to." They straggled in over the next few days, some fording the creek to camp on the far side, ready to head west onto the Great Plains. Given the flat bottomland of Northwest High, it looked as if a Huskies' home run might trace an arc over Kimball's first camp. Four days later, most of the original party of 148 had crossed the Little Papillion—143 men and boys, 3 women, 2 children. With them came 72 wagons, 93 horses, 52 mules, 66 oxen, 19 cows, 17 dogs, and several cages of fat laying hens. Besides personal effects and foodstuffs, the wagons carried cooking utensils, tools, implements, and musical instruments. For road noise, it must have been hell, not counting fiddles or flatulence.

The weather ran cold to pleasant, with a skin of ice on the buckets one morning and fresh breezes the next. By April 13, they regrouped twenty miles west at the Elkhorn River, waiting for their leader to show up. Most were high-minded Yankees full of Puritan flavors—visions, prophecy, Godly community. A handful were from Dixie. Mentioned in the manifest are three servants: "Hark Lay, Oscar Lay, blacks" and "Green Flake, black." Early on April 14, the man they were waiting for crossed the Little Papillion, driving hard to catch up, reaching the Elkhorn River a little before noon on the 15th and overtaking Kimball's party three hours later. Overhead, the sky flattened to slate gray, the weather turning "gloomy, windy, and cold."

He was unassuming. The lid of his left eye drooped as if half of him was falling asleep. Thick-bodied as an oak stump, his eyes were blue-gray under a wide forehead, his lips thin over imperfect teeth, which explains why, in photos taken later in his life, he never smiles. His nose was almost beaked and his face "somewhat bloodless." He liked baked potatoes and buttermilk and never drank "anything stronger than a glass of thin lager-bier." By 1860, when the famous British footpad Sir Richard Burton met him, "his followers deemed him an angel of light; his foes a goblin damned."

Goblin or saint, he once controlled one-fifth of the continental landmass of the United States. Challenged by the U.S. government in 1857, he held at bay the Fifth and Tenth U.S. Infantry, two batteries of artillery, and the Second Dragoons, before hammering a U.S. president into a face-saving compromise. Called the "Lion of the Lord" by the Mormon prophet Joseph Smith, he caught fire in the summer of 1827 while scything hay in the fields of Colonel George Hikok's farm, three miles north of my home above Canandaigua Lake in New York. By the time his flame burned out in 1877, he had altered the course of American history and redefined Promised Land. A bogey in the best of times, he had a hard way with words. When a religious blowhard, Bishop Gladden, challenged his leadership, he fired the blunderbuss of great religious retorts: "I can fart better prophecy," Brigham Young said, "and shit a better prophet."

• • •

Three days and 138 years later, I crossed Little Papillion Creek at noon, dodging cars to get to Military Road, the name that usurped the eastern stretch of the Mormon Trail when the U.S. Army began supplying its western forts during the Indian Wars. Beneath a shady canopy of cottonwoods, two feet of almost clear water ran in the creek bed, but on either side of the bridge the creek was choked with junk—tires, a hubcap, two failed hot-water heaters, and the usual litter of plastic and paper.

This fouling of America was noticed early by Prince Maximilian zu Wied on his way to visit the Mandan villages on the upper Missouri River in 1833: "By way of settlement, we may preserve here in America neither the aborigines nor the wild beasts, because the beginning of civilization is the destruction of everything," he penned. The Mandans went first, followed by the buffalo, followed by the land. When the fragile topsoil of the plains blew away during the dust bowl years, it carried with it a piece of Tom Jefferson's plow-crazy agrarian democracy. Today, it's still washing off the fields—100,000 tons every twenty-four hours. The Osage once put it to better effect at the grave of William Clark (Lewis and Clark) above the Missouri River in St. Louis's Belfontaine Cemetery. Fuming at the squalor of abandoned factories below, he erupted.

"We ought to change R.I.P to R.I.T. Rest In Trash!"

Halfway up the grade, across from the shopping center's griddle of asphalt and downwind from a McDonald's, I stumbled across a gaudy, dilapidated farmhouse turning tricks as a quick-stop, a solitary pickup camped on its postage-stamp lot. A tangle of used refrigerator truck boxes held an overflow of returnable empties, and a smeary hand-lettered sign announced "Bait and Worms, Minnows, Picnic Supplies." A cootlike man stumbled out, a six-pack in each fist, eyes squeezing shut at the sudden glare. A breeze stirred; two empty McDonald's drink cups shuffled across the road like hermit crabs. I took out my camera just as Mr. Six-pack looked up.

"Can I take a picture of this place?"

"Fuck off," he said.

• • •

Many people mistakenly think that's what the United States said to the Mormons. It didn't. There's no doubt they fell upon hard times and persecution at the hands of their neighbors. If anything, political leaders like Stephen Douglas and Abraham Lincoln tried to offer them a way out of their troubles, suggesting resettlement in the far reaches of the American West—Oregon, for example. They wouldn't have been pushing wagons over the future Military Road, Douglas County, Nebraska, if their religion had been an American love affair. For most nineteenth-century Americans, contact with Mormons was certainly steamy, but, truth be told, the Mormons did themselves few favors in courting their frontier neighbors. In a nation heady with one-man-one-vote, Mormons voted in a bloc as "advised" by their prophet. Showing a remarkable facility at misunderstanding the dynamics of frontier politics, especially the expanding role of newspapers in a fledgling democracy, they were quick to set themselves apart as God's own elect—a reincarnation of the Children of Israel led out of an American Egypt by a latter-day Moses to Promised Land.

Insofar as Brigham Young led the Mormons out of the United States to squat on *Mexican* soil, the metaphor is apt; but it was marital extravagance, not self-righteous hyperbole, that turned the tide against them. Rumors that Joseph Smith had "reinstated" polygamy stirred the pot of Christian-perceived sin, no matter that hot-and-heavy Christian revivals, sexual excess, and "camp meeting" bastards

FOLLOWING THE WRONG GOD HOME

abounded among other faiths on the frontier. Americans were aroused—a few incensed. By some tallies, Joseph Smith had as many as forty-nine wives, although it's hard to get a leg over the exact figure. Brigham Young topped off at fifty-six.

Mormon polygamy was a self-inflicted religious wound for half a century until the fourth Prophet, Seer, and Revelator, Wilford Woodruff, bargained it away in 1890 for statehood. *Bargained* is perhaps too condemning a word; Mormons were hectored, bullied, and hounded into submission by a government that called Utah Territory "the biggest whorehouse in the world." Even today, in remote reaches of Arizona, Colorado, and Utah, where a person can parboil among vermilion rocks in August, polygamy still festers—a pus for which there's no antibiotic.

None of this excuses the savagery with which Mormons were treated. Not a violent people, they met with violence in large doses at the hands of their neighbors, building and abandoning three communities in the same number of states— one the largest city in Illinois.

But if their neighbors proved intolerant, Mormons were equally intransigent. Convinced of the truth of their "restored" gospel, many were blind to Smith's failings. When he made a shambles of early church finances, proving that a prophet was no guarantee of financial wizardry, he was set upon in Kirtland, Ohio. Tarred and feathered, he headed west to Independence, Missouri, but he fared no better in the Show Me State.

In Jackson County, Missouri, the sudden influx of so many bloc-voting Yankees threatened older settlers. Missouri was Daniel Boone country and suspicions ran high, especially at the ballot box. When matters reached flash point over the Saints' follow-the-leader bloc voting, a vexed Missouri governor, Lilburn Boggs, ordered Smith and his followers "exterminated"—the only time in history when a group of U.S. citizens was threatened with government-ordered genocide. In the Missouri fracas, several Mormons were murdered at Hawn's Mill, the prophet was jailed, and a hitherto unknown strategist—Brigham Young—led them to safety.

In Illinois, encamped on the banks of a swamp at the edge of the Mississippi, they hustled up the largest city in the state. Freed from his Missouri pokey (he was allowed to escape), Smith called his new city Nauvoo, interpreting the word as "beautiful place." Missionaries scoured Europe for converts, and the down-and-out from England and Scandinavia came in droves, swelling the city to over ten thousand, lured as much by Manifest Destiny as by the Mormon faith that was one of its many incarnations. Smith's "City on a Hill" became a prospering outpost of his intended Zion, its citizens courted by Stephen Douglas and young Abe Lincoln—so large a bloc of potential votes for Whigs or Democrats that the

Illinois legislature obligingly coughed up a charter giving Nauvoo the powers of a city-state and arming the city's militia. Appointed lieutenant general of the Nauvoo Legion, Smith blustered around on his big stud, Charlie, dressed in epaulets, gold braid, buff trousers, high-top military boots, ceremonial sword, and "a handsome chapeau topped with ostrich feathers."

Nauvoo might have survived but for megalomania and excess testosterone. In 1843 Smith petitioned the government to become "Governor of the Federal Territory of Nauvoo," hoping to create an independent state. Growing more grandiose, he appointed "a council of fifty 'princes'" and had himself crowned "King of the Kingdom of God." In 1844, when he threw his hat into the ring for U.S. president, his candidacy was electric with the home folks, but outside Nauvoo it had the appeal of a venereal disease. Some historians claim that Joseph had no illusions about winning national office; it was a last effort to gain justice for the Mormons, who were falling again on hard times. He talked of heading west to the Rocky Mountains: open road seemed his only way out—again.

Smith's bubble burst on a prick of fate: someone got wind of his gusto for plural wives. In particular, William Law objected to Smith's courting his lawful wife, Jane, and Law was an influential Mormon who threatened to grind his axe to a fine edge in the first (and only) edition of his newspaper, the *Nauvoo Expositor*. Newspapers had increased dramatically in America—from roughly 75 in 1790 to 1,400 "voices of the people" by 1844. The *Nauvoo Expositor* was a new "voice" in the Mormon-controlled city and clearly a threat to King Joseph's doctrines.

Smith's wife, Emma, had already denounced "The Principle," which Joseph courageously introduced to her using his brother, Hyrum, as front man. But it wasn't the first time she'd come out swinging against her husband's peccadilloes. She'd discovered his dalliance with their maid, Fanny Alger, and beat her from the prophet's home with a broom; but when William Law made good on his threat, publishing a tepid accusation of Joseph's doctrine of "plural marriage" in the *Expositor*, Smith made a fatal blunder. He declared the newspaper "a civic nuisance," Law an apostate and renegade, attacked the newspaper, destroyed its type, and burned every issue he could lay hands on. Polygamy had reared its head. "The cat is out of the bag," Heber Kimball said, "and that is not all—this cat is going to have kittens; and . . . those kittens are going to have cats."

What came out of Smith's bottle was no servile genie. Out of wishes at last, his action unleashed a statewide explosion. Anti-Mormons declared Smith's journalistic pyromania an affront to the U.S. "holy Constitution," while the nearby *Warsaw Signal* yawped, "War and extermination are inevitable!" With the citizens and the state militia "beyond legal control," Illinois governor Tom Ford feared civil war. So intense was the heat that the charge leveled against the Mormon prophet was treason.

Fearing for his safety, Smith slipped the state, crossing the Mississippi into Iowa in an effort to save his bacon. But on the advice of his counselors, he relented and recrossed the river to give himself up since Governor Ford promised him a fair trial. Some claim Smith was sure of an acquittal if he could get a just hearing; others said he was inwardly certain of martyrdom. The former is more likely; the latter smells of the already forming saintly myth that grew around him. Whatever the truth, the prophet allowed himself to be jailed in Carthage, Illinois. An anxious Governor Ford rushed to Nauvoo to calm the Saints, assure them of their prophet's safety, and argue for due process.

But Ford was deceived. One by one, Smith's supporters were isolated, driven from Carthage as access to the prison was cut off. Abandoned by his guards, Smith was left in a second-story room with his brother and two others. A few minutes past 5:00 P.M. on June 27, 1844, while Ford was still in Nauvoo, a mob stormed the Carthage jail. Joseph Smith, Jr., age thirty-nine, "Prophet, Seer, and Revelator" and "King of the Kingdom of God," was gunned down and passed into myth and history.

Smith remains an enigma; to Mormons, he remains God's prophet. Generous to a fault, gregarious in the extreme, he was by all accounts a man of the people— plain talking, charming, genial, warmhearted. "Not a hair-shirt prophet" was the way his most notorious biographer put it. But it was left to Josiah Quincy, the son of a U.S. president, to sum him up best: "If the reader does not know just what to make of Joseph Smith, I cannot help him out of the difficulty. I stand myself helpless before the puzzle."

So did I. Still do.

• • •

By three in the afternoon, I was lost in a tyranny of numbers. The streets ran west into the hundreds; Omaha throbbed like a nasty hangover. Between 122nd and 129th Streets, still walking the meander of Military Road, I witnessed landscape being carved into checkerboard squares, the kings in play being developers. Earthmovers and bulldozers, choking in their own dust, reduced prairie fields to featureless "homesites" with black ribbons of new asphalt marking out as-yet-nameless streets.

Out of sorts, I wanted to be somewhere else—perhaps in Booche's Bar, a favorite Osage haunt in Columbia, Missouri, listening to the soft *whrrr* and *thuuck* of pool balls pocketing in the old Brunswicks, green hot sauce on a pork tenderloin, mouth afire, cold beer in hand, the Osage thrumming conversation. A ruffle of westerlies came up; dry and hot as oven's breath, they hit full in the face, coating the inside of my nostrils with grit. Out of water, I stopped at the home of Hubert Newhouse, a man of few words. He led me to a hose out back.

"Hot," I ventured.

"Yep."

"Too hot."

"M'be."

I filled my canteen with cool water.

"What's the forecast?"

"Hot."

"Thanks," I said, corking the canteen.

"Y'betcha."

As I reached the road, he called after me.

"M'be rain."

I thought the state department could use a man like Hubert to keep life-and-death negotiations to a minimum.

· · ·

I ran out of light trying to skip the suburbs. When I spotted a likely campsite, it was two hundred yards off Military Road. Up close, I saw a tidy brick house set well back among a stand of cottonwoods. Desperate, I crunched up the gravel drive and knocked. No answer. I knocked again. The door opened, then closed to a slit, anchored to its chain. A woman's voice spoke softly from the darkness. "Yes."

I explained.

Yes, there was room at the inn. Yes, I could set up my tent down by the creek. Yes, I could fill my canteen from the hose out front. It would be no trouble—no trouble at all. The door shut; a bolt shot into place. I was too relieved to notice anything odd.

My lightweight tent went up without a hitch. Two hundred feet from the house, I sat bent-legged as a yogi in the opening and fired my tiny Svea stove. In the darkness, it chortled to life with a reassuring hiss, blue flame lapping at my one small cooking pot. I "reconstituted" freeze-dried potatoes, made a cup of coffee, cut a chunk of cheese, and gorged. Nodding off, I decided on bourbon and another cigar to celebrate day one. A gill of George Dickle cut through any remaining road

　　　　　　　　FOLLOWING THE WRONG GOD HOME

dust, rearranging my point of view from owly to less. I took long, lazy draws at the second of Charlie's nicotine logs; smoke drifted through the "no-see-um" mesh door, floating toward stars. Sleepily, I drifted with it—too far.

I jerked awake.

Two revolving red eyes glared from the field. Still clenched in my teeth, the cigar had burned neatly through the "no-see-um," leaving a round, quarter-sized hole. A voice said, "Take it easy." Then a flashlight beam settled on my nose, dissolving the scene to white glare.

I eased the cigar back through the hole. "What's up?" I asked. I knew damn well what was up.

The flashlight wobbled away from my face, its beam cutting behind me to the contents of the tent—backpack, cooking gear, boots, a sprawl of sleeping bag. The officer's bulk, square, black, and backlit from the car's lights, framed the door. He swatted at gnats with his free hand. Hatched in unnatural spring heat, they flitted in the headlights like dust motes in Bob Harpster's feed mill, biting with pin-prick fire. "Nasty sons-of-bitches," he said, flailing away. "Got some I.D.?"

I reached for my pack, and the flashlight followed my hand into a side pocket. Unzipping the "no-see-um," I handed him my wallet. He flipped through the contents with one hand and walked backward to the car. I could see the safety flap on his sidearm holster was undone. "This'll take a minute," he said.

I heard his radio stutter inside the patrol car. He talked with the windows rolled up, his face a yellowy smear above the flashlight, the hand holding my driver's license still whacking at gnats. It was a young face with an older man's voice—a voice used to one- or two-word details, each spoken in a monotone as if his larynx had aged from too much experience too soon on sheriff's patrol.

My cigar had died, so I relit it. He squinted at the flaring match, keeping his eyes on me until the radio sputtered back a hissy message. This time, when he got out, he kept the beam of the flashlight on the ground, his boots pooled in light as he crushed through the grass. "You got a record," he said. "Illegal border crossing in North Dakota."

"I was trying to get out of the country ... back home to Canada," I said. "They thought I was trying to get in. They made a mistake."

"You got a green card?"

"Under the driver's license."

"What's a guy like you doing out here?" he asked.

I knew then he was buying time: my university ID was under my green card. "Taking a long walk." I explained things.

"Mrs. Bivens up at the house forgot her husband was getting home late," he said. "He's down to Lincoln. Asked us to check. I'll tell her she's got nothing to worry about. Has she?"

"I'm harmless."

"That's what they all say." He handed back the wallet and looked at the hole in the net. "Put a Band-Aid over that," he said, "or you'll get the shit bit out'a you." He fanned at more converging gnats.

"Y'betcha," I answered.

3

Wotan, the chief of the gods, . . . was wont to walk the world disguised as a wanderer.　　　　　　　　　　MILES JEBB

We traveled on about four miles and came to the river Horn, forded our teams across, the wagons on a raft. This stream is about 150 feet wide.　　　　　APPLETON MILO HARMON,
APRIL 15, 1847

At noon sharp, I limped into Elk City. A red plastic pinwheel whirled crazily on a dirt mound next to the road. Some wiseass had lettered "Greater Metropolitan Area" on the sign, announcing the hamlet's presence among the lesser burgs of America. If you combined twenty miles an hour with a sneeze, you'd miss Elk City on the first *whonk*. Stripped down to a blue silk T-shirt, reeking sweat, I set a limping course toward a neon Budweiser sign, hit the door, and hitched myself to Elk City's only oasis—the Ponderosa.

"Beer," I ordered into the darkness.

It was the cave of the ice bear—twin air conditioners whooshing full blast and the temperature minus meat locker. Worried all morning about sunstroke, I shifted now to pneumonia as cold shriveled my silk tee and settled in a pool around my ankles. A sandpaper voice came out of the dark. "From the size of your load, I'd say you was making a slow getaway."

Eyes in glare-to-gloom mode, I made out a quartet—two denimed and booted cowboy types playing eight ball under dim wattage, an over-the-hill wrangler in a western designer shirt, and a thirty-something blonde behind the bar, all four pop-eyed in my direction, mouths round and rubbery as diaphragms. The bar was padded with a Naugahyde crash cushion in case someone went down from one too many. Fancy Shirt owned the sandpaper voice. "Take a load off," he said.

Unhitching the pack, I bent over to stash it against the bar, then moved to belly up. Problem was, I couldn't belly—a key had turned in the small of my back, locking the hinge. For a moment, I leaned with one arm on the Naugahyde, head down, riding out the spasm. When I straightened up, a large rubber armadillo lay on the bar sucking a make-believe bottle of Bud. Penny, the blonde publican, slid a cold Schlitz across to me, pointed to a hand-lettered sign on the wall.

> Elk City is too small to have a town drunk.
> So we all take turns. When it's your turn
> be sure to be here.

Nodding toward Fancy Shirt, she said, "Red's leaving soon. You gotta fill in until another drunk takes the shift."

"What's the pay?"

Fancy Shirt laughed, wheezy as the hinge on a rusty screen door. "Hell, there's no pay. It's civic duty . . . but none of us are leaving 'till we hear your story. Are we boys?"

Forewarned, the two cowboys bolted for the door, letting in a blast of furnace air, dust boiling at floor level in the vanishing slant of light. When things settled, Penny said, "Strangers make the locals nervous." She propped her elbows on the bar. Eyes the shade of blue jeans, her face, too pale and beginning to wear like fading wallpaper, was a mask of sad indifference. Behind her, against the cash register, was another sign, hand-lettered:

> Please Be Patient
> I only work here because I'm too old for a
> paper route, too young for social security,
> and too tired to have an affair.

Fancy Shirt said, "A man on shank's mare with a pack that big is either screwed over or screwed up." He offered his hand. "Red Martin. Tell me about your slow getaway."

Red Martin had a face with so many lines in it that a rubbing of it would look like a spider's web with eyes—a personal history wondrously spun. He drank beer slowly, with respect, like an experienced hand who's been nipped more than once by unexpected teeth in the hair-of-the-dog. What was left of his wavy red locks was now thin and high on his forehead, and the etched face was folded around button-sized eyes on either side of a beef-colored nose. He had ears and earlobes of a man twice his size, tipped out from his head like whisper-catchers.

He listened the same way that he drank beer, cautiously, savoring my words and getting my intentions straight. He had no interest in Mormons, but his eyes full-mooned whenever the talk came around to journeys. I spoke of the Osage and his recent travels, how a man can rearrange his life on closer inspection of native land.

"I was raised in North Dakota," Red told me. "One summer, I went to visit my uncle on a horse ranch in Alberta. God almighty, I love horses . . . just the look of 'em. I go to sixty, maybe seventy, horse shows a year. We all think we're cowboys outside of the Omaha city limits."

He drained his last two fingers of beer and I offered to buy him another, but he waved me off, looking into his empty glass as if reading the leftover lace like tea leaves. His eyes took on distance and his features the weary patina older men get when they've been rubbed wise by experience and memory.

"One day my uncle saw me admiring his stock. 'Red,' he says, 'You can have any three of them horses so long as you can ride 'em home.' I jumped to it. Made me up a pack and rode four hundred miles from Alberta to North Dakota. I still think of that trip . . . every day."

I ordered another beer and two hamburgers. Red propped his elbows on the padded Naugahyde bumper, watched me eat, and whimsied on. "Once a fella gets to looking around . . . then to moving around . . . it catches him up. So I got hold of a used Piper Ponca and started buzzing over flatland. Me and my brother had to fly low over elevators reading the town signs painted on 'em . . . trying to find out where the hell we were."

"How did it end?"

"In the U.S. Air Force . . . Iceland, Newfoundland, Europe. Once I flew back stateside through the Azores just to pick up a load of cheap wine. But I'm sure as hell grounded now."

"You've still got horses."

He laughed, almost bitterly. "And you got Mormons. I'll take a green horse . . . hell no, I'd take a damn green mule any day over Mormons. You can't break a Mormon." He swung off the bar stool and held out his hand again. "Take it easy," he said. "Here's to a good road."

"And horses."

"Whatever suits."

FOLLOWING THE WRONG GOD HOME

After he slid into the afternoon glare, Penny brought me the check, and slid a small card into my hand.

> I am a creature from outer space. I have
> transposed myself into this piece of paper.
> I am now having sex with your fingers. I can
> tell that you like it, for you are smiling.
> Please pass this along. I am really horny.

· · ·

Walking Highway 36, I dropped toward the Elkhorn River with pressure building under the balls of my feet, each step a small agony. When I passed local patriot J. Whalley's place (his name was neatly lettered on his mailbox), Old Glory was snapping due east in wind-driven salutes while gusts blasted full in my face. Closer to the river, the going was somewhat easier, but an eerie wind coiled around the budding crowns of the cottonwoods, sobbing or moaning with each blast. By the time I reached the bridge, I knew I had serious problems with my feet, so I climbed the guardrail and trudged through sand until I found shelter among the trees.

Snugged between sandbanks, the Elkhorn River was no more than thirty yards wide—shrunken by sixty feet since 1847. Ta-ha-zouka (Elk's Horn), the Omaha chief from whom the river takes its name, figured in a 1796 treaty with the Spanish governor of Louisiana. Sand spits rose in midchannel like parallel archipelagoes, and silt-choked water oozed steadily toward its junction with the Platte below Elk City. Downstream from the present bridge, the Mormons had rafted the river, then angled northwest to camp on the banks of the Platte south of Fremont. A bullet fired due west along Highway 36 would fall within yards of the old site.

I stripped off the Karloffs and socks. Damage assessment: two dime-sized blisters under the ball of each foot, both broken, both raw, neither bleeding. Rubbing antiseptic cream into the sores, I stretched the broken skin back in place, gluing it down with two patches of adhesive moleskin, praising providence for Dr. Scholl. Then the wind died. I mean *died*. Riffles on the water disappeared, and the cottonwoods, bowed eastward a moment earlier, ceased their wracked mourning and rose up by still waters. Uncannily still.

By the time I climbed back onto the highway, it seemed half of Nebraska was in the air. To the southwest, the sky was smeared oily black, and new wind streamed unchecked as eighteen-wheelers, gust after gust, rolled east along the highway. Between bursts, fat rumbles of thunder shuddered the afternoon; through an ochre haze, dust devils rose from plowed spring fields across six flatland miles of the delta between the Elkhorn and the Platte. I beat my way forward. Three times I was saved from foundering by the steadying influence of Roadmaker; three times Roadmaker righted my keel, otherwise I would have capsized on the gritty shoal of Highway 36. Then the wind turned murderous. Bits and pieces of debris whipped along the concrete, hacking at my ankles. Above me, wires bowed crazily between their poles, screeching in tongues of wind. I leaned into it, trimming my body like a sail, spurting forward between windwalls, dirt lodging in my hair, nostrils, and mouth. Blown back, I took to the ditch and clung to a telephone pole. Southward, the sky boiled to darkness and daylight turned yellow.

I didn't see the car, only heard the faint sound of a horn drifting past. When I looked up, he was calling to me from the far shoulder through the Ford's open window. Not a syllable reached me, but I read the panic in his eyes, let go of my mooring, and skewed across the asphalt. Up close, his words were shredded, like bits of paper.

". . . pack in trunk. Tornado warn . . ."

•   •   •

Benny Stave, who rescued me that afternoon, told me that "Congress and Reagan are letting savings and loans get away with murder," a prophecy that came true in spades. The bitterness in his voice startled me at the time, but the bilking of America by the likes of Charles Keating (later convicted; he won on appeal) proved his point. Like Nebraska winds that afternoon, lives and families were blown away by high-velocity greed, extravagant lifestyles, and unethical neglect. When the multibillion bailout came, the Staves, like most Americans, were shook up and shaken down.

Benny (a banker) and Helen (a county superintendent of schools) retired to Fremont after working in Montana, the Dakotas, and Nebraska. I could see Mrs. Stave was uncomfortable; she picked nervously at the sleeve of her blouse. She said, "We never . . . usually don't . . . pick up hitchhikers."

"But when we saw you leaning into the wind . . . hanging on that pole," Benny said, gently correcting her intention, "well . . . I decided."

I thanked them. But I knew what Helen was driving at. I was unwashed, smelly, begrimed, a risk.

By the time we reached the junction of Highway 36 and U.S. 275—a stone's throw from the old Mormon camp on the Platte—Benny's car was bucking the wind, dust so thick that motorists had their lights on. Across the Platte, a seething sheet of black was closing fast on Fremont. Benny turned right onto 275, and the tailwind made his driving seem as if he'd thrown caution to it. We curved around a new cutoff on the east side of town as the first ugly slaps of rain splattered the windshield and promptly died away. In the parking lot of a Super 8 Motel, we said hasty good-byes. Helen looked back and waved as Benny pulled into traffic, her face a grid of concern.

Minutes later, the storm hit, shrieking at my window and howling to get inside, drowning the streets and scouring the parking lot with micro-explosions of pea-sized hail. For half an hour it rumbled, slamming the building with shock after shock, drifting finally east toward Omaha. Safe, I lay down on the bed and dozed. Later, in the bathroom mirror, a wet finger traced a line through the dirt on my forehead, my beard stiff with grime as if dipped in egg whites. I showered for twenty minutes, courage dwindling.

Of Nebraska's spring weather, Willa Cather wrote, "There was only the throb of it, the light restlessness. . . . One could not get enough of the nimble air." "Nimble" is hardly the word for it. For at least 20,000 years, Nebraska's topography has been shaped by water, wind, and ice. After the great Kansan and Wisconsin glaciers withdrew—the last a mere 10,000 years ago—alluvial outwash from melt-waters carried deep silts that formed the plains. The Sand Hills region, the Cheyenne tablelands between the North and South Platte Rivers, and the fat hand of loess covering all of eastern Nebraska were shaped by water and great cyclonic winds. Not exactly *nimble* air. It's a chills-and-fever state where temperatures range between 47 below to over 100 above. "Generally healthful," is the way the 1930s WPA Guide puts it, although the word *generally* might worry a sane man with limited experience of the Cornhusker State. "Spring," says the Guide, "has changeable weather," but self-promotion is always built on exaggeration or understatement.

· · ·

Next morning, I took a cab back to where Benny and Helen Stave had rescued me from hail and high water. As I walked the shoulder toward Fremont, the air hung languid; heat waves shimmered off the highway like reflections in a fun-house mirror. Near the junction with U.S. 275, two men were propping up a blown-down highway sign—Bennington 15, Omaha 25.

"Helluva wind," one called out.

"Tore the shit out'a things," the other said.

By the time I reached the Platte River bottoms and turned north toward Fremont, oily clouds were piling up again and new winds rocketed over the flats. Half a mile away, along the river, cottonwoods slammed and shuddered in the on-again, off-again blasts. Then, almost as quickly as they had begun, the winds settled and the clouds moved to the southeast.

Tired of breathing exhaust fumes, I left the highway and took to the parallel railroad tracks. A freight rumbled past with a long string of cars brimming with coal, the most common cargo on the plains. In three months, hundreds more would pass me. I imagine them still, and feel the earth move under me. For almost two months, I slept close to the main line of the Union Pacific, listening to the thrum of big diesels, which became as comfortable and familiar as a bedmate's nocturnal muttering and tossing. I'm still pleasured by the salutatory wave of an engineer or brakeman or by long lines of train cars, wobbly and screechy as drunks trying to walk a straight line. One joy of a solitary walker is that everything on wheels overtakes and passes him, leaving in its wake silence and space for reflection. Thus is he drawn into the world around him, not merely through it.

I walked into Fremont under full steam, crossing a viaduct over the railroad yards, heading for the city center and my home away from home. Next to the tracks, a grain elevator blazed white in the sun; from the nearby Hormel Packing Plant came a reek of pig droppings and a stench of rendering hog. A billboard porker, plump as an overstuffed feed sack, advertised "Licomix for Healthy Hogs." A second billboard hawked conspicuous consumption courtesy of the Columbia Federal Bank: "Go Ahead, Buy It With Our Money." A jeep throttled past, lidless, radio blasting Dream and the Boss: "Born in the USA."

· · ·

At the corner of Military Avenue and First Street, I came face-to-face with two inheritors of the "Camp of Israel." Dark suits and dark, leather-bound books announced them as surely as if they wore Phrygian caps. Richard Owen Thomas and D. W. Bagley were retreating from a porch of a nearby house whose occupant had closed the door—abruptly, from the look of it. Each young man had a black plastic nametag pinned to his lapel. I waved them over. "Mormons?"

"Latter-day Saints," elder Thomas corrected. "We don't use 'Mormon.'" (In 2001, LDS leaders issued a press release advising the media that they were henceforth to be referred to as the "Church of Jesus Christ," not "Mormons"; "Latter-day Saints" was optional. Politely, the media told them to take a hike.)

I apologized. "You realize, of course, that we're standing at the center of your history," I said.

Bagley looked at Thomas, Thomas at Bagley—an odd, knowing look as if they'd just realized Mr. Demented was hanging off the back of the bus; but in ten minutes, Mr. Demented brought them up to date on vital Mormon lore.

Thomas was from Houston, Texas, and Bagley from Twin Falls, Idaho. Curiously, they were out of touch with the history under their feet that afternoon, which made the moment more prescient to me, as if they'd missed out on some necessary training in missionary boot camp. Even more curious, they were the last Mormons I talked with until I walked into Utah.

4

A plague on my accursed feet!   WALTER STARKIE,
                                     RAGGLE-TAGGLE

Brigham told me to rise up and start with the pioneers in half an hour's notice.   WILLIAM CLAYTON,
                                                                                        APRIL 14, 1847

Shuffling along the shoulder of the old Lincoln Highway (U.S. 30), I cleared the Fremont city limits west of Little Audrey's Transportation, a trucking company fresh out of trucks, its lot vacant. According to the Omaha paper that morning, farmers were going broke fast, but Victor's Farm Equipment was doing a brisk business, offering opportunities for more red ink in its advertising for a new line of tractors: "Case Has a Fresh Team for Today's Farmer." No doubt they'd teamed up with the Columbia Federal boys downtown to further the crisis, so I muttered, "Go Ahead, Buy It With Our Money," and passed on.

By the time I reached Fremont Lakes, I was walking into a damp wind with clouds hanging overhead like soggy gray blankets. In the roadside park, I pulled on my Gore-Tex rain jacket and took a load off the Karloffs. Beaver had toppled several of the cottonwoods lining the banks of the pond-sized lakes. When the Mormons passed by, they made no mention of the world's second largest rodent; the lakes were crowded with ducks, which made up their dinner.

Evidence of an older natural world close at hand startled me. In a way, the American West began with John Jacob Astor's quest for a beaver hat. In 1811, sailing around the Horn, members of his American Fur Company reached the mouth of the Columbia River, where they established Astoria. The next year, in February, a party following the Lewis and Clark route arrived by land, and a second ship, aptly named *Beaver* for Astor's American Dream, reached the post in May 1812.

New World trade in beaver pelts was already two hundred years old. Carried on by the French, Dutch, and English from the early 1600s, it reached the Mississippi and Missouri Rivers as early as 1700, where the Osage's ancestors traded pelts for cheap metal tools. After 1812, trappers ranged throughout the mountain West, their names synonymous with its history—Jim Bridger, "Broken Hand" Fitzpatrick, Jedediah Smith, Peter Skene Ogden. (Bridger later caused Brigham Young to lose sleep and was most likely the first white American to see Great Salt Lake.)

In three decades, trappers stripped rivers and creeks of their flat-tailed harvest, sending pelts back east along the Platte River, roasting beaver tail over campfires, and turning it into a mountain man's succulent dinner; but with demand falling and the beaver trapped out, the fur traders' routes to the West became roads of settlement. The California, Oregon, and Mormon Trails were coexisting routes to the riches (some say *plunder*) of Dreams of empire "across the wide Missouri." By 1985 the beaver population had regrouped, at least in the Fremont Lakes—*Castor canadensis,* to be patriotic about the hardy species.

• • •

That morning, Bill Cioni and his wife, Joan, were fishing for pike. "We got beaver in here that weigh seventy-five pounds," Bill told me, "but the fishing's way off. No luck this spring."

We talked in the lee of Bill's blue Chevy pickup, weather and the future on our minds. Bill had recently been laid off from his job as a welder. A "Windy City" native who married a Fremont girl, he had a vampire's hairline and the handsome, beaky face of a character actor; raven-haired Joan had the blood to tame a vampire; and I had the impression that Bill would live anywhere Joan took a shine to, including Transylvania.

"Watch out for straight-line winds," Bill advised as I pulled out. "Those suckers come up fast this time of year. They'll tear you up."

Minutes later, a gray tongue of cold rain licked across the Lincoln Highway, but the Gore-Tex waved it aside. Behind it, a wind rose, shredding soggy clouds overhead while I listened to the creaks and rattles of the pack and Roadmaker tapping the asphalt like a metronome.

• • •

For three days the Mormons camped near the site of Fremont, using the time to repair wagons and shoe horses—going to ground as I had done to settle down after an uncertain beginning. Ahead, the bottomland was soggy from recent rains,

FOLLOWING THE WRONG GOD HOME

difficult to cross. Meanwhile, Brigham dashed back to Winter Quarters to round up wagons and cash, but particularly to see John Taylor, who had just returned from England with "two barometers, two sextants, two artificial horizons, one circle of reflection and one telescope." When he rode back into camp, instruments neatly boxed, Brigham brought with him a former Liverpudlian of moody temperament—a man who suffered greatly from toothaches and, to hear him tell it, lack of respect. But William Clayton was nobody's fool and a damned good scribe to boot, so Brigham and others high or mighty used Clayton's talents to invent their "personal" records of the journey, especially Heber C. Kimball, Brigham's New York neighbor, whose writing and spelling make even the semiliterate wince. It's to Clayton that historians of the Mormon Trail owe their greatest debt; *William Clayton's Journal* remains the jewel in the crown of Mormon overland travel accounts. I carried it in my pack and read it nightly.

Up ahead, a Nebraska state historical marker hove into view. I read it in the rain, three paragraphs of what turned out to be unsettling as snake oil.

> The Great Platte River Route West
>
> The north bank of the Platte River from the 1830's through the 1860's, served as a major overland route to the West. It was used by fur traders, soldiers, gold seekers and other emigrants. The expedition of Major Stephen H. Long passed through this area in June 1820. Just north of the river were the last villages of the Pawnee nation, prior to their being placed on a reservation. Fremont was named in honor of General John C. Fremont, when settled in 1856. This trail is usually referred to as the Mormon Trail, as they were the first to use it in great numbers.
>
> This route was also known as the Omaha-Fort Kearney Military Road, and the stage between Omaha and Salt Lake City also ran here. It became the line of the first trans-continental telegraph in 1861. A few years later it became the route of the Union Pacific Railroad, the first trans-continental route. The railroad reached Fremont in 1866 and, in a few years, the Platte Valley of Nebraska ceased to be a frontier, becoming a prosperous farming region.
>
> With the development of the automobile, this route became U.S. Highway 30 or the Lincoln Highway, the first trans-continental road. It was completed to San Francisco in 1913, though

a portion of the road west of Fremont was not paved until 1920. Begun as a major road to the West, it developed into and remains an important route to the East as well.

Standing on old main line America, I felt drop-in-the-bucket. This was a road before the Mormons, layered over by successive use and, as I came to understand later, a road before history as we know it. But even without rain the signage was all wet—factual, to be sure, but skewed. Except for *one* line about displacing the Pawnee, an entire Native American people were missing. So much for their Dream. Months later, talking with the Osage, I discovered what it was that worried me.

"It was a *toll* road," I suggested. "Only we never paid full price to ride. Everything we took or bargained for we got cheap . . . and treated it all like that. Even the land blew away."

"You got it," he said.

• • •

Any American on the road can usually count on historical markers ("hysterical markers," I call them) to tune the facts to a popular wavelength that creates the least static and suits whatever harmonics of Dream that are currently in vogue. Nowhere in bronze does it state that James Buchanan, the fifteenth president, was probably gay or that Nebraska's best-known writer, Willa Cather, was lesbian. As James W. Loewen points out in *Lies across America: What Our Historic Sites Get Wrong*, "America has ended up with a landscape of denial." The result is selective mental amnesia. "It may be more important to understand what the historical landscape gets wrong than what it gets right," Loewen suggests.

Only once have I come across a historical marker with a sense of humor. I was outbound for Washington State with the Osage when we came to a rest stop on Interstate 15 near Dell, Montana, where many town names (Kidd is just up the road) are monosyllabic because uninterrupted beauty marks its dominion over anything fanciful that a man could Dream up:

> Along in early 1840s, Americans were like they are now—
> seething to go somewhere. It got around that Oregon was quite
> a place. The Iowa people hadn't located California yet. A wagon
> train pulled out across the plains and made it to Oregon. Then
> everyone broke into a rash to be going west.
>
> They packed their prairie schooners with household goods,
> gods, and garden tools. Outside of roaring prairie fires, cholera,

famine, cyclones, cloudbursts, quicksand, snow slides, and blizzards, they had a tolerably blithe and gay trip.

When gold was found in Montana, some of them forked off from the main highway and surged along this trail aiming to reach rainbow's end. It was mostly one-way traffic but if they didn't meet a back-tracking outfit there was plenty of room to turn out.

I have no idea who wrote it, but he or she is a kindred spirit. Although Native Americans were left out again.

· · ·

A green Oldsmobile passed me heading east, the driver's hand raised in a salute, head under a black Stetson. I waved in return, shouted a greeting into the mist. I heard him brake but kept on walking, in no mood for strangers. The car shot past, now heading west, braked, did a one-eighty and pulled to a stop on the shoulder in front of me. His face was startling, edged round in salt-and-pepper beard, its length exaggerated and drawn to purplish circles under eyes red-rimmed and haggard. Wedged into the Stetson, his head seemed to float above the glass, loosely attached to a yellow shirt and blue sweater. He powered down the window.

"The gods of this world are all travelers," he said.

"Yeah?"

"Travelers have wings of archangels."

A basket case, I thought. Just my luck.

Another broom of gray rain dusted the highway, moved on, a companion sound to the man's voice, like a whisk scratching a wooden table. "A traveler is a man who's bailed out of everything in order to find out who the traveler is. Am I right?"

"Could be."

"That's why we're both on the road. What's *your* story?"

His story seemed more interesting. Then again, perhaps he was high on uppers or wired with coke. I eased a pocket-sized notebook and pen from my shirt.

"You first," I said.

· · ·

A mile back, at The Outpost, a hoedown bar with the atmosphere of an empty warehouse, we drank draft beer into midafternoon. If he had a story, it was scrambled. McCarthy said he was a teacher, a musician, a mystic, a psychic, and a drunk, in that order. The last I believed since he had the emaciated look of a man who's known extended periods of liquid nourishment. "That's OK, too," he muttered frequently, excusing himself with the sadness of a man who knows better but can't help it. "I learned music from angels . . . all of it a reflection of my life."

Angels were an important part of McCarthy's cosmology. Bound for Omaha, flush with cash, he tumbled big bills onto the table like wads of crabgrass, leaping up to buy a round for the regulars, cocking his cowboy boots on the rung of a bar stool, full of the facial tics that overtake a man running from something. When he trailed back to the table with a curious woman, husky voiced as himself, they were talking about what to name their babies.

Shelly was a woman with a bottomless cup of coffee—a bleached blonde with a story of rescue from the temptations of free drinks and McCarthys, a mother who named her six-year-old Pip, "because he gave me 'Great Expectations,'" who survived marriage with a "Hell's Angel who beat me until blood run from my eyes," and who had a habit of saving dimes at the rate of $11.10 exactly in each cast-off aluminum cigar tube from Garcia Vega. She talked about salvation by Alcoholics Anonymous, about old habits dying hard ("I did speed and everything else"), and about her odd Dickensian son at his uncle's wedding.

"When the minister came to the line, 'Until death do us part,' he up and yelled 'Who cares!'"

Both Shelly's and McCarthy's eyes were lusterless as clay marbles in dark pouches, but when Shelly smiled—something McCarthy didn't—it came out under pressure, like a slow leak, and had nothing to do with McCarthy or me.

"When you smile like that," McCarthy said, "you grow a flower."

"I ran out of flowers," she said.

When I hefted the pack to leave, McCarthy hustled outside. Standing by his Oldsmobile, he said, "I'd like to write a play . . . a musical. It's about people who come to a place where there are no rules. You write the words, I'll write the music."

"I'm no good at plays."

"That's all right too." Everything was all right with McCarthy. Desperately all right.

On a whim, I asked, "Do you have an American Dream?"

He took a moment to answer, fiddling uncomfortably with his smoky beard. "You get what you wish," he said. "I dreamed I retired and lived in a cat house. It all came true. Married a widow with seventeen cats." Then he got in, revved the engine, and punched the Oldsmobile toward Omaha, waving his Stetson out the open window like a bronc rider. One cat too many, I thought. Or one woman.

The day turned cold. Red Martin was right; mine was a "slow getaway." Bill Cioni was right, too; I was walking into a "straight-line wind." Discouraged, I went back inside the bar and sat down with Shelly. Her bottomless cup was empty.

Any person undertaking . . . a long journey on foot is sure to be looked upon and considered as either a beggar, or a vagabond, or some necessitus wretch.   KARL PHILIPP MORITZ,
                                    JOURNEYS OF A GERMAN IN ENGLAND, 1782

At 5:00 in the morning the bugle is to be sounded as a signal for every man to arise and attend prayers before he leaves his wagon. Then cooking, eating, feeding teams, etc., till seven o'clock, at which time the camp is to move at the sound of the bugle.
                                    WILLIAM CLAYTON, APRIL 18, 1847

All morning I walked under low, muddy clouds scudding east. The temperature hung in the mid-forties, and wind, driving out of the northwest, caught the backpack, forcing me to tack in awkward directions. Head down, I followed the rails due west, eyes sheltered by glacier glasses with leather side flaps to keep out dust. Bill Cioni's caution began to make sense; these were "straight-line winds," rocketing across the prairie with a velocity to suck the wind out of a man, like being hit in the chest with the flat surface of a frying pan.

During lunch in the hamlet of Ames, a fat boy in T.J.'s Café said, "If I owned Oklahoma and Hell, I'd rent out Oklahoma and live in Hell." A crowd was talking Big Eight football, and the land where "the wind comes whistling down the plains" was high on their hate list. Prophecies of renewed bloodletting when Cornhuskers met Sooners next fall were stacking up like baloney sandwiches; a sign over the chipped laminate counter read: "Don't Huck With The Fusters." Nobody hucked with me.

That spring, Nebraska's football crazies were naming streets after Coach Tom Osborne. "Only two letters separate Tom and God," a gridiron guru told me, punctuating his pigskin theology with a thump on the table that bounced a hamburger off his plate. With T.J.'s savory lunch of ham sandwiches, stinging horseradish, and scalding but tasteless coffee having revived me, I nodded in agreement like a jack-ass. Not the right time to flaunt Mizzou's colors. Later, refreshed and back on the Union Pacific tracks, I was searching for "the foothills of the Rocky Mountains."

· · ·

To a stranger's eye, Ames looks the kind of town where construction costs for a bowling alley are reduced to an absolute minimum. Laid low, *flat* is an over-statement. The hamlet grubs out its daily existence next to the tracks, stitched together by a thread of small shops, a feed and farm supply store, and the faded memory of high hopes that entwines all railroad towns scattered along a main line. Yet, for the U.S. government, Ames, Nebraska, was the place where the Rocky Mountains began. Fact.

When the first Union Pacific train rumbled over the site with its cargo of top-hatted government commissioners and Union Pacific con artists (April 16, 1866), the railroad was out to extend an already generous land grab. By government con-tract, it was entitled to every odd-numbered section of land (640 acres to the sec-tion) for *ten* miles on either side of the track from Omaha to the Rockies—a hefty federal subsidy to help defray construction costs. The idea was simple: the rail-road could sell the land to settlers and recoup expenses from the gullible.

But the contract contained a caveat. Whenever the Union Pacific struck "the foothills of the Rockies," it could lay claim to every odd-numbered section of land for *twenty* miles on either side of the right-of-way. Sensing opportunity and a profitable scam, an enterprising company man, Clark Ames, spied a mound ris-ing near the future site of Ames. Think of it as an egg yolk on a plate half the size of Kansas. "Here, gentlemen, the foothills of the Rockies begin," he said solemnly—and Uncle Sam bought it. Naturally, the "foothill" town was named after Ames. So, by Union Pacific connivance and U.S. government concurrence, the Rocky Mountains begin exactly 47 miles west of Omaha and the Missouri River—500 miles east of Denver. Now rising at the astounding rate of 8.4 inches per mile, I was mountaineering west.

An hour later, fed up with eastbound freights and stumbling over railroad ties, I crossed a field of stubble to a parallel dirt road running straight to the horizon. Ten minutes later, rain swept in, cold and driving. It came in waves and sheets again, turning the shoulders of the road into foaming, dung-colored creeks; walk-ing in the sodden muck became torturous as clay balled under the Karloffs, throwing me off balance. I took to the tracks again, but the frequent trains drafted so much water that I huddled under a railroad overpass, content to be dripped on rather than washed away. Wind plowed riffles across the surface of a slough, lashing its edging grasses. As space between earth and sky narrowed, fields loomed dark and ominous. Whatever I'd been Dreaming about when I hit the road was rapidly turning to nightmare.

· · ·

Orson Pratt deemed the Mormon campsite near Fremont "a very pleasant grove which we called Paradise." By April 17, 1847, when the Mormons camped close to the site of the Ames post office, the weather abruptly changed, turning on them as it did on me. "It was so cold in the morning," Appleton Milo Harmon wrote, "that it froze ice one-half an inch thick." That day and the next, they were bothered by "disagreeable winds," as was I. When the bugle called the camp to order, Brigham struck a military mien. Taking over where Joseph Smith left off, he named himself lieutenant general of the Nauvoo Legion while granting on-the-spot promotions to Stephen Markham (colonel) and John Pack and Shadrack Roundy (majors). Below these were fourteen groups of ten foot soldiers, each with its own captain.

"After we start from here," the now-official commander in chief ordered, "every man must keep his loaded gun in his hand, or in the wagon where he can put his hand on it at a moment's warning."

Spooked by the Pawnee, whose villages were nearby, Brigham was covering his bets. Huddled under a railroad overpass, spooked by cold and rain, I wondered if I could cover mine. Charlie Roemer, I suspected, stood to lose cash to the Osage.

· · ·

North Bend, Nebraska, was grim indeed. Like most Nebraska towns that were hustled up along the railroad, it seemed dumped from a moving freight—a cluster of frame, brick, and stone with pale, glassy eyes turned toward the tracks, begging for crumbs. As Lord Dunraven said of western settlements, it looked "as if providence had been carrying a box of toy houses, and had dropped the lid and spilt the contents. The houses have come down right-end-uppermost, it's true, but they otherwise show no evidence of design . . . dumped down anywhere, apparently without any particular motive or reason for being so situated." Dunraven was British nobility and upper crust, which accounts, of course, for his umbrage and pique. A tagalong servant shined his boots.

North Bend had burned twice and frozen solid three times since 1856. When I walked in, late that afternoon, it was waiting for one or the other to happen again. I voted for conflagration. The rain had stopped, but the cold hung on, gnawing a man's best defenses, which are never *that* good in the best of times. For two hours, I holed up in a busted bank doing business as a doughnut emporium and coffee shop. The Last National Café (my naming) was stonily imperial, but when I asked for a sizable withdrawal of hamburgers and fries, one of two elderly cook-tellers set to with a passion. Sadly, the vault was barren of doughnuts, but forty or so monogrammed cups on pegs gave the place the air of a community center, and two silver-haired gents, swapping yarns over coffee, now and then glanced in my direction as if I was an intruder in a private club. They talked in rising, childlike tones that older men get when lying becomes a way of life and dentures a petty inconvenience. For a three-buck fee, a man could hang his cup on a wooden peg and pay wholesale for a refill. Mine came at premium prices, along with the food.

"The way that boy eats could make a famine," said one of the grandmotherly cooks. I fancied being called "boy," just as I'd appreciated Red Martin calling me "son."

"Saw him comin'," the other one intoned, "like a starved critter to a trough."

As for insignificant history, well deserved, North Bend is the town that built the "World's Largest Fly-Trap," a device tested in 1913 by a local druggist, John Tapster. Of its mechanics, I'm wholly ignorant. Of its existence, I'm positive. Records have it that Tapster snuffed 10,000 flies in a single day, although who actually did the counting or what species went belly-up isn't clear. Consider this: there are 16,144 species of Diptera in America, including sand flies, net-winged midges, black flies, wood gnats, snipe flies, deer flies, horse flies, stiletto flies, robber flies, and humpbacked flies. As for the other 16,134, I felt related to two—the *flatfooted* and *thick-headed* flies.

• • •

If Joseph Smith had stopped in North Bend for a cup of coffee, he wouldn't have prohibited it and Mormons today might be the largest stockholders in Starbucks, worshipping cappuccino with the rest of us. Weak and enfeebled as Nebraska coffee is, it poses no menace to the human nervous system, ranking right up there with warm tap water. In the Last National Café, I drank flagons but still couldn't bestir myself.

In the Midwest, coffee beans are less *roasted* than *toasted*, and lightly at that, so as not to stir up too much color or flavor that might lead to excess. Across the prairies and plains the preferred "restaurant blend"—served with commercial zest, I must admit—is made by an Omaha roasting company claiming descent from two fraternal sons of the soil, advertised on the label as brothers. In Nebraska, a Mormon is under more threat from drowning in his cup than death from an overdose of caffeine. Smith never actually denounced coffee by name, revealing only his antipathy for "tobacco, strong drinks and hot drinks"; it was Brigham who tacked coffee and tea on the prohibited beverage list, ignoring hot chocolate (Mormons swoon for it), hot lemonade, and hot cider. But in 1847, Mormons headed for Zion were still imbibing questionable hot brews and whiskey as well. Sacks of coffee and barrels of the hard stuff were tucked in their wagons.

Next to water, coffee was by far the most universal drink on the road west. In his famous how-to-get-there-from-here book, *The Prairie Traveler*, Randolph Marcy advised fifteen pounds of coffee per head on the trip across the plains. Like those of every other westbound wanderer, Mormon beans were carried green in ten-pound sacks and roasted in a frying pan. Whiskey was carried in jugs or wooden firkins, ready for quick tapping against all manner of bites—frost, snake, and mosquito—or for an occasional "constitutional." Mormon journals are curiously silent on these matters, enough to suggest revisionist history. In "A Bill of Particulars" issued at Nauvoo for Mormon "emigrants leaving this government" (a very telling line), each family of five was advised to take a pound of tea, five pounds of coffee, and one gallon of alcohol *per person*. Assuming the suggested manifest applied to the first 148 to hit the road, the gross totals of coffee beans and booze might have run as high as 725 pounds of the former and 148 gallons of the latter.

Today's Mormon abstinence from alcohol was less a "Word of Wisdom," as Smith's brainchild became known, than a child of its times. There was very little *inspired* about it. By 1840, "temperance" was everywhere in the air. America was a nation of soaks and tosspots, Mormons among them; and American Dreamers were tossing back an average of five gallons of whiskey per head in 1830 (the average is well under two gallons today), and most folks felt very, very good during their waking hours. Hot alcoholic drinks were the rage, usually brandy-laced toddies, and it was this bibulous excess that the prophet had in mind, having borrowed almost every other currently circulating idea—including Masonic ritual and mystical practices of the Jewish cabal—to get his "ism" off the ground. Unfortunately, coffee got caught in the crossfire, in part because Brigham couldn't get a monopoly on the trade in Utah. Never a "dry" man, Joseph Smith once opened a bar in the living room of his home in Nauvoo (his outraged wife, Emma, promptly closed it down); so whatever his "dreams of empire and indulgence," as Fawn Brodie calls them, they were partly fueled by coffee and alcohol, to name two ingredients in his prophetic punch. When one of the faithful, Almon Babbitt, came before a local Mormon judge, accused of excessive familiarity with sour mash whiskey, he argued in self-defense that "he was only following the example of President Joseph Smith."

When Brigham headed west, Smith's Word of Wisdom hadn't yet fully caught fire, and, outbound for Zion, Mormons had their share of tipplers, coffee drinkers, and devotees of what William Byrd once called "that bewitching vegetable"— tobacco. Arrived in Utah, Brigham soon embarked on a rough-and-ready whiskey business with Gentile passersby. With what could be called a "bottoms-up interest" in a distillery that manufactured a particularly virulent rotgut known as "Valley Tan"—made from molasses and green tea—you might say he "soaked" his visitors. Today, nondrinking Mormons live longer than the rest of us, but on the road to Zion they were fellow travelers.

. . .

I skipped North Bend with a growing urinary problem and relieved myself in a copse outside of town. It isn't easy finding a copse on land scabbed off as a parking lot. When one showed up, I drained all six cups in a rush, about the same color going out as going in. Two miles west of town, cottonwoods were rife with birdlife, and the sun, smeary as egg yolk on a plate, broke through tatters of cloud. A jay, some nuthatches, finches, and a woodpecker were up among the mouse-ear buds crowning the trees, trying to make the best of things. Away from any sign of a house, I climbed a fence, crossed a field to the Union Pacific tracks, and scrambled another mile or two before finding a snug, grassy patch off the main line. Light was going fast when I fumbled the tent into position, put down my sleeping pad, and squeezed into the sleeping bag. I sat with my back against the pack, listening to a sigh of wind running the tent's nylon walls, marking the day's walk in red on my maps, drinking the last tot of my bourbon, and making jottings in my logbook. Finished, I pulled on a warm vest, lit my candle lantern, and spent twenty minutes reading from *William Clayton's Journal.* That day, our paths had been almost identical. Somewhere nearby, perhaps a stone's throw from where I was reading, Clayton had lain down to his rest: "I slept with [Howard] Eagan in Heber's wagon, Heber [Kimball] being gone to sleep with President Young," he wrote. "All peace and quietness."

In the night, Union Pacific freights rattled through every thirty minutes, rumbling with the commerce of the prairies, cycloid headlights sweeping the tracks, wheels screeching steel to steel like giant fingernails clawing at a blackboard. The earth heaved beneath me. If the gods of this world are all travelers,

FOLLOWING THE WRONG GOD HOME

as McCarthy believed, they'd get little sleep by the Union Pacific tracks and no Dreams at all.

6

I would show . . . with a pair of strong boots you can get to Rome. Good-bye all ye vampires of modern travel.
ARTHUR COOPER, "THE WALKING VICAR," CIRCA 1880

I walked some this afternoon in company with Orson Pratt and suggested to him the idea of fixing a set of wooden cog wheels to the hub of a wagon wheel, in such order as to tell the exact number of miles we travel each day. WILLIAM CLAYTON,
APRIL 19, 1847

East of Schuyler, the trail sagged south across soggy fields toward the Platte, forcing me to keep to the railway tracks on a rifle-shot course toward white grain elevators in the distance. Under warming skies, volunteers poked through the loams of the river bottom like devilish green tongues, corn sprouted from last year's crops, struggling vainly for a foothold before spring plowing. Two miles from the Colfax County line, Marvin McGinn eased out his front door, crossed his yard and the twin tracks of the Union Pacific main line to meet me. "Anybody walking my land, I want to talk to," he said, his voice soft and apologetic. I asked how anyone living fifty feet from the UP main line could sleep at night.

"Y'know," he said, "In one ear, out . . ."

Marvin's caution was prudent, since he rented fifty lots for summer cottages along the river and kept an eye out for would-be felons. When I explained myself, he offered me lunch. "Not much, but you're welcome to it."

Marvin's head held a lot of territory under one PAC Seeds cap. When he hung it on a peg behind the kitchen door, a weather line circumscribed his forehead like a cranial equator. His wife, Irene, served sandwiches, and Mike, their six-foot son with a smile like sunshine on the side of a barn, stuffed two extra in my pack "for later on . . . y'know . . . sort of a snack." The McGinns plant seven hundred acres of soybeans and corn every year, and, as Mike told me, "early heat means a late frost." Marvin pegged it for May 9. "Don't get rid of your long underwear," he advised.

But that noon the McGinns were waiting for a delicacy to arrive. "Any day now," Irene said.

"Any day," Mike repeated.

"Soon," said Marvin.

Then, preaching a gospel of spring's bounty to an obvious heathen of nature, Marvin quoted McGinn family scripture: "When the leaves on the cottonwoods are as big as squirrels' ears, comes the sponge mushroom."

"Any minute," Irene said, revising her schedule.

Mike dropped his ham sandwich as if it were dog meat. Irene and Marvin bowed their heads in a moment of prayer as the collected McGinns paid homage to an edible member of the class of Ascomycetes—the common morel. Later, I realized they were bestowing a gastronome's blessing in the fervent hope that I wouldn't be left out come the day of harvest. As it turned out, the McGinns' God was good to me.

· · ·

Back on the UP main line, I kept my eye on the cottonwoods lining the Platte. Close by, the Mormons had nooned on April 20, 1847, and the night before Brigham savored the luxury of a "fine brandy." Porter Rockwell, Joseph Smith's onetime bodyguard and erstwhile bartender, known as the "Avenging Angel," had galloped back to Winter Quarters to fetch a high-proof cask of the stuff—a gift from the Mormons' old friend Thomas Kane of Philadelphia. Along with Rockwell, the booze arrived in the company of a murderer—Nathaniel Thomas Brown.

Tom Brown was a Mormon hard case if there ever was one—"a grain of that violent outlaw individualism so common on the frontier and so infrequent among the Saints," Wallace Stegner wrote in *The Gathering of Zion*. Wanted for murder in Iowa, Brown made the mistake of leaving his trademark knife in his victim's chest. Yet Brigham took him in.

Tom Brown claimed no long-term interest in the story of the Mormons; a few months later, he was knifed to death in a brawl near Council Bluffs, Iowa. (Mormon history claims he was "accidentally" shot.) Hearing of his predictable demise, Brigham Young said that "Brown's old shoes were worth more than the whole body of the man who killed him." But walking through the landscape of Brown's first day with the Mormons, I saw him as archetypally American—part of the Dream that makes up a westerner's rough-cut libertarian inheritance. Less outlaw

FOLLOWING THE WRONG GOD HOME

than outcast, it's his frontier mindset that still marks much of our conception of the West and not the community that Mormons came to represent in its dead vast. Individualism and community were frequent, if often incompatible, fellow travelers on the trails west—twin specters of the forming Big Snooze.

Bill Bonney, the Iowa sheriff who later made Brown infamous in *The Banditti of the Prairie*, understood too well the Saints idea of "community" and the way it closed around a man, tucking him into the shadows like a ghost disappearing through a wall. In Illinois, it twice saved Joseph Smith from the long arm of Missouri law when agents tried to snatch him for questioning in the near-fatal shooting of the state's governor, Lilburn Boggs, who had ordered the Mormons "exterminated."

After Smith resettled in Nauvoo, the hated Missouri governor was three times ventilated in the head by an unknown assassin. Although Boggs survived the attack, rumors of his death burned through Nauvoo like flames through chaparral. When Smith heard it, he shouted, "The Angel did it!" Two days later, Porter Rockwell rode back into town. By one account, Rockwell regretted that he hadn't killed "the son-of-a-bitch." Years later, when I asked his great-great-grandson—a Mormon whose shoulder-length locks are meant to imitate those of his notorious ancestor—if attempted murder was in the family tree, he smiled and denied it. To this day, the evidence is inconclusive.

Watching shadows drifting on the river, I realized that the McGinns had inadvertently given me a metaphor for this bifurcated American Dreaming. When I finally looked up *morels* in the Peterson *Field Guide to Mushrooms*, I was surprised and delighted. The entry read, "morels fruit in spring, either solitary or in clusters, on rich soil and in moist places, *individually* on the river bottoms or in lowland *communities*." Seems sponge mushrooms grow and fruit handily—"*alone or together*." Textbook American Dream. The individual morels that sicken the body have names of greatest beauty—Elfin Saddle, Wavy Lorchel, Ivory Candle. Or, like Porter Rockwell, the Avenging Angel.

• • •

Near Rogers, a gandy dance was in full swing. A yellow-cabbed Pettibone laid rails for the roadbed gang, its mantislike crane arm and dangling electromagnet picking up old rails and laying down new, banging out a steel chorus like a giant's wind chime. Trailed by another track-straddling behemoth that welded rail ends, it formed quarter-mile sections of CWR—continuous welded rail. Sparks sluiced and hissed along ribboned steel. Gandy dancers pushed old rails off the right-of-way and bull-handled new rails into place. Now and then, a man would swipe a forearm across his eyes, brushing sweat from his brow, toting and lifting in the heat. Where CWR met the ties, another crew with eight-pound mauls sledged it home using twenty-two-pound cinch plates, each taking six spikes—three outside, three inside. Dark faces shone at me, eye meeting eye. Native American faces. One answered my nod. They likely didn't know that Pawnee *women* built a mile of the original Union Pacific grade near Fremont, hauling fill for the roadbed in baskets.

Along the main line, rail traffic was squeezed to a single track; east and westbound freights rumbled past, drafting dust. When I clambered off the track onto a parallel inspection road, dodging between parked company vans, I turned for one last look, thinking of Karl Bodmer's images of Native Americans, of rich dentalian shell and beadwork necklaces, of proud vermilion Mandan faces on the upper Missouri, of ebony hair decorated with eagle feathers, and of the Pawnee whose villages once lined the Platte. Gone forever. What were Americans Dreaming then?

In Rogers, a young widow sold me a beer. It sobered me up.

· · ·

Later, a woman showed up on the tracks holding out a quart-sized Styrofoam container with a straw sticking out of a plastic lid. "How about a chocolate malt?" she asked.

"Couldn't refuse," I answered, flabbergasted.

Up close, she had large, intense eyes and the nervousness of a sensible female in the middle of nowhere with a total stranger. But gutsy Kate Freeman, who worked as a stringer for a North Bend weekly, somehow got downwind of a story and photo op, no doubt from something I'd let slip in the Last National Café while swilling enfeebled coffee.

In the half hour we spent together, I did my best to answer her questions, but it was subterfuge: I was in the dark myself. Yes, I was trailing Mormons (my reasons seemed murky as the Platte); yes, I'd done my homework before leaving the East (true); no, I hadn't been hassled (one cop didn't count for much); yes, I might write about it (and might not); and yes, I'd left my family in upstate New York while I hit the road for history's sake. Meanwhile, I slurped greedily at the gift malt.

As writers will, Kate confided, "I took a course from the poet William Kloefkorn. Have you heard of him?"

"We once sang a duet together."

In the "small world" category, Kloefkorn and I sang a duet on my forty-seventh birthday at Bullwinkle's Tavern in Rochester where Nebraska's white-maned poet laureate was a passable baritone even under the influence of New Yorkers. Blue-jeaned and booted, he had the cragginess of advancing middle age carved into his face like blowouts on a tallgrass prairie. I admired his earthy lines from "Platte Valley Homestead":

> Punch a thumb into this Platte Valley soil,
> and if the thumb is longer than a moment
> you'll strike a mother lode
> far richer even
> than a good rainwater cistern.

What Bill Kloefkorn meant by "mother lode" is the Ogallala Aquifer, the largest reservoir of freshwater in the world. Early on, American Dreamers like Zebulon Pike and Stephen H. Long rode, unknowing, over its treasure and promise. Crossing the plains of Kansas and Colorado in 1806, Pike bemoaned, "These vast plains . . . may become in time as celebrated as the sandy deserts of Africa." Hugging the Platte in 1819–20, Long and his botanist, Edwin James, took up the same "barren and uncongenial" refrain, dubbing the region "unfit residence for any but a nomad population."

Like other Americans confronting the West for the first time, Pike and Long suffered from nightmares of a land without trees. Under the hooves of their horses lay two billion acre-feet of water (one acre-foot equals 325,810 gallons), eighty times the annual flow of Rocky Mountain snowmelt draining from the Colorado, Missouri, Platte, Republican, and Red Rivers. Sooner or later, someone was bound to wonder why twenty million buffalo could grow fat on "The Great American Desert."

• • •

At last light, I crept through a fence opposite the Reed Mill and Elevator Company, walking on packed sand and scrambling among the scrub for high ground to put down my tent. Fifty feet off the tracks, I cut away a brushy overhang with the miniature saw in my Swiss Army knife, finally managing to get the tent centered on a lopsided patch of uncertain grass. Surrounded by sand, it was like camping on a desert island.

After a dinner of two McGinn gift sandwiches, I rolled in and promptly rolled out. For an hour, I squirmed on uneven ground, trying to relax while lights from the mill cast moving shadows of branches across the nylon. Free from the pack, I was tormented by the memory of its straps, my shoulders and spine still compressed into a nagging, unyielding ache. Two aspirin only drove it into a loose knot. Toward morning, I slept to the sound of distant thunder. A few miles away and fourteen decades earlier, chilly and insomniac under a wagon, aspirin was what William Clayton hadn't. That night Luke Johnson pulled Clayton's infected tooth and botched the job. "He got only half," Clayton wrote sourly, "the balance being left in the jaw." Unable to eat, he "could not sleep for pain till near morning."

7

It requires a direct dispensation from heaven to become a walker.
HENRY DAVID THOREAU, "WALKING"

About 2:30 the rain began to descend heavily, accompanied by heavy peals of thunder and vivid lightning which continued till about 4:00 o'clock. A strong north wind blew up, the rain and thunder ceased and the weather grew very cold.
WILLIAM CLAYTON, APRIL 21, 1847

About 7:00 A.M., the sky opened and Niagara washed over my tent—icy, unforgiving, relentless. Outside, the runoff created yawning gullies, forming and reforming under the load of water, eroding the sand beyond my grassy island. Witless, I'd camped in a catch basin. When water pooled and began a steady climb toward the tent, I moved. No time to lose. Pulling on my Gore-Tex rain suit over the nifty polypropylene long johns I'd slept in, I plunged into the downpour, barely managing to get the tent down and stuffed in my backpack before water lapped at my boots. They mired almost to the ankle, making sucking sounds as I slogged toward the tracks.

At 7:30, I floundered into the Top Notch Café to a litany of bitching, the place choked with farmers who'd been driven from their fields by the ongoing downpour. An elderly sodbuster in a begrimed green raincoat, with a two-pronged steel hook where his left hand used to be, squinted in my direction, eyes thin as razor blades. When I closed the door behind me, conversation dried up, the only sound the *plock, plock* of water dripping off my clothing. For fifteen seconds, I stood for dress inspection from the generals of the fields. *Asshole* in every eye. "How far to Columbus?" I asked the waitress.

FOLLOWING THE WRONG GOD HOME

"Sixteen miles," she answered.

I ordered ham and eggs, then sat alone in a corner. One by one her customers drained away, gone home to watch television, wrung out of complaints. By ten, I could tell she was getting nervous having me around, so I ordered sandwiches to go. When I got up to pay, she finally smiled and looked into my eyes, a plains woman in her late thirties, simply dressed in jeans and sweater, no makeup. Her good looks and naturalness made me homesick for my wife. She knew what I was thinking and looked chastely away, but at least I could keep her in mind for a couple of miles. Outside, rain hammered at the glass.

• • •

I made eight miles in three hours and twenty minutes. Freights grumbled through every half hour, drafting ice water, but it was better than the highway with its continuous wash from eighteen-wheelers. I'd lost my gloves, so I covered my hands with two nylon stuff sacks, tucking them up under the cuffs of my rain gear. Bone cold and wind whipped, I washed up on the shores of another flyspeck village under glowering skies and a dull, crepuscular light.

Richland, Nebraska, was a hamlet of dark humor, perfectly suiting the day, but at least there was a café. Two good old boys loading feed into a pickup at the Farmers Co-op hailed me through the drizzle. "You walk all the way from Schuyler to eat in that place?"

"From Omaha," I answered.

"Shit, are you gonna be disappointed!"

Above the café's counter, a sign threatened: "We have sold our cow, so we don't need your bull."

I didn't need two greasy hamburgers either, but I had to get out of the rain and it was a pay-up-or-keep-moving kind of place—no shoes, no shirt, no service—and the boys at the Co-Op were right about disappointment.

• • •

Two miles east of Columbus, my feet finally blew.

From Richland, I'd limped out five mean miles. Sheltered in the lee of a line shack, I took a look—a grim tally: blisters on both heels, the little toe on my left foot a ballooned, watery mass. Wet feet hadn't helped; the soles were gray and wrinkled as soggy newsprint, so I changed socks and gave up. Taking a side road, I limped north to U.S. 30 and stuck out my thumb. What the hell, I rationalized, even the Mormons had taken to their wagons in foul weather. The guy who picked me up didn't talk much at first; jacketed against the cold, grimy from his labors, and mud-covered to his knees, he had the essential grimness of a man temporarily dispossessed. Yes, he would drop me at a motel. "Bet you see a lot," he volunteered gloomily, trying to make conversation.

"Not much except rain."

Without warning, he erupted, "Would you believe those farmer sons-of-bitches are ripping out the shelter belts! I'm takin' their money to do it! Ain't that fuckin' somethin'!"

I wanted to commiserate, perhaps sound suffused with vulcanism, but I was flat worn-out. *Humor him*, I concluded, managing a feeble protest.

"Them trees done more good for this county than all the farm subsidies in history! Kept the wind from blowing this state away. You tell me I'm right." He glared at me briefly, his eyes inflamed knots. Maybe he'd been drinking.

"Damned right," I said, plucking up. "What's behind it?"

"T'git more ground t'plow. Farmers owe the fuckin' banks."

It was a refrain I'd heard before. Perhaps an extra strip of ground added enough cash crop to float a failing mortgage or pay down a good loan gone bad. I said as much.

"Yeah, they're hurtin'," he sulked. "But it's still a fuckin' shame to cut them trees."

At the Super 8 Motel, he said, "Sleep fuckin' tight."

I could hope.

· · ·

At the front desk, the clerk gave me a bovine blink, surprised when a hobbling, grimy geek handed her green plastic. She looked at the credit card ("American Excess," I sometimes call it when trying to curb an impulse), then back at me, then back at the card. A suspicion of larceny floated into her eyes while I dripped quietly on the carpet and she checked me out with credit card central. When the approval came back, she seemed still uncertain, watching me sign on the dotted line as if worried that I would scrawl an "X."

In the room, I emptied my pack—including a couple of cups of water that had somehow defied the ingenuity of the pack's makers; but I'd been hasty that morning in exiting swamp city, and leakage wasn't entirely the manufacturer's fault. Stuff sacks that held my clothes were dry, but everything else was either damp or soggy. In damage control mode, I dried everything as best I could with bathroom towels, including the sand-begrimed tent that I washed in the bathtub. Finished, I draped the lot over desk and chairs, sleeping bag as well, until the place looked

FOLLOWING THE WRONG GOD HOME

like wash day at summer camp. Letting the humor of my predicament spill into the room (I was almost fifty, for God's sake), I belly-laughed for the first time in two days—rasping, wheezy, choked.

. . .

I limped over to Barnie's Pizza and pigged out on his Thursday night buffet for $3.62, not including the buck gratuity that I grudgingly added, not being in a gratuitous frame of mind. The listless waitress looked as if she'd been wrung out by hand, and the pizza she served me drooped over the edges of its pan like soggy canvas. Back in my room, I thumbed on the television and got this encouraging update: "A monster spring storm, folks. Some places in Colorado could get as much as twenty inches . . . and that's the white stuff."

All night rain hammered on the uncertain balloon frame construction of the motel, drowning the parking lot and choking drains and gutters. Lights in a nearby shopping plaza appeared, disappeared, and reappeared, smeared between blowing curtains of water. Now and then a car punched through, lights blazing, winking out, lost. A semi, revved to a scream, sent a wall of water arching high over the street. Toward morning, I sat up and laughed again—bitter, indignant, self-mocking. Having sold my cow, so to speak, I didn't need this bull either.

. . .

George Dodds caught me staring at his midriff. The rain had passed, leaving a morning streaky with high clouds and pale sun, but my feet agonized at walking. On my third cup of flavorless coffee (more Fraternal Sons of the Soil), I noticed Dodds's belt buckle.

"Coca Bola," George said, which sounded like a Tahitian greeting-of-the-day.

"Beg pardon?"

"Coca Bola."

"Susquehanna," I said, returning the greeting.

"Coca Bola," he repeated, pointing to his buckle, certain now that I was dense as Asian mahogany. "It's the way you cut it."

Marge, his wife, came over and topped off my morning cup of hot water, frazzled at the pace she was pouring refills among the flavor disadvantaged. I estimated that Daylight Donuts would go under by dark unless they changed coffee suppliers. The deep luster of her husband's belt buckle stood out against his plaid shirt like gemstone, the kind of pattern you stare into, not at.

"Polished stone?" I queried.

Without answering, George bolted for the door, his chair wobbling on one leg until it settled again.

"Now you done it," Marge said, a friendly woman with a fragrance of fresh baked bread and pale eyes round as a cherry tomato.

"Did I offend him?"

"George? No. He just wants to talk up his hobby."

Back from wherever, George laid a case in front of me that could have held a brace of handcrafted dueling pistols. He snapped it open. "Wow," I said.

· · ·

George Dodds's passion is jewelry—not lapis lazuli, garnet, jade, topaz, opal, tourmaline or turquoise, but something equally fine and perhaps more rare, with the beauty of cat's-eye agate, scarlet-flecked opal, and lustrous carnelian—brooches, earrings, pins, clasps, buckles. All *wood*. Each piece brilliantly polished. Not a stone or gemstone in the lot.

"Manzanita," George said, fingering one gloriously burnished piece. "Got hooked on it in Casa Grande, New Mexico." He pronounced it *Case'a'Grand*.

Dipping into the chest, he lifted out another ethereal sample and held it up until light dazzled its grain. Honey locust, mesquite, Nebraska cedar, Mexican ebony, tulip wood, Osage orange, and buffaloberry had all seized on George like a grand mal.

"Natural finish, that's the secret," he confided. "Nature puts the art in it before I ever touch it. Cut the grain one way and you get beautiful color. Another way, you may not get it." His eyes turned smoky. "After you're at it for a while, you feel it on the inside. Never crosscut fine wood. Go with the grain. That's its beauty."

When I asked him his favorites, two answers popped out of his mouth like cherry pits. "Paduc . . . and myrtle. Some call paduc 'African purple heart.' Myrtle grows in only three places . . . Oregon, California, and the Holy Land." He saw me admiring his work. "Go ahead," he said, "take a belt buckle on me."

"I'll pay you."

"I been paid."

I protested, but George insisted. When I chose the buffaloberry, rich as Oloroso sherry and a Great Plains wood into the bargain, George's marquee smile flicked on.

"Figured you for that one. There's spirit in it . . . an' it's been places, too. I've had it for a while."

Outside, we lounged against the cab of his truck.

"God almighty," he said, "I love people with places to go. I try to keep Marge and me moving most of the time. We got us a thirty-five-foot Sunflower trailer with one of them tippy-out sides, a washer-dryer, tee-vee, you name it. If I could,

I'd go with you. I'd drive until the damn road runs out. You could walk and me and Marge would go ahead and set up camp. It'd be a hell of a trip!"

I told him I might not make it, that I had a bad attitude and blisters. At that moment, I confided, I didn't much give a damn one way or another.

"Don't believe that crap for a minute! No way! Seems to me you're headed in the right direction. Isn't that right, Marge?"

Marge had stepped outside to get George to help her at the counter. "They're drinking coffee faster than I can make it," she said. She still had the carafe in her fist. In the full light of day I swear that coffee looked like something from a weak kidney.

"George is right," she said. "You can make it." She leaned toward me, suddenly confidential, as if the handful of customers wolfing the daylights out of the doughnuts and swilling watery coffee might hear what she had to say and suddenly bolt the place. "This here's only temporary for us. We came up from New Mexico to save our daughter from a bleeding ulcer."

"Sorry to hear it. I hope she's better."

Marge winked, grinned. About half a cup of urine slobbered from the carafe onto the concrete. "She's OK now. We found out what was causing the trouble . . . and got rid of him."

George snorted.

• • •

Altogether, I spent thirty-six hours in Columbus, a big farm town with all the charisma of a stripped Ford pickup trying to dress itself up with extra chrome, roll bars, and mag wheels. Commerce and "boosterism" were squandering its fine old town square, feeding a cancer of concrete block shopping malls and commercial strip centers along a four-lane highway on the north side. The four-lane highway—a bad Dream—connected a two-lane highway on the east with a two-lane on the west. So far as I could tell, its main connection was from developers to their bank accounts, the resulting architectural travesty what H. L. Mencken called "the American lust for the hideous."

The seat of Platte County, Columbus lies at the junction of the Loup and Platte Rivers. By 1847 it was already a site for hammering out business deals, as the Mormons soon discovered. On the day their wagons rolled by, a grand chief of the Pawnee waded across the Loup. "Several hundred" others were poised on the opposite bank to make sure the parley turned a quick profit. Brigham bargained out of harm's way by gifting the chief tobacco, lead, gunpowder, salt, and fishhooks. But the Pawnee sulked, claiming the gifts were paltry and the white man a cheap date. Besides, he said, whites would kill the buffalo and rob his people of their livelihood—a prophecy that came true. Brigham, however, rightly detected a worm in this bad apple and gave it a name—Peter Sarpy. An Indian trader and no friend of the Mormons, Sarpy was sighted among the Indians across the river. Whatever his role that day, an old and familiar stench wafted into the Mormon wagons—spite and persecution.

. . .

Shucked to the cob, Columbus became for me a metaphor of Thomas Jefferson's Dream of an agrarian republic going sour, a cornucopia that began with the "noble farmer" and seemed to be ending that spring with depleted resources and broken Dreams. While Willie Nelson was singing for Farm Aid, Uncle Sam was offering a Band-Aid, and all across Nebraska, farmers were eager to vent their dilemma. "If you can't beat 'em . . . and you can't . . . you gotta join 'em," one told me. "Either line up for the federal dole or sell out to the bigger guys."

Oddly enough, the pan that fried small family farms was heated with the good intentions of a Mormon, Ezra Taft Benson, whose grandfather (the original E. T.) came west with Brigham in 1847. As secretary of agriculture under Dwight Eisenhower (1953–61), Benson promoted "agribusiness," the streamlining of crop production and other efficiencies for farmers that paved the way for today's giant "corporate farms." Benson's unintentional legacy meant small farmers needed to think like corporate CEOs. With enthusiastic help from local banks, they added land and equipment, consolidated operations, and went into debt in an attempt to stay ahead of the agribusiness game. Land prices shot up, along with costs for chemical fertilizers, fancy new machinery, and interest rates. Overproduction followed, commodity prices fell, land prices bottomed out, and foreclosures ballooned on a scale not seen since the Great Depression.

Still, going broke was always a farmer's second occupation on the Great Plains. Although a long drink of water the size of Lake Huron lay under the Nebraska sod, getting to it was a problem. In the 1870s, south of Columbus, a parched traveler spotted a sod house with a hand-dug well and made a beeline for the bucket. He licked his lips and let the bucket down. Instead of a splash, he got a hollow *thunk*. Then he spotted the sign:

> THIS CLAIM FOR SALE
> Four miles to nearest neighbor.
> Seven miles to nearest schoolhouse.

Fourteen miles to nearest town.
Two hundred feet to nearest water.
God bless our home!
For further information address
THOMAS WARD, OSKALOOSA, IOWA

*Journeys alone have a life of their own. . . . Given time, I thought,
I could walk anywhere.* JOHN HILLABY

*There has been no trouble from the Indians. . . . The cannon was
prepared for action, and stood all night just outside the wagons. . . .
From southeast to southwest you can see the course of the Loup Fork
for a number of miles.* WILLIAM CLAYTON,
APRIL 22, 1847

The name "Loup" is a French translation of the Pawnee word *skidi*, meaning
"wolf." This largest tributary of the Platte is formed by the union of the North,
Middle, and South Loup Rivers, which drain a soggy web of streams from the
water-rich Sand Hills region of Nebraska—country made famous by Mari Sandoz in her book *Old Jules*. The Mormon route up the north bank of the Loup was
dictated by necessity; there was no good fording place at its confluence with the
Platte.

When French trappers arrived on the Loup in 1715, the Pawnee were already
living along the river and had been for at least a hundred years. Their unique
earth and timber lodges—"a perfect circle about forty-four feet," as William Clayton described them, were strung like beads on a silver string of water from the
Loup's confluence with the Platte at Columbus to the present site of Fullerton,
thirty miles to the west. Between the Loup and the Platte lay a V-shaped wedge of
Pawnee land. Think of it as a neck, with the Platte and Loup as strings on a necklace and Columbus, at the confluence, its pendant.

On May 19, the Mormons passed an Indian battleground, picking their way
through a broad patch of graves "several hundred yards wide"—remnants of a

recent Pawnee encounter. By the evening of April 21, when the vanguard prepared its cannon for action "just outside the wagons" (most able-bodied men stood on "picket guard" through a frigid night), the Pawnee were on a fast track to nowhere. A growing worry to Brigham, they were beset on all sides. A year before, they'd been decimated in a Sioux raid. A month after Brigham passed, eighty-three were butchered—again by the Sioux—at the mouth of the Cedar River. In 1849 they lost one-fourth of an estimated 10,000 to cholera carried west in pioneer wagons. By 1869 only four clusters of Pawnee lodges remained on the Loup, all huddled along Beaver Creek, near today's town of Genoa. By 1906 only 640 Pawnee had survived (all in Oklahoma's Indian Territory), and today they have all but vanished.

In Caddoan (Pawnee) sacred myth, they came from a hole in the ground along the Loup River (Old-Home-in-the-Darkness) and were led by the moon to the earth's surface where they took human and animal forms. In his classic Pawnee ethnology, *The Lost Universe*, Gene Weltfish notes their "elaborate round of rituals" involving well-practiced performances, special costuming, and high drama; all of which supported a "complex philosophy of the creation of the universe and of man and their ongoing nature"—a description that, when I thought of it, perfectly suited the Mormons.

Festooning themselves in feathers and multicolors, the Pawnee gave sacred names to participants in their annual "cult" celebrations—an elaborately *staged* "Grand Opera." Part of a "ceremony of creation at the first thunder," it reenacted their sacred creation myth. In a ritual that early struck terror into the whites, they sacrificed a maiden (usually a captive Sioux), calling on the powers of the sacred Evening Star.

· · ·

Like the Pawnee, the Mormons were stargazers, ordering life and death around the sun, moon, and stars—a cosmological theology that deserves a brief mention. Crossing Pawnee ground near Old-Home-in-the-Darkness, it struck me that given the brevity of his life and his high-voltage imagination, Joseph Smith's divinations would be of interest to the Pawnee and, possibly, to Stephen King.

Americans have long been aware that Mormonism is tinged by the seemingly bizarre. For years, in their temples, they reenacted a miracle play recounting the Mormon myth of creation (it's now on videotape, but still required viewing), using locals in the roles of Adam, Eve, and Old-Snake-in-the-Grass. But it's Joseph Smith's take on the "complex philosophy of . . . man and (his) ongoing nature" that would get a round of applause from the Pawnee and give Stephen King pause.

According to Smith, mankind's "ongoing nature" under the stars is *physical* and a man's physical nature is *forever*. Smith's suspicion of the "immutability of matter," which, he claimed, could not be changed or added to ("the same today and forever"), led to Mormon extraterrestrial theology. With less physics than intuition, Smith proclaimed, "As man now is, God once was. As God now is, man will become." If matter is forever, he reasoned, taking a step further into a Twilight Zone, then God is a *physical* being, only "perfected."

Since a man can become a *physical* God and God is a *perfected* man, Smith reasoned that any man-God surely needs a celestial home. Where else but among the stars and planets? Assuming a man embraced the Mormon faith to a T, he (not she, however) could evolve to become *perfected* and emerge "in the fullness of time" as a god of his own universe—all body parts attached. Better yet, Smith argued, multiple universes can accommodate multiple Gods. (He was a fan of all things plural.) Women weren't left out of Smith's celestial revelation of perfected beings, although they were subordinate and required to stand by their man-God. To boot, a perfected man-God could conduct business from a planet of personal real estate. Labeled as *prophecy*—which it could have been, for all I know—it seems . . . well . . . out of this world.

Just the thing to give a down-at-the-heels walker a reason for a time-out. I settled my back against a railroad switch box, and mused on the possibilities of religion and science fiction, considering the disadvantages of being forever a physical God—celestial blisters, for example. As I mole-skinned my ragged heels, I was thinking that Smith's enthusiasms were a lot like an advanced course in American Dreaming, although more along the lines of Isaac Asimov who, come to think of it, had an equally star-struck quality to his writing. Anyway, thinking about the possibilities of Smith's revelations made an otherwise dreadful day stimulating, although I suspected that news of men hoping to become gods had already reached my wife.

• • •

Even more stimulating was how Joseph Smith worked out his signposting on the road to Glory. Mormon glory is achieved by degrees, he argued—Telestial, Terrestrial, and Celestial in ascending order, depending on where you're seated on heaven's bus. Liars, adulterers, thieves, and "the endless hosts of people of all ages who have lived after the manner of this world"—most of us, that is—get off at the first stop where accommodations are much less *stellar*, although there's a lot of classrooms where one gets to make up the courses he's missed. Those "accountable persons . . . who die without law" (this includes lukewarm Latter-day Saints, assorted backsliders, and folks who didn't know the bus ever existed until it unexpectedly showed up) get off at the second stop—more upscale, trendier classrooms, with a better choice of restaurants. Only those who have practiced "complete obedience to gospel or celestial law" disembark at the third stop, described as a place of "transcendent beauty" and "the gate through which the heirs of that kingdom will enter."

A closer look at the famed Mormon Temple in Salt Lake City shows this creative and unique Mormon fascination with things extraterrestrial. Sun-signs and moon-signs decorate its exterior (as they did on the Nauvoo temple), all borrowed from Joseph's brief sojourn into Masonic ritual, including the all-seeing eye and the carpenter's square and compass—the same all-seeing eye, by the way, that shows up on the U.S. one-dollar bill since many of the founding fathers were Masons. Mormons seldom point out these symbols on the temple, let alone explain them to visitors, but on its surface, one can read the remarkable Dreamlike evolution of Joseph Smith from New York farmboy to prophet, and from "King of the Kingdom of God" to a wannabe God of his own universe. Joseph Smith, one might say—and I will—was a veritable "shooting star."

. . .

Feet tended to, I hefted the pack and carried on climbing the Loup River necklace. With the Pawnee long gone, its beads had changed hands, now a lackluster but congenial grouping of farm towns. Free of Columbus's fading jewel, I walked with an equally fading will, my two-day rest having given only temporary ease to my feet while bolstering a false courage. A fast-moving front, black and menacing as cast iron, piled in from the west, shrinking the sun to an achromous disk. Cold before the cold came, I pulled on my bunting vest. Next came two translucent aborted fetuses, probably canine, stuck to the pavement at highway's edge; then a sullen, curse-spewing man and a wraith-woman with a swollen purple eye ordering me away from a house amid a jumble of abandoned cars where I'd stopped in search of water.

"Clear off!" he yelled. "No bums allowed!"

In a wailing voice, the woman echoed, "Clear off! Clear off!"

. . .

In 1889, Leander Gerrard gave Columbus the boot, moving to a patch of prairie thirteen miles away. Announcing that no town had been named for President James Monroe, he promptly cleped his burg-to-be accordingly, overlooking, in his rush to glorify his hero, Monroe, Michigan; Monroe, Wisconsin; Monroe, North Carolina; Monroe, Louisiana; and Monroeville, Alabama. When a brother joined him, his backwater Dream was launched. By the time I arrived, it slumbered uneasily as a dustyard dog under an on-again, off-again sun. When I reached what seemed to me an accommodating lane, I walked toward a neat frame house and into a miracle.

"You can put your tent in our back forty," Charlotte Gottsch said, eyes brimming concern. "There's some cottonwoods next to the railroad tracks. I'll send my husband down later to see you get settled." Half an hour later, as I dozed off in the tent's lazy warmth, the miracle arrived with a rustle against the nylon and a tentative "Hello."

The kid outside had eyes the size of banjos, a one-size-fits-all cap advertising Agri-Bolt and Cabinet Company, a fire-engine-red sweatshirt, and a smile that made him look like a pint-sized John Wayne. He handed me a paper plate wrapped in tinfoil. "Mom sent 'em," he said. "She just cooked 'em. They're hot."

I tipped back the tinfoil. "Praise Jesus," I said, and meant it.

• • •

There are moments when the predestined slaps you upside the head. Or, as the Osage said while staring at his moon-sign on a Missouri limestone bluff: "Anytime you get coincidences clumping around a theme, you're getting marching orders." The present coincidence (or miracle) in hand clumped around a "theme" first voiced by the family McGinn. Given more faith, I should have taken their odd reverence for spring communion as Holy Writ. Now McGinn prophecy had come to roost (more accurately, to tent), arriving in the hands of eleven-year-old Cory Gottsch. Sponge mushrooms. Morels fried in butter. A heap. A feast.

Between mouthfuls, Cory and I talked of spring in Nebraska, of pioneer trails (the Mormon Trail passed across the Gottsch farm), and why a sighing wind comes up at dusk. Cory traced his finger over my footsteps on the maps and over the places where my footsteps would fall, curiosity welling out of him like water from a clear spring. Half as old as his next oldest brother, he was poised on the drop edge of growing up, and I had the feeling that a stranger arriving unexpectedly with a tale of journeys and destinations could tip him over the edge. Then it would be like swimming, doing the Australian crawl across the depths that life and Dream allows. Truth is, I met Cory at a fatal moment—he at the edge of his life, me foundering in the ocean of mine. That night, going under in the cool dark, I heard a single manic shriek, but my slumber was easeful and deep, dreamless and clear.

• • •

"It would mean a lot to Cory," Ted Gottsch said next morning. Blue-jeaned and thickset, Ted's handshake was strong and his smile shy. Under dark-rimmed glasses, his eyes sparked contagiously. Snoopy and Rover, ragtag family mongrels, set up a furious sniffing; uncovering remnants of my morel feast, Snoopy took off with the paper plate clamped in his jaws, whirling out of reach of Rover's yapping pursuit. "If we got started by eight, we'd have time for breakfast at the house," Ted said.

That settled it.

Fried eggs with high yellow yolks awaited us in the Gottsch kitchen ("Farm fresh from Mother's place," said Charlotte), along with steaming mugs of coffee, toast, and apple juice that still had the crisp and snap in it. The morning was sunny-side up, too. I mentioned that shriek in the night.

Charlotte blushed. "That was Scott's wife, Sandy. Come over to pick rhubarb. Scott . . . that devil . . . snuck up on her in the shadows. Worried all night about what you thought."

What I thought was that the Gottschs were a remarkably close family, held together like individual swatches in a finely stitched quilt, and when Ted confirmed it, winking at me across the table, his voice went furry. "Times like that got us four boys . . . three grandchildren." When he looked at Cory, his eyes nearly brimmed. When he looked at Charlotte, she blushed again.

Between mouthfuls, when the breakfast talk turned to Mormons, Ted mused. "There was Mormon graves over on Hugo Fitchie's place . . . about a mile west of town. Hugo was what you'd call egg-centric. Had 'em marked to suit himself. The secret died with Hugo."

"The Mormons never lost anyone until they reached Salt Lake," I said. "A child drowned in City Creek."

Ted went on. "Course there's Indian graves all over the place. When the highway came, it cut through barrow pits. Found heaps of bones. Over on Clear Creek, they dug up a skeleton sitting up and facing west. Had big knuckles with an arrow in the hip . . . everything complete but one big toe."

A skeleton sitting up in death was a curiosity worth noting, but what Ted said next hooked me as easily as a carp in shallow water. "Rumor has it the Mormons fought with the Indians near here . . . maybe Pawnee. Some got buried where they lay. You know anything about that?"

Unless it was a scrap of myth about their march through the Indian battleground at the Loup fork, I didn't at the time. "The Mormons cut the Pawnee a lot of slack," I said. "Brigham took a wide berth around trouble. They never actually fought with Indians along the trail. Meetings, yes. Battles, no. It doesn't make sense."

FOLLOWING THE WRONG GOD HOME

"No telling how rumors get started," Ted allowed, "but there's always something to a rumor."

. . .

Reacting to a threat of intrusion by French trappers into Spanish territory west of the Mississippi in the spring of 1720, the Mexican government sent a detachment of troops with Apache guides north from Santa Fe to check out the rumors, taking with them gifts to mollify any hostile tribes they might encounter—"short swords, knives, sombreros, and half a mule-load of tobacco." Intended to flaunt Spanish power in the face of French attempts to penetrate as far as the Rocky Mountains (they soon did), as well as fend off revolts by the natives against their Spanish oppressors, the expedition was commanded by Pedro de Villasur, a subordinate of Governor Antonio Valverde Cosio.

By mid-August the expedition had traveled at least "three hundred leagues" without seeing any signs of the French; but when it crossed the Jesus Maria and San Laurentius Rivers, its luck took a nosedive when it ran into the ancestral warriors of the Pawnee. Sensing his danger, Villasur, his soldiers, and the Apache guides fled east along the north bank of the San Laurentius, finally crossing the river to spend the night of August 13, 1720, at its confluence with the Jesus Maria. By morning, Villasur and thirty-five of his Spanish contingent were dead, ambushed and strewn among the grasses between the two rivers—now identified as the Platte (Jesus Maria) and the Loup (San Laurentius). A handful of survivors, mostly Apache, most likely buried them "were they lay"—ten miles or less from my camp on the Gottsch farm.

The massacre is depicted on an Indian skin painting acquired by an eighteenth-century Jesuit missionary to Sonora Province, Mexico—Father Philipp Segesser—who sent it to Switzerland where it remains today in the von Segesser von Brunegg family of Lucerne. In 1890, a mile north of the Loup, a French settler found "parts of a bridle and the crest of a helmet said to be of Spanish origin"; in 1904, a cache of period Spanish coins was dug up in Monroe by a settler sweating over a post-hole. Brass discs similar to those used in Spanish armor were unearthed in 1914, and in nearby Genoa a brass chain of Spanish workmanship turned up along with more brass plates.

As Ted Gottsch said, "There's always something to a rumor."

. . .

At 9:00 A.M., I walked into Betty Hebda's fifth-grade class at Monroe Elementary School to work off my debt. Both boys (15) and girls (3) wore sweatshirts advertising the twin expectations of American education—rampant consumerism and upward mobility. Yamaha, Camaro, Nike—even Heineken—festooned their togs. Only one, a bespectacled lad with the look of a future corporate lawyer, presented a dead-on-the-mark brief: centered on his T-shirt was a large Mickey Mouse.

Hawkish Betty Hebda, with large oval glasses and an orange plaid jumper, reminded me so much of my own fifth-grade teacher, Miss Madge Patterson, that déjà vu is understatement, and the classroom smell (carbolic and chalk) vaulted me four decades back when a wide-eyed son-of-a-barber was tutored by a formidable woman who clings to my psyche like burrs on a woolen shirt.

With Ted and Charlotte squeezed into kid-sized desks beside Cory, I talked about history on the land, of Mormon hopes and tribulations, of my home in upstate New York. But the kids asked about ordinary things. What did I eat? Where did I sleep? How many miles did I walk in a day? Where would I sleep tonight? Was I afraid? Did my feet hurt? What they really wanted to know was the question they hadn't yet formed: what's it like out there? Will I be safe when the time comes?

Time is a cheat. Looking into their eyes, I was startled again by the curiosity of innocence. The long road to middle age, which doesn't seem that long when one gets there, fills up with survival, and the clutter we mistake for a life pulls childhood from us in direct proportion to our self-deception. Innocence we expect to lose; curiosity, never.

In the photograph I took that morning, they stare into an unsettling moment in my life, strangers to a stranger. The American flag droops in the background, almost a shadowy afterthought. Since then, I've looked often and with regret at that photograph, and this I know: the children are more beautiful than any Dream. Because I've lost a son of my own, I've come to that conclusion, aware at last of the dangers of the self-centered, self-indulgent life—the beginnings of which we so idly let pass on the sweatshirts our kids wear, turning children into billboards, planting the seed that mortgages their future.

Even the Osage managed to get himself into that moment; the kid with the Yamaha T-shirt grips my handmade walking stick below its filigree of the sacred circle and the four roads, clutching it as if Roadmaker will take him outbound at any moment on his own journey. Betty Hebda is fixed in that moment, too, also tucked into the background behind the life her young charges are stepping out to meet. And then there's Cory kneeling on the front row.

When Ted Gottsch met Charlotte in a Columbus bus station, Cory's destiny arrived as surely as the 5:05 from Omaha. I never asked, but Ted might have felt he'd been run down by the bus. Maybe Charlotte felt the same—spark enough between them to populate a village. The three older Gottsch boys were evenly spaced, perhaps in hope of a girl. But Cory was a different matter entirely—a ticket not bargained for, a journey with nothing beyond love and the unexpected to account for him.

I had a son like that—and almost lost another. Sometimes, for comfort, when I can't sustain the grief, I reread the closing lines of Thornton Wilder's *The Bridge of San Luis Rey:* "Even memory is not necessary for love. There is a land of the living and a land of the dead and the bridge is love."

Perhaps that's why, among the fifth graders of Monroe Elementary School, in their ring of light beyond Old Glory and before their future, I understood for the first time what was happening to me. Living deeply, I was learning to die.

9

I like solitude. The soul of a journey is liberty, perfect liberty, to think, feel, do as one pleases.   WILLIAM HAZLITT,
                    "ON GOING ON A JOURNEY"

After dinner we forded Beaver Creek which is about thirty feet wide and two feet deep. Traveled eight miles and camped at the old Pawnee village or missionary station where we found plenty of hay which was very acceptable.
                    APPLETON MILO HARMON, APRIL 22, 1847

That afternoon, when I crossed the meandering scour of Looking Glass Creek, a sheet of mist slid overhead, turning the sun dim as a headlight in fog. Looking Glass Creek stunk of manure; svelte as a snake, it lapped at its banks, flowing through bankside grasses with a hiss. Looking down, I saw nothing reflected in its murk, the promise of its name a lie.

Gathering darkness, a slurry of winds blew in from the southwest: full in the face, they brought little relief from the heat. Overhead, a feeble sun burned at its curtain of mist. Nearby, William Clayton had sat on an Indian grave "from whence is a splendid view of the country," he wrote. Curious, I left the road in search of higher ground and, like him, saw "the course of the Loup Fork for a number of miles." Lightly brushed with dwindling light, its ruffled surface seemed a sweeping of broken glass. The "skirt of timber" on its banks and the "vast plain" that Appleton Harmon saw were still there, stretching as they had in 1847 "eighteen or twenty miles distant." Fields and farms dotted the landscape now.

Clayton's sense of solitude gripped me. About the only thing missing was the "lone Indian" who came walking toward the Mormons that day—that and an image of Pawnee wading the river earlier at the Loup Fork demanding "powder, lead, salt and tobacco." The encounter had spooked Brigham, as Ted Gottsch's strange "rumor" spooked me. If the Mormon ramble through a Pawnee grave-yard that day wasn't the source of the rumor, perhaps some whisper from Pedro de Villasur's brush with the Pawnee in 1720 was the germ in Ted's notion that Mormons and Indians had clashed and the dead were "buried where they lay." Rumors sleep long on the land, only to be awakened when least expected.

• • •

Truth be told, Mormon history is haunted both by the unexplained and unexplainable. The bizarre, lurid, and strange have been its bedfellows since the church's beginnings in 1827. Polygamy accounts for some of it, and the Mormon belief that God lives on a distant planet is bound to be considered a trifle *alien*—one reason it's hardly surprising that the Mormon sci-fi writer Orson Scott Card takes many of his plots from *The Book of Mormon*. Mark Twain called *The Book of Mormon* "chloroform in print," but could find "nothing vicious in its teachings." Even today it remains a Mormon curiosity.

At ground level, rumors about Mormons rise like shibboleths left behind in the shadows of their passing wagons—fuzzy, out of focus, and skewed. It's as if Americans can't get them to come clear, viewing them through cheap binoculars. Walking up the Loup and Platte Rivers toting my pocketful of questions, most Nebraskans I queried came up blank about Mormons. When I raised the subject, many pointed out the nearest bridge to the river's south bank (the Oregon Trail), which they knew a lot about, often in great detail. Although the Mormon Trail passes through many a Nebraskan's back forty, knowledge of it remains obscure, taken over by the hype associated with the all-American rush to Oregon and California. While the sesquicentennial reenactment of the Mormon exodus (1997) revived popular interest in the trek, few in the Cornhusker State seemed to give a damn about it in 1985. Not that I could blame them: religious eccentrics are seldom remembered as part of the Dream.

However eccentric the faith, the Mormon effect on the United States was profound. Joseph Smith and Brigham Young influenced the course of American history as much as, and perhaps more than, other Americans of their generation. The opening of the West and the political, social, and economic destiny of six states—Utah, Idaho, Arizona, Nevada, Colorado, California—were all stirred in a Mormon pot of empire. Mormons adapted Native American irrigation to the deserts, pioneered and wrote the nation's riparian water law, laid out and settled the West's arid regions, and created the most successful social, religious, and economic experiment in U.S. history—all held together by the "community" glue of a self-proclaimed "peculiar people."

Unknown to many, it was a Mormon battalion that helped wrest California from Mexico in 1846 (Brigham used the payroll to finance the exodus of the Saints to the Great Salt Lake), and another Mormon, brash but thrifty Sam Brannan (later ousted from the church), who bounced a no-account Pacific burg named Yerba Buena into a factious boomtown named San Francisco—all because another Mormon, James Marshall (he died a drunk), put his hand into the water at Sutter's Mill on the American River near Sacramento on the morning of January 24, 1848, and came up with a "malleable rock of very odd weight" that changed the destiny of American Dreaming forever. After boiling his find with vinegar in a soap kettle, he exclaimed, "Boys, by God, I've got it," and the damnedest gold rush in history was on. Salt Lake City became a major way station on the road to riches, and Mormons cleaned up, among other things, on the whiskey trade.

But in spite of their incredible history, I kept tumbling headlong into "rumors" about them, like a man wandering at night in a field of abandoned cellar holes. Some were bitter, cramped, crooked, or edged with meanness. Most folks claimed they knew nothing about Mormons, blinking like a cash register showing a full row of zeros and asking for whatever cash flow I had to offer. Like Ted Gottsch, a few summoned a meager reserve of Mormon lore, offering up an unidentifiable lump like James Marshall's nugget, but seldom shining.

• • •

Half-baked Mormon "rumor" shows up when least expected, a left hook rocketing out of nowhere. In the autumn of 1984, the Osage and I stood on a ridge above "Cutnose," Iowa, looking across a half-moon bend of the Mississippi, eyes fixed on the old Mormon city of Nauvoo—the same dizzy height from which numerous artists sketched Smith's saintly city in the 1840s. Through drizzle and a slash in the trees, the city looked faded as a sepia postcard. On the bluff below us, traces of roses planted by Louise Honere Tesson in 1790 still lingered—the roses that colored the view on June 27, 1844, the day Joseph Smith was murdered in Carthage, Illinois. It was Tesson's seasonal smear of ruby that caused Iowa settlers to abandon the Indian name, Cutnose, for Montrose—Mount of Roses.

We stood on the site of an Indian village that by 1900 had become a Chautauqua summer camp. In those days, steamers piled in at the Montrose wharf, off-loading visitors for Bluff Park where they were entertained by the likes of Miss Evelyn Bargelt, "with a winsome smile and a power of gripping human hearts." On the Illinois side in 1900, Nauvoo was a sleepy ruin at the edge of a cattail marsh, its dwindling Mormon memory drifting in the mind of Montrose irregulars like scum floating on the river. By 1984, Nauvoo was considerably revived, bought up and rebuilt by Mormon dollars. "A Williamsburg on the Mississippi," a descendant of Heber Kimball told us.

That morning, the Osage (himself a Chautauqua notable) educated me in no uncertain language about "lollygagging in unseasonable rain and cold," especially rummaging in a remote corner of the Hawkeye State in an "all-day drizzle for dope on Mormons." In blue jeans, plaid shirt, denim vest, but cloaked indignant under glowering skies, he'd managed to stir up a pint-sized beagle. The pup dove at Osage legs, yap-yip-yapping until man and menace whirled in the chill morning air.

Glenn Gerdes, who owned the beagle, came out of a frame house perched high on bluff's edge to "see what all the infernal barking is about," a rough-cut, middle-aged man with watery eyes the color of streaky peanut butter and hair sprouting from under a stained baseball cap. A minor tremor along the New Madrid fault would topple Glenn's house into the river. He collared the beagle, asked our business, and, in the middle of explanations, roundly cursed industrial America. Upstream, the Armour Packing Company, noted for its high-volume production of what Glenn called "Vienner sausages, them little goobers in a can," had turned the river reedy from its soupy effluent.

"Before the dams and flood control, there was rapids just below the cliff," Glenn told us. "The river's wide now."

I asked about Mormons.

"As a boy, I was told how they got John Smith," Glenn said, rubbing one watery eye with a goober-sized pinkie finger. "It was a whiskey mob. Tied him to a tree ... middle of town. Cut off his privates. Bled to death."

The Osage's eyes rolled. "Who?"

"John Smith," Glenn answered, "the Mormon leader. Had all them wives. Cut off his ... y'know." He made a circle around his genitals.

The Osage grimaced, the pup whimpered and scratched himself, and the rain began in earnest. "Cut 'em clean off," Glenn said.

"The only thing missing in that tale," said the Osage as we drove away, "was the part about a dull knife."

• • •

Rumors and half-truths like Glenn's "whiskey mob" castration of "John" Smith rise on wings of a murky past—remnants carried in a substratum of memory like a faint sediment in some ancient, eroded geology. It was a similar faint but unbelievable sediment in Ted Gottsch's story that interested me. Mormons seemed stuck to it like woozy afterthoughts in a drunk's dream. Nestled in the grass with the Loup River spread out along its margin of prairie, I brewed a cup of coffee on my Svea stove and thought about it. Nothing came clear. It was the immediate world that drew me back. Silver dollar leaves on the cottonwoods were startled by rising wind, the air turned heavy again, and the Loup churned with riffles, edged as knives. As for me, I was now deep in the killing fields of the Pawnee.

• • •

When John Treat Irving visited the Pawnee villages in the fall of 1833, he was astounded to find "the hills black with masses of warriors," encircling his party "in one dark, dense flood" with "closely shaved heads." In decoration, they prized the colored feathers of birds, painting their faces vermilion and coating their bodies with ocher mud. Most were naked. Some wore necklaces of bear claws, and "a plume of the bald eagle floated from the long scalp locks of the principal warriors." Awesome, beautiful, and terrible by degrees, the Pawnee so captivated Washington Irving's nephew that he confided in his journal, "There is something in the fierce, shrill scream of Indian warriors, which rings through the brain and sends the blood curdling back to the heart."

But it was the annual Pawnee fertility rite that struck terror into the white man, as widely reported by 1847. Women captured from the Comanche, Sioux, and Cheyenne were sacrificed to appease the Pawnee spirit Morning Star. In 1833 John Dougherty, Indian agent to the Pawnee and Otoe, tried to rescue a fourteen-year-old Cheyenne girl. He failed. The child's body was "torn to pieces" as the Pawnee, "galloping their horses madly ... whirled pieces of bloody flesh above their heads on leather thongs." As late as 1838, similar human sacrifices took place.

Rumors of Pawnee cannibalism only added to white fears. As early as 1832, traders were so hostile to the Pawnee that they carried vials of smallpox-infected pus to spread on tobacco, blankets, and clothing. That year, nearly all Pawnee over thirty died in the villages of the Loup Fork, a visitation that continued until the end of the decade, ravaging the once proud nation like scythes mowing a wheat field. Among Pawnee braves, there lingered a long festering hatred of the white man. It lingered still, I thought, in shadows on the land.

· · ·

Later, I angled off the highway to follow the Columbus-Genoa canal, tracing a gentle grade along the big ditch that skirted sandy hills as the Mormons had done. Along its banks, wild plum blossomed and a gaggle of mallards rocketed skyward, honking at the intruder, velvet heads beautiful in flight. Here, too, was evidence of beaver. Along the river, cottonwoods were greening fast, new leaves tremulous in the wind.

When the road turned sharply west, the first drops of rain fell—lazily at first, like fat polliwogs, thudding into the dust. A glance skyward told the tale. Too absorbed again in Ted Gottsch's "rumor," I hadn't noticed massing thunderheads, black as braids of tar. In the distance, I made out Genoa's tree line, but in rapidly failing light I couldn't make out any buildings. When the air stilled, thick as paste, a sliver of lightning snapped and a cannonade of fat thunder trembled the air, a bone-rattling blast so close that I heard an after-sizzle before I was momentarily deafened. I lunged ahead, tried to run, but duck-waddled under the weight of the pack, fearful that its metal frame, the strapped-on tent poles, and even my boot grommets would jolt me into eternity, the kind of storm torment that gets to a man, say, with a metal plate in his head.

But the rain held off. Closer to town, I called out to a woman who had rushed outside to close the windows on her Buick. "How far to the center of town?"

A rising wind carried my voice. Only half of hers came back. "Four! . . ."

"Blocks," I made out, lip-reading.

And then the hammer fell—a weight of steely rain so dense the town disappeared. The dirt road exploded on impact, sending dust clots into the air, tiny mushrooms that germinated, sprouted, and died in the nanosecond before rising water crawled over my soles. I was alone in a sodden, griseous world.

Almost as suddenly, Genoa swam back into view. Turning a corner, a hand reached out and hauled me to safety. My lifeline was the Redwood Motel where Wally and Buzz Bozak snugged me into a warm berth for a mere eighteen dollars.

FOLLOWING THE WRONG GOD HOME

My relationship with the Bozaks began with an act of faith. I asked Buzz if she'd take a check. Her eyes widened ever so slightly at this suggestion—especially since it was drawn on an obscure bank unheard of outside of Ontario County, New York.

"To conserve my cash," I ventured.

"Anyone fool enough to walk across Nebraska in the spring is worth a risk," she said, adding cautiously, "I think."

No sooner was I tucked inside when the sky-cork over Genoa blew out a second time, shaking the windows with a battering wash. Safely out of it, I showered, then turned in for an hour's nap between clean sheets with the air conditioner on low to cut the humidity. Later, when the rain died down, there was a timid knock at my door. On the other side was a pretty teenager holding a tray. On it was a melon-sized mound of spaghetti and meat sauce, a large green salad, several slices of buttered bread, and a fist-sized helping of strawberry cobbler with whipped cream. "Dad thought you'd be tired and hungry," the Bozaks' daughter said. "Mom says enjoy. Oh, welcome to Genoa."

• • •

That night, I woke up with shinsplints, thanks to my duck waddle run for cover. Outside, the Redwood was taking another lashing, winds veering around her edges, groaning her timbers, curtains luffing from an occasional full-blast draft. On top of my spaghetti ballast, I sucked down two aspirins and pulled on a blanket for good measure. When I woke again at six, it was still raining, scouring like a brush at the windows, street awash, gutters sloshing. With the barometer rising, I decided to lay over in snug harbor and went back to bed.

IO

Spider Woman said, "Be still within yourselves, and know that the trail is beautiful. Whenever you are in danger walk carefully and quietly."   HOPI LEGEND

At 12:15 we arrived on the east bank of the Beaver River, having traveled about ten miles. This stream is about twenty to twenty-

five feet wide; swift, clear water and pleasant tasting. The banks are tolerably well lined with timber.

WILLIAM CLAYTON, APRIL 22, 1847

At noon, under a continuing drizzle, downtown Genoa looked like a mouthful of broken teeth. At the local grill and pool hall where I combined breakfast and lunch, a hangdog group of Butch and Sundance types malingered over beers and cards in its dark, cavernous interior, most waiting for the afternoon to wring itself dry so they could get back to work. It was a day not meant for voices, so silence hung on in Rock's Bar and Grill like a winding sheet, broken only by the occasional flare of a match or a few damply whispered requests that set the owner into slow motion. I was courteously left alone, eating in one shadowy corner, grubbing through my borrowed newspaper, a stranger within the gates.

That day, the *Omaha World Herald* told me the Mormons were taking lumps. Myth and magic were in their rumor mill—again. A recently discovered letter from Martin Harris, a New York farmer who bankrolled the publishing of *The Book of Mormon* in 1827, claimed that a spirit in the shape of a white salamander attacked Joseph Smith at the moment he attempted to retrieve the golden plates from a hole in the ground near his family farm in New York. Mormon leaders were worried and scurrying for cover. First they bought the spurious document, next tried to conceal it, then denied they had it, and finally admitted they had—red faces all around, no doubt embarrassed at having been flummoxed by Mark Hoffman, a Salt Lake documents dealer turned forger and murderer.

• • •

Back on Main Street, I poked through the drizzle until I found the public library. Behind a storefront façade, I found Kathleen Harris with a smile that bathed me in welcoming BTUs. Dressed against the cool and damp in slacks and sweater, her brown hair neatly cropped, she blinked when I asked for information on "Old Genoa . . . you know, Mormon Genoa."

"What's left of it is under the corn next to the Beaver River. West of town," she said. "But if it's Pawnee culture you're looking for, you'd best ask Allen Atkins."

"I'll settle for both," I said.

Minutes after Kathleen Harris called him, Allen drove by to pick me up.

• • •

When Chicago's Field Museum opened its exhibit on the Plains Indians, they turned to Allen Atkins for information on the Pawnee. "We've got an earth lodge," they said, "but we don't know much about Beaver Creek culture." Allen advised and consulted, then flew to the Windy City for the opening.

Atkins's interest in the Pawnee began in the 1950s when he was fifty-five. Thirty years later, he was just as avid about his subject but was showing signs of wear—a frail man recovering from what he termed "a bad spell." At times, his arms seemed to short out, gesturing suddenly as if misdirected energy was trying to mend a path through damaged circuits. Shushing over the back roads of Nance County, he had a way of talking in incomplete sentences as if I could fill in the rest by intuition.

"Pawnee land . . . plowed . . . started using fertilizers," he said, ". . . field hands if they, y'know, knew . . . stone piles and such . . . to come and tell me. I'd go looking."

Allen uncovered so many Pawnee artifacts in the fields around Genoa—pottery, tools, arrowheads—that when he got control of a belly-up local bank building decorated with columns and fake marble, he saw *museum* written all over it and stuffed it wall-to-wall with his passion. So the former Genoa National Bank became First National Pawnee—or something like it. Citations from state and civic organizations followed. Eventually, Allen was interviewed on *Good Morning America*.

Near the cemetery, Allen braked onto a soft shoulder, staring at what looked like pumping stations. "Deep wells," he said, one voltaic arm sweeping the scene, "site of Pawnee lodges. Most powerful Indian nation . . . 1820s. Ten . . . maybe fifteen thousand here . . . along the Loup."

Around the deep wells, on land now plowed for spring corn, I imagined Pawnee crops—maize, beans, squash—to feed a people who raided along the Santa Fe Trail as far south as the Mexican settlements on the upper Rio Grande. Looking over the site of Genoa's water supply, I was hard pressed to imagine this ground as the apex of a confederacy that gave Brigham the shakes and once controlled the prairies and plains between the Niobrara and Arkansas Rivers—a people who, it's said, invented the calumet (peace pipe), stole the sacred arrows of the Cheyenne, struck fear into John Treat Irving, and whose ancestors decimated the envoys of New Spain at the junction of the Loup and the Platte. Harder still was imagining it as the center of a people for whom the stars held the key to cycles of life. But I felt Allen Atkins's grief. On the drive back to town, I noticed several large buildings huddled together like old shoes and asked Allen about them. His face brimmed with sadness.

"Government Indian school. Closed up. It, well . . . a high wire fence around it to keep 'em inside. Bed count."

His voice slurred, thick as sorghum, so I left it alone.

Back on Main Street, Allen fiddled a key into the lock of the First National Pawnee. It was damp as a tomb inside as he searched through odd nooks and crannies to find light switches. Standing at the crammed display cases, I finally understood what *artifact* really means—not "a simple object, as a tool or ornament, showing human workmanship" as the dictionary defines it, but "a deep pain from the recognition of skeletal remains, as in the ruin of nations." By no feat of imagination could anyone make those shards live again.

For half an hour, I stared at the artifacts of a vanished culture, at arrowheads shaped to resemble sacred animals—wolf, buffalo, eagle—and more deeply at faded photographs of the last Pawnee chiefs—Pawnee Dick, Eagle Chief, Riding In, Walking Sun, White Eagle (who toured with Buffalo Bill), Frank Ship-She-Wano. Moldering in a defunct bank, Allen's collection was an expression of suffering and ruin, like a loan gone bad or a lost deposit. Looking back, I remember Allen best at Beaver Creek—no longer the "swift, clear water" Clayton saw, but a dun-colored glide. Near the site where the Mormons crossed, Allen came at last into the luxury of full sentences, his voice peeling back the years.

"Pawnee women ferried goods across the Beaver for settlers and Mormons," he said. "They wore hide dresses and waded across. When I was a boy, an ol' fella told me the dresses would rise up, all billowed out, and float on the water. Can't you see 'em? All billowed out?"

I could, and was buoyed by the image.

• • •

Later, under Kathleen Harris's watchful eye, I read that the Genoa Indian Industrial School opened in 1884 and closed in 1934, one of several government attempts to enhance the "assimilation process." By 1932, the arbiters of "assimilation" had lumped many old enemies together. Of 533 students, the Sioux triumphed with 218, followed by the Omaha with 99 and the Pottowatomi with 51. In decreasing numbers came the Winnebago, Ponca, Sac, Fox, Crow, Iowa, Shoshone, Arapaho, Chippewa, Kickapoo, Cheyenne, and Modoc. The Choctaw, Oneida, Gros Ventre, Mandan, and Pawnee were down to one each.

Life at the school was based on a military model. Girls and boys wore uniforms—ankle-length wool dresses with a navy collar for the girls or striped pants, military jackets, and Sousa-style pillbox caps for the boys. Reveille, roll call, and taps were daily occurrences. Both sexes were formed into companies and taught "Christian" virtues of teamwork, discipline, competition, and precision drilling, with dollops of vocational training ladled in for good measure—

farming, blacksmithing, carpentry, tailoring, baking, and laundering. "Many would be ailing when they entered school," one forlorn pupil wrote. "If it was found they could not be helped, they were sent home. Some died before this could be done."

"Assimilation" ended at graduation. Students returned to dirt-poor reservations "unable to communicate in their native tongue," and since tribes resented white ways, many "no longer fit." In one surviving photo, government retainers lurk like jackals in the background while Indian boys in close-cropped haircuts and starched collars, jug-eared as bankers, stare into a brave new world with dead or dying eyes. What happened to the lone Pawnee, last of the warriors, I never found out.

• • •

That Beaver Creek was "tolerably well lined with timber" caught Brigham's fancy when the Mormons nooned on its banks on April 22, 1847. He liked the flats along the stream so much that ten years later he was back in the spirit of enterprise—the second time Mormons illegally squatted on Indian land. Beside the Beaver's "pleasant tasting water," opposite the ford where Pawnee women once waded in billowing hide skirts, he built a way station to assist Mormons on the road west and a wagon stop to service his BYX (Brigham Young Express) freighting company. Growing prosperous in Utah, the Mormon leader had garnered a government contract to ferry goods to Salt Lake City and put money into his budding theocracy.

On Brigham's orders, Andrew Cunningham and Nathan Davis surveyed a town site. Mixing religion and commercial opportunity (a characteristic of the church), Brigham sent Apostle Erastus Snow on a "mission" to superintend the way-station settlement. By late spring, Mormons had felled timber along the stream and built a community of log and sod shelters and earth-heaped dugouts, not unlike those at Winter Quarters. By the end of June, two hundred acres of Indian land were enclosed and two hundred planted. The next summer, one hundred families were living on the site, enough to apply for a post office. Asked where he lived, one grim settler replied, "In yonder graves."

From the beginning, it was risky business, since Brigham was legally a day late and a dollar short in the real-estate department. Two years before Cunningham and Davis showed up, Congress granted the land to the Pawnee. In exchange for a new "homeland" of 288,000 acres, the Pawnee ceded 30 million acres to the United States for two cents a pop, but they were surrounded by enemies, especially Sioux. On all sides, they were going under.

Perhaps Brigham took advantage of the weakened Pawnee to settle inside their territory. Perhaps the Pawnee thought the presence of whites offered protection from the Sioux, but the site Cunningham and Davis surveyed was three miles inside the reservation boundary. The advantage of good water, an easy crossing, and ready timber wasn't lost on the "Lion of the Lord." A sawmill was up and running on Beaver Creek within weeks.

Brigham's plan might have worked, except sentiment against Mormons was pumped to fever pitch in 1857. Disturbed about the distinction between *church* and *state* in Utah (the former was the latter), President James Buchanan undertook some hasty and ill-timed political surgery, removing Brigham as governor of Utah Territory and replacing him with Alfred Cumming of Georgia. To sharpen the insult, Buchanan dispatched fifteen hundred U.S. troops from Fort Leavenworth, Kansas, under Colonel Albert Sidney Johnston with orders to bring Utah to heel.

When Mormons got wind of Buchanan's strong-arm tactics at their annual July 24th blowout (the date they entered Salt Lake Valley in 1847), all hell broke loose. Fearing another Missouri-style massacre, Young barricaded Utah canyons, sent bands of guerrilla fighters to burn the army's supply wagons, and, burning his own bridges behind him in a scorched-earth policy, forced the exhausted U.S. Dragoons into winter shelter on short rations at Fort Bridger, Wyoming, which the Mormons torched beforehand and abandoned.

"If you persist in sending us officials from the tag, rag and bobtail of whore houses, grog shops and gambling hells," Brigham thundered at Buchanan, "we shall take the Yankee liberty . . . for the first time of using up that class of officials strictly in accordance with their desserts."

Martial law was declared in Utah. By spring, five companies of U.S. infantry and riflemen arrived at Fort Bridger to shore up government forces. Bloodshed a-brewing, only the diplomacy of the Mormons' old and faithful friend Thomas Kane saved the day. Arrived in Salt Lake from San Francisco, Kane hustled east to parley with Johnston, whose army, by now, had empty bellies. As a peace offering, Brigham sent supplies to the hungry troops and the "Mormon War" was settled by an uneasy compromise. On June 26, 1858, Johnston's army marched into a nearly deserted Salt Lake City.

But hatred and suspicion flowed back and forth across the trail. A scent of Mormon polygamy drifted east. In 1859 a subagent for the Pawnee, Judge Gillis, had a nose full of Mormon stink, ordering them off the Indian lands, thirty days

FOLLOWING THE WRONG GOD HOME

or else. By winter, most had gone, moved east over the reservation line where they built the hamlet of Zig-Zag. An occasional name on the land is all that's left to remind anyone of the illegal Mormon settlement on the Beaver River.

• • •

At 6:00 P.M., Kathleen and Jim Harris picked me up at the Redwood Motel for the annual Future Farmers of America dinner—an invitation (Kathleen's doing) that I couldn't turn down. Tall and outgoing, Jim Harris had unpretentious good looks, right down to the Cary Grant cleft in his chin. Under horn-rimmed glasses, he looked more like a college professor than the manager of a local credit union.

"Big night in Genoa," he said, shaking hands. "I hope you know what you're getting into."

Totems of ten warring tribes covered the walls of the Genoa High School gymnasium where the medicine bundle of the Genoa Orioles was an exercise in sums: "Teamwork + Cooperation = Victory." In Allen Atkins's day, Genoa High battled the Indian Industrial School, and it wasn't until Allen's senior year that the combined tribes were finally beaten back. The gaudy banners of Genoa's rivals—Fullerton, Osceola, Stromsburg, Shelby, David City, East Butler, Nebraska Lutheran—hung like scalp locks on the walls, and the gym held faint echoes of war dances and thunder drums. Many balls had passed through the sacred hoops.

"Assimilation" was still on the menu in rural Nebraska, showing up in second- and third-generation names on the program—Drozd, Nelson, Lempek, Smith, Korys. Blue uniforms were still in vogue as well—corduroy jackets, dark pants, white shirts, and ties (blue skirts and blouses for girls), with the FFA crest above the heart and the name over the breast. Moms and dads clustered around the tables, slicked up in frills or cardboard suits, nervously chattering with their future farmers.

"You asked for it," Jim said.

"Anything for a free meal."

"Men," Kathleen said, shaking her coif.

Looking over the program, it seemed to me that FFA training was run along similar lines as the Genoa Indian school—Home and Farm, Ag Sales, Fruit and Vegetables, Poultry Production, Soybean Production, Sheep Production, Horse Proficiency, Feed Grains—images straight out of Crèvecoeur's *Letters from an American Farmer*. Middle-of-my-road, Genoa welcomed me, its friendliness all-American with a Norman Rockwell trace of nostalgic Dream touching down.

Genoa was like small towns I'd known everywhere, and starched up for a night out, its people were reminders of evenings in English village pubs or taking in local fairs or church socials in my native Canada. Yet that Rockwellian trace of nostalgic Dream nagged me. I'd never known a "Canadian Dream," never needed to convince myself or my friends that my country, above others, contained infinite promise or that my destiny was more manifest. Other than a vague allegiance to the queen, no advertising was needed to remind me that talent and achievement know no borders, although education and opportunity too often do. As a registered alien in the USA, I often felt like a character in J. J. Fiechter's novel *Death by Publication*, who said, "I sometimes had the impression that I had a Siamese twin living inside me and that I was waiting to hear from him, to find out what he wanted me to do."

Would I have been less free had I stayed in Canada? Denied some justice available only in the United States? Was there less "community" or regard for the "individual" in my homeland of permafrost? Lacking a "Canadian Dream," would there have been less pork in my frigid barrel? Less frozen chicken in my frosty pot? Try as I did to understand it, the American Dream seemed rabbit-from-a-hat, an illusion promising too many vague "rights," tainted by contradictions and self-indulgent promises of a good thing. Only the Dream could give so many blurry associations so tenuous a shape—and dreams are what happens when you're not awake. Besides, how much hope or opportunity can be melted in one pot?

"Enjoying yourself?" Kathleen asked, looking at me with a knot of concern in her eyes.

"You betcha," I replied.

But Kathleen's simple question struck me as desperately "American," as if a cloying uncertainty lingered in her mind, not about my experience in Genoa, but about her experience of Dreamland. "Mythologies are huge cairns of anything and everything that helps explain a people to itself," the Canadian writer Robertson Davies claims. "Some of the rocks in the cairn are ugly boulders and others may be quite smooth pebbles. It doesn't matter so long as the cairn rises above ground level and serves . . . as a home for the Gods." Still, I felt that if I was to voice doubts about American Dreams, someone with similar doubts would leap to his feet to argue, obstinately, as Americans will, that "everything's up to date in Kansas City"—anything to keep Dream's illusion alive.

This isn't to say that Canada—my huge cairn of rocks—has avoided any doubts. In an essay, Robertson Davies wrote: "Canada was not so much a coun-

FOLLOWING THE WRONG GOD HOME

try one loved, but a country one worried about." Davies claims the name, *Canada*, came from an offhand remark by a Spanish explorer—"Aca nada"—meaning "nothing there." That's probably inaccurate, but it's revealing about Davies: the ability *not* to love one's country too much is very Canadian.

U.S. President Ulysses S. Grant once called Canada "a semi-independent and irresponsible agency." Maybe to Ulysses, but it's never had a revolution (several rebellions), a civil war, or a New Deal, Fair Deal, or Square Deal—not being a nation given to slogans. None of its leaders have been assassinated, although several of its prime ministers carry self-inflicted wounds. As a chunk of real estate, Canada spans 4,545 miles from Atlantic to Pacific, crosses one-quarter of the world's time zones, and, south to north, stretches three thousand miles—farther than from Los Angeles to New York. Forty percent of its northern territories remains unexplored. Canada contains 30 percent of the world's freshwater in a million lakes, rivers, and countless streams; and its forests are six times the size of France. The second largest nation on the globe, Canada is the United States' largest trading partner—a benefit to both, although some Canadians think otherwise. Canada's "Great White North" (that's everything above two hundred miles north of Buffalo) is one and a quarter times larger than India and contains no more people than you could find at a major league baseball game. You could drop Texas and its cowboy-booted blowhards, including the latest, into Quebec and still have room for Connecticut and Rhode Island, two more civilized states. Canada's freshwater, vast untapped mineral and oil reserves, and cheap hydroelectric power make the United States weak-kneed with jealousy. It's a nation with reasonable handgun laws, having determined, unlike the United States, that an "organized militia" means a state-supported trained army and not any six guys on a block with arsenals in their basement who carry concealed handguns to shop at Kmart.

That said, even "Canadians rarely see or . . . think of what lies behind their thin line of population," writes Andrew Malcom, a Canadian correspondent for the *New York Times*. "But like some unseen, dark, powerful presence in a midnight *dream* (italics mine), it is felt"—and rarely bragged about, I might add, this being an exception. Dead on the mark, Malcom asserts, "If their frontier experience convinced Americans that anything was possible, the geography of Canada taught its captives true skepticism, that everything, except themselves, has limits"—not including the hot air flowing north from south of its border. That seems limitless. So stuff it, eh.

· · ·

After dinner, FFA members stood to be recognized and accept awards—Star Green Hand, Gold Harvest, Star Chapter Farmer— twenty-eight in all, not including individual certificates for "special achievement." In a room of achievers with parents incandescently proud, Jamie Nygren, FFA state officer, rose to give the evening's homily—"The FFA in Community." A budding version of Ernest Borgnine, Jamie looked like a young man whose middle age could run beefy.

"Dolly Parton has grown into a figure we can all admire," Jamie began to uncertain laughter, "but the Future Farmers of America, with five hundred thousand members, offers each of us a choice for development and individual benefit."

I don't suppose anyone else caught Jamie's ironic shift in emphasis—from *community* to *individual*—but his needle skipped a groove, toppling him into the troubled waters that pestered me all across Nebraska. For fifteen minutes, he drowned in a river of "individual benefits" flooding from his youthful association with the Future Farmers of America. Alas, *community* came in a distant second until, too little, too late, he floated a concluding analogy on his all-but-forgotten topic.

"An Indian chief wanted to get his allies together to fight against their common enemies," he said, "but they wouldn't do it. Each felt they were better off alone. The chief asked the head of each tribe to take an arrow and break it. Then he asked each of them to give him an unbroken arrow and bound them together with rawhide. No one could break it."

Surely no people knew the power of bound arrows better than the Pawnee, who stole them, and the Cheyenne, who lost them, and no one had broken the old communal clans, tribes, confederacies, and bloodlines better than American Dreamers on their *individual* roads west, Mormons no exception. But most early Mormons were bound in a tribal bond of *community*, denying *individual* rewards for a common theocracy. It hadn't worked, of course. In the end, they were forced to compromise with mammon.

Back at the Redwood Motel, on a nosedive toward sleep, I suddenly pulled out and sat up, stirring uncomfortably in the Mormon past, trying to see the Pawnee from Brigham's point of view as dark-skinned failures of the Lost Tribes of Israel, cursed like Cain. Then I imagined them from John Treat Irving's first sighting, a people of awe and wonder, "peculiar" themselves. At first light, I saw the trouble. Who exactly was cursed?

Somewhere, Dan McAdam writes, "The devil had a good deal to do with the making of the West if we believe its place names—Devil's Gate, Hell's Half Acre, Devil's Slide." Truth is, there's always a devil in the Dream.

II

My bones cannot be dry bones . . . or I could never be able to endure such walks.   Ellen Weeton, Wales, 1825

Arrived at the intended crossing place. . . . My feet were so sore and blistered I could not walk for some time after I got there. The sun is very hot and no wind. At 3:20 the wagons arrived and prepared to ford the [Loup] river.   William Clayton,
April 23, 1847

On April 23, 1847, the big news in the Mormon camp on Plum Creek was that "President Young and the others are gone to the river to ascertain where we can best ford it." Separated from the main Platte River Road and wandering deeper into Pawnee territory, Brigham grew wary. With Pawnee warriors coming and going around him, he decided to ford the Loup and drive south to meet the Platte where the Camp of Israel could travel along its north bank, keeping the width of the Platte between it and the despised Missouri "pukes" and Illinois "suckers" who were heading west on the Oregon Trail that spring. "Pukes" and "suckers" had badly mauled the Saints, the first pummeling them from Missouri and the second from Illinois. A fever of animosity and persecution ran hotly on both sides of the Platte that spring.

When the sun rose on the Loup River, Mormon wagons were circled on the site of the abandoned Plum Creek Mission, where a a botched Presbyterian attempt to educate the Pawnee in God's saving graces had ended in grief and murder in the autumn of 1846. Caught in a fatal melee between the Pawnee and Sioux, the mission was deserted, its missionaries having fallen back to the Missouri River settlements in battered retreat. Bathed in the "Blood of the Lamb," they were now bathed with blood of the Pawnee whose slaughter they aided and abetted. A quarter of a mile below the abandoned mission stood a gutted government farm—"two double log houses and six single smaller houses with pig pens," wrote Thomas Bullock. With its fenced fields, weedy corrals, and a "beautiful little creek of Soft Water," Bullock described it as a "pleasant retired spot for a farm." With "two ricks of good hay" for the taking, it was a natural spot for the Mormons to make camp.

But a dark slash in the nearby hills worried Brigham more than the bloody history of the place. He took one look at a shadowy defile running in from the north and added Sioux to his list of things that go bump in the night. So O. C. Tanner hustled the cannon into place and drilled the guard, while Clayton, having a good night for a change, talked up his idea for a "roadometer." "Several caught the idea and feel confident of its success," he confided to his journal. His enthusiasm faded overnight; he woke up with another toothache and sore feet.

• • •

So did I. The toothache wasn't much—a discomforting twinge and a slight sensation of swelling above an upper left incisor—the kind of irritation one notes but quickly forgets. Washed by a warming wind, I headed out under a powder-blue sky. Crossing another irrigation canal, I scuffed along a service road smelling Nebraska spring for the first time: an olfactory explosion of earth, grass, buds, blossoms—the best day for walking since I'd left the Missouri River. With the Loup to my left and the Burlington and Northern Railroad to my right (the Union Pacific followed the Platte at Columbus), I was free of blacktop highway with its stink of exhaust. Soon I passed a retired yellow caboose marooned in a meadow, gaudy with startling red trim. It seemed in frolic, like an octogenarian grandmother dolled up on South Collins Avenue in Miami Beach.

Farther along, I came across two piscatorial statesmen sitting on the canal's bank, each bobbed and baited, each with a can of beer and a high-tech fishing pole tucked between his knees.

"How's it going?" I hailed.

"How's it s'posed to go?" one hailed back.

"It's supposed to be fun."

"Hell, is it?" the other called, slapping his friend on the arm and almost toppling him into the ditch. He steadied himself and punched back. "This lyin' sonofabitch told me we was workin' today."

L.S.O.B. tweaked the back of the other's hat, tumbling it over the man's forehead where it snagged on his sunglasses. The head beneath was bald, white as old putty and shiny as a saucer. He snatched at the cap, plopping it back onto his head

FOLLOWING THE WRONG GOD HOME

with one hand while tipping his buddy's hat off with the other. Neither stopped laughing. I halted across from them, the twenty-foot span of water between us moving sluggishly as air in a Georgia heat wave. "What do you catch?"

"Not a damned thing. When we do, it's catfish."

They stopped pounding each other long enough to give me their full attention. One had a cast in his left eye, the other a twisted, cauliflower ear, suggesting they'd been battering each other since childhood.

"Where you from?" L.S.O.B asked.

"New York."

"Where you goin'?"

"Utah. If I make it."

"Jesus Christ!" they yelped in unison. "You wanna beer?"

"Sounds like a good idea," I said.

"Well, there's a store up ahead in Fullerton. . . ." They both gagged on laughter and started throttling each other again. "Just foolin'," L.S.O.B wheezed, digging in a cooler behind him and coming up with a cold one. He looked at his friend, "You wanna toss it over, Merv . . . or is your shoulder still out after all these years?"

Merv snatched the can, cocked an arm, and let it go. Later, I thought that with one bad eye, he probably aimed too far to the right. But he had distance. I could taste the faint hoppiness of Coor's "wet air" as I watched the can arch over the canal, glint briefly in the sun, and pass over my head. I was still tasting it when it hit the ground ten feet behind me and exploded in a seeth of foam. By the time I reached it, burdened as I was by the pack, there was a mouthful left. They both saw loss and longing in my eyes.

"Aw hell!" L.S.O.B said. "Merv was always strong as a high school quarterback, but not that accurate. Go ahead, Merv, tell the man those football lies you're always tellin' me. Your friends ain't around and the coach is dead. It's just a fella from New York and they know all about bullshit."

So Merv told the truth. I didn't have to like it.

"You missed the pass," he said. "We're gonna have to go with a new wide receiver."

• • •

Half an hour later, forced to cross a timber weir ("Warning: Dangerous Water"), an umber flow roiled and hissed over a spillway—the only time I'd heard hydrological volume on the walk so far, an uncommon sound on the prairie where most streams meander in slow, silent ease across flatland. I picked my way across, stopping dead center to feel the planks vibrate, legs trembling above the roar.

Downstream, the surface peaked into sucks and boils—currents that could pull any man under as gently as a velvet hand.

Turned out it wasn't an irrigation canal after all, but a conduit that sluiced water from the Loup River through the turbines of power companies in Genoa, Monroe, and Columbus. I wouldn't have tumbled to the high-voltage resource underfoot, except I ended up talking to an honest-to-God plains sailor named Leonard Kush. With no celestial navigation skills required to float in a straight line, Leonard and a crew of twelve ply the "big damn ditch," as he put it, a few feet a day in the barge *Pawnee*, sucking sand from the inflow of the Loup. What Leonard and his mates try to do is reclaim the conduit's wandering silica and anchor it into a more or less permanent place along its banks, an impressive stretch of wannabe beachfront property for the Cornhusker State. When I asked Leonard if bottles with messages ever washed up, he looked at me with the humorless expression of a man confronting the *New York Times* crossword for the first time.

"We suck up beer cans," he said. "That's about it."

The purpose of this inland voyage, according to Leonard, is to dredge the big damn ditch lower than the bed of the Loup River (gravity siphons off the water) and keep it from filling up with the detritus of several counties. After eighteen years with the company, he'd watched the barge Pawnee heap up the "largest manmade sand pile in the world," a leviathan of grit running for miles, much of it rising above the cottonwoods. The sandsucker creeps forward at nearly minus knots, hooking itself to effluent pipes with mouths the size of garbage cans and tanker-sized hoses that stretch like pythons across Nebraska's landscape.

"How much sand sifts back into the canal?" I asked. "How often do you dredge up the same stuff?"

Leonard put two fingers under a greasy cap and scratched thoughtfully, as if hearing the question for the first time. He avoided my gaze, looking downstream, as if the correct answer could be read only long distance, perhaps by semaphore. "Beats the hell out'a me," he yelled above the noise. "It just keeps comin'."

Which was how I felt about Nebraska.

• • •

I crossed Council Creek with nothing around but breeze, grass, and sky, all harbingers of essential prairie. Half a mile away, a cluster of cottonwoods marked the junction of old "Plum Creek" with the Loup. Near the site, Clayton first noticed a rich, loamy soil that "would yield a crop of good corn." Fact is, it already had. Now almost dead center on the site of the abandoned Presbyterian mission where Brigham spent an uneasy night, I tried to imagine Clayton's view as he recorded it, but the "good number of log houses" had vanished into history and the fields "enclosed by rail fences" were now alfalfa meadows. Old "Plum Creek" was now Council Creek on the map, the two having exchanged names and geography sometime during the last century.

Behind me, I looked for the ravine from which marauding Sioux spilled onto the unexpecting Pawnee. Something like a dark *defile* was there, so, for history's sake, I chose it. Then I sat down in the grass, lit another of Charlie Roemer's *hecho a manos*, and watched smoke drift skyward, my mind in the past. Overhead, a jet-liner traced contrails at thirty thousand feet. On bloodied ground, the hair was standing on the back of my neck.

• • •

The Plum Creek Mission was bad news from its beginning in 1841 when Tom Harvey, superintendent of Indian Affairs, gave the go-ahead for a Presbyterian mission and government farm on Pawnee lands—a volatile cocktail mixing church, state, and Native Americans. Converting "heathen" went hand in glove with Yankee emigrants whose Christian virtues trooped west with them on the overland trails. Like white man's whiskey and cholera, a stiff-necked Christian superiority traveled the routes of settlement and commerce, infecting and eventually displacing almost every Native American it touched, including the Pawnee.

By 1842 three missionaries showed up on Plum Creek—John Dunbar, Samuel Allis, and J. B. Gaston, soon to be joined by a fourth, James Mathers. Dunbar and Allis are described in the history books as "simple-minded, plodding Christians," the type who make good followers but unfortunate disciples. Unlike Gaston and Mathers, they had their heads screwed on more or less straight, and with "commonsense conduct" attempted to move the Pawnee cautiously toward Christian culture. They quickly built the mission and government farm and persuaded the Pawnee to build a new village of forty lodges on nearby Council Creek. Gaston and Mathers, on the other hand, do-gooders who made both bad disciples and worse crusaders, ignored these efforts in favor of a more "muscular" Christianity.

Allis sent warriors through the villages to "smoke out" Indian children, who were then driven to school like cattle. Sweating in long shirtsleeves, Allis pointed at oversized letters on a blackboard and "shouted the name of each letter in turn, the children yelling the names in chorus." This was accompanied by an "anvil chorus"; blacksmithing was hammered out next door, another Christian virtue reserved for the Pawnee. Finished with the alphabet, Allis led the children in "good old Presbyterian hymns" turned "into rough-and-ready Pawnee."

Oberlin College graduates, Gaston and Mathers had other plans for Pawnee salvation. Gaston was the "crusader," while Mathers combined brutal "practical farming" with "a mighty zeal for improvement." Both had "no experience and no patience," the combined virtues of bigots encountering alien cultures for the first time. By 1844 they were lashing the Pawnee into submission. As his Christian duty, Mathers took to "knocking the Indians down with his fists," while Gaston "whipped" Pawnee women in the corn fields. When one of Mathers's sons beat a Pawnee woman to death, he was quietly sent away to work in other fields of the Lord. When another son gut-shot a young Pawnee brave for filching a few ears of corn, the newly appointed Indian agent, Daniel Miller, took the view that "colored people, Negro or Indians . . . must be handled firmly and forced to do what was for their own good."

Big Horse, chief of the Grand Pawnee, was the first to recognize danger within and without: the site of the mission was already being overrun by Sioux, 250 Pawnee having been killed between March and July of 1843. Then, on June 27, 1846, a band of 500 mounted Sioux warriors burned half the Pawnee village to the ground, littering the site with corpses. All four missionaries stood by, afraid or indifferent, as the slaughter continued. Bold with blackboard and whip, not one lifted a finger to help, even withholding ammunition from the mission's stores. By now, the Pawnee seethed with rage.

Soldier Chief took up the argument, so enraging Mathers that he hacked off the Indian's arm with an axe. Bleeding to death, Soldier Chief wrenched the axe from Mathers and hurled it into the back of Mathers's son, who died on the spot. Then the remnant Pawnee rose in fury, torching the farm and burning most of it to the ground. Gaston and Mathers fled east, followed by Dunbar and Allis. Dunbar returned to Missouri, an embittered man. Allis faded into history. Gaston and Mathers were defrocked, but the damage was done. "Muscular" Christianity had run its wicked course on the Loup River, and the Pawnee had long memories.

• • •

When Mark Twain met Brigham Young in Salt Lake City in 1870, the Mormon prophet seemed to him "a quiet, kindly, easy-mannered, dignified, self-possessed old gentleman of fifty-five or sixty, and had a gentle craft in his eye that probably belonged there."

Nowhere was Brigham's crafty eye more obvious than at the abandoned Pawnee mission and government farm where opportunity knocking made him sit up and take sharper notice, especially considering the litter of farm implements and other dry goods that were left behind in the missionaries' retreat—a harvest for the taking. To get around the problem of looting what was, technically, government property, Brigham latched on to a fellow Mormon in his party—James Case.

Jim Case had worked as a "government farmer" at the mission in 1846—a $300-a-year job that also came to grief. Whether he was fired because he joined the Mormons (his story), left of his own accord, or headed for the Missouri River when the Pawnee burned the farm is uncertain, but when he mentioned that he "was denied his last payday," Brigham ruled that Case was entitled to a portion of the abandoned goods as payment due in arrears—a rough, if ready, justice Brigham style. The Saints were beyond the government's reach, and cash money, always in short supply anyway, had little useful value on the plains. Tools and implements mattered, so Case collected his back pay from the mission's stock. Mormon history claims that Brigham instructed the others not to take "one cent" worth of tools or equipment, but Case was granted an exemption in the prophet's court of appeals. With no post office closer than Saint Joseph, Missouri, Case promptly fired off a letter "to whom it may concern" explaining what he considered a fair deal, considering his overdue paycheck. Mail service, however, was "irregular" beyond the Missouri River, and any "post" depended on occasional encounters with traders or trappers headed east to the "settlements." No letter from Case to Uncle Sam is known to survive.

• • •

In 1847 the Loup River was four hundred feet wide, flowing in two channels with a sandbar in the middle. Currents in the channels that April were dangerously high and the water waist deep. On the first attempt to cross, Mormon wagons mired in quicksand; others had to be lightened before they could get across. Amid squall and tumult, foundering oxen were unhitched midstream, roped and hauled to safety on the far bank. Brigham's wagon had been built watertight for such emergencies and was pressed into use, floating goods and people over the flood; but removed from its axles and rigged as a makeshift ferry, the "Revenue Cutter"—now a skifflike box—was no match for Case's heavy implements.

So perilous was the crossing that Brigham ordered it halted, electing to build two rafts for use next morning. A few managed to cross further upstream, finding the going easier once the wheels had packed the sandy bottom; so, by sundown, all but a handful were on the south bank, dry and delivered. That night, six men were left shivering on the north bank of the Loup to guard the off-loaded mission goods, each taking his turn watching over the others, vigilant against Pawnee attack.

"I stood guard in my wet clothes half the night," Norton Jacob wrote, "and slept in them the other half."

12

The walking of which I speak has nothing in it akin to taking exercise . . . but is itself the enterprise and adventure of the day.
HENRY DAVID THOREAU, "WALKING"

At 3:00 p.m. the last wagon was over on the solid sand bar, and about four o'clock all the wagons and teams were safely landed . . . on the south side of the Loup Fork.
WILLIAM CLAYTON, APRIL 24, 1847

That night I was watched over by two Australians—Cujo and Chip—both with a dogged suspicion of strangers. Cujo (blue heeler) and Chip (red heeler), took up positions to the left and right of my tent, one under a bush, the other squared off in Merlin and Judy Frenzen's driveway waiting for me to make a move. I was bedded down on their owners' lawn and, toward morning, when I had to take a godawful whiz, I tempted fate. I was draining my bladder against a nearby tree when they suddenly shifted position, cutting off my retreat, raising their upper lips in that intimidating long-toothed smile of canines who know you've made an ass of yourself. I feinted right, then left. Neither moved. So I tried talking them out of it as a stupid man will, first slathering baby talk as if dogs are idiots, then taking them into my confidence like a father having a man-to-man with newly pubescent sons. No movement, except that Cujo scratched his privates in an insulting sort of way.

I wasn't ignorant of dogs. I had three of my own, two permanently attached to our New York household, and one with unlimited visiting rights. All three, I'm proud to say, were fine American mixed breeds who would listen to reason. Not Cujo and Skip; they had the willful stubbornness of Australians in their genes and no amount of wheedling, whining, or whimpering moved them. For twenty minutes, they held me at bay, panting steadily under moonlight like steam engines building pressure. Dogs with less sympathy I have yet to meet.

FOLLOWING THE WRONG GOD HOME

Making bold, I sprinted to the left heading for the Frenzens' house. They burst into silent pursuit. Wheeling sharply right, I described a parabola around the tent, so confusing their dash that when Cujo turned, his paws slid sideways on the dewy grass and he sprawled out of control. But Skip cut me off. I dove over him, headfirst into the tent.

Neither followed. Instead, they mustered themselves again for guard duty, this time closer to the tent, all gruff and whuff and obviously pleased to have herded me back into my pen as cow dogs are trained to do. Pride wounded, especially when Cujo came over to nuzzle my hand, I bluffed back. "Listen you Aussies," I said. "You've been outsmarted by a Canadian."

• • •

A few hours earlier, I'd sat down to dinner in the Frenzens' kitchen. Taking pity on a stranger, they'd offered me the use of their yard and threw in a hearty supper of noodles with beef chunks, corn so sweet it tasted like candy, fresh green onions, bread and butter, brimming glasses of iced tea, and strawberry pie. It was 9:30 P.M. when we tucked into Judy's home cooking.

"We don't get to dinner early," Judy said. "We use up all the daylight in daylight savings time first." She wore a dark skirt, a bright-red blouse with white piping, matching collar, and a splayed red choker—the costume she'd worn to her day job at the county extension office. Three sons—Kent (18), Scott (17), Kurt (11)— were evidence of an ongoing Frenzen romance.

Merlin and his brother bought the farm in 1961, expanding it from 320 to 2,400 acres—1,200 in pasture, 500 in corn, and the rest in wheat, sorghum, oats, and alfalfa. As I walked into the west, farms took on more and more acreage as land dried out and irrigation took over. Now a new kind of survival confronted Nebraska's farmers, one requiring better use of limited natural resources, especially water, while expanding acreage to harvest a square meal *and* a profit. When I turned the subject to hard times, Merlin stared down at the wreckage of dinner, stabbing now and then at a stray piece of macaroni on his plate. Compact, barrel-chested, with a head round as a cabbage, he had a wide ring pressed into his hair from where he'd forced his hat down over it. His jack-o'-lantern smile was missing its candle.

"Nance County's averaging about one farm sale every day," he said. "A lot of people have to quit altogether. It's bad. Real bad. I swore a year ago I wasn't goin' back in a farm subsidy program. Too much hassle. But this year, I did. We got a payment up front. It helped with cash flow and fertilizer, things we need."

"Why the misery?" I asked.

"Too much production. Prices fell. Most farmers don't want to be in a federal subsidy program. They wish the free market was such they could avoid it . . . but they need help to survive." He took a long pull at his iced tea. "A number have gone under and are now working for other farmers who are getting bigger all the time. That's bad enough, but at least we got no prudent shell farmers yet."

That seemed a new crop to me. "What's a prudent shell farmer?"

"Insurance farms," he explained. "Owned by big companies like Prudential. I call 'em 'tax break farms' . . . only in agribusiness for a write-off."

Thunderstruck, I asked, "Is it legal?"

"Sure," he said. "Anything's legal if you've got big bucks. Small farmers get caught in the middle . . . don't count." He looked away, eyes bitter, perhaps regretting he'd said it.

But a tone was set, a grinding discord I came across again and again until I was deep into Wyoming and ranch country—big-time "agribusiness" controlled by companies like Prudential Insurance that put millions into land only to harvest a loss. I had no idea how to heal a wound like that. Nor did Merlin.

• • •

Fullerton looked nonviolent to me, its Main Street dozing in sunshine, the civic equivalent of a hog in a wallow. Walking into town on a back road past stark white silos of the Farmers Co-op, I was visited by a tawny kestrel hovering above a fencerow and a redheaded woodpecker tub-tub-tubbing in a tree next to an abandoned farmstead. Nearby, pumping memories of water, a rusting Aermotor windmill rattled its vanes in the morning breeze. Underfoot, I kicked up skuffs of dust, thinking of a cool longnecker and a hamburger for lunch.

Instead, I headed for the county extension office (Judy's suggestion) since I needed a short course on prairie grasses. Other than big and little bluestem, which the Osage taught me to recognize, I was brain-dead on plains and prairie botany. Judy's office was in a neat building on Main Street with the kind of official smell that, if one could can it under pressure, would work better than mace.

"Meet Susie Oldfather," Judy said when I showed up. "She's good with grasses."

• • •

The *Oldfather* name (Susie married into it) was a first for me, literally medieval and ranking right up there with monikers like *Gildersleeve*. Susie didn't look like a woman raised in North Royalton, Ohio—practically a suburb of Cleveland. (North Royalton is only a stone's throw from Kirtland, where Joseph Smith got

FOLLOWING THE WRONG GOD HOME

into banking trouble and was tarred and feathered before heading for Missouri in the dead of night.) Decked out in faded jeans, boots, striped jersey, and sunglasses, she had casually managed brown hair, but her smile was polite, even skeptical. "Dude," it registered as she looked me over.

So far, the women I'd met had most of two feet in the East, but Susie defined a boundary: her style and manner implied "West." She possessed what I later came to understand as a ranch woman's grace and poise—femininity with edges. When I probed, her story came out.

"Tomboy, I guess," she said. "I ended up at the University of Wyoming in agronomy. Loved it. Studied range management at Nebraska . . . and here I am." Even more interesting was this: "I married a banker."

Crossing the Loup and heading for open ground, Susie rammed a battered government pickup over county roads and up a steep farm track, pulling off next to a fence. We walked to the crest. Grassland trailed westward like a lush blanket, tattered and thrown down carelessly in gentle folds and humps. Rusty patches stained its fabric. To the north, the Loup traced a lazy arc, disappearing into the distance.

"Beautiful," was all I could manage.

"It's a transition zone," Susie said. "Tall and shortgrass prairie meet here. Big bluestem . . . or turkeyfoot . . . thins out. Little bluestem takes over. There's still turkeyfoot here, but it's too early yet. It needs warmer soil."

She waved her arm across twenty or thirty miles of sweeping landscape, stretching to horizon. "Anything that looks rusty in April is probably a native grass. Anything green probably isn't. Western wheatgrass is the only exception . . . greens up early. That rusty looking stuff over there is little bluestem. Two hundred years ago these plains were covered with it. Millions of buffalo got fat on it. That's why it's called 'buffalo grass.'"

Humpbacked folds and grassy swale told me I was still in the Loess Hills, tightly packed dunes of silt blown eastward by cyclones after the age of glaciers. In places it was 200 feet deep, 7,000 square miles of it.

"What else is growing out there?"

"Crested wheatgrass . . . but that's not native. Some oatgrass and redtop. Maybe quackgrass and some early brome. Brome moves in when the land's been overgrazed."

She pointed to a concave patch of bare, sandy earth below the slope of a nearby swale, a breeze catching her hair as she spoke. "That's a *blow-out*. Wind erosion is what you get when range has too many cattle on it. That patch isn't too bad. It's filling in again with ripgut or grama most likely."

"Why overgrazing?" I asked. I'd concluded the answer was greed but I got an unexpected reply.

"Fences," she said.

• • •

Once again, I'd come face-to-face with man's ugly signature in the Dream—a debt America owes to Joseph Glidden, a man who borrowed his wife's coffee grinder to twist two metal strands into what we call "barbed wire." Open range was a good deal when herds were large and men scarce in the West. Wide-open spaces supported ranchers, settlers, cattle, and bison. But more men, more ranches, and more cattle per acre meant less profitable ground, so six million bison were killed off and the land was surveyed and fenced to keep bovine outsiders out and a man's herd of insiders in. With cattle in wire cages, ranchers built herds too large for available space, and they chewed the land to ruin. Homestead to homeland, fences and borders define us, separating *mine* from *yours* and *us* from *them*. Inside those confines, it's easy to overgraze, despoiling our pasture while keeping the world at bay: "Private Property. Keep Out. Protected by Smith & Wesson."

"Over here!" Susie called, dropping to one knee, fingers in the swale. "Snowy gromwell . . . a sure sign of spring."

Yellow rises first in a prairie spring and riots on into summer—golden pea, buttercup, tumblemustard, butter-and-eggs, sunflower, pricklypear, snowy gromwell. Under Susie's fingers, crinkly edged petals stared up through spikes of green, a plant whose roots the Pawnee ate and whose purple juice they used to make a vermilion dye. Here was the first cousin of an old Missouri friend, known to the Osage as "puccoon."

• • •

In the first six inches under prairie topsoil lie between six and seven thousand pounds of root structure per acre, from which we get our sense of permanence, as in "putting down roots." Grass, burned in the caloric furnaces of horses and oxen, made it possible for Americans to power themselves west. With over six thousand grasses in the world, only a small number produce food for animals and man. Over millennia, we have winnowed our human preferences to seven edible grains: corn, wheat, oats, rye, rice, millet, and sorghums. Of these seven, two predominate—corn and wheat—and the failure of one of these two grains would create massive starvation.

The American heartland grows native grasses of great variety—buffalo grass, wheatgrass, bent grass, threeawns, gramas, reedgrass, saltgrass, and the bluestems. Common varieties sprout poetry: bent grass is "ticklegrass," one of the threeawns is "arrowfeather." Gramas include "sideoats" and "hairy," while bluestems like "broomsedge" and "splitbeard" dance on the tongue.

But today, intruders have taken over the heartland. Called "interlopers," they are transplants from other continents, true melting-pot grasses. Quackgrass came from Eurasia; redtop from Europe; meadow foxtail from Asia; tall oatgrass from North Africa; rescue grass from Argentina; smooth brome from China. Bermuda grass originated in India, and "weeping lovegrass" was first broken-hearted in South Africa.

Prairies and plains are home to plants other than grasses—native and not. These include legumes, which fruit in pods, like beans; and forbs, which are anything that isn't a legume or a grass. Many legumes are edible (prairie acacia and leadplant come to mind), and many are not. Wooly loco makes most animals just that and horses, in particular, high. Bundleflower, birdsfoot trefoil, and blue lupine are nutritious to livestock besides beautiful to name. Alfalfa and clovers are legumes harvested for hay.

The forbs, however, are full of evil names with reputations to match—bitterweed, water hemlock, fleabane, buffaloburr, snakeroot, sneezeweed, deathcamas, and black nightshade. Poison runs in the family. Even those disguised by verbal beauty—larkspur, snow-on-the-mountain, prince's plume—are dangerous to man and beast. Only a select few make a tasty dish for livestock. Cattle go nuts for gayfeather, compassplant (which native Americans used as chewing gum), and coneflower.

Chemical warfare is the standard tactic against the pesky forbs. There's no Geneva Convention in this war, and no letting up by either side. Forbs fill in the empty spaces where grassland is overgrazed, and humans retaliate with chemicals rendered into toxic soups. But forbs fight back with a twisted chemistry of their own—trementol in snakeroot, euphorbon in snow-on-the-mountain, glycoside solanine in black nightshade, which paralyzes the lungs. Cicutoxin in a pea-sized bite of spotted water hemlock will kill a man. Alkaloid zygadenine in Nuthalls deathcamas begins with violent pukes and ends in coma.

In the war for survival, the forbs are winning.

• • •

I left Fullerton a little after 2:00 P.M., crossing the Loup for the second time that day. My mood was better, since I'd had a good lunch that left me dull-witted as a cow in clover. Only the day seemed to matter; for once, my feet didn't nag and I kept my eye on a ridge to the south. Up there, at prairie's end and plains's beginning, I could sleep under stars.

At dusk, when I came to the Peterson place, below the ridge I'd chosen for a campsite, Mr. Peterson was mowing his yard. Eyes heavy lidded, dark, he stopped mowing as I hove into view and watched me until I was in his yard, a man with the look of a comfortable sweater. Retired, I guessed. I pointed to the prairie. "Would you mind if I camped up there tonight?"

"Suit yourself."

"I don't make fires. I'll be gone early."

"Suits me."

"Me, too," I said.

"Anyway, it ain't my land," he said.

I wandered until I found a flat nest of new grass with hummocky prairie on three sides and a long view toward the river. With the tent up, I sat in its opening eating peanut butter and crackers, washing them down with mouthfuls of hot coffee. Camped by the river, William Clayton used Orson Pratt's telescope to see the rings of Jupiter "very distinctly never having seen them before."

One October, the Osage and I walked across the Flint Hills of Kansas, crossing the last of the natural tallgrass prairies. Grazed to ground level, the hills were rusty with autumn's spent turkeyfoot. For three days we trekked through another century, dozing in the concave moons of still visible buffalo wallows—once to watch a boil of sixty hawks overhead, both too amazed to speak. At night, we put our fingernails on the sky, scratching at the stars—so brilliant, cold, and deep in space that we fixed our position by the sextant of the heart.

"At home in the universe," the Osage said.

Deep in Nebraska, I fancied this: in a "transition zone" a man might change in spite of himself.

13

It is the simple story of joy on legs.   CHARLES LUMMIS,
A TRAMP ACROSS THE CONTINENT

Arose soon after five, shaved and changed some of my clothing. . . .
Our course for the last seven miles has been about southwest. We
are about 14 miles from the main branch of the Platte river.

WILLIAM CLAYTON, APRIL 25, 1847

Things did change. It began with an unbroken view of the plains, sun splashed over its greens and russets like patches on a grandmother's best quilt, and a ribbon of quicksilver when morning's bright needle caught the thread of river and stitched it across the valley. Up early, I meandered over hills and crossed fences under a nearly cloudless sky, dropping toward the river at midmorning to pick up a road west.

For three halcyon days, I walked across the thick wrist separating the Loup and Platte River watersheds, part Nance and part Merrick Counties. This was the best of the Nebraska spring, and I felt as languid as the poet Vachel Lindsay, strolling across Kansas in 1912: "I have mounted a little hill on what was otherwise a level and seemingly uninhabited universe . . . patterned like a carpet with the shadows of clouds."

The road underfoot was packed sand, and the farms I passed slumbered in sunshine. At noon, with my back to a cottonwood, I listened to a jay's squall while reinventing a lost history from a crude sign with welded letters on a nearby post: "Site of Sunrise Post Office, 6-8-1899/11-7-1906"—a sad glyph that someone's Dream had begun here, only to have its promise burn out eight years later. The haunt of Sunrise so harried me, that when I later checked a dictionary of American place-names, the name wasn't listed anywhere, although Texas managed both Sundown and Sunset.

Nearby was a windmill so short that a toddler could flip a penny onto its deck from ground level. Water here lay close to the surface: "The shorter the windmill, the shorter the draw," I was told weeks later in Wyoming. Later, I passed an abandoned one-room schoolhouse—an aging divorcée down on her luck—with rusting swings and sagging basketball hoops. When I sat on one of the swings, it screamed from the unexpected weight and I fancied I heard ghosts of children.

Late that afternoon, when I waved to a farmer rocking on his tractor, Joe Santin cut the engine, climbed down, and walked over to greet me. The tractor was hub-deep in a soggy field, pulling a multiwheeled seeder straddled on both sides with green plastic tanks of liquid fertilizer. "Wet spring," he said, eyes dark as anthracite, thick hair salt-and-pepper, an old friend's manner of speaking in his voice. Two minutes later, I had thirty square feet of Santin real estate on which to pitch my tent, an offer of dinner, and an invitation to take in the annual high-school play in nearby Palmer.

The Santins' brick ranch house stands barely above floodplain on the Loup—sturdy as a French barque, trim as a well-kept ship. From their rear deck, evening splayed across the fields, turning them a deep watery green, so close to the Mormon Trail (Brigham slept nearby on April 26, 1847) that I might have counted the cracks in William Clayton's chapped lips as he passed. Like most families who live along the trail, the Santins' memory of Mormons had long faded, but an appreciation of their history, renewed by conversation, was genuine.

The daughter of a French Canadian turned Nebraskan, Loretta Santin was an Omaha girl when she met and married her dark-haired Joe. Catholic grandparents put the kibosh on her father's proposed marriage to a young Protestant in rural Quebec, and when the girl died, her love requited but Loretta's father broken-hearted, he crossed the U.S. border for a less Roman Catholic Dream. A head shorter than her husband and pale from a recent illness, Loretta's eyes were the color of gooseberries; coiffed for the night out in Palmer, her sandy hair was almost opaque in the dying sun.

On the ride into Palmer, Joe talked of family and their past. "My father remembered the Loup when the river was still clear. You could throw a stone across it. Back then it had fewer islands or sandbars. Once you plow, water runs off faster. Ditches and culverts get water to the river quicker . . . and the runoff carries more dirt."

He looked across the floodplain at the smear of water threading through the valley. "In the old days," he said, "it was deep and clear and good to fish. In the old days . . ." His voice trailed, drifting in some down-the-drain enchantment.

•   •   •

Palmer had the look of a town that started out with high hopes but got caught in a sudden squall. Older houses stuck up from the plains at odd angles, listing, sinking, or trying to right themselves. Downtown, a man could roll keel up in a stiff wind. Home to the Dimsdale brothers, two agribusiness success stories and owners of a string of small-town Nebraska banks, Palmer had a rudderless look in ocean prairie.

The high-school play was a drifting hulk of angst, its drama unappreciated, thank God, by most of the Palmer audience. Pimps, prostitutes, drug addicts, and murderers hived on the hometown stage. The play (*Juvie* by Jerome "let's-hope-he-never-writes-another" McDonough) takes place in a juvenile detention center in the Bronx. Local thespians, teenagers all, addled their lines and, at times, appeared embarrassed. All handsome or beautiful or somewhere in between, it was impossible for me to imagine a pimp, pusher, or hooker in the lot. With each new revelation of Big Apple depravity on his hometown stage, Joe sucked in wind, the audience coughed nervously, and Loretta stared at her shoes. Mercifully, it ended.

"None too soon," Loretta critiqued.

Agony over, I tarried in the thespian disaster zone long enough to have a word with the drama coach, a fidgety younger man. I asked why he'd chosen McDonough's *tour de farce* for the town's annual off-Broadway extravaganza.

"The students chose it," he answered, adding lamely, "They wanted to send a message."

I pushed the envelope: a stranger, I'd be gone by morning. "Let's see if I can get the *message* straight. Palmer teenagers are considering careers as pimps, pushers, and prostitutes?" I knew better, of course.

Worry lines knotted his forehead into a damp, crumpled dishrag; his eyes narrowed like a man fearful for his financial future, no doubt thinking I'd taken things literally and might possibly have a word with the principal. Applause had surely been sparse, and the theater had emptied quickly, the audience carrying gloom onto the streets.

"Drugs are everywhere," he answered, emphasizing each word in case I missed the point.

I didn't argue. "What about rapes, murders, and kidnappings . . . in Palmer, that is?"

"Drugs . . ." he began again, looking around for any salvation near at hand and spotted some. "If you'll excuse me . . ."

He bolted in the direction of a huddle of parents who looked as if they'd relish having an unkind word with him. Outside in the sweet plains air, I volunteered to put a New York playwright out of his misery—little enough to promote *community.* "After all," I said, "McDonough shot your drama coach in the foot."

"Do him a world of good," Loretta said, through her French Canadian-American smile.

• • •

"You tell anybody about these asparagus beds," Jack Wegner said, "and you're dog meat. That's a fact."

Now he was threatening a stranger. We were battering our way over Nebraska back roads in Jack's pickup, dust boiling behind us like a jet's contrail, lost in Nebraska's deep space as far as I was concerned, but headed for the Ark of the

Covenant in Jack's temple of edible immigrants—asparagus. Like most of our ancestors, *A. officinalis* arrived from the Old World and, although tamed on the farms in California's Imperial Valley, it still grows wild in many parts of America as it once did in the sandy meadows and fens of Essex, England. Asparagus crossed the Alleghenies with the Dream and followed the pioneers onto the plains, and Jack knew the "best damn spot" in the county where asparagus Dreams came true.

"Not a word or you're in deep . . . manure."

When we passed the farm where his uncle Don was blown out of his boots by lightning and struck dead, Jack's blue eyes took on the peculiar cast of a man with a treasure map in his head where "X" marks the spot. He braked, cut the engine, and tumbled out into God knows what part of the Cornhusker State (I swear it, Jack! Your secret's safe!), shunting into the greensward like a switch engine in a railroad yard. Then he dropped to his knees. "Look at this!" he said, coupling his hands around slender stalks.

Infrequently, I admit, I eat the store-bought variety that grows double the size of the wild stuff and makes your pee stink. But on the sandy soil of the Loup watershed that morning, wild stalks looked as delicate as a pianist's fingers, barely reaching eight inches—a field of the stuff. With manic hustle, Jack snapped the stalks and stacked them neatly in piles. Before we'd carried the first two armloads to the truck, we'd eaten a couple of fistfuls raw—succulence impossible to describe but better than stolen New York apples fresh from the tree.

"Not a word!" he ordered as we hefted more asparagus into his pickup, cradling the harvest in baskets. "Some secrets are best kept . . . y'know what I mean. Or else." He said all this while smiling.

• • •

Jack Wegner is addicted to using *Zygomaticus major*—a man who can't keep from smiling. He seems to have little or no use for the *Corrugator supercilii* muscle, since he seldom frowns. Straight as a six-foot oak plank and almost as thin, he radiates a clement disposition, not unusual for a kid born in Hayward, California, who looks more like a beach boy than a Nebraska farmer. When I met Jack six miles south of the Santin spread, his smile climbed down off his tractor before he did and made me momentarily nervous. I was sitting in a swale by the roadside brewing up a pint of my usual road-warrior coffee and comforting myself that Mormons had done the same before they became sanctified, when he rumbled to a stop.

"You look all beat-up," he said, climbing down off the tractor, loping after his smile.

"Afternoon jump start," I answered, pointing at my cup. "I'm out of beer."

"We can fix that," Jack said, which led to an offer to tap a keg at a local tavern later in the day and stay overnight. "You can sleep in Granny's brass bed. Take a shower. Talk my head off."

Invitation accepted, I headed on while Jack lurched away in a crunch of gears trying to get his day's work done. It was prime seeding time. Around me, corn was going into the ground and tractors grumbled in the distance, straining through fields with farmers hunched in their cabs hoping for salvation by bumper crop. When the gravel turned to a rutted, tree-lined farm lane, still running true to the surveyor's chain toward the Platte, a teenage girl on an ATV growled through the ruts, hesitated long enough for me to see fear in her eyes, then gunned past bouncing in her mechanized saddle like a bronc rider, her ponytail smoky colored as her stinking exhaust. Thinking she was a landowner's daughter, I quickly shuffled on, hoofing south.

Toward dusk, shaky with fatigue, I arrived at the section line road where Jack had agreed to meet, and found him dozing in his pickup, a dusty bill cap pulled over his eyes. When I tapped on the door, he popped up like jack-in-the-box and grinned. "Catch it when you can," he said.

We rattled overland to Johnny's Place, a veritable tabernacle of the gospel of brew. Situated in the burg of Worms, named after the city of Worms, Germany, Johnny's Place was awash in "wet air" beers—Schlitz, Budweiser, Miller—and filled with eccentrics, punsters, card sharps, and friendly assorted swill-bellies. I felt right at home. Our mutual pleasure was cold, frequent, and punctuated with laughter, tall tales, even sadness, especially when Jack, noted for his fine baritone voice, spoke of singing at the funerals of children and how dying friends would ring up with last requests.

Later, enveloped in the ministrations of "Granny's" brass bed, listening to Carol Wegner's own melodic voice settling their children to sleep and Jack's low, easy laughter easing the night away, I was suddenly choked with loneliness for home and family—perhaps the only time on the walk that the Dream laid a hand on me. Mormon regard for "family" is well advertised; a core sample taken from bedrock Mormon will turn up a thick stratum of "family values" anchoring their future hope. In the great pantheon of religious beliefs, Mormon defense of families seems an anchor in America's troubled waters, but in life their statistics fare little better than the rest of us come time to divorce. I admire Mormon families, but, having viewed them firsthand and often in larger-than-average numbers, I'd offer Mormon parents Russell Baker's sage advice: "Don't try to make children grow up to be like you or they may do it."

Next day, under a streaky cyan sky, I trudged toward the Platte refreshed and full-bellied. By noon, a draggle of clouds had shunted eastward, and heat fell over the land with a promise of better tomorrows. All day, I marveled at the lush Nebraska green, and once, when I wiped sweat from my face, the Cornhusker State seemed less a picture than picture perfect. When I stopped for my midafternoon jump start, I fetched Clayton's *Journal* from my pack and read the entry for his day—straight out of the Keystone Cops.

Turns out that four Camp-of-Israel "scouts" (Porter Rockwell, Tom Brown, Joseph Matthews, John Eldredge) came close to soiling their shorts when "fifteen Indians sprang to their feet, all naked except for the breech cloth." By Clayton's reckoning, each Indian was armed with "rifles, bows . . . and about twenty arrows," a remarkable mathematical calculation since the skirmish lasted less than two minutes. Which "scout" made the head count of enemy and armaments isn't clear, but how so precise a number of Pawnee managed to wield bows, arrows, *and* rifles at the same time without stumble-bumbling over their weapons remains an unsolved Mormon Trail mystery—at least to me. Rockwell reportedly waved his rifle; Matthews brandished a cocked pistol. At the sight of Mormon small arms (told with a straight face by Clayton), the fifteen Pawnee cowered while "the brethren turned their horses to come to camp." "Turned" and "come" are words lacking an impression of immediate hustle and velocity.

Quickly, Clayton's account gets more amusing; all "fifteen" Indians opened fire from "150 feet" on the *backs* of the four Mormons "coming" to camp, but not a single shot struck home; not one horse's derriere was punctuated, and the "brethren did not shoot at the Indians, even when the Indians shot at them"—a remarkable example of Mormon resolve, if true. The intrepid "scouts" were on a flat-out gallop across the prairie—at least 1,150 feet out of range, by my estimate, when shooting commenced—all heading for "camp" in a rush with t-t-t-tall tales to tell.

But Mormon guns weren't entirely silent that day. Their hunters managed to hit three targets—a rattlesnake (shot by Luke Johnson), an antelope (shot thrice by a trio of Deadeye Dicks) and a jackrabbit—"nearest like the English hare of any," Clayton wrote. Rattled by the Pawnee menace, John Brown accidentally shot Lewis Barney's mare in the foreleg, set Barney's wagon on fire, and turned Brigham's attention to the hazards of "brethren" with firearms. Was it history, myth, or comedy? Whatever, tall tales, like Dreams, are always better in the telling.

"This is a help-yourself kitchen," Adeline Houdek said.

So I did. Twice. Chicken salad sandwiches. Bread and jam. Salad. Lemonade. Dragging a full plate to the table, nobody looked surprised; all the others—Ray, Adeline, three boys and their wives—were putting it away grand style, a family so large, they shoehorned me in and hardly noticed. Albeit sober, my luck was holding; I'd landed on my feet in another good woman's kitchen. Dream come true, but Mormanesque, you might say—no coffee, no tea, no smoking—but with one saving grace. It was home to a herd of genial Democrats.

Full-bellied Ray Houdek spoke up. "I'm not much on Ronald Reagan," he said. "The man still thinks he's in the movies."

"He is," I answered between mouthfuls. "The lines are from a script but the screen's smaller."

I slept behind the machine shed with Blue, the family mutt, for company. We stirred frequently in the dark, squirming into our respective comfort zones, listening to a restless spring wind mourning in the cottonwoods. When I headed toward Grand Island next morning, Blue rubbed against my legs as if he'd found another stray a home, nudging me back toward the fulsome brick house in which the Houdeks had raised their alcohol-free brood and sheltered a wandering Canadian. The generous Houdek clan was a semicolon in my north-south sentence between the Loup and Platte Rivers—"a degree of separation between the comma and the period." Having completed one part of a geographical parallel construction, I was now beginning another—the long walk up the Platte River valley. Heading west again, the emotion of that morning I later found in a line from a John Harvey novel: "He hung on the edge of something he could neither ignore nor fully understand; something that, even when he closed his eyes and ears, still echoed discordantly inside his mind."

14

Cross country on foot, miles are always misleading; the hours are
what counts.   COLIN FLETCHER,
                                        THE MAN WHO WALKED THROUGH TIME

We travel on the first bench about three quarters of a mile north of . . . Grand Island. There are many wild geese.

WILLIAM CLAYTON, APRIL 30, 1847

I sat on the front porch of Henry Fonda's boyhood home staring due west. On the street, wind lifted a skim of dust, twisted it to a funnel, and dropped it again. For a while, nothing moved, not even the fragile leaves of the cottonwoods, the morning torpid as a muggy day in August. I listened to my breathing, regular and deep, and took in what was once an expanse of prairie, the kind of space that caused folks to throw a shielding hand over their eyes as if to frame the awesome and unknown within some recognizable horizon—a landscape Stephen H. Long called "unfit for cultivation" and O. E. Rølvaag called "the great stillness where there was nothing to hide behind."

Like Grant Wood's depiction of a midwestern farmhouse in *American Gothic*—plain, framed, uncluttered—Fonda's boyhood home was much like the actor himself. There was nothing curvilinear in Fonda's acting; he played each role with the grain, never against it. When he graduated to Westerns, he came into his own—tight, sparse, gnarly. He looked a dude, but a tough one, and like Americans a century before, it was a westering vision that led Fonda from Grand Island to California. There's a telling photograph of Henry standing on the front walk of his boyhood home during his later Hollywood years, smiling grandly; but his eyes are distant and fogged, as if he's smiling in present tense, but seeing in past. In *On Golden Pond*, the same haunted look shows in his portrayal of a confused old man teetering on the edge of the dark.

Although Fonda lived *in* the house, he never lived *on* the site. The building was moved from Grand Island sometime in the 1970s. Now part of the Stuhr Museum of the Prairie Pioneer, it's tucked into a collection of cribbed and cobbled buildings—a fake "pioneer" village—which might account for the haunted look on his face on the day he was photographed by local paparazzi, as if his beginnings and endings had come down to sets on a Hollywood back lot. The real Henry Fonda (he hadn't yet died in 1985, the year I sat on his porch) was first and foremost a media creation whose life was defined by roles, as mythic in effect on twentieth-century America as Manifest Destiny, the Corps of Discovery, or the gold rush on the nineteenth. At the core of Fonda's craft was a talent for deception, of make-believe; at the heart of his movies lingered a West of the imagination. Now, settled in a make-believe town, his boyhood home had also become a fantasy, the stuff of which, when I thought about it, Dreams are made and from which Fonda made a good living.

. . .

It was inevitable, I suppose, that this carefully assembled make-believe town turned me gloomy, as if a shadow creased the sun. Not that history didn't interest me, but I was fetched up against that old bugbear, myth, sucking at my heels like scummy bath water circling a drain. The further away we are from an event, the closer we approach myth, tidy and sanitized. Minus horse manure, outhouses, unwashed bodies, drunks whizzing in the streets, tobacco juice splattering saloon floors, syphilis, gonorrhea, and families carried off by influenza, smallpox, diphtheria, tuberculosis, or any of the other realities of the West's "good old days," our contemporary interpretations of America's past come neatly packaged to suit marketing needs.

One way or another, the mythic West is always a version of *High Noon*, *Stagecoach*, or *Gunfight at the O.K. Corral*. Good triumphs over evil and we get a sack of popcorn and a Coke into the bargain. (There's a yarn about *Cheyenne Autumn* that's a legend in Gallup, New Mexico, where John Ford hired local Navajo to play the Cheyenne. Asked to speak "Indian" in scenes, they obliged. As long as they sounded authentic, Ford assumed, it was okay for a Saturday matinee. Today, *Cheyenne Autumn* is a cult classic among the Navajo, who laugh themselves sick over what grandfathers Begay and Yazzi really said on camera, usually something colorful like, "Listen you paleface turd, you'd sell your sister if you could make a peso.")

Half a block away a vintage steam locomotive chuffed, gave a shrill and forlorn shriek, and caterwauled away, wheezing around the museum grounds. Part of an American hallucination gone belly-up and "built of dreams of Klondike Gold," it was manufactured near the end of the Klondike gold rush in 1908—a strike that attracted thirty thousand miners, hustlers, and whores in 1896 when the White Pass and Yukon Railway was built from Skagway to Whitehorse as a supply route to the diggings across 110 miles across Alaska, British Columbia, and the Yukon Territory. Fresh from the Baldwin Locomotive Works in Philadelphia, Locomotive 69 (134,369 pounds) was shipped in pieces and assembled in Skagway to link towns that had sprung up before the claims played out. In its dotage, it wound up in Nebraska. Grieving over its final destination, I bought a ticket to ride. As the antique train made its wheezy circuit around Prairie Village, the only thing worth the fare was that no fake train robbers burst from the underbrush to "stage" a holdup.

· · ·

Excerpt from the *Grand Island Times*, July 15, 1874: "About six hundred Mormons passed through here on Sunday morning for Utah. They were a dirty, stinking and beastly looking set, and needed soap and water more than anything else."•

Like most towns along the Mormon Trail, Grand Island was born rolling when the Union Pacific marked out a town site and hammered rails westward. It took its name from a forty-five-mile-long sliver of land in the Platte River named by early French trappers. By the time the Mormon wagons meandered over the grassy flats above the river, parts of the island were beginning to erode, although one remnant thumb in the Platte was forded and used by the Saints to pasture and feed livestock. Mormon Island, as it's known today, is a state park.

The founders of Grand Island were delusionary rather than visionary, which is about what you'd expect from people who bought land from a railroad company that convinced Uncle Sam the Rockies started forty-seven miles west of Omaha. Settled in 1857 by five Yankees and thirty-two German immigrants on the usual "plan of speculation" (read scam), the town stood at "the very edge of civilization." The "speculation" was to get an advance leg up on the proposed transcontinental railroad, but the handful of Germans alternately shivered and fried in prairie limbo until the Union Pacific finally came through in 1866 and dropped off some new neighbors. It was rough and tumble from the start. The first town meeting ended in a fistfight.

In 1939, when writers for the Works Progress Administration summed up the place, "most of the elements in Grand Island that represent respectability, tradition, and small-town life" lived south of the tracks. Churches, businesses, and homes of the genteel hived like Pharisees between the UP and the river. North of the tracks lay an industrial area with "dingy tenements where washing is hung out to dry on lines strung along the porches." Beyond that was "a dismal expanse called *Foggy Bottoms* with its row of shacks and cheap frame houses where the poorer white and Negro working men live." Rear-of-the-Busville.

From its location almost dead center in the heart of the country, the town fathers reasoned that Grand Island was a sure bet to become the nation's capital; but when that hand didn't play out, they opted out of the game: "one died in the poorhouse, one shot himself, another took strychnine, and one was run over by a train." No mention is made of whether the Dream-killer train was east or westbound, but I'd bet the latter, since the rails, like most Americans with a busted flush, headed in that direction, like Fonda and Spangler Arlington Brugh from Filley, Nebraska, who became known in the movies as Robert Taylor.

Naturally, some Nebraskan entertainers missed the train entirely but deserve honorable mention—Jake Eaton, for one, "champion gum chewer of the world." On a good day in Grand Island, Jake could chew three hundred pieces of gum at once, which says a mouthful about the state of entertainment in Nebraska and why Henry Fonda and Arlington Brugh scraped up enough money for a ticket. When I dropped into a drugstore for a tenpack of Wrigley's Spearmint for the road, the clerk was historically nonplussed when I mentioned Jake.

"Three hundred!" she said, jawing on her own nimble wad. "That's a lotta gum!"

"How many tenpacks would that be?" I ventured as she took my money. Her pretty face pruned under the strain.

"Thirty?"

"And how much would it cost today?"

When I hit the door, she was still smiling, groping with multiplication.

• • •

Across the West, at a line drawn roughly at the Missouri River, towns take on a worn and scuffed look, like old shoes scattered across a rug. Along my line of march, even established towns like Grand Island seemed tossed together, as if things started off right, but once streets were laid out, confusions, misalignments, and maladjustments took over. For a month, on the long haul up the Platte, I walked through communities trying their civic best to hold hearth and home together—agricultural towns glued down by farmers co-ops, implement dealers, feed stores, and small-town banks.

Walking up the Platte River for the next couple of weeks, I passed through a litany of monotonous town names, each strung out on a road map, chipped beads on a string. Some rang alliterative (LeMoyne, Lewellen, Lisco) but most rang tuneless as their namesakes (Gibbon, Brady, Maxwell), and the solitary one-syllable name (Darr) was as ugly to the ear as it was to the eye. Water played a significant role in Nebraska place-names along the Platte: Wood River, Elm Creek, and Willow Island all evoke a tall glass of promise or the possibility of shade. Nebraska's treeless space was stark to those who first settled the place, so it was foreordained that Nebraska should become the home of Arbor Day. Like stitches in a tedious fabric, these towns sewed a piece of the nation together, creating another patch on an incomplete quilt. But what to make of the patch? As late as 1862, an American dragoon, Lieutenant William Hazen, wrote: "We may as well admit that Kansas and Nebraska . . . are perfect deserts."

Wright Morris, the late, great writer of things Nebraskan and Kansan, puts the best possible spin on dry life on the high plains: "In the dry places, men begin to

dream. Where rivers run sand, there is something in a man that begins to flow. West of the 98th Meridian—where it sometimes rains and it sometimes doesn't—towns, like weeds, spring up when it rains, dry up when it stops." Unlike Hazen's dust bowl description, this is terrific writing, but both are bullshit, one filled with fear and the other with Dream. Nebraska's towns aren't weeds but seeds in a dry land still hoping for flowers.

. . .

I ambled over to Nightser's Bakery for eggs, potatoes, toast, more plains enfeebled coffee, and something called a "chop suey roll" that a curious man couldn't resist, but that other aliens in the state should—advice offered here as a public service. It turned out to be a pustule of fried dough and maraschino cherries, neither of which explained its odd name nor connected it with anything oriental, unless it was body parts left over from a Tong war. A more dedicated man would have "sueyed" the owner for defamation of ethnic food. Still, there was something stolidly Nebraskan about yellow tables and red chairs. At another table, two middle-aged grumblers bellyached nonsense about marijuana.

"They put it in pillowcases and dry it in the dryers at the Laundromat," one lamented. "My grandkids get high drying their clothes."

I asked the name of the laundry. I had washing to do.

. . .

Before putting Grand Island in past tense, I dropped in to visit the Stuhr Museum of the Prairie Pioneer again. The museum is a jewel in the immense scape of Nebraska, rising from a patch of silver water as if grown on a lily pad from a windblown seed. Agleam in the center of a reflecting pool, the museum's contemporary architecture is glassy and angular; the building is approachable only by a bridge over a moat, which gives visitors the impression that the state really isn't in a deepening thirst. Nearby, Mormons felt the first effects of dry air as it shriveled their nostrils and shrank the felloes in their wagon wheels.

Jack Learned, the museum's director, was kind enough to give me an audience. A cadaverous, chain-smoking man inside a rumpled white dress shirt with sleeves rolled to the elbows and wearing a stained tie, his capacious feet rested on his desk and his nicotine addict's eye seldom wavered from a pack of Pall Mall cigarettes. Between exhausts of tar and carbon monoxide, he said, "If it's history you're after, Bob Manley's the man you want to see. I'll introduce you."

When I shook hands with the museum's resident historian—a beetling man who would look at home on a professional basketball court—"Dr. Bob," as he's called, gazed down on my balding pate with the intimidating self-confidence

common to the extremely tall. His passion runs deep: in a word, *Nebraska*. He also totes a fine-tuned guitar. In schools throughout the state, he's known as the "Singing History Professor."

But Dr. Bob puts scant emphasis on Mormons or their trail. "They were long gone when Nebraska's towns began sprouting," he explained, left hand fingering imaginary frets. "Mormons had a superhighway goin' through here by 1855. They started a 'road ranch' culture . . . supply stations that helped out other Mormons heading for Salt Lake. By 1860, there were eleven or twelve road ranches across the Territory . . . not all of them Mormon . . . but all trading with emigrants."

To understand Nebraska's settlement, Dr. Bob told me, a person has to understand water, the railroad, and American Dreams in that order. "An apparent lack of water made the territory an imaginary dust bowl. Emigrants wanted to cross it quick. Most never looked back. By 1869, the railroad made it easier for folks to hop off a train and ponder Nebraska's possibilities. If they didn't like it, they could get back on. Nobody much hopped off until the early 1870s."

"Sounds reasonable," I said.

"Hew Pee," he said.

For a second, I thought he was ordering me to the men's room, but he was merely mouthing the initials of the Union Pacific Railroad in plains dialect.

Nebraska was a classic late bloomer, and the Union Pacific came late in its story—sixty years after the land was first crossed—bringing with it sharps who sold off land to anyone willing to magnify a fragile hope. "Nebraska's settlement comes down to demographics," Dr. Bob intoned. "Demography shows the future . . . and demographics in this state still comes down to available aich-two-oh . . . plain old water." He leaned on the wall as if to anchor his lankiness and emphasize his point by turning himself into an exclamation point. "Go north or south of the Platte today and average age goes up as land values go down. Everything . . . I do mean everything . . . comes down to the Platte River Valley. It's the only game in town. Always has been. Always will be." In Manley's book, *The Town Builders*, he points out that there were places in pioneer Nebraska where towns were "supposed to 'loom up' . . . only they didn't 'loom.'" When they did, it was along the Platte.

"People who settled this state weren't drifters," he argued. "Nebraska wasn't a 'Hell, Ma, let's strap the plow to the wagon and head further west kind of place.'"

Now I protested. "But some of that must have gone on. Go West, young man, go West . . . that kind of thing. There's a lot of Nebraskans still moving on."

Dr. Bob tapped his skull, looked down at my tonsils. "When folks took root here, they mainly stayed put," he said. "Mormons were history. Memories in Nebraska aren't about moving through or moving on. They're about great-grand-father Nils Hansen . . . somebody like that . . . who got his start in a Nebraska sod house."

That part was true. Across Nebraska, it seemed that everybody claimed descent from nightlife in a "soddy." The rest were transients, a mere fragment, at best, of the Cornhusker ancestor Dream. Yet, if there's a place that marks an American Dream with more simplicity than the Stuhr Museum, I've yet to find it. Inside its walls, I saw the hopes of all immigrant peoples writ small but elegant on a handmade Swedish trunk: "Kari Hellekson Moen, Newman Grove P.O., Madison County, Nebraska, North America." I admit it put a lump in my throat.

15

There is much to be said for lazy walking.
J. BROOKS ATKINSON, "ON WALKING"

A very Strong North Wind blowing, & being dark, [it] caused the Camp to halt for the night. . . . President Young gave liberty for the brethren to have a dance & enjoy themselves, as they had neither wood to warm, nor good water. THOMAS BULLOCK,
APRIL 30, 1847

In the Gas'N'Git in Wood River (I'd slept under the town water tower the night before), I bought a cup of java, forced myself to drink it, and spread my now grimy maps on the counter. Business was slow and the tidy woman tending shop didn't mind the disorder. Watching me drink, her eyes looked sympathetic. When she asked and I explained what I was up to, she said, with a tincture of holier-than-thou, "Good Mormons don't drink coffee."

I pushed the cup across for a refill. "Then they're not missing much flavor."

She blinked lazily into the sunshine like a frog warming on a lily pad. "The first refill's free," she said. "Then you pay for your poison."

Over the Gas'N'Git's two cups of beige-colored hot water, a creeping indeci-sion settled on me, compounded by my obsessive rigmarole having to do with charts, guides, and gazetteers. I was weighted down with paper—books, maps, journals, diaries—altogether, when I later weighed the stuff, six pounds. I needed them. Or did I?

Did and didn't took up an hour while I fidgeted over my mother lode, laying each out, pruning like a tree surgeon in a scruffy orchard. In the end, I decided to hell with maps. All I needed was old advice—follow the Platte to the Sweetwater River and the Sweetwater to South Pass, Wyoming. I found a box, off- loaded the unnecessary weight, and headed for the post office. Once across the Continental Divide, I'd worry about further directions.

· · ·

Don Sloan walks the Union Pacific tracks from Wood River to Gibbon (four-teen miles) once each week wearing a bright yellow hard hat and carrying a six-pound steel spike maul. When I met him near Shelton, he was wearing a sleeve-less T-shirt, leather gloves, boots that could kick the you-know-what off a statue, green aviator sunglasses, and jeans that would never come clean. He sauntered toward me, muscled as a plow horse, with the maul tossed lazily over one shoulder like a man carries a fishing pole. Considering the vagaries of Nebraska weather, I asked him what he wore in winter. "About five layers," he answered.

Don told me he rarely finds "anything serious" on the UP main line. "Now and then a broken rail . . . but we find something wrong with the switches almost every week."

His idea of "anything serious" seemed flawed to a layman. Images of Casey Jones came to mind, but instead of death with a hand on the throttle, I flashed some of my newly acquired track lore. "But this is CWR . . . Continuous Welded Rail," I said. "If it's broken, how do you fix that? You can't sew it together like a torn shirt."

Don looked me over the way a bank manager does when nay-saying a loan to a felon. "Hell you can't," he said, waving the maul in my direction like a tooth-pick. "They got a machine. Comes out, heats up the rail. Puts new steel over the break. It's the future of rail tick."

"Rail tick?"

"Yeah. Technology."

But it was the past, not the future, that came blasting past, six-foot drive wheels grinding the rails, streamlined under green metal sheeting, smoke belching—the

Union Pacific 8444—the fabled steam engine that hauled the Overland Limited, Portland Limited, and Los Angeles Limited in the heyday of rail travel. Its vintage cars tailed away down the track, ass end wiggling as trains will. Don Sloan smiled at the look on my face.

"Grand," I said, a word I overuse, but it was perfect for the occasion. I was a kid again, lining up pennies on the hometown tracks, waiting for the noon train to flatten them into copper moons—the same Canadian National train that would one day carry me partway to the United States of America.

"She's headed for North Platte or the Cheyenne yards," Don said. "They keep her there. Goes on tour twice a year. She's comin' back from the World's Fair in New Orleans."

When he walked on, I knelt down and put my ear to the rail. I heard the dim grumble of the Overland Limited, steaming across the Mormon Trail it usurped. *Trails. Rails.* Take away a single letter and one is the inherited reflection of the other. Ahead of me, the tracks blurred in the heat.

• • •

I stank. The three ladies who ran the Daisy Queen (not Dairy Queen) in Shelton looked at me ominously. Wet clear through my shirt, six eyes said in unison, *Drifter.* I bought an ice cream cone. *Lick 'n leave,* the eyes said. So I moved on, found a café where I lingered, joking with a waitress as endowed as the Venus of Wollendorf. I asked her to come along. She refilled my tea, chuckled.

"I can't go camping today," she joked.

Somewhere nearby the Mormons had crossed Wood River, but I didn't give a damn. It wasn't much of a crossing anyway and sore feet have a way of focusing one's attention.

• • •

When Frederick Piercy crossed Wood River on his way to Salt Lake in 1853, he found a slapped-together bridge "composed of branches of trees and foliage thrown into the river . . . about 3 or 4 yards wide." Twenty-three and from Great Britain, Piercy documented his trek in drawings from New Orleans to Salt Lake City. They remain the only detailed renderings of the Mormon Trail in its prime. Before he died in virtual obscurity in 1891, his work was exhibited eleven times at the Royal Academy of Arts in London—portraits, landscapes, sculpture. Of the Portsmouth-born artist, Fawn Brodie writes: "Green as his countrymen, before the trip was over he had learned how to drive the stubbornest mule, and . . . without any medical training he had set the broken leg of a friend so skillfully it mended without complications."

But young Piercy was reticent. At a time when Mormon polygamy was creating a national heartburn, the non-Mormon was curiously silent about the practice. Except for two or three oblique references in his journal, he never mentions it, sidestepping the "hysterical denunciation" going on at the time. He wrote with "quiet detachment," Brodie argues, in part because his trip "was arranged by Mormons in Liverpool who later edited and published his book." Piercy's *Route from Liverpool to Great Salt Lake Valley* remains a classic, but he lingered in Salt Lake only long enough to sketch the city and a likeness of Brigham Young, a rendering in which the prophet looks more pussycat than Lion—a portrait Young disliked for the rest of his life.

• • •

Brigham crossed Wood River on the morning of April 29, 1847—a chilly Thursday. Facing strong winds, it was 48.5 degrees by Orson Pratt's "detached thermometer," a day "cold and gloomy." Men donned overcoats while grubbing the wagons and oxen forward. Clayton suffered quietly from toothache (as did I) and Orson Pratt's horse was bedeviled with "bots"—a parasitic fly whose tormenting larvae burrowed into its tongue and gums. Eight miles from their last camp, they came to a forced halt "some distance from the river," where they ate a sullen supper.

But cold was relieved by a simple discovery: *shit burns*. Or, as Clayton put it: "the camp . . . found a good substitute for wood in the dried buffalo dung which lies on the ground here in great plenty." This miracle, like loaves and fishes, came at the right time, an incendiary inspiration that settled on Heber Kimball, who "invented a new way of building a fire . . . well adapted to the use of this kind of fuel." Quickly grasping that firing buffalo scat had as much to do with draft as dung, the one-time potter promptly invented the Kimball Scat Furnace.

Heber dug three pot-sized holes four inches apart and eight inches deep, linking them by narrow trenches to funnel the draft toward the center pothole. Tom Bullock made a crude sketch, impressed by the efficiency of the invention.

Stuffing the middle hole with buffalo chips, Kimball fired them with powder and flint, placed "two wagon hammers" on top to hold his cooking pots, and sent somebody to gather more "prairie coal." There was plenty of it to go around and six million factories producing at least two or three lumps a day on the plains; but the idea was understandably slow to catch on, so Hans Hansen fiddled while the men danced or wrestled to keep warm. When Clayton tucked in, his tooth raw and inflamed, it was under a solitary quilt. He shivered, bone cold, all night.

A gaggle of Muscovy ducks wranked and wrangled in a pen. "I eat 'em," Charles Wood told me. The ducks shrieked, fuddling together, as if an unexpected dinner was imminent.

Wood was a heavyset man with the openness of a pilgrim. His eyes floated in his face under thin eyebrows, a baseball cap with "Lockheed" in red letters (a gift from a brother in San Jose) pulled down tight against his ears, and a blue work shirt with stained pockets tight across his chest. The afternoon I hobbled in, he was planting a truck garden to sell roadside produce—"sweet corn, potatoes, come harvest time." A Korean war vet (U.S. Air Force), he's "a make-do man," who "farms some" using "the stuff that modern farmers cast off."

"Got me an ol' two-row planter for corn . . . the kind they used in the Forties."

A Canadian once removed, his easy grace of hawking a local yarn accounts for my liking him. Over coffee, he jawed about Junior "Termite" Blumenthal who lived "over to Denman," and got his nom de guerre "from carvin' his name in restaurant tables." Frustrated by long Nebraska winters and an uncertain cash flow, "Termite" would hop a UP coal train near Gibbon, "throw off coal for all he was worth for more'n a mile," then catch another freight back, jumping off "when they slowed down for the main line." He collected his contraband in burlap sacks, delivering them weekly to his modest house by the tracks. "Them big chunks of Wyomin' kept him warm all winter."

Wood's Scottish grandfather migrated first to Nova Scotia, but moved on to homestead in Nebraska in the 1870s where he died intestate, leaving behind "a heap of trouble." In 1939, the home place was sold and the family headed for Gibbon, whose economy is now largely supported by death. In local plants, 1,400 cattle meet their Maker every day, and God knows how many turkeys go drumstick up every twenty-four hours. Charles kindly let me camp next to his driveway, less than fifty feet from the Lincoln Highway and, beyond that, another fifty to the main line UP. As we stood in the dusk, chatting, we ignored the flush of passing traffic and the rumbling overture of steel wheels; but he left me laughing.

"Ol' Alvy Hawke, well, he talked to himself. Answered himself, too . . . like there was always some other fella' with him. Had a regular conversation goin' on. Up north of here, was a cattle feeder name of Jim Clark, who kept Alvy when he got past his prime. Jim went up to Alvy's shack one night and knocked. Alvy was all by himself in the shack. Alvy called out, 'Come on in, Jim. We was just talkin' about you.'"

That night, coal trains stirred me from sleep, but it was a restful stirring. I had "Termite" and "Ol' Alvy" for company as I went under. Now and then, I came up from a deep pool, drawn back by the rumble of marathon freights. Once, wind got in the tent and moved things around like a big woman moving in a small space. She was warm and friendly, large breasted and soft to the touch, but she didn't linger.

16

If your heels are blistered
  and they 'urt like hell,
drop some tallow in your socks
  an' that will make em well.   RUDYARD KIPLING

Soon after we started this morning three buffalo were seen graz-
ing . . . this being the first day buffalo has been seen.
                    WILLIAM CLAYTON, MAY 1, 1847

In 1860, two miles west of Gibbon and thirteen years after Clayton warmed his breakfast over burning buffalo scat, the front wheels of Edward Oliver's wagon "ceased to track." It was mid-July, a sweltering day, and Oliver had watched the axle warping all the way from Joseph Johnson's Mormon Trail pit stop on Wood River. A Mormon like Johnson, Oliver had hobbled into the road-ranch with his family of nine, dragging a broken front axle and dwindling hopes. Like other weary Latter-day Saints bound for Utah that summer, the Olivers needed fresh fodder, fresh vegetables, and a fresh start.

Johnson did his best. With no seasoned wood to be had, he cut a green ash from a stand near the river and jury-rigged a new axle. A few miles into the heat, it began to bow, slowly at first, like a sag in a clothesline. Oliver noticed it when his oxen began straining in their yokes; the front wheels toed out and the green axle arced dangerously out of line. At the top of their rotation, the wheels dug into the wood of the wagon box, locking up. In a daguerreotype taken in his native England, Oliver looks a lot like Burt Lahr as the Cowardly Lion in *The Wizard of Oz*.

A mane of thick hair is pulled back from his forehead and drapes over his ears; muttonchop sideburns girdle his neck, and his head protrudes from a hairy muff. A broad upturned nose and wide mouth enforce the similarity. His full, fleshy lip seems ready to tremble.

Although temporarily waylaid, Oliver was no coward. A zealous Mormon convert, he hauled his family—including his wife's twenty-two-year-old maid—back to Wood River Center, where they shivered through a plains winter in a hastily built log and sod hut. Come spring, when the snows drew back and a properly seasoned axle was ready, he made plans to move on to Zion. But Mrs. Oliver and the kids (their oldest boy was twenty-eight) wouldn't budge. Seems relationships had changed during a long winter in the confines of the "soddy."

Some argue that Sarah Oliver lost her faith, seduced by an abundance of good water, wood, and grass along Wood River; but the truth is that polygamy struck and she balked; Sarah's maid was comely and Edward was willing. When Sarah refused the union, Edward pleaded, but it fell on deaf ears. Not one to look back, Edward took the maid along to Utah; Sarah and her brood became a founding family of Buffalo County. One letter to Sarah from her husband remains, written in a flowery hand from Sessions Settlement, Davies County, Utah, in June 1862.

> Dear wife and children:
> I again write you these lines to you [*sic*] hoping they will find you all in the enjoyment of good health and every other blessing that will tend to your joy and future happiness. Since I received your letter in Jany I have wrote three times to you and never received any answer to any of them and I think it very unkind of you, if you don't wish to hold any correspondence with me that you might at least send me word so that I might know what course to pursue. Ever since I have been in this place I have made it my continual study to prepare a house for you and do the best in my power to make you happy and comfortable the remainder part of our days, and my prayer to God every day I live is that we may shortly be together again and live in peace and enjoy many happy days together. . . . You might come up this year if so will try please to answer this letter and let me know your intention.

Sarah never wrote so much as a single line to Edward again. She and her family prospered, but she never remarried. In Utah Territory, where several women could marry the same man, Edward and his comely maid set up house. On the slopes of the Wasatch, they planted "three acres of garden vegetables"—beans, peas, and "cucumbers ready to get . . . by the fourth of July." Their trees were "loaded with fruit," and "the prospects . . . good for a very fruitful season." He named the place after his abundant hope—Bountiful—and sired a second brood of six daughters and a son.

• • •

The guy riding shotgun in the green Ford pickup shouted through the open window. "Dickhead, you gonna get wet!"

"Tell me something I don't know!" I hollered back.

Clouds had gathered all afternoon, first like a thin film over a dingy window, soon piling up into resplendent dark masses with inner hints of rose or silver. Only on the plains is there such awesome beauty in electric mayhem, boiled energy piling on the horizon, sucking up air and water, poised as a hammer to flatten or flood. I thought about the safety of town, but hoped for rain. Hot all morning, I felt like parchment: anything written on my skin would last for centuries.

Outside Kearney, lightning zagged earthward, slapping so close that thunder was instantaneous. Hands over my ears, I checked traffic, crossed into the hitchhiker's lane, and walked with the flow, determined to meet the gray curtain rushing toward me head on. When it hit, it felt like stinging beads of glass. A red Datsun pickup pulled onto the shoulder ahead of me; a door popped open. Waved inside, I met Craig Snively, a thirty-one-year-old semiemployed electrician, and sat with the dripping pack on my legs—a cold, sodden burden. Ahead, the road simply disappeared. Craig waited until it cleared some, then ground back onto the highway. He didn't talk much, so I felt obligated.

"How'd you get into the electrician business?"

"Ad in the paper."

"You had experience?"

"Never done it before."

"Like it?"

"It's a job."

Sometimes I think most Americans answer to the Dream that way.

• • •

Like most towns north of the Platte, Kearney's businesses were drifting south in a strip city edging closer to tourist and trucker money hammering across Interstate 80. Four lanes ran south from the center of town to cross the river and hook up with the road that Eisenhower built, as if the city yet harbored a forlorn hope of becoming a metropolis by shifting directions. But Kearney surprised me; bland as oatmeal, it was a town I liked, rescuing me from a septic self-pity that often accompanies the solitary walker. Fact is, I'd self-indulgently internalized my problems—long days alone, sore feet, having to give up stimulating new friends too soon, little contact with family back home—all of which made me overlook what J. Brooks Atkinson, an avid walker himself, calls "the deeper mystery of the map."

That was about to change.

• • •

It was Alice Howell, white-haired past president of the Buffalo County Historical Society, who matter-of-factly mentioned that "the Mormons in Kearney are all reformed."

"From what?" I asked.

"Not reformed from anything," she replied, coolly. "I mean Re-formed Mormons." She made it sound as if local Latter-day Saints were badly molded to begin with and their Silly Putty had to be prised into a more perfect shape. Then I got it.

"You mean Reorganized Mormons."

"That's right," she said. "They reformed or something."

But I knew that, having been raised in a Reorganized Latter Day Saint family. As a child of an offshoot of Joseph Smith's odd religion—one I'd abandoned in my twenties—my walk was about history and lingering familiars. Anyone who comes from a Mormon background and has given it up knows what I mean: one never *gives up* the Mormon faith so much as one *fights it off*.

It was Sunday morning in Kearney, my last after a two-day patch and repair job, and Alice Howell agreed to pick me up at my motel and escort me to the Trails and Rails Museum where she rustled through files in a back room and handed me faded blue mimeographed pages on equally faded historical topics. Much of this chapter I owe to Alice, particularly the story of the Oliver family.

"Those Olivers were just wonderful people. United Brethren, you know," she said guardedly, putting Sarah and her brood back within acceptable Christian fields, forgive and forget. That Sunday, having come from church, Alice was dressed to the nines in a raspberry suit, polka-dot blouse, hose, and heels, her silver hair an ornament and her face grandmotherly pleasant behind large glasses.

In the distance, thunder rumbled. When she dropped me back at the motel to pick up my pack, I snapped her photograph. Clouds had moved in, a long rolling darkness with more rain on the way. In the photograph, her hair is lifted on the wind and her smile pert as an exclamation point. I thanked her.

FOLLOWING THE WRONG GOD HOME

"Don't mention it," she said. "It was my pleasure. Put in a good word about the Olivers." No mention of Mormons.

• • •

After 1844, when Joseph Smith was murdered, Mormonism mutated into multiple factions as bizarre and numerous, at times, as species of fungi. The charge of "cultism," frequently leveled against the LDS people, is aided and abetted by notoriety from one or more of its fringe elements—over the years, more than 240 splinter groups and schisms. Present or extinct, a sample of Mormon-derived factions includes the Congregation of Jehovah's Presbytery of Zion; the Israelite House of David; the Church of Christ with the Elijah Message; Zion's Order of the Sons of Levi; the Church of the Firstborn of the Fullness of Time; the Watchman on the Towers of Latter Day Saint Israel; the Bride of the Lamb's Wife; the Priesthood Company; and the Homosexual Church of Jesus Christ.

Next to the Utah-based Church of Jesus Christ of Latter-day Saints (note the hyphen and lower case in the official name), the Reorganized Church of Jesus Christ of Latter Day Saints (no hyphen, upper case), is the largest of Mormonism's many factions and (believe it or not) the legal successor to the religion founded by Joseph Smith as recognized by U.S. courts—which makes it not a faction at all, but something akin to Mother Church. Headquartered in Independence, Missouri (and having recently changed its name to the Community of Christ), its 200,000 plus members have had little, if any, success in arguing the fine points of the U.S. court's decision with 11 million adherents—and still growing—of the Utah-based church.

Along with rejecting Brigham Young as their prophet, the Reorganized Church also rejected polygamy and any other emerging doctrines—baptism for the dead, for example—that shimmered eerily onto the Mormon scene after Smith's death. Secluded in Utah, Mormon doctrine took on ethereal highlights that later helped focus its self-proclaimed "peculiar" nature.

But there are other differences between the two groups. The RLDS accept the Holy Trinity, a belief on which their Utah brethren take a pass. They also know how to make a decent cup of coffee and ordain women (Utah's Latter-day Saints are strictly patriarchal in matters of holy orders), although for years they forbade dancing. Brigham's followers are nimble-footed on the boards.

The RLDS faction originated in 1844 with an acrimonious rejection of Brigham Young as top dog following Smith's demise. In 1852, eight years after Smith's murder, a cluster of the disaffected "reorganized" under the leadership of Smith's oldest son—Joseph Smith III. Until recently, all prophets of the Reorganized Church have been direct male descendants of Joseph Smith, except its current president—a Canadian (suits me)—who is no relation whatsoever, the line of male descent or the gene pool having crashed. In the 1990s, the RLDS built a temple to world peace in Independence (Harry Truman's hometown)—a curiously out-of-place but beautiful conch-shell-like structure that is open to everyone, in contrast to the Utah faith whose temples, worldwide, are closed to all but the elect.

Compared to some schismatic strains of Mormonism, the RLDS practice innocuous stuff. Not so with other Mormon derivatives. When the United Outcasts of Israel's Dream failed in 1960, it replaced itself with American Indian Restoration Enterprises (AIRE), a part-religious, part-racist self-help movement. The chief AIRE head, Noel Pratt, advocated a Mormon-style temple to the Great Spirit, in which Native Americans would be restored to white skins.

Last heard from in Utah County, Utah, Paul Solem—another glow-in-the-dark Mormon Dreamer and self-styled fundamentalist—took an interest in the infamous "John Koyle Dream Mine," a well-known Utah scam that sold stock in a lost "Nephite" treasure revealed—you guessed it—in a Dream. Solem claimed the site was sacred to angels from the planet Venus who were extraterrestrial members of the Ten Lost Tribes of Israel. First contacted by flying saucers in 1944, Paul Solem continued to receive angelic visitors from outer space, until he was invited to preach full-time in the Idaho State Mental Hospital in Blackfoot.

John Leabo—a former RLDS—founded the New American's Mount Zion movement and what's been called "a religiously oriented scientific and political association." Operating Antarctica Development Interests, Leabo's corporation "was begun in order to attract interest in the Lord's development of Antarctica by the righteous people who reside there"—and he didn't mean the scientific researchers already in residence. Leabo and his handful of followers believe there is an unknown race of people on the planet, possibly inhabiting the South Pole. Like Paul Solem, he claimed several UFO sightings.

Bruce David Longo claimed to be the Holy Ghost, perhaps because he was so seldom seen in public, and was excommunicated by the Latter-day Saints for blasphemy in 1960. A decade later, he reappeared as Elohim and had his divinity again rejected along with all seven of his followers. Despondent at not being recognized as God incognito, he gassed himself in a Utah canyon in 1978 while his wife drove to a downtown Salt Lake City hotel and pushed their seven children from an eighth-floor balcony before leaping herself. One child survived.

Mormon Dreams have a dark side.

. . .

Each of the above nightmares took shape in the ferment of Mormon "revealed" scriptures—surreal curiosities to outsiders even today. Smith dabbled in all manner of questions that aroused the interest of nineteenth-century Americans. What became of the lost tribes of Israel? Who were the ancestors of the American Indians? Was evidence of ancient mound builders in the Ohio and Mississippi valleys also evidence of lost American civilizations? As Mormon scriptures evolved through Smith's revelations, so did answers—nowhere more apparent than in the *Book of Mormon.*

Often described as a "record of the Lost Tribes of Israel," the *Book of Mormon* is nothing of the sort. It's a migration tale of later-wandering Hebrews—Lehi and his kin—who wash up on American shores in 600 B.C. after escaping the Babylonian destruction of Jerusalem. Lehi's sons turn out to be the Cain and Abel of the New World: Laman sires a "dark and loathsome" people and Nephi a light-skinned and "righteous" band of brothers. (Skin colors change back and forth according to the degree of righteousness in either group.) The resulting family squabble—good versus evil, the standard Hollywood plot—plays out over centuries. A record of this extended family mayhem is kept on metallic plates (usually called "golden" in Mormon myth) until, at a last apocalyptic battle, the "Nephites" are wiped out, but not before the plates—now "abridged"—are buried in a New York drumlin near Palmyra, New York, where they await discovery and "translation" by Joseph Smith, thus providing Biblically minded Yankees with a *new* or *imaginary* history—depending on one's point of view—of pre-Columbian civilizations in the New World. Alone on a now dark continent, the dark-skinned "Lamanites" are neatly transformed into the ancestors of the American Indians and remain the sole possessors of the Americas until Columbus sets foot on dry land in 1492.

But the Lost Tribes of Israel were definitely on Smith's agenda. Anyone who studied the Old Testament—which Smith and other Americans did aplenty—knew they had been taken captive and scattered by Schalmanezer into Assyria around 720 B.C. But into what void had they gone after that? Smith's revelations, collected into yet another Mormon scripture, *The Doctrine and Covenants*, provided Mormons with an answer. In two musings, Smith claimed they had scattered "to the Lands of the North" or "the North countries." In a flash, popular

Mormon myth had it that the Lost Tribes were hidden behind the ice at the North Pole. (John Leabo's South Pole fantasy seems no more than a busybody's attempt to be contrary.) Given Smith's actual words, the North Pole is a stretch, but in "the last days," he prophesied, when all the remnants of Israel would come together, the Lost Tribes would "smite the rocks," ice would "flow down at their presence" and a "highway be opened up to the great deep." If this sounds to you like the emerging nineteeth-century dream of a Northwest Passage to China, you're not alone.

As for flying saucers, Smith once claimed that a large chunk of the continent had been flung into space, leaving the ocean to flood the Gulf of Mexico. Mormon-style enthusiasts of extraterrestrial continental drift, such as John Leabo and Paul Solemn, took it to heart. Followers of their nearly lost "tribes" think the real Lost Tribes of Isreal were taken along for the ride and are adrift in the heavens. Flying saucers and UFOs, they claim, are attempts by the Lost Tribes to contact earth. Of course, down-to-earth Mormons don't talk about this stuff because they're as sane as the rest of us on a good day. But still, "What wonders hath God wrought?"

Among polyester-clad diners in a restaurant near my motel, an hour before I left town, three customers seemed out of place; they swilled beer as fast as other diners sucked back iced tea. The big guy had shoulder-length hair, biceps the size of gallon jugs, and a T-shirt with sleeves rolled up to hold a pack of Kools. Maybe thirty-five. A girl was parked against his beef, braless under a thin cotton tank top and not minding who noticed. Maybe twenty. The greasy sidekick who never gets the girl was imitation Johnny Cash—black shirt, ebony belt, raven pants, and side-zippered dress boots the color of boiled tar. Over his upper lip was a thin moustache that looked as if it had been drawn in No. 2 pencil.

The sidekick said, "Ol' Rubber, he come off the line at three grand RPM. Smoked them t'ars."

Tossing back a hank of hair, the girl squealed approval; in the vise of Mr. Kools' bicep, her head looked like a walnut with hair. Mr. Kools said, "After it was all done, Rubber come over and sucked down half a case o' beer . . . half a fuckin' case!"

The girl oozed, "He could'a sucked a keg!"

"Them boys may be dumb, but they make a damn good c'or," said the sidekick.

Mr. Kools said, "I don't trust his paint jobs none."

"Who gives a damn about paint jobs?" the sidekick asked, drawing a finger over his upper lip as if checking on his manhood. "All I care about is that Ol' Rubber can smoke the t'ars."

When I paid the cashier, I looked back. They seemed as out of place as I felt. I wished I had the courage to ask them to take me somewhere where a man can "come off the line at three grand RPM." I gave the girl one last glance. She gave me a smoldering smile. Smoked my tires.

17

They say if you shut your eyes while walking you retain an image of where you're going to tread for eight paces, after which your brain loses confidence and you have to look again.
CYNTHIA HARROD-EAGLES, *KILLING TIME*

A Frenchman came from the opposite banks of the river, having seen us in the distance. He informed us that he was from Fort Laramie, having traveled the distance in sixteen days.
ORSON PRATT, APRIL 4, 1847

Dead center between Boston and San Francisco on the old Lincoln Highway is the 1733 Ranch, a legacy of H. D. Watson, an early Nebraska boomer and oddity who deserves to be called the "fodder of his country." The Lincoln Highway— U.S. 30—was the first developed "rock" road to cross the United States. Finished in 1923, much of its original route is now occupied by Interstate 80, although parts of it remain. Most of the route was pioneered when Horatio Nelson Jackson, a Vermont doctor, banged a two-cylinder Winton from San Francisco to New York in 1913.

Watson's original 8,000-acre ranch was the locus for his numerous agricultural experiments in "dry farming," from which he stumped the state preaching a Trinitarian crop doctrine of Alfalfa, Alfalfa, and Alfalfa. Nebraska ranchers came forward in droves to be saved by the gospel of the Great Haymaker. By the 1920s, with H. D. deep-sixed and most of his spread sold off, what was left of the 1733 Ranch became a popular midcontinent pit stop for motorized pilgrims. Hupmobiles, Packards, Tin Lizzies, and Studebakers dusted up to the place regularly, their drivers and passengers basking in the illusion of being equidistant from trolley cars and baked beans.

On the day I passed the ranch house, its homeliness was in painful and con-spicuous contrast to the new 1733 Estates, a development whose house facades seemed sucked from the four points of the compass by the Vacuum School of Architecture: California chic, New England saltbox, southwestern ranch, and northwestern cedar, with occasional design nods toward Tudor, Swiss chalet, and Spanish colonial. A development that should, perhaps, be gone with the wind—the only thing missing was Tara.

* * *

Near the site of the 1733 Ranch, buffalo fever hit the Mormons and caused a highly irregular Mormon whoop-up. Seeing buffalo on the plains, Clayton "counted with my glass, 72." By noon, the number had multiplied. Horses shied. Men skit-tered among the wagons for firearms. Women and boys stood on the wagon boxes to gape at the strangely lumbering, hump-shouldered beasts. In all the confusion, Luke Johnson lost his hat and "could not find it again." Feelings were "strung up to the highest pitch."

Taciturn as a doorknob, Heber Kimball borrowed Howard Egan's "fifteen shooter," and headed full-gallop into the herd, "inspired," said Clayton. Porter Rockwell was the first into the melee, blazing away at a cow, but it was Heber who dashed in to finish her off, firing the "fifteen shooter" over his horse's head. The mare reared and pitched down "a bluff like lightning." Kimball lost the reins, yaw-ing in the saddle like broom straw in a gale. "Precarious to the extreme," Clayton put it. But the wily New York potter managed to stay aloft, righting himself at the last second.

Charged by a "large and furious bull," Porter Rockwell shot it in the skull "with no other effect than to make it smoke a little, some dust fly and the raving animal shake savagely." (In the best of times, head shots weren't easy for Porter. If he did put three slugs in Missouri governor Lilburn Boggs's noggin and Boggs lived, it meant both his accuracy and averages were off.) A notorious hard case who died drunk in his office at the Colorado Stables after a stint in a downtown Salt Lake City tavern, Rockwell remembered the buffalo hunt all his life.

After the dust settled, the harvest came to "one bull, three cows and six calves." By my reckoning, a kill that size would dress out at over 2,400 pounds, 50 pounds for every man, woman, and child in the camp—enough to cause, as it did, severe intestinal problems for the Mormons next day. A quarter was given to each com-pany, and the camp feasted on fresh meat, "every fire loaded." Kimball's steak could have been grilled over its own scat.

* * *

In 1530, Alvar Núñez Cabeza de Vaca, the first white man to record *Bison amer-icanus*, mistook them for "cattle" on the plains of Texas. Eleven years later, Pedro de Castenada, traveling with Coronado, supposed them "bearded large goats" with "the mane of a wild lion." For the Plains Indians, they were sacred crea-tures—the source of clothing, footwear, implements, and food.

Fifty years after Rockwell and John Pack finally brought down the buffalo bull, six million bison had all but disappeared from the continent, most squandered for sport and greed. Sadly, Mormons and most other emigrants who followed the Dream into the west had a hand in squandering the buffalo, although the Mor-mons were much less responsible for the slaughter. After the first whoop-up, Brigham had the good sense to limit hunting parties to kill no more than was needed, and mightily smote any Saints who didn't heed his admonition—a dis-cipline that Mormons generally obeyed. Mari Sandoz, the famed Nebraska writer, tells of "two old-timers who helped to destroy the last of the Republican herd . . . by building fires along the South Platte—and shooting every buffalo that approached the river in his desperate thirst." When the iron horse split the great herds, providing easy access to railheads, the slaughter intensified. Carcasses were stripped for their hides and left to rot; the hide trade was soon followed by the bone trade, and carnage in the West became a symbol of Promised Land.

If the slaughter is hard to imagine, even more difficult is the indifference to natives who depended on the buffalo. For Yankee-bred cattlemen, buffalo were nuisances competing for scarce grass, and the Plains peoples, also regarded as nui-sances, were deliberately worked into the extermination plan. With the buffalo gone and the land claimed for the whites, Indians could more easily be herded onto reservations. By 1890, when they tried to Ghost Dance the lost buffalo back into existence, threatening to unite Native Americans, the government response turned into the killing fields at Wounded Knee, South Dakota.

"Now the dream of the buffalo, too, was done," Mari Sandoz wrote. Another Dream took over.

•   •   •

Was there a connection between Ghost Dancers and Mormon Dreamers? The Ghost Dance began in the 1870s among the Paiute of Walker River, Nevada, with "a prophet known as Wodziwab." If his people danced, he claimed, they could commune with their ancestors who would rejoin them to "sweep aside" the whites and aid in the return of the buffalo. On the Columbia Plateau, Smohalla, another "prophet" of the movement, had as many as two thousand followers among the Palouse, Nez Perce, and Northern Paiute, even merging some Christian elements into his ceremonies and creating a "Pom Pom" (Dreamer) religion. Eventually, the Ghost Dance united tribes from California, the Great Basin, and the Columbia River Plateau, finally spreading onto the Great Plains where it gained strength among the Cheyenne and Sioux. By 1880, Wovoka (a son of one of Wodziwab's "apostles") was on the scene, igniting the message of the Ghost Dance before its fires died with the massacre of the Lakota Sioux at Wounded Knee in 1890—the final clash "in which the Indian dreamers were earmarked for doom as in a classic Greek tragedy," writes David Humphreys Miller, "an inevitable step in the juggernaut advance of our so-called advanced civilization."

But any Ghost Dance connection to the Mormons has less to do with "prophets" than with sacred Mormon ritual and ceremonial dress, since Mormon *missionary* influence in the Great Basin after 1847 had an impact on the native tribes in the Great Basin and regions surrounding it. Mormon attitudes toward all Indians came gift-wrapped in the millennialist trappings of *The Book of Mormon:* Native Americans were the remnants of dark-skinned "Lamanites"—damned descendants of Lehi. The Dream of Indians redeemed—even Indians restored to white skins—circulated widely among Mormons and became a Mormon obsession. Even Joseph Smith had organized "missions" to the Indians.

But under Smith, Mormons had adopted rituals that included elaborate ceremonial dress; symbol-laden aprons, signs, and tokens of the Masonic Lodge were incorporated into Mormon temple rituals, and a sacred "temple garment"—an amulet—was early on adopted. Worn *beneath* the clothing, like underwear, these "garments" were said to protect the wearer from evil and death, even bullets. With their influence rising in the Great Basin and extending as far as California, Mormons missionaries came in contact with many tribes—Ute, Paiute, and Shoshone among them.

By 1880, the Ghost Dancers had adopted an amuletic garment—a ghost shirt revealed in a vision. Said to withstand bullets at close range, the shirts were "made of unbleached muslin or sheeting," writes Miller, and "were cut like old time ceremonial war shirts, fringed and shaped alike but marked distinctively, each with an individualized pattern of symbols and markings." Miller also argues that the ensuing conflict—which assigned the Ghost Dance to oblivion—was "actually sparked by grave misinterpretations of the teachings . . . of Christ, for messianic conceptions had no place in native Indian religions but were taught to the red men by white missionaries," Mormons among them in the Great Basin, Arizona, and Nevada.

Given the extent of Mormon influence in the West by 1880, there's an implied, if not real, connection between the use of Mormon temple "garments" and the adoption by the Indians of sacred ghost shirts. Mormon myth is rife with examples of the miraculous powers of their sacred temple "garments" in shielding wearers from death-dealing missiles—an attitude that was carried by many Mormon soldiers into both world wars. While the similarity between the two sacred garments is startling, proof of a connection is hard to come by. Conjecture must suffice. Nonetheless, Mormon fervor in Nevada, Utah, and Idaho between 1847 and 1880—especially in frequent "missions" to convert the Indians of the arid regions—may have had something to do with the millennial fervor of the Ghost Dance and the "bullet proof" ghost shirt. There's no doubting that the "flare of religious excitement" that swept through the tribes between the 1870s and 1890s had roots in a twisted Christian millennialism, just as the massacre at Wounded Knee had its roots in an American obsession with guns and conquest. It was the Gatling gun that slaughtered many of the Lakota Sioux.

· · ·

Efficient killing is always improved by technology, and the "fifteen shooter" that Howard Egan lent to Heber Kimball was part of the soiled American Dream and remains so today. It was the first of an improved breed—a "slide rifle" (also called a "harmonica rifle") crafted in Nauvoo by a Mormon whose name is forever associated with weapons of conquest and mass destruction. At the time, his best intention was to improve on a tool needed to claim and hold a raw country, but by the mid-1900s, Jonathan Browning's heirs had amassed a fortune in the firearms trade. Browning's patents included the lever-action repeating rifle that John Wayne carried in his scabbard and the machine guns that spewed death in two world wars.

In 1842 Browning converted to Mormonism and moved from Quincy, Illinois, to set up shop in Nauvoo. His gun shop, now restored, survives. Self-taught, he copied the "fifteen shooter" used by Heber Kimball from the 1838 Nicanor and Kendall "slide repeating rifle," which sported a rectangular steel bar "with five chambers at right angles to the bar's axis." Think of it as a "harmonica" with five .44-caliber holes, each primed with black powder and loaded with a rifle ball. Browning's version had as many as twenty-five chambered "slides" in each "harmonica," which were manually pushed through a slot to line up each chamber with the rifle's bore, which explains why Kimball dropped his reins: it took one hand to steady the heavy rifle and another to slide the "harmonica." How the inventor of the scat furnace managed not to fall face first in fresh flops is a mystery or a miracle. Take your pick.

· · ·

"Don't stir up my ox's," Nick Ponticello said.

As if anyone could: they hadn't moved a millimeter since 1932 when Reverend Shaw, a Seventh Day Adventist, hitched them up as a roadside attraction for his Covered Wagon Gift Shop. Cast in concrete, with heads the size of oversized wrecking balls and crazy circles painted around their walleyes, the duo were tethered to an oversized prairie schooner—also concrete—sunk halfway to its hubs in Nick's front lawn. (Shaw had kept a coke- guzzling bear in a cage out back, but it had long gone to bruin heaven.) One ox stared grimly west, doing its best to look manifestly destined; head down, the other had spent fifty-three years staring at one square foot of Nebraska.

"Still pulls 'em in," Nick said, slapping a concrete flank and nudging me with a bony elbow.

Nick is the essence of "bantam." In short, short. Nick's height never came up in our conversation, nor did I question his being "a sort of unofficial basketball coach" at Kearney State—the first because it seemed a delicate subject and the second because it seemed astounding given Nick's personal elevation above sea level. To document our encounter, I got Nick to pose with me next to his concrete oxen, the only time I've ever been able to put my arm around another full-grown male and have the top of his head at shoulder level. On a day when the barometer's rising, Nick's four foot ten. Elfin.

"Maybe you'd like a couple of postcards," he suggested, looking up my nose, "I got some nice ones inside."

Inside the gift shop, Nick's living quarters had seeped into the business space. Among tables of souvenirs (decorated ashtrays, plates, mugs) lay a handful of souvenir-sized birch-bark canoes giving off the same sickly scent I remembered from Cheshire's Five and Dime in my Ontario hometown. At the first squeak of the door, Nick's wife greeted us with a decibel level set at ultra forte or fortissimo.

"A customer, Nick?" she bellowed.

An inch taller than Nick and hard of hearing, Rose has Kewpie-doll features and wide eyebrows that flare over innocent, ebony eyes. When she blinks, it's as if someone pulled a blind over an open window.

Unwittingly, I'd walked into a love story.

• • •

Rose Ponticello is a Nebraska girl who couldn't give up the Cornhusker State, although she tried, for Nick's sake. The U.S. Postal Service is entirely responsible for their romance. During World War II, she met Nick when he was stationed at Lowry Air Force Base in Denver—the kind of low-altitude airman who, when told to "fall in," left a vertical gap in the line. Think of it as a smile missing half a tooth. From New Jersey, Nick had the appeal of a man from another planet for Rose—talkative, athletic, and perhaps the only technical supply sergeant under five feet in the U.S. Air Force. Rose's letters followed him to England, and by the time he was stateside after the war, love arrived daily via the mail, so Nick let his momma in on the romance and sent posthaste for Nebraska Rose. So the daughter of a Sand Hills rancher who "choked to death on oysters" (Rose had a photo of her daddy in his coffin) was married in the Garden State, but even an Italian mother-in-law's cooking or bribery couldn't keep Rose from her beloved Cornhusker State. "His momma gave me a big fur coat to stay on with 'em," she boomed. "It didn't help."

So Nick and Momma gave up. Nick moved to Wellfleet, Nebraska, and opened a grocery store. "I was a beach bum anyway," he said. "Rose gave me something better to do."

Corn Flakes and crackers were good business, but in 1957—"the year the dust started to fly bad ag'in,"—money dried up, along with meat and potatoes, and Nick signed up for a second tour of diminished duty, this time in Texas. Rose stayed behind, keeping the store "on a cash basis." When Nick came back from the Lone Star State, they held on until 1964, selling out only when Nick was accepted at Kearney State College—a freshman at fifty. In 1984, having completed a slow-motion curriculum, Nick graduated with a BA in physical education and geography, in the meantime becoming a Kearney State icon. Full of high-voltage energy, at seventy, he still ran four miles a day.

But the Ponticellos never had children. "Sterile," Nick said, unabashedly. "I was taking twenty-five-dollar shots. Nothing happened."

Except Rose, I reminded him.

• • •

But it was Nick's twenty-year "register" of road warriors that fascinated me—a history in signatures of every oxen-smitten oddball who turned up on his lawn. His finger traced a legacy of tumbleweeds and footloose wanderers—Rob Sweetgall, for example, who passed through a couple of weeks earlier on a fifty-state walk for a shoe company. Nick couldn't remember which company, but Sweetgall "was heading east."

"Walked 6,870 miles in 233 days," Nick told me.

(When Rob Sweetgall crossed the Brooklyn Bridge on September 5, 1985, he'd walked 11,208 miles and used up "364 days, twenty million footsteps, and three pair of shoes," as a reporter for the *Evening Gazette* in Worcester, Massachusetts, put it. Sponsored by the Rockport Shoe Company, he carried only a four-pound waist pack.)

"Here's a fella rode in on a horse," Nick said, fingering another entry. Bill Emerton, an Aussie, rode through in 1978, part of a Pony Express celebration. "Talked funny," Pete said.

"G'die" I said.

"Yeah. Like that."

On a round-the-world bike tour in 1976, Dr. Bill Marquart pedaled through. "Never made it," Nick said, his face bunching sorrowfully. "Got run down and killed in Massachusetts."

But the signature of the most interesting tumbleweed eluded him and struck sorrow into me. Nick couldn't find the name of "an Englishman who came through in '67 or so walking backwards across the country." I don't put any eccentricity past the Brits, who are the world's best ramblers, but I must have looked incredulous.

"It happened," Nick said, defensively. "Wore the toes off his shoes first. Backed up the highway headin' for California."

· · ·

On the highway again, I pondered the monotony of walking backward, considering a view of the world receding from me step by backward step, finally dropping off the horizon in front as new geography floated into my peripheral vision, slid into focus, and drifted away. Walking forward, the future slides past and the scene enlarges; walking backward it slides away, grows distant. In our straight-ahead, eyes-to-the-front, quick-march world, I felt a beguiling spontaneity in thinking about traveling ass-end first. Perhaps if we'd walked backward across America, we might have bumped into a Dream by accident, and instead of inventing and claiming it, have let it claim and invent us, the way Rose and Nick had come to claim each other.

· · ·

Darold Halliwell stood in the middle of the Lincoln Highway wearing a foamy sort of smile, swabbing sweat from his face and holding out "Colorado Kool-Aid." Wet air in a bottle.

"Figured you could use a Coors," he said.

On the ground where thirst first teased the Mormons and dry air cracked William Clayton's lips, sweet mercy fell into my hand —frosted, chilling, delicious. Odessa, Nebraska, came to my rescue, a-spit-in-the-bucket burg, but friendly on a Sunday afternoon. "You might as well come in out'a the heat . . . that's if you don't have anything better t'dew," Darold suggested.

And so the Odessa Bar opened its arms and welcomed me back—at least they claimed I'd been there before. "Everybody's been here at least once," someone said. "You was with 'em. I'm certain of it. Darold, wasn't he the bearded guy who come in here telling lies about your wife?"

Chilled air flowed all the way back to the pool tables where Freddy Blevens and Pete Brammer strummed and lowed cowboy songs in the murky dark, looking each other straight in the eye. I shot the breeze and gradually came to believe I'd known these people before, my whole life, maybe. Darold and his brother, Don; John and Shiela Syotos (flowered in mauves, greens, and blinding bird's-eye yellow); Jerry Hiltibrand; Pam Silvers (who lost seventy-five bucks playing a game called "pickle"); Todd Gant (it was his money Pam lost); Martin Armstrong, "Your Used Horse Dealer" (on his business card); and anyone else that time had forgotten.

"Just another Sunday in Odessa," Darold said.

By five o'clock there were so many lies going around that I wrote a couple down to keep from using somebody else's when my turn came, so deep into it that a pitchfork and hip boots couldn't have saved us. When Martin Armstrong handed me a wooden mule with a pencil where its tail should be, I pressed down on the eraser (it came out under the belly) and wrote my name and address down for him with a No. 3 graphite penis.

"Can't write with mine," Darold said. "Every time I do, it bends in the middle. Ever try it, Martin?"

"Sure, but my lead keeps breakin'."

Late that night, Pam Silvers and Todd Gant, a winsome couple, took me to dinner at the Sapp Brothers restaurant across the river. A trucker himself, gap-toothed Todd punches a Kenworth Detroit Diesel from South Dakota to Texas hauling hay, oats, or corn to horse farms in three states. Sitting in Sapp's, Todd told me his father shot himself. Todd was six at the time. After dinner, he and Pam took me home and gave me their waterbed for the night. Sober, I sloshed toward sleep. Pam and Todd bunked on the couch. I don't know if I dreamed that night, but as I went under, something else began gnawing at me—a night creature I couldn't quite make out.

● ● ●

I woke before dawn and saw its face. He'd been in and out of the Odessa Bar all Sunday afternoon, no mistaking his full blood or the ring of privacy that gathered around him—a palpable distance between him and the others in the crowd. That I hadn't noticed him until evening wasn't natural, as if he was more spirit than real.

"Apache," John Syotos called him.

But Nekiia was real and really drunk—a study in black, with two gold teeth and a sheen of jet hair draping to his shoulders, wrapping the Native intensity of his face. I imagined him walking toward me on the Llano Estacado, a spectral warrior. There are cases on record where enemies killed themselves out of fear of the Apache. So I walked over to see Apache death up close.

"I'm not full-blood Apache," he said, glad for some company. "I'm half Navajo. Born in New Mexico."

"Which blood gets the upper hand?"

"The one I need most."

When I asked if he ever went home, his face hardened to a bas-relief.

"Hardly ever," Nekiia answered.

Don Halliwell slid off a bar stool and walked over to our table, red-eyed under his Terra Gator bill cap. He said, "You're the best damn Indian I ever met . . . and the only one, Nekiia. Know what I like about you? Nothin'. No. I'm kiddin'. You're the best, buddy." Beer talk.

Nekiia reached out and shook Don gently by the arm, a generous Navajo gesture, but his eyes looked faintly Apache. "Forget it," he said. "I'm just drunk and on the way down."

Later, when he asked to be helped to his car, it was Don Halliwell who guided his steps. I trailed after them. Outside, the night air was sweet from a passing shower, and a clearing sky let the stars through like blurry candles. A dog came up to nuzzle my hands. Don talked to Nekiia in gentle, remonstrating tones and bedded the Apache cum Navajo down in the backseat of his car. Don kept the keys.

"Done it again, buddy," Don said. "We both done it."

Nekiia was the only full-blood Native American I talked with in ninety-one days crossing the home of the Osage, Kansa, Omaha, Pawnee, Sioux, Cheyenne, Arikara, Shoshone, and Crow.

God forgive us.

18

Talking tends to make men aware of their differences; walking rests on their identity. Talking may be the same on a fine day or a

FOLLOWING THE WRONG GOD HOME

wet day . . . walking varies according to each and every one of these
conditions.   A. H. SIDGWICK, *WALKING ESSAYS*

The prairie . . . is still burning ahead of us, supposed to be set on
fire by [Indians]. . . . We traveled on about a half an hour and
found the prairie all in a blaze.   WILLIAM CLAYTON,
                                                         MAY 5, 1847

John Syotas hoisted his cup. A hairline crack on one side looked to me like a bad
omen. "Here's to another day of getting rich in Odessa," he said, blinking into the
overcast beyond the window, watching rain brush the highway and whisk away in
the wind. Festooned in a godawful rose-flowered shirt with his thin lips turned
down at the corners, he had the pained look of a man suffering with piles. At 11:30
A.M., the Odessa Bar looked like the town drunk and I felt like it. John adjusted
squarish spectacles, poured me a cup of tarlike java, and put both elbows on the
bar—a melancholy day all around. Syotas's coffee had the chemistry of witch's
brew, so hot and acidic that I worried about the enamel on my teeth, one of which
was aching again, perhaps in sympathy for William Clayton's having suffered
from the same. I told John the truth. "That's the first cup of good coffee I've had
since I left New York."

"Then it's on the house," he said. "I made it last night."

Overnight, tornadoes had damaged thirty-two farmhouses and outbuildings
in Buffalo County. Mid-bitching, a soggy farmer dripped in for a breather. "Boys,"
he complained, "over to Overton it hailed buckshot. Alfalfa's drove so far down,
you cain't swath it. Clipped trees like a hedge trimmer."

"Hell of a way to run the Great American Desert," I griped.

Both men looked at me as if I was short a hinge. When I hit the door, John
called after me, "See you in the next life." That seemed about right. The way I felt,
I was already in it.

· · ·

It took the Mormons six days to cover a forty-mile stretch of Nebraska (Gibbon
to Lexington) that froze them, sparked tempers (especially Brigham's), spooked
them, sickened them, and burned everything around them. Brigham rightly fingered the Indians for the flames; they annually torched dry spring grasses to
encourage summer growth. But mild-mannered Erastus Snow caught hell when
Brigham lost his "forty dollar" spyglass. The Lion of the Lord roasted Snow for
mismanaging the camp's cattle and causing a frenetic chase to separate them from

the buffalo herds. Amidst the bovine brouhaha, a fumble-fingered prophet dropped his expensive telescope. Erastus and Brigham exchanged a few words, although just how the cussedness went is left out of approved records.

Having roasted Erastus, Brigham wouldn't rest until the entire camp agreed with him, so he put peevishness to a vote. All in a row, they voted "unanimously" that Snow "was not in the line of his duty in taking care of the cows." Chastised by theocracy in action, Snow apologized. It wasn't enough: Brigham wouldn't let up. "The best man in camp that undertakes to stick his nib against the authorities," he carped—meaning him—"will slide off like Warren Parish and Sylvester Smith." Parish and Smith were well-known "apostates" from the days in Nauvoo or, in plainer words, men that marched to a different drummer than Brigham. As the day wore on, matters turned even more "windy." Having gorged themselves on fresh buffalo meat the night before, the Camp of Israel, including the prophet, came down with an extra measure of gas.

• • •

Odessa behind me, the rain never let up. By the time I reached Elm Creek, it poured so relentlessly that I couldn't see the street from my seat in a down-home café, smothered with attention by three silver-haired Florence Nightingales who kept the coffee hot, if weak, and the cheeseburgers coming. Topped off in the grease department, I hoped for a break in the weather, mulling through a dog-eared copy of *Field and Stream*. When none came, I plunged back in, slogging between gusts of wind and water. To pass time, I concentrated my thoughts on intrepid Rob Sweetgall, since he was no doubt trudging in similar weather, begrimed, dripping, gritting his teeth—taking it on the chin. For eleven years, Rob Sweetgall remained an icon stamped large in my memory of footsore heroes until, in 1996, rummaging through a used book bin in Portland, Oregon, I discovered the truth and nothing but.

Turns out Sweetgall phoned a report to the *Worcester Telegram and Gazette* each week where a local Massachusetts reporter, John Dingham, turned it into a weekly human interest column. A year later, Dingham and Sweetgall published *The Walker's Journal*—reprints of Dingham's columns with brief "Foot Notes" by Rob summing up every two weeks of his walk. A section titled "Eating Off the Highway" gave me the impression that Rob survived on roadkill—something even vegetarians could admire.

But it wasn't so. Rob flew to Boston regularly for R and R, where the University of Massachusetts Medical Center provided checkups and stress tests to measure the cardiovascular benefits of walking. (Was there ever any doubt?) He took every weekend off. Sweetgall's diet was checked and rechecked. In towns with salad bars, he ate "as many colors as possible," including red, orange, yellow, green, white, maroon, purple—tomatoes, carrots, spinach, cauliflower, kidney beans, beets, mushrooms. I forgave him that. But to my dismay, Sweetgall was followed every step of the way by a paid driver and a sag wagon, which carried foodstuffs, water, Gatorade, state-of-the-art rain gear, extra clothing, socks, and a plentiful supply of shoes provided by his corporate sponsor, not to mention furnishing the obvious benefit of emergency shelter. His touted "thin waistpack" probably contained a handkerchief and a couple of aspirins.

In period photos, Rob Sweetgall appears a wiry young man whose face radiates all the sag-wagonny determination that helped him cross the Cascades in winter and the Rockies in early spring. Trudging through Nebraska, he mused on high winds, a tornado, and bouts of icy rain. But did he ever huddle, dripping, under a railroad overpass? Or sleep in a sandy catch basin? No. It was motels all the way—and chauffeur service. In my book—no pun intended—Rob comes dangerously close to being two links short of a chain in matters of weather. Take this pithy prose, for example:

> Early in the journey, I used to feel sorry for myself on those miserable mornings when I'd have to climb out of my motel bed, dress, pack, and step out into dark rain and puddles—30 miles of it perhaps. . . . As the walk progressed, my attitude changed. I began liking those nasty days. Not that I prayed for them, but when they did come, I accepted them. "Rob, these are the days you'll remember," I'd say to myself.

Really. Below his "Foot Notes," Sweetgall leaves a fill-in-the-blank section for readers who want to make personal observations on his on-the-road tidbits of wisdom. This is mine: "Get real." But I agree with Rob in this: he dubbed Nebraska U.S. 30—the Lincoln Highway—the "Longest Monotonous Stretch of asphalt in the U.S.A."

Nothing much about the extremes of daily toilet shows up in the diaries and journals of western travelers, but it's well known that loose stools ransacked many emigrants on their manifest roads west. Fortunately, there was a lot of unpopulated ground to fertilize, although women no doubt had a harder time with so much open space and not a lot of privacy. But there's a patch of more vibrant green along the Lincoln Highway that owes its exceptional verdure to me.

Outside Lexington, an elevator in my lower intestine broke its cable. Whether it was from John Syotas's day-old coffee or from something wriggly in the Sapp Brothers' cuisine the night before, I don't know, but I'd felt queasy most of the morning and fought it back—one reason for stemming the tide with a belly-load of hamburgers in Elm Creek. But pressure kept building—not nausea, but a nasty grumbling in my guts. Suddenly merciless, it cramped violently as rain danced off the highway, not a tree in sight. Desperate for relief, I took to the grass, aiming for a shallow depression, hoping to conceal myself, but made it only a couple of feet beyond the shoulder before urgency forced me to drop my drawers. In the movie *The Dresser*, Albert Finney says to Tom Courtenay, "I asked for thunderbolts and you gave me farts." This was more like both. A car streaked out of the rain, swerved crazily at the sight and screamed away while someone's banjo eyes stared in disbelief. I let go, amazing grace, how sweet the sound. Saved a wretch like me.

• • •

I made Lexington with Gore-Tex awash, stopping frequently at service station restrooms to ventilate. When venting finally subsided and a semblance of appetite returned, I floated to the nearest restaurant, hoping the local health board had given it a passing grade, where, mightily relieved, I picked over a dismal dinner while seated at a table under a stuffed moosehead. On the opposite wall a sign provoked me: "Our Chicken Is Out Of This World." Mine tasted as old as the Big Bang.

Lexington, Nebraska, got its start as "Plum Creek," a trading post on the Oregon Trail that became an infamous rendezvous for gamblers, thieves, and holdup artists. When the Union Pacific came through, Plum Creek shifted allegiances, hopped the Platte River, changed its name, cleaned up its act, and seemed to me as respectable as any retired madam. But the banditti hadn't changed; considering what I shelled out for "out of this world" chicken, it was still big into highway robbery.

I retrieved a newspaper, reading by dim light with dimmer expectations. In New York, gravediggers were on strike, keeping a hundred corpses a day above ground in refrigerated trucks while raising Cain with city hall over "health and pension benefits." Made perfect sense to me. With so many folks going underground each day, health benefits would naturally come to a gravedigger's mind, along with the hope that he might survive outside long enough to have a few animate months in retirement before having to go back in permanently. Rob Sweetgall was now averaging thirty-three miles a day—another piece of news that put me off my feed. Hoofing through drizzle in hope of any improvement in my mental health, I washed up at a Super 8 motel and claimed a room—something in common with Rob Sweetgall that night. Sleeping wasn't a problem.

• • •

Next morning, I tramped into a second day's downpour; but if I couldn't wring out the damp in my shoes, I could wring out my spleen, and did, grumbling mile after soggy mile. Cranky and contentious, I soon turned morose, passing the site where Turkey Leg, a Cheyenne chief, ripped up a culvert and derailed a Union Pacific train in 1867. Upset that steel rails of the iron horse had halved the Buffalo hunting grounds, Turkey Leg emphasized his point in blood by killing an engineer and a fireman before breaking into freight cars and filching bolts of bright calico, which his Cheyenne braves tied to their ponies, riding into the sunset trailing ends of the rainbow. For a feeble instant, the Cheyenne had cut into Manifest Destiny—which didn't include Turkey Leg or his kin.

Nearby, the Camp of Israel were scared almost witless when William Empey returned "at a pretty smart trot" after topping a rise and running into "300 or 400 Indians," all mounted. Brigham countered this immediate threat by making sure that somebody took notes and wrote down the rules of the camp and, possibly, was later given a test. If anything went wrong, there'd be a record of what was supposed to go right; so a scribe, possibly Thomas Bullock, was set to the task of writing up the Mormon's first line of defense. To ensure against spooks in the night, the cannon was unlimbered and belched twice into the dark to warn away any lurking Turkey Legs. Still skittish next morning, Brigham ordered strict military rule: no man was to go further than "twenty rods" from his wagon without orders. "Let every man have his guns & pistols in perfect order," Tom Bullock remembered him saying as they moved out "in close column regimental style."

• • •

My own cannon having fired, so to speak, I summoned up a "regimental style" of my own—one leaden footstep after another in not-so-quick time. Ahead, the road seemed empty; but at 7:30 P.M., on May 14, 1985, under a clearing sky, I floundered into Cozad, Nebraska, and crossed the Kalunga Line.

PART **2**

Across the Kalunga Line

19

I have two doctors, my left foot and my right.

GEORGE TREVELYAN

During the night the Lord sent a light shower of rain which has put the fire out . . . and made it perfectly safe traveling.

WILLIAM CLAYTON, MAY 6, 1847

I sat with my right foot in the East and my left in the West; the 100th meridian ran between my legs and bifurcated my two best intentions. From my vantage point by the UP tracks, with my back propped against my pack, the highway shimmered with heat in both directions. Up Meridian Street, Cozad, Nebraska, dozed in a sweet relief of sunshine.

Among the Makongo natives of East Africa, there's a line separating the living from reflections of the spirit world. On South Carolina graves, Makongo descendants place shiny objects to reflect spirits on the other side; the Kalunga Line is the edge beyond which life and death is but a hazy reflection—a mirage.

More or less, America agreed that the 100th meridian was its Kalunga Line dividing humid East from arid West, a demarcation of Dream reflecting "spirits" of hard going or hope. Beyond lay a desiccated region encompassing 40 percent of the new nation, a land reflecting the wiles and temptations of Old Scratch. Like most lines in the sand, it was an arbitrary decision. East of the meridian average rainfall increased; west of the meridian it declined—twenty inches of rain or more to the east, less than twenty inches to the west, with the meridian running from the Mexican to the Canadian border and passing roughly through Laredo, Texas, and Minot, North Dakota. Today, U.S. 83 generally follows the meridian. Technically known as the "isohyetal" or "mean annual rainfall line," it was where

Dream turned to nightmare for many Americans in the mid-1800s until the Sierra Nevada or the Cascades were crossed. Nonetheless, blowhard promoters like William Gilpin waxed salubrious about the anhydrous West. "Yapping in the van of the continentally confident," was how Wallace Stegner put it.

By 1860 Gilpin saw the West "through a blaze of mystical fervor," undaunted by a "capacity for inaccuracy." Paraphrased, Gilpin's blather went something like this: "By God, boys, it's not a desert at all. It's a paradise in disguise. No need to bring a plow. Artesian water! Land for all!" Stegner colored it "the sunburst dazzle of Manifest Destiny."

. . .

If the West had a living prophet by 1868, it wasn't William Gilpin *or* Brigham Young. It was John Wesley Powell, a one-armed son-of-a-Methodist who became the first man to run the Colorado River and who tried to talk Washington into common sense about land and water use in a nearly dry hole. Powell—who often posed for photographs as if a corncob was stuck up his vent—was perhaps the smartest dude to explore the West and the first to clearly understand its limitations. Without blowing smoke about life beyond the dry line, Powell effectively "did in" the notion of the "Great American Desert," but he also made it clear that what little water existed couldn't be used to satisfy the pipeDreams of a nation raised on eastern notions of more abundant farming. Where Brigham prophesied "Zion" in the desert, Powell prophesied "drought." Powell's prophecy came true.

In his classic study *Lands of the Arid Region of the United States* (1878), Powell argued for settlement that wouldn't overstuff the West with "pioneers" with extravagant expectations that its limited water couldn't provide. In short, he suggested that ignoramuses like William Gilpin take a hike. Eventually, Brigham Young became Powell's ally, hoping to sustain his own kind with what little water the arid West had to offer; but growth and greenery won out. Phoenix, Salt Lake City, Las Vegas, and Los Angeles have all but sucked the pipeline dry, creating cities where deserts should be. Today, not a single drop of the Colorado River reaches the Gulf of Mexico. Water is used, abused, and reused trying to grow eastern trees and Kentucky bluegrass where they weren't intended: California's desert valleys are turning into saline, unfertile basins because forced irrigation has leached minerals out of the soil while fertilized crops have poured in more poisons.

In much of the West, water conservation is too often given lip service while thirsty economic development projects are given handouts. With God and mammon aligned in both corporate church and corporate politics, developers—both Mormon and non—are continually trying to prime the pump on a well that's fast

FOLLOWING THE WRONG GOD HOME

drying up. Water is becoming a scarce commodity along Utah's Wasatch front, and the politics of water is always on the boil, simmering a political soup that too often favors a palate for unchecked growth. Critics complain that too many of Utah's growth-at-any-cost conservatives get off the ground with only a right wing and a Mormon prayer, and the more extreme of these have been lampooned by Bob Kirby of the *Salt Lake Tribune:* "Having a bomb shelter in your backyard and a testimony that Bo Gritz is one of the Three Nephites barely gets you a second look. So long as you don't start wearing a helmet to church, they regard you as little more than eccentric." (The Three Nephites, by the way, are the Larry, Curly, and Moe of Mormon folklore, mythic immortals that mysteriously appear out of nowhere to serve the needy and save the day.) By some accounts, Utah uses more water to groom its lawns than the combined agriculture of Wyoming and Nevada, and using Scott's Turf Builder four times a year is the equivalent in parts of the state of having a Mormon "testimony."

• • •

The U.S. government had a hand in turning the intermountain West into a dryer hole—at least in the short run. After the Civil War, encouraging a bad migration habit, the government gave away a quarter section of land (160 acres) to anyone fool enough to reclaim the "Great American Desert." In the fecund East, 160 acres was an Eden capable of providing a living for kith and kin; beyond the 100th meridian, it was hell on earth. It took up to forty acres per cow to get a glass of milk and hundreds more to get a crop that would pay out—if you had water and time enough to work it.

When the Homestead Act (1862) proved a false start in a parched land, Congress enacted the so-called Kinkaid Law (1904), which urged settlers to cross the 100th meridian by upping the ante to 640 free acres of Nebraska sand hills—a 300 percent increase in potential misery. Away from the Platte River, as Dr. Bob Manley pointed out, a handful prospered but most went bust, although the Kinkaid Law effectively broke the High Plains monopoly of cattlemen. With a population on the move whose national punch was spiked with an inebriating dose of "better times," Americans crossed the dry line with boozy congressional blessings and adopted a drunk's delusion of a never-empty jug.

By Franklin Roosevelt's era, the delusion was still alive and well, evolving into millions of tons of concrete on western rivers and going by the name (so says the *Oxford History of the American West*) of "the Reclamation Dream." Water was packaged and sold behind great dams—Hoover, Grand Coulee, Glen Canyon. Another Gilpin clone, William Ellsworth Smythe, boasted, "Irrigation is a miracle." Anyone who doubted him had only to look at Mormon accomplishment in Utah, often served up as proof that a desert could blossom like a rose. As early as 1899, the Rio Grande Railroad took one look at the green Salt Lake Valley and produced a map comparing Canaan and the Dead Sea with Mormon country and the Great Salt Lake. But sitting astride the Kalunga line, I knew this: Cozad, Nebraska—and what lay beyond—was once part of a Great American Wet Dream.

. . .

I ended up at the Hendee Hotel searching for a child's initials carved in a door-jamb. The hotel itself is long retired, but looks as if at any moment Marshall Dillon and Miss Kitty will step outside blinking after a quickie. Built by the town's founder, John J. Cozad, a mysterious gent who stepped down from the Union Pacific one hot summer Sunday in 1872, it had an unusual attraction. Dressed in a wool swallowtail suit, cravat, diamond stickpin, and top hat, Cozad walked six miles from Willow Island toward his future, striding confidently and sporting a gold-headed cane. John Cusak, a Union Pacific section boss who happened across him that morning, remembers Cozad's "tails flying in the wind." Dude to the max.

He was a mysterious gent from the start—tall, dark, and sharp-eyed. Never referred to by his given name, he was "Mr. Cozad" to those who knew him. His specialty was town building (Cozadale, Ohio) and gambling. Legend has it he was the best dressed, shiftiest, and hardest to pin down faro master on the western circuit. Rumor had it he'd been barred from the floating gambling palaces on the Mississippi and Ohio Rivers.

For openers, he bought forty thousand acres of land from the Union Pacific and recruited his neighbors from Ohio. In 1873 he filed a homestead claim on Cozad and shipped his Virginia-born wife, Teresa, and his two sons, John and Bob, to his newly founded town by the tracks. The first building was a salvaged railway car with "Cozad" painted on its side. When his in-laws came west, they arrived in the middle of a prairie fire and, like other settlers, made do in "soddies" until timber could be shipped from Wisconsin. In the relentless summer heat, the Cozad family set up hammocks in the cottonwoods by the Platte River to catch the breeze. It was a pat hand—well, almost.

The town ran hot and cold. At one time, only five families held out for better times while others, "et out" by a plague of grasshoppers (the same happened to the Mormons in Utah), scurried back East for solace and shade. But John Cozad waited out his bad hand. For openers, he built two hotels (the first burned), moved his family into one of them, and began to advertise back East: "Ho! For the Great Platte Valley." For thirty bucks, a Cincinnati salesman with a yen for starting over could buy a round-trip ticket to snake-oil heaven. Against the odds, Cozad's hand played out.

But the wild cards in John's deck were temper and pride. When he drummed up his town for the county seat (too loudly and too often) and disdained the cattle culture for letting herds graze roughshod through the gardens of his new town, he brought enmity to the table in the form of a rough and raw plainsman named Print Olive. Olive was a "grass man," in a place suited to cattle, not fences, and he wasn't much for swallowtail suits or diamond stickpins. When Cozad got into an argument with Alfred Pearson over money, the cattleman went for a knife. Cozad shot him. "Murder," cried Olive, and the rancher was a roughcut who could back up a threat.

Some say the gambler turned coward, but John J. wasn't about to be deep-sixed with his cravat and gold-headed cane; he borrowed a horse and lit out. Next day, his top hat was found in a coyote den. When he didn't return, Teresa sold the hotel to a man named Hendee (hence its name today), forsook her hammock by the river, and left town with the boys.

Betty Menke helped me locate the initials of John Cozad's son. Faint filigree in a doorframe, there was nothing artistic about them—the kind of entertainment a lonely plains kid might take to on a boring afternoon. Yet nobody tumbled to their significance for almost a century, until H. B. Allen, a local historian, finally asked, "What happened to John J. Cozad?" Seems John, Teresa, and two sons disappeared into thin air. When Allen finally ran their history down, it turned out to be one hell of a good yarn, which Nebraska writer Mari Sandoz promptly told in *Son of a Gambling Man*, proving that a top hat in a coyote's den isn't proof of foul play.

• • •

In *The Art Spirit*, Robert Henri (pronounced "Ahn-ree") writes: "a work of art inspires. . . . For an artist to be interesting, he must have been interesting to himself." The founder of the Ashcan school of art and a luminary in the infamous New York Armory Show of 1913, Henri argues: "Freedom is indeed the great sign which should be written on the brow of childhood." It was written on his. Henri was creative, self-absorbed, passionate—his "art" based on deception, and his brilliance on mystery, intrigue, and illusion, like his father before him.

Robert moved with his parents to Atlantic City, where his father bought land next to the boardwalk and opened a gambling hall named Lee's Fort. Overnight, his parents became Mr. and Mrs. Richard Lee with no forwarding address from

Cozad and no return visits to Nebraska. His older brother studied medicine and set up his shingle as Dr. John Southern. Young Bob skipped to the next state to study at the Pennsylvania Academy of Fine Art—a long way from carving his initials in a Nebraska doorframe. The rest, as they say, is art history.

· · ·

On Betty Menke's advice, I walked from the Robert Henri Museum and Walkway over to Sam Schoolby's pig yard (long gone), where once richly manured ground has matured into a town park. Cozad's citizens have created a miniature Prairie Village on the site, complete with a nineteenth-century schoolhouse and a log Pony Express station (oldest of the remaining originals), which was resettled from its site at Willow Island—the spot where John J. Cozad stepped down from the Union Pacific train. Built in 1849, two years after the Mormons passed, the Willow Island station was first used as an Indian trading post. When the trade played out, so did it until, for two brief years, it was resurrected to serve fast horses and U.S. mail heading for San Francisco. On the day I saw it, the "hysterical" marker out front was true to the Dream: "May the spirit of those hardy pioneers who blazed a trail to the Golden West never die."

"Do you suppose any of us could beat the idea of the Golden West to death with a baseball bat?" I asked Betty Menke.

She looked up from under a mop of blond hair and said in her gravelly Garbo voice, "It's not so golden these days. We've had hard times around here. Suicides. Some very sad stories."

On that note, I left town. As Cozad slipped away, I heard the peewee bird trilling prophecy—at least I imagined I did. When the phoebe sings, expect cold weather. It isn't called the "weather bird" for nothing.

20

In the morning when I tramp through the country I feel hard as steel and as firm a lord over myself as Julius Caesar. But towards evening I become more mellowed. WALTER STARKIE

From a lunar distance of moon from sun, determined the longitude to be 100 deg. 5 min. 45 sec., differing only 2 sec. of a degree,

FOLLOWING THE WRONG GOD HOME

or ten rods from the longitude determined by Captain Frémont . . .
detached thermometer 41 deg. A high wind renders the weather
cold.   ORSON PRATT, MAY 7, 1847

Out of sorts, I stuck grimly to the highway, nursing a headache that stabbed at
my jaw like an ice pick. Even joyous sunshine didn't lift my gloom, although a
dizzying dose of aspirin fought back the pain. As the day steamed on, I dripped,
daydreamed, and longed for a diversion. All walkers do. Dour Walter Starkie, a
Scottish professor hoofing to Budapest with a violin in his backpack, persuaded a
woman to dance naked for him while he fiddled around, but her husband showed
up at the last minute and he scuttled out a window. Something lively like that, I
imagined, could brighten an afternoon.

I wobbled into Willow Island and stopped at its post office (a house trailer)
where I mailed a letter to my wife. I wasn't sure what it contained, since I'd written it back at the Odessa Bar, but I was confident that any form of communication would go a long way toward cementing family values. An air conditioner
hummed inside the PO, gnawing steadily at the heat.

Why Barbara Yoder worked at the PO wasn't any of my business, but I did ask,
"How come there's no town here?"

A handsome-looking woman inside her aluminum and rubber-wheeled crate,
Mrs. Yoder sized me up, but smiled when I asked for a first-class stamp. "If you
count everybody," she replied, "there's probably thirty-five or thirty of us in Willow Island."

I found it interesting that Mrs. Yoder mentioned the higher count first: at the
rate her mind was depopulating the burg, Uncle Sam could be out of business in
five minutes. A reasonable person must admit that a post office on wheels seems
suspicious and suggests a pessimist's planning. A lack of conviction on my face
prompted another revision: "Well, maybe twenty-five," she confessed. "But we've
been here for a hundred and ten years. Zip code six-nine-one-seven-one. Serves
four local businesses—two feed lots, Stapp Irrigation, and a John Deere plant."

"Well hidden," I observed.

Mrs. Yoder stripped a stamp from a drawer and pushed it across the counter
with a stiletto finger. Outside, the only thing that moved was dust. Willow Island
looked the kind of place where, if I lived there, ran for mayor, and voted for
myself, I'd have a 50 percent chance of winning—assuming Mrs. Yoder was a permanent resident and a Republican. No doubt about it: I was in a Twilight Zone.
Doing some quick math, I reckoned that on a heavy "first class" letter day, all

thirty-five of Willow Island's out-of-sight citizens would max out on stamps at about three bucks a week each—roughly $7,000 a year. Toss in packages and cookies from Mom to her boy in the state prison, and you might double it in a leap year. I mentioned these financial conjectures.

"A lot of truckers stop here," she said politely, frowning as I licked the stamp and positioned it upside down on the envelope. "Then there's the business trade. It adds up."

I waited around hoping a trucker would pull in with a fat wad of mail to post, but it didn't happen. I craved for an embodied "citizen" to stop by. No such luck. I scanned for FBI "wanted" posters. In vain. On the walls of United States PO Zip 69171, nobody was wanted by the Feds. Meanwhile, the air conditioner yammered, outside the afternoon turned steamy, and the road ahead was empty.

Luckily, only half the trailer was rented to Uncle Sam; the other half was doing duty as a quick stop. Mrs. Yoder sold me a candy bar and a Coke, but asking a federal employee to dance nude would have taken things too far in a rented government facility. Munching a Hershey bar and sucking at the coke, I fiddled on down the road.

• • •

On the 1843 map of the West that Brigham used, there were only two named habitations—Fort Laramie on the Laramie River and St. Vrain's Fort (near present-day Platteville, Colorado) on the south fork of the Platte. Including the North and South Platte, there were ten known rivers, ten named creeks, two sinks, two springs (one warm, one hot), two peaks (Laramie and Long's), and six geological landmarks running west on the Oregon Trail—Cedar Bluff, Chimney Rock, Scott's Bluff, Red Buttes, Rock Independence, Devil's Gate, and Table Rock. The map ended at South Pass in today's Wyoming. Between South Pass and the Sierra Nevada lay the dead vast.

Near Willow Island, the Mormons walked onto the edge of semiknown territory. Until then, the map they used was reasonably detailed—a copy of the first expedition map of John Charles Frémont ("Freemouth," the Osage calls him), who explored the West in five journeys between 1842 and 1853. Drawn by a melancholy and splenetic German named Charles Preuss, who traveled with Frémont and later hanged himself in a fit of depression outside the nation's capital, it was a basic guide—an early Rand McNally.

Preuss's contribution to the opening of the American West is immense. It was Preuss who first mapped the territory between the Mississippi and the Pacific Ocean on modern principles of geodesy and cartography. Except for the overbearing Frémont, he might have stolen more of the show—and deserved it. In his wagon, Brigham carried Preuss's maps in seven sections, but only one—the 1843 *Map to Illustrate an Exploration of the Country Between the Missouri River and the Rocky Mountains on the Line of the Missouri and Platte River*—was of daily importance to the Mormons until they reached the Rockies. Laid out on a barrelhead each evening, it was used to get a quick read of the territory ahead.

In 1846, a year before Brigham and the Mormons hit the road, Preuss produced a series of seven maps of the West that included Great Salt Lake floating in an expanse of unknown space. The *Topographical Map of the Road from Missouri to Oregon Commencing at the Mouth of the Kansas and Missouri River and Ending at the Mouth of the Wallah-Wallah in the Columbia* was a compilation of fact and fancy from Frémont's explorations after 1843, combined with materials from the Lewis and Clark expedition and observations of fur traders and trappers. For Brigham, it was a reference to outer space. At a scale of ten miles to the inch, it was the best map of the region to date, and Brigham needed only four sections (2–5) to get from the 100th meridian, over South Pass (the Continental Divide), to Fort Bridger, Wyoming.

· · ·

In one of his diaries, which lay unknown for years in a German attic, Charles Preuss bit the hand that fed him: "This morning Frémont set up his daguerreotype to photograph the rocks; he spoiled five plates that way. Not a thing was to be seen on them. That's the way it often is with these Americans." In Frémont's hymn-to-the-West, Preuss heard atonal refrains—not the ebullient notes of an American spirit of freedom but the twang of moral superiority: "They know everything, they can do everything, and when they are put to the test, they fail miserably."

Preuss mistook Frémont for an ordinary American explorer and erstwhile incompetent when he was *extraordinary* at both—at one and the same time an archetype of Manifest Destiny and a metaphor for the delusions of grandeur that came with it. He deserved Preuss's scorn. As a tireless self-promoter, he had few equals; as an explorer, he was the first to range widely throughout the West, whipping up enthusiasm for the push to the Pacific and carping it to the winds.

Frémont faded after 1846: riding a falling star, he took up an ill-fated political career as an also-ran. Given to hyperbole, "the Great Pathfinder" eventually became a national embarrassment, flickering on and off like a light bulb short-circuiting in the warehouse of U.S. history, a man whose aspirations never matched his abilities—arrested for disobeying orders, court-martialed, and convicted (Washington, 1848); briefly senator (California, 1850–51); nominee of the Republican Party for president (1856—his campaign slogan: "The Twin relics of barbarism: Slavery and Polygamy"); Civil War major general commanding the department of the West, relieved of command (1861); belly-up investor in railroad ventures (1870); and son-in-law to that zephyr, that rising gust, that monsoon of senatorial wind, Mr. Manifest Destiny himself—Thomas Hart Benton. When Benton's lovestruck daughter, Jessie, eloped and married Frémont, her chagrined father jump-started him to prominence by getting him command of his first expedition; but as Frémont burned out, Jessie frequently bailed her husband out of poverty with the proceeds of her own writing (*The Story of the Guard, Far-West Sketches*) until he was rescued by political cronies and made governor of the Arizona Territory (1878) where he was out-of-sight, out-of-mind. At last.

Mormons, especially, owe Frémont a debt, since he was among the first to describe the Great Basin—information that helped Brigham Young to settle the Mormon's destination. An American mythic hero (the Babe Ruth of bombast), he lives on in the rodomontade of politicos, in reputations built on rabid self-aggrandizement and in the self-congratulatory rhetoric that winds platitudes around national Daydreams.

• • •

Unlike Frémont, the Lion of the Lord was a curiously Dream-less man. Brigham had both Yankee feet on the ground. Wrapping the instincts of a colonizer around the wiles of a pragmatist, he led less by Manifest Destiny than Manifest Efficiency. Although he was trying to get shuck of the United States when he walked onto Preuss's map of the West, he ultimately became the western "hero" that Frémont wasn't. A determined and occasionally ruthless colonizer who could rightfully claim extraordinary success in shaping his piece of the West, Young explored the Great Basin and planned a Mormon kingdom, but wound up creating the nucleus of the forty-fifth state. Except for U.S. expansion into Mexican territory, Utah might have turned out a theocracy (some claim it's never been anything else) with only a toehold on democracy.

• • •

"I gave up on rodeos and bronc busting after receiving two messages," Dallas Coder said, "a bad fall that broke my arm and a horse that kicked me in the head."

Even with the last impairment, he seemed sane to me. Twenty-seven, lean and sandy haired, with a touch of western bow in his legs, and the ice blue eyes of a Swede, he looked like roadkill after spending a sweaty day at the irrigation company where he worked setting up "center pivots," those mantislike monsters of pipe, steel, and oversized rubber tires that rotate around a well-hole dripping the

FOLLOWING THE WRONG GOD HOME

dwindling Ogallala Aquifer onto green circles in the sand. Standing beside a battle-scarred Nissan Z that grunted like a wounded boar, Dallas tugged a grimy baseball cap low on his forehead and gave me the bemused once-over of a man for whom strangers offer relief from living in Gothenburg, Nebraska. He slapped the Z on its rusted flank and said, "This is all I got left from the glory days. Bought it new."

Minutes later, we were cooling off at a local watering hole. "The thing about small towns," he said, "is that everybody thinks they know your business . . . but it's all a combination of fact, rumor, and bullshit. I liked Denver at first. Who wouldn't coming from Gothenburg? But you know what? I prefer to know the people I'm walking toward on the street. It's better."

Dallas is a product of the collision between the Old West and the new age of consumerism. You can find him multiplied in almost every small town west of the 100th meridian. To hear Dallas tell it, everything he'd done in life reflected the passing of the old and an adjustment to the new. He'd ridden the range, sort of, broke cattle and horses, sort of, and done time in Vail, Colorado, saloons trying his hand as a ski bum. When nothing took, he Z'eed back to Gothenburg and took up where he'd begun, working a dry land. Sooner or later, I suspected, he'd end up where he belonged.

Dallas's predicament was part failed romance (he'd lost the affections of a high-rolling butler's daughter in Vail), part failed cowboy (the rodeo circuit broke him), and part failed rider-of-the-purple-sage. He wrangled cattle on a county-sized feed lot near Greeley, riding "mostly in circles," for the Monfort Packing Company, and the irrigation business was going to fail him, too, I suspected, because he knew the price for it was paid in ruined land.

Dallas taught me something unexpected about the Dream. When I told him I'd been walking up the Platte Valley trench for the past month, that the river bottoms were full of irrigated trees and that I'd like to get up over the rim and onto the edge of the plains, he spun off his stool. "Know just the place," he said. Minutes later, under a dying red sun, we topped a ridge in his smoking Z to where land was more brown than green, rolling on forever, unbroken and seamless.

Basking on an edge of high plains, Dallas pulled over by a postage-stamp cemetery. High above the Platte River valley, it held three graves, all belonging to a Swedish settler's family. Above each was a handwrought iron cross, pitiful with loss and love in that shelterless sweep of grass.

For most of my adult life I've haunted cemeteries for history's sake, often standing at monuments to the famous and not so, but those monuments paled beside these simple crosses crafted out of grief. Two of the iron crosses were

decorated with stars or hearts cut or punched into the metal, one with an elabo-
rate arch enfolding a cross inside. The rough, hammered inscriptions were in
Swedish. One bore a newborn's nameless inscription: "Fod August 8, 1887 Dod
August 19, 1889."

"Remember this place," Dallas Coder said. "It tells you something there's no
words for."

21

*The mind can form no larger idea of space than the eye can take
in at a single glance. Things near us are seen of the size of life:
things at a distance are diminished to the size of understanding.*
WILLIAM HAZLITT, "ON GOING ON A JOURNEY"

*"From Winter Quarters, two hundred ninety-five miles." . . . I
have repeatedly suggested a plan of fixing machinery to a wagon
wheel to tell the exact distance we travel in a day.*
WILLIAM CLAYTON, MAY 8, 1847

Brady's Island in the Platte River was named for a murder, the memory of which
accounts for the Nebraska village of Brady, site of the Mormon campground on
May 9, 1847. Five years earlier, John Frémont and Christopher "Kit" Carson were
camped across the Platte, which they reckoned a half-mile wide "with the water
nowhere two feet deep," the spring runoff from the mountains having already
flushed to the Mississippi. Like the Mormons, Frémont saw buffalo "swarming in
immense numbers" (Preuss mistook them for trees) and, par for his mouth, waxed
superlative of his foray into the herds for the kill. "My horse was a trained hunter,
famous in the West under the name of Proveau," he gushed, "and, with eyes flash-
ing, and the foam flying from his mouth, sprang after the cow like a tiger." Such
feline cunning in a bangtail sounds more like horse manure, of course, which our
hero knew how to spread around.

Frémont's account of the Brady skullduggery and murder in his account of his
exploring expeditions goes something like this: "Some years ago" a company of
three hunters, hard cases all, camped on the spot where the village now stands.

FOLLOWING THE WRONG GOD HOME

While one rode out to bag dinner, Mr. Brady and a fellow slacker stayed behind, frontiersmen who "frequently quarreled." Back from banging at buffalo, the first amigo found Brady dead from a gunshot wound, possibly in the back. Not one to meet his Maker due to a second "accident," the first hunter helped bury Brady, "but the wolves had torn him out," Frémont wrote, "and some human bones lying on the ground we supposed to be his."

· · ·

On my trek toward Brady, I walked all afternoon toward a bottleneck with the Platte. Bluffs on both sides of the valley squeezed river, roads, and tracks into an ever-narrowing trench. Choosing the tracks, I ambled past river bottoms rife with bird life, cattails, and dusky-leafed Russian olives, preferring the occasional draft of freights to the drag of big trucks on narrow asphalt. When two bikers flashed by on candy-apple Harleys, radios blasting and saddlebags bulging, they revved a welcome into the muggy afternoon.

So far as I could tell, Union Pacific mile marker 257 west marks the Platte River valley at its narrowest point. Past and present is compressed into a corridor less than a half-mile wide—the Oregon-California Trail, Interstate 80, the river, the Union Pacific, the Lincoln Highway, and the Mormon Trail. Nowhere else on the route west is so much history laminated into so small a space. In Clayton's day, this was desolate country; today it's become what the naturalist Paul Johnsgard calls "the shoreline forest."

In this part of the state, avian cultures collide—and some were hard at it that afternoon. Indigo and lazuli buntings, rose-breasted and black-headed grosbeaks, Baird's and semipalmated sandpipers, Bullock's and Baltimore orioles, all flutter along the Platte in "one of the hotbeds of genetic contact between eastern and western birdlife." Meadowlarks, sandpipers, red-winged blackbirds, and sparrows all hold sway near its waters, sharing space with killdeer, snipe, and plover. Geese, ducks, gulls, and terns float the river, each taking advantage of protected mid-channel islands and grassy banks. On the route of a major avian flyway, the magnificent sandhill crane crowds the Platte's waters each spring before heading north for the arctic.

But love for the river does not come easily. Known to the Pawnee as *Kikautz* (shallow water) or *Kisparuksti* (wonderful water), emigrants found it "the meanest of rivers—broad, shallow, fishless, snakeful" with "quicksand bars and muddy water." I found it enfeebled, hobbled, and frequently out of sight: today, the river's braided channels have been tamed to a trickle. On foot, you can't see the river for the trees—none of which existed when Brigham passed.

Oddly, the Platte is the only American river ever to have been hiked. Returning to the East with a harvest of beaver pelts, a band of dimly endowed trappers got the idea to float their booty to the confluence with the mighty Missouri, all the while harboring a delusion that the Platte had a main channel. In truth, its flow resembles the runoff from a pancake with multiple competing channels, each thin as a ribbon and shallow. Navigating crude buffalo-hide boats, the trappers bogged down, finally taking to pulling their loads from sandbar to sandbar—thus qualifying as the only persons in history to have hiked down the middle of an American river.

· · ·

A better-documented story about this stretch of the river is that William Clayton came up with an idea that saved him from committing suicide (perhaps homicide) in the Camp of Israel. For two days he'd been counting the revolutions of Heber Kimball's wagon wheel. Dizzy work, at best. As camp drudge and resident scribbler, he'd been assigned by Brigham to estimate the mileage of each day's travel, a responsibility that frequently put him out of sorts since he was a fastidious scribe. By the reckoning of others in camp, he was usually "two and sometimes four miles" a day off the mark—a nagging concern for any anal-retentive. So he measured Heber Kimball's wagon wheel and determined it had a circumference of 14 feet 8 inches, "not varying one eighth of an inch," and, working things out, discovered it took precisely 360 turns to the mile. On May 8, he planted a cedar post on the trail with his best guess of progress so far: "From Winter Quarters, two hundred ninety-five miles. May 8, '47. Camp all well. Wm. Clayton." Then he eyeballed the wagon wheel around and around for 1,800 revolutions (five miles) and made a more exact calculation next day, which he posted "on a small board": "From Winter Quarters, three hundred miles, May 9, 1847. Pioneer Camp all well. Distance according to the reckoning of Wm. Clayton."

By my reckoning, this earns an Englishman bragging rights to the first five miles of accurate mileage recorded west of the Missouri River. After washing his socks and taking a cool bath (he was covered with dust), some of Clayton's dizziness lifted and another revelation washed over him that put him forever into the history books of Mormon Trail ingenuity and for which, to hear him grouse about it, he never got a full measure of credit.

Clayton "repeatedly suggested" that the Camp of Israel construct a mechanical device to count the revolutions of Kimball's wagon wheel—a gifted and practical idea, especially since it would keep him from throwing up before lunch. Anyway, the idea festered and that night, having gyrated all day with Kimball's wheel, he had a (lowercase) dream. He saw himself paddling the Platte River in a leaky skiff, skimming the current "like a railway carriage." To his astonishment, both his paddle and rudder turned out to be large feathers—subconscious wish fulfillment, obviously, since he'd had about enough around-and- around and probably wanted to fly the coop.

But Clayton's idea stuck. Naturally, coming from a British point of view, he encountered American skepticism. As appointed scribe, he was supposed to write things down, not make things up. Seeking succor from on high, he mentioned his idea to Orson Pratt, "the best educated of the Saints and one of the principal intelligence's," who was likely miffed that his own "principal intelligence" hadn't tumbled to the possibility ahead of the camp scribbler. Eventually Pratt forgave Clayton for being bright, and came around, taking over the idea and sketching a workable mechanism. Pratt suggested they call it a "double screw," which was how Clayton felt when the project (and more of the credit) was handed on to Appleton Milo Harmon, "an experienced mechanic." In Mormon lore, the invention was the America's first odometer.

This is a description of a double screw: "Each six turns of the wagon wheel would cause a screw to make one revolution. The screw in turn moved a smaller wheel with sixty cogs. By the time this 60-tooth wheel made one complete turn, the wagon had covered one mile."

At full screw, a racy invention.

22

Happier life I cannot imagine than this Vagrancy.
THOMAS DE QUINCEY, WALES, 1802

I completed a roadometer and attached it to the wheel by which we could tell each night the distance traveled through the day.
APPLETON MILO HARMON, MAY 1847

In 1985 more humping was going on in North Platte, Nebraska, than in any other city in America. One man was the cause of it all and the city made him a hero. North Platte wasn't getting much until a native son, Bill Jeffers, started putting on the moves, first by becoming president of the Union Pacific Railroad and, second, by choosing his hometown to build the largest railroad hump yards in North America—a vast complex of interconnecting tracks that disconnects and rearranges freight cars heading for sensitive points in the nation. In Grand Island, you can get humped for New York, Kansas City, Los Angeles, San Francisco, New Orleans, or Chicago. If Biloxi or Boston is on your manifest, they'll be on top of it in no time.

North Platte felt more "West" than towns I'd passed through in the eastern part of the state—exactly what you'd expect from the home of Buffalo Bill Cody. The title of its first newspaper, *Pioneer on Wheels*, gives an indication of its restless mood, as if the place threatened to come unglued like a badly licked postage stamp. Incorporated in 1871, the town nearly burned out in 1893 when a prairie fire was started by hot cinders from a passing train. Barns, homes, and the pride of its three thousand residents went up in smoke.

On May 18, when I rolled into town, North Platte was more or less burning again. Worse, Santa Claus had been sentenced to a year in the state pen for "first-degree sexual assault of . . . his elf," an AP story hot off the wire in Saturday's *Telegraph*. No one likes to think of Santa fondling a thirteen-year-old girl in the back of a donut shop, but a wit in the café where I'd filched the newspaper quipped that "with time off for good behavior, Santa should be out for Christmas." Ho. Ho. Ho.

And Estel Lyle had died. The former North Platte postal worker and retired bishop of the local Latter-day Saints church went south, permanently, in Manti, Utah. By the time the news reached the obits in the *Telegraph*, he'd already spent the better part of a week underground. When I phoned the LDS church on a whim, hoping for better information on the Mormon Trail in Lincoln County, it was picked up by a woman who gave me the living bishop's number—at least she claimed he was living. When I called him, I had doubts. Speaking in tones from the Great Beyond, he was polite but uninterested, didn't seem to have a clue, but finally coughed up a name and an apology.

"I don't know much about that," he admitted. Amen.

Back among the living, I rang up an eighty-two-year-old Mormon elder with *some* kick to him who strained to remember details about the route. More talkative than his bishop, and still warm, he spoke in a gift of tongues, hemming or hawing over tangled words as he thought about it until the right ones stuck and a complete sentence came ripping out like machine-gun fire. Friendly as a grandfather, and affable as a Mormon elder should be, he gave me the gist in a twenty-one word burst.

"Near as I can remember, the trail ran north of the river, on the other side of Buffalo Bill's Rest Ranch."

· · ·

Over dinner, I fussed about what Mormons don't know about their history, just as I fretted that the dynamic duo I'd met back in Fremont—Thomas and Bagley—knew next to nothing about the ground on which they daily walked, eking out converts where their forebears had struggled for survival. In 1997, twelve years later, when the Mormon Trail Sesquicentennial reenactment made news and Americans learned more about Mormons than they probably intended, both newspaper accounts and television documentaries about the trek made international headlines, crossing state lines and lighting up the tubes and boobs who watch them. This boob followed it daily. Mormon wagons again rolled west, this time with cameras, hired wagon masters, and a caravan of twenty trucks toting grub, toilet paper, and fifty porta-potties—the past served up in period costume but with conveniences. I expect Mormons also learned something new about themselves, many for the first time.

PBS, among others, put a human face on the largest religious exodus in the nation's history, and in the euphoria over the reenactment of the 1847 march, Mormon authors gave the event Dreamy titles like "Trail of Faith" or "Journey of Hope." Less pilgrimage than media event, the documentary focused its cameras on the Mormon triumph over long odds while all too frequently avoiding the bigotry that caused it. In 1963, before flying to an appearance in Salt Lake City, the British novelist T. H. White met Mickey and Goofy in Lotus Land. "Disneyland came out of the brain of one man," he wrote in his *America at Last*. "What a mouse's fart it seems beside the whole of Utah, which came out of the brain of Brigham Young."

· · ·

The first woman Admiral of the Great Navy of Nebraska is about the size of Horatio Lord Nelson (5' 1") but is unlikely to end up pickled in a keg of brandy as Nelson was on the return trip after his victory and death at Trafalgar. Admiralty status was conferred on this strict Baptist teetotaler by the governor in recognition of her promise to canoe Nebraska's Dismal River, which is. She did. "The Dismal isn't a river at all," she told me, truthfully. "It's got high banks, but at places isn't more than six feet wide."

Prior to her elevation in rank, Nellie Snyder Yost was a colonel in the Cody Scouts and an honorary colonel in the Nebraska National Guard, but she held gold braid in personal maneuvers—winner of the AK-SAR-BEN (Nebraska spelled backward) Award, Western Hall of Fame Award, the Golden Spur Award, the Western Heritage Wrangler Award, the Levi Straus Golden Saddleman Award, and the Mari Sandoz Award for occasional services to her home state such as "bringing dignity and honor to the history and legends of the West."

On the warm Sunday afternoon we met, Nellie was decked out in a red taffeta dress, polka dot scarf, domed hair Texas-style, and nickel-rimmed bifocals. Frank, her husband of eight months— a Mississippi riverman who gave up skippering tugboats on the Father of Waters for Nellie—still had a shock of black hair and a youthful gait, although he'd grown some in the middle. An unimposing silver-haired woman, Nellie suffers from lateral scoliosis, her spine misshapen but her manner straight. Nellie's books—*Buffalo Bill: His Family, Friends, Fame, Failures, and Fortunes; No Time on My Hands; A Man as Big as the West; Keep On, Keeping On; Pinnacle Jake*—are based on the recollections of family, friends, and the far-fetched in cattle country. Her father, Jake Snyder, once broke horses for Buffalo Bill.

"Dad turned down forty dollars a month to ride in Cody's Wild West Show in England," she told me. "Didn't go because he could make forty dollars a month right here in North Platte. Jake Snyder stuck to a place."

So did his daughter. Born in the Sand Hills, Nellie was raised on Jake's Ten Bar ranch. When she was two weeks old, she was driven home in a buggy; it broke down and she finished the journey on horseback in her mother's arms. "I have an understanding of old-time ranch life," she said with pride. "My books are about history and high times on the plains."

In 1929, Nellie married Harry Yost, had a son, and raised him "in the big lonesome canyons south of Maxwell." Harry died of Parkinson's disease, but when her boy, Tom, earned his driving license and drove off more frequently in search of what young men are always looking for, Nellie took to writing, tapping her father for raw material, grubbing out ranch stories for her first success, *Pinnacle Jake*.

Here's a Jake Snyder tale:

> One night that summer I stayed all night with Oley at Sam Marant's place, and in the night I heard some jars and stuff falling off a shelf along the wall. The shelf was just a two-by-four along the shack wall and Oley kept some glass jars of stuff setting there, only they were on the floor that morning, and one or two was broke.
>
> "Oley," I said, "what was makin' all that racket and knockin' those jars off that shelf last night." "Damn that bull snake," Oley

grunted. "If he don't quit doin' that I'm a-goin' to put him out'a here." And that was the first time I knew I'd slept with a bull snake in the same room with me.

Eleven books later and a month shy of eighty, Nellie was at it again, this time writing "the most gruesome true story you can imagine." When I got it out of her, it was a tale fit to kill most women of her age, a story full of deception, treachery, mayhem, murder. Take a homicidal crone, a blasphemous daughter, a crooked judge, a compliant doctor, a full measure of greed, ready money, and a house full of elderly wards of the state and see how fast you can kill them off—bludgeonings, poisonings, drownings. True crime. A forensic feast.

"Worked those helpless people with a buggy whip," Nellie mourned. "That woman had a hold on people—a judge, a county commissioner. She killed so many. Wouldn't let some of them wear shoes, summer or winter."

"Murdered them, you mean?"

"Totally evil."

One bleak night, the crone's blasphemous daughter snarled at her mother one time too many and the old lady hurled a cast iron stove lid, crushing her daughter's skull. Nellie grimaced. "The undertaker signed 'accidental poisoning' on the death certificate . . . but that woman put her own daughter in the coffin *on her side* to cover up what she'd done! When the mother died, people bought mattresses from the place . . . tore 'em open looking for money. Left an estate worth eighty thousand."

"Who got it?"

"The attorney."

A person with a passion for Nebraska's plains will one day write Nellie's life since the complexities of her words are best understood by someone with deep roots in Sand Hills culture—someone for whom dust, grass, water and a tedium of space stir romance or desire. Mari Sandoz would fit the bill, but she's long slipped into the dark; and so would Wright Morris, who's gone the same way recently, leaving us short-changed of his talent. Like Nellie, such a writer must love grassland snoopery for its own sake while listening patiently to some aging grandchild of a sodbuster jawing on until something pops out that makes all the difference. The Osage knows about that; the man could get stories from a stone.

· · ·

On May 12, 1847, near the confluence of the North and South Platte Rivers, the Mormons entered a "valley of dry bones"— detritus of bison left to bleach in the

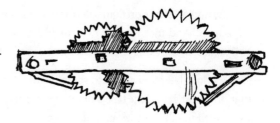

The "endless screw" odometer. From *Appleton Milo Harmon Goes West*, ed. Maybelle Harmon Anderson (Berkeley, Calif.: Gillick Press, 1946), 12.

sun. Crossing north of the present city of North Platte on ground where Buffalo Bill Cody later built his famous "Rest Ranch," they came across hundreds of carcasses, most skinned for their hides by Sioux or Cheyenne. The stench sickened the women.

Orson Pratt's "double screw" had by now gone through three hands and, having constructed the device, Appleton Milo Harmon attached it to the "nigh rear wheel" of Heber Kimball's wagon, ending Clayton's dizziest days. Lacking a basic understanding of the device, Brigham wrote that "Ap Harmon has made some machinery to put on a wagon wheel by which Wm. Clayton can tell the miles traveled each day." But Clayton wasn't off the hook entirely: "I shall only have to count the number of miles, instead of the revolution of the wagon wheel," he confided to his journal. Pratt revised his description and now called the device the "endless screw." It consisted, wrote Clayton, "of a shaft about eighteen inches long."

⋅ ⋅ ⋅

Monday morning, I left main roads behind. From North Platte to Ogallala, Nebraska, U.S. 30 skips to the south side of the river, linking a necklace of small towns—Hershey, Sutherland, and Paxton—before heading toward Sidney, the Colorado border, and the Rockies. North of the river is an open expanse of sparsely populated ranch land, dirt roads, and jeep tracks; a two-day walk that revived my spirits, bolstered my hopes, and offered up a first compelling sense of the Great Plains as they must have been. Along the way, I glimpsed bison on the hoof, sampled two culinary delicacies not experienced in my half century of living, and had a detailed conversation with Buffalo Bill Cody.

The bison belonged to Ted Long, an artist whose work has decorated homes of the rich and famous, among them Henry Fonda and John Wayne. Long is a "full" man, neither fat nor skinny. Decked out in lizard boots, jeans, plaid western-style shirt, and a Stetson, he looks the image of "West." Self-taught, but with an eye for "western light," Long hails from a family of homesteaders. His paintings dazzle, brilliantly suffused with waxing or waning sun, full of detail that ties itself to a big land and its people, with nothing to confuse perspective but an immensity of open space.

Long's subjects are based on history and myth—mountain men wintering near Casper, Wyoming, or the first meetings between white traders, trappers, and Native Americans. That morning his easel displayed a lush painting of John Colter's historic meeting with Manuel Lisa at the mouth of the Platte. A longtime trapper and experienced mountain man who traveled west with Lewis and Clark, Colter was the first white man to see Yellowstone with its mud pots, sulfurous pools, and geysers. "Colter's Hell," he named it. Stormy Manuel Lisa pioneered the western fur trade, an entrepreneur who helped sell eastern slicks on beaver hats. In Ted's painting, Colter and Lisa are face-to-face, opening up between them half a continent to plunder.

Ted's studio—a restored log cabin from Bridger County, Wyoming—looks out on four head of bison who appear in many of his paintings with the artistic refinement of old friends. The walls are adorned with Ted's personal collection of western art and artifacts—Native American beadwork, decorated buffalo skulls, arrows, parafleche, fringed buckskins, braids of wild turnip, moccasins, and buffalo robes, as well as taxidermy of bighorn sheep, antelope, wild boar—all bagged by the artist.

"I go to the site of an event and spend time there," Ted told me. "Sometimes a week or two. I often can't get it right until I stand in the other guy's footprints. Times change but a landscape holds up."

"Maybe even dead artists got somethin' to do. Maybe they paint the clouds," Charlie Roemer had said at Winter Quarters cemetery. Maybe. But Ted Long paints in colors of the Dream.

●　●　●

Buffalo Bill Cody waited under a spreading cottonwood in his yard, tweaked out in trademark fringed and beaded buckskins and looking not a day older than when I last didn't see him, which was possibly around 1898, the year my father was born. The old scout struck a pose as I stepped down from the pickup, one hand on his hip, black Stetson cocked to one side, complete with string tie, shoulder-length silvered hair, mustache and goatee that identified him as the one, the only, the straight shootin'est, wa-hooin'est frontiersman to ride in a circus of lies, half-truths, and sideshow Dream ever to make it to Madison Square Garden.

"Bill, I'm honored." I held out my hand and he shook it.

"You're late," he said. "I expected you over an hour ago."

I apologized to the man who sold tickets to the West of popular imagination, the sly fox who put "western" in the movies, the entrepreneur who handed *rootin'* and *tootin'* on to Hollywood, who put the *Hoot* in Gibson, the *Roy* in Rogers, and the *Gabby* in Hayes.

"Boy, come on up to the house and let's talk. Have some icetee. You look t'ard."

When we got to the white frame house, Bill's wife made me comfortable in the kitchen, poured me a tall, cold glass of refreshment, and waited for me to launch an interrogation, since I had pen and notebook in hand. Across the table, I stared into the eyes of an American icon, dark as anthracite but ready to spark.

• • •

Charlie Evans's grandfather "proved up" on his Nebraska homestead in 1879, as required by the Homestead Act to get title to a free chunk of Dream, arriving on the Great Plains from Virginia to work as a section hand for the Union Pacific. Charlie lives on part of the original spread, ranches eight thousand acres, checks his cattle with a 1947 lemon-yellow Piper Cub that his son uses to dive-bomb strays and flush them back into the herd, check gates and stock tanks.

"I got drafted for Buffalo Bill in 1963," Charlie told me. "It was the Centennial Pageant for Fort McPherson. That was the end of it, I figured, until the high school called me to do football games. I had the look and the same build as Bill. I got to ride around and shoot off my guns." Sounded like the Dream to me.

Charlie hit it big in 1974, when Pan American Airlines and the Bank of America rustled him up for a promotional campaign in Europe. "Flew us to Frankfort, Düsseldorf, Berlin, and Paris . . . Monty Montana and me," he said. "We took two Indians with us and put on a western skit. Navajo Charlie did a hoop dance, Monty did rope tricks, and I did Buffalo Bill. Had us a country and western singer, too."

In those halcyon days, Charlie wore a "stick-em-on wig and beard," but during a "Wild West commercial" for Sears Roebuck filmed at Buffalo Bill's Rest Ranch not far from where we sat, "the wig kept a blowin' off." (The commercial, Charlie assured me, "showed all over the world.") After that, he grew his own hair and beard, making Bill's hirsute attributes permanent.

Charlie's Buffalo Bill togs are also authentic; his fringed buckskin jacket is a copy of the real McCoy that he discovered in a museum at Signal Mountain, Tennessee. When he asked to take measurements, the curator said, "G'wan, take it home. Send it back when you're done with it."

"What's it worth?" Charlie asked.

"Let's just say some fella from Texas offered fifty thousand for it," came the reply.

Back in Nebraska, Charlie had the jacket copied, right down to the beadwork thunderbird. "I wear Bill's clothes real well," he said. "I've worn several things of his. I mean, the real stuff."

Later, bedded down on Charlie's lawn, I pondered what it would be like to go to bed at night and wake up next morning with a borrowed identity. The Osage had done that, and it changed his life. John Cozad did it too, emerging a new man in Atlantic City. Even Brigham Young, once a chair maker, pulled it off.

· · ·

On Thursday, August 8, 1844 (Joseph Smith was a month in his grave), Brigham took to the ring in Nauvoo to fit himself for the prophet's mantle. Claiming the title in a knockdown debate with Sidney Rigdon, a feeble contender to be sure, he made certain there wouldn't be any rematch: after hitting the mat Rigdon was excommunicated. According to witnesses, not only did Brigham appear "in the likeness of Joseph," but he also "spoke in Joseph's voice"—a physical and vocal transformation that is now embedded in Mormon myth. It being extremely hot that August, heatstroke was a possibility and, perhaps, an explanation. Whatever, Brigham assumed a new identity he was to be granted fully on the way to Utah: "Prophet, Seer, and Revelator" of the Latter-day Saints.

· · ·

Over breakfast next morning, Charlie's wife mused about the twilight of her husband's career. "Can't ride no more because of bone breaks," she said, "and he's got *flee-bite-us* in his leg."

Charlie's eyes flashed. "Hell, I don't even know what *flee-bite-us* is," he said. "Anyway, Bill had to ride in a buggy his last years."

We parted company, Charlie playing himself under a pale morning sun and me playing the loneliness of a long-distance walker. In his own garb—jeans and worn plaid shirt—Charlie Evans was a kindly man, hobbled by a bad hip, soft as rainwater, and comfortable as a grandfather. I'd spent a day with Buffalo Bill, but only met Charlie Evans at breakfast. I never saw Charlie again, but I did see Buffalo Bill on NBC News a few years later, standing behind Ronald Reagan wearing the same smoked tan and beaded thunderbird jacket that he did on the day we met, his silver hair tugged by a breeze and his head corkscrewed into the black Stetson while the Great Communicator misinformed a North Platte crowd about his intentions for a second term. No offense, but it was one flimflam man to another.

23

Next day I trotted gaily down the canyon, climbed over the western wall . . . and struck out. Now I was truly in God's country . . . which is peerless. CHARLES F. LUMMIS,
A TRAMP ACROSS THE CONTINENT

About eleven, the camp started, being obliged to take a winding circuitous route, over . . . a broken succession of hills and ravines, very much resembling the tumultuous confusion of ocean waves, when rolling and tumbling in all directions by violent and contrary winds. ORSON PRATT, MAY 14, 1847

In 1884, when Charles Lummis walked over the "western wall" and found himself in a peerless "God's country," he described a vision of American Dreaming that comes up again and again in the experience of those who choked the overland trails three decades earlier. Entering a country that all but defied description, emigrants painted it in every color that simile, metaphor, and hyperbole would allow an unknown geography, their imaginations stimulated by a landscape so changing and vast that even numbing Yankee pragmatism turned to occasional inspiration. Lummis was ending a walk across the continent (3,500 miles with detours) that landed him in California, where he went to work as city editor for the Los Angeles *Daily Times*. At foot pace, Dream had seeped into him like a slow drip into a bucket of sand.

Early western artists like Alfred Bierstadt graphically lied about the country, creating majestic phantasms in light and color to portray the dementia that hit most travelers heading into the unknown. The "West" was a country to change perspectives and did, mile after mile expanding emptiness until the sky enlarged and those who crossed it saw the true curve of the earth. Less journey than contagious wonder, it spun words by the millions from the pens of settlers; the same ethereal quality exists in accounts by Apollo astronauts viewing earth from the moon.

In what's been called its "Colorful Period" (1840–1900), the West adopted language that described its mythic appeal from A to Z—Alamo, bonanza, cow town, dead man's hand, eating dust, fandango, ghost town, half-breed, Indian lover, jamboree, kick the lid off, last roundup, maverick, neck-tie party, outlaw, panhandle, quick on the trigger, rustler, saloon, ten-gallon hat, underbrush, vamoose, wagon boss, XIT brand, yellow belly, and zapato—the last a term for foot gear. Every plains boss, Bible puncher, range bum, dude, greenhorn, muleskinner, and cowgirl who entered it folded its lingo around them like a pair of chaps. Empty space, you might say, was tamed on the tongue.

From language flows myth. In no time flat, the "West" was transformed into dime novels, tall tales, dude ranches, and Disneyland—each an extension of early saccharine descriptions and sarsaparilla imaginations. Its history is laced with trappings of conquest: it was "tamed," "conquered," or simply "annexed" by "pioneers," "forty-niners," and "gunfighters." In Dreamtime, it was "won" when, in fact, it was seized and exploited.

· · ·

The idea of conquest has its roots in Elizabethan England where two dominant ideas of the history of civilization held sway—the *progressive* and the *retrograde*. Virgil and Plato argued both. The *retrograde* viewed history as having declined from a golden age—a eulogy to an ancient world. Its image lingers in the classical naming of American cities—Athens, Rome, Cincinnati, Sparta, Antioch. *Progressivists* believed that civilization was moving steadily uphill—that "progress" was constant and continual.

No matter which side of the fence an Elizabethan clung to, both led to "an identical feeling: history must be a continuous *reformation*." People aspired either to regain the old or to progress with the new and inevitable, a notion that led directly to British Dreams of expansion and empire. Included in the welter of Elizabethan ideas that eventually washed up on American shores is this justification from Thomas More's *Utopia*: "When any people holdeth a piece of ground void and vacant to no good or profitable use; keeping others from the use and possession of it . . . by the law of nature, [it] ought thereof to be nourished and relieved." Elemire Zolla calls this Old World point of view "a straightforward opportunity for piratical trade." The propagation of faith was simply another of the various devices employed to extol the idea that trade and civilization must be spread along with the Christian religion—a practice common to both seventeenth-century Catholics and nineteenth-century Mormons.

But hiding behind this so-called Christian aim was economic plunder, pure and simple. Over the bodies of Incas and Aztecs, the gilded treasures of the Americas had been sent to Spain by Cortés and his ilk; and following the path of the conquistadors—after having brought back tobacco from Virginia—Sir Walter Raleigh set out on a voyage to Guiana in 1595, taking with him a hundred "gentlemen, soldiers, rowers, boat-keepers, boys, and all sorts," hoping to find the mythical city of El Dorado. His "purse," he said, "was wasted with charge" (empty) and "the empire of Guiana is adorned with temples and treasures." Eventually, in the name of God, profit, progress, and America, the "only good Indian" became a "dead Indian"—no matter what other western lingo we wrap around it.

· · ·

Somewhere beyond North Platte, the Mormon quotient for Dreamtime began to expand: they entered *moonscape*. That they weren't overly imaginative is evident from their surviving journals, most of which are compendiums of dullness edited and sanctified by their descendants. But a few Mormons stuttered into figurative language.

Orson Pratt began his description of "West" on May 14, 1847. Normally as linguistically challenged as any seat-of-the-pants scientist, he began to wax fulsome beyond the confluence of the North and South Platte. A line of pure poetry creeps into his journal. His description of western hills as a "tumultuous confusion of ocean waves, when rolling and tumbling in the winds," is metaphor, and his description of the "roily yellow waters" of the Platte is a strikingly vivid image. The same day, William Clayton was tripping over similes, noting sandhill bluffs "like large drifts of snow," and "flowers, not unlike the violet, and very rich."

Like Pratt and Clayton, many temporarily disoriented emigrants often focused on bright colors in an otherwise expanding monotony of dry land. On his way to California in 1850, Byron McKinstry noted the abundant prickly pear—"especially yellow ones." Arrived at Ash Hollow two years later, a more abundant imagery caught up John Wayman: "The bottom bedecked here . . . with Grey Ash, Dwarf Cherry, Current and rose bushes, making the air fragrant with their odor"—all sights and smells that he called "pleasant associations of home." But for Mormons, "home" became a destination in an unfamiliar space, and the images they recreated in Utah's harsh landscape, all monuments to their handiwork, are reminders of a lost world. Once in the West, they revived the bloom of the East, making their desert inheritance "blossom as a rose."

· · ·

The West was a space that Mormons went deeper and deeper into until they emerged on a semirecognizable but possibly habitable surface. Utah was mysterious, its colors hauntingly unorthodox—russets, ochers, lavenders, vermilions, and bile greens leached from the earth's crust. Much of Utah was dolorous tan; some of it was blackened where vulcanism once held sway, and such strange colors seeped into their already iridescent faith. Paul Shepard caught the doctrinal implications in his book *Nature and Madness*: "The most antiseptic and fire-purified earth is the desert, so Christians took it along everywhere. Introspection turned the wetland of the natural self into a dry rectitude."

Shepard's "dry rectitude" seems a most Mormon thing. It was "desert" rectitude that they stored up in Utah in an unorthodox lifestyle and doctrine that Bernard De Voto called a "dizzy sacerdotal system" that Joseph Smith's mind "wove into a crazy quilt of dogma." Harsh, to be sure. But De Voto is on well-charted ground when he claims that Mormonism was a "great catch basin of evangelical doctrine," most of it stirred up from the new religious flavors of the nineteenth century, much of it caught in the crossfire between a *retrograde* view of lost civilizations and a *progressive* insistence on new and better worlds. Doctrinally creative and experimental, Mormon faith rose from a seething of American Protestantism, as individual as the Republic itself and, like the West, wreathed in unusual hues.

Certainly the Mormon faith is indebted to the doctrinal botany of the Great Awakening, which provided the hybrid seeds that caused it to blossom; but on the journey to Utah, Mormons were ambushed by an awesome landscape and that landscape distilled into their theology and lifestyle, eventually changing the pigment of Mormon beliefs into an American Dream of a unique kind. Alone in Utah's vastness, Mormon doctrine congealed with unusual tints. Beliefs about life after death came to include an expectation of a glorified and perfected existence on other planets—something Joseph Smith had hinted at before his death. In so septic a space as Utah, any image of resurrection—shade trees, blossoming flowers, lush gardens—was a miracle. Baptism for the dead arose more easily from its semi-dead landscape, a watery temple-in-the-desert ritual offering the Mormon promise of salvation to generations of the long dehydrated and deceased. Although Smith Dreamed of a refuge in the far West (Stephen Douglas had suggested Vancouver Island and Abraham Lincoln Oregon), he didn't live to experience the landscape that matched his fertile imagination. Who knows what might have taken shape in his visions if he had ever got hold of so bold and evocative a country?

・ ・ ・

Before I ran out of back road, I waded into the hills and crossed a wide swath of original Mormon Trail ruts—the best extant in Nebraska. In 1997, an overzealous television crew documenting the Mormon Trail Sesquicentennial destroyed a section of these—another loss of memory written on the land. As I topped a rise, I saw a "beautiful and extended prospect opened on every side" where "the surface of the country exhibited a broken succession of hills and ravines." The vision is Orson Pratt's as he crossed the same ground on May 14, 1847.

Where the road ended, I walked onto a sandy farm track and came across rangy Roy Lunkwitz, as spare, attenuated, and toughened a fellow as you'd ever want to meet, quintessentially western under a Stetson, with his jaw full of chew and a bouquet of pencils sprouting from the pocket of a faded blue shirt. He wore a single roan leather glove on his left hand; his bare right hand—worn and exposed—looked not much different. A collie, Susie, sniffed around my legs, licking at my ankles, and, as well-mannered dogs do, warming to an unexpected stranger. Roy was fixing an enfeebled door on a faded and peeling clapboard one-room schoolhouse, long abandoned and full of manure, but his respectful attention to it held my interest. Raised three miles from the dung-infested wreck, Roy had walked five days a week as a boy to the schoolhouse he was mending.

"Never got more than eighth grade," he said, drawling out the words slowly, as if some language was still trapped in a long-ago reverie.

"Here?"

"Yup. Right here."

He climbed into a distressed Ford pickup, turned for a last prideful look at his tottering academy, and pointed at the door.

"I put that door on years back," he said, waving and spinning his wheels in the sand as dust spewed. When he hit the first turn, Susie was still open mouthed in a frame of rear window. Roy's head shot out of the driver's side window and deposited a hefty ecru wad in the road. Toad size, it lay in the sun and steamed. How a man can get that much chew in his mouth, I can't say. But this much I can: it was impressive.

An hour later, when I walked through Larry Hoatson's back forty, he was nosing a tractor blade through his corral, cleaning out what comes from the stern end of a mustang. It was ripe. I'd come in following a cut of old trail, still laid down for the eye to trace. Larry didn't mind that I crossed his land and, once he got my story straight, he took his hat off and scratched the back of his head, just like Henry Fonda did in the movies.

FOLLOWING THE WRONG GOD HOME

"Always wondered where those ruts come from," Larry said. "They been here all my life."

Overland again, I crested a sandhill rise, looked down at the junction of Clear Creek and the Platte, and counted twenty-nine big carp fanning in a sand-bottomed pool five feet deep—an oasis surrounded by reeds and willow brush. The carp looked strangely out of place in a land of limited rain, their tails waving me in their direction. I scrambled down through brush, stripped off, and joined them. As I washed my hair, they nudged my legs, cool and rubbery as water-filled balloons. When I submerged into their world and looked at them, they didn't seem at all startled by my staring, but watched me through round, Jello-y eyes, yellow-bellied as watermelons. Afterward, I lay on a rim of pool, stretched out in the sun, watching a curlew quick-stepping across a sand bank. Ten feet away, arid hills rose to meet the trail. For a few minutes, I napped in an oasis, but climbing up the sandy track, refreshed, I sensed I was entering the West at last. At Mick McFadden's place, I got my first clue. I'd crossed into Mountain Time.

24

I had not yet learned the secret of that swinging walk. . . . On the contrary, I limped, dragged, now walking with great strides, and now loitering at a snail's pace behind.

JOHN BUCHAN, *SCHOLAR GIPSIES*

I discovered that brother Appleton Harmon is trying to have it understood that he invented the machinery to tell the distance we travel, which makes me think less of him than I formerly did.

WILLIAM CLAYTON, MAY 15, 1847

When Vera Sillasen came up from the cellar with a whole chicken under glass, all body parts attached, I was impressed. Later, she brought up a quart of canned beef, but because of its source (she'd cut it up plenty), the original was rendered unrecognizable. What parts of it I ate were savory, and I do believe, given the cooperation of the Mason glass company, that Vera could "put up" a whole cow and get in the *Guinness Book of World Records*.

Bottled meat was born of necessity on the plains, where long winters without stable refrigeration became a way of life for early settlers. Distance from the nearest town was another incentive, so anything grown in season on the home place went into jars—fruit, vegetables, and anything that clucked or hoofed it. Free-range chicken, the slopped hog, and the fatted calf, all stewed in juices under a good plains woman's ministrations. For all I knew, there was a jar of mountain oysters in Vera's cellar, but I hadn't the nerve to ask.

What Vera knows about critter canning is a hand-me-down from an older ranch world where a wide sweep of chilling winter ran the eye to horizon with nothing on it but a woman, her man, some kids, a few bunkhouse "hands," and a multitude of the four-legged dumb where once the buffalo roamed. If Nebraska's plains are a hot, mesmerizing sweep in summer, they're a cold, hell-frozen-over sheet of geography come the winter solstice. Ball and Mason jars were a consolation.

Vera and her husband, Jim, run the Nevens Ranch, a 19,000-acre spread connected to civilization by a sand cut across the plains to Keystone, a dusty hamlet ten miles to the west. I walked in from roadless hills, coming upon the white frame ranch house—a refuge in boundless grass. When I asked for water and a place to put down my tent, I got dinner, an evening's conversation, chicken and beef in a jar for appetizers, another high brass bed with cool, clean sheets, and a ranch breakfast. At dinner they fed me salad, steak (naturally), fresh onion, radish, rice, and a rhubarb cobbler with ice cream.

Vera and Jim Sillasen are a well-matched couple who show the weathers of many seasons in strong, agreeable features—Jim square-jawed with a wide mouth easily given to smiling, and Vera with cropped brown hair, put-you-at-ease eyes, and a look of well-tempered patience. Both are soft-spoken, reserved, and wary of, but warming to, strangers. Openness comes naturally to ranch families, I discovered, as if contact with so much surrounding space rubs off, leaving an almost serene sense of self-reliance that leaks out in conversation, as when Jim quoted his grandfather: "You can never imagine the activity of the sky until you've night-herded."

What Jim meant—whatever majesty was implied in his spare, venerating language—I wouldn't understand until I was deep in Wyoming when I saw my own universe move, an emotional high point at which my journey either ended or began, I'm not sure which. Nor could I fully grasp the loss in Jim's voice when he said, "We never ride at night anymore and we cheat a bit on horses. We use pick-ups and horse trailers to get to the range, and pickups to get to the cows. We honk and the cows follow. They eat right out'a the back."

. . .

Most of what I imagined about ranching came from a sheltered small-town childhood—a snoop into Zane Grey novels, a generous smattering of Roy Rogers and Gene Autry movies, followed by adolescent doses of John "Duke" Wayne. Any use of wheeled vehicles in place of Trigger or Champion didn't fit into my fantasy anymore than did cattle lowing under the diamond glitter of starlight while munching out of the back of a pickup. To me, riding "tall in the saddle" meant being bowlegged atop Old Paint.

Of course, horses wouldn't be involved in American Dreaming at all if Native Americans hadn't stolen them from the Spanish conquistadors who first imported them along with cattle around A.D. 1500. Horses eventually made the Apache, Comanche, and Sioux the terrors of the plains—an image of Armageddon that helped turn a West Coast tar pit into Hollywood and Nebraska's Henry Fonda into a quick draw on the silver screen. But with millions of buffalo grazing the plains, "longhorn" Spanish cattle were virtually ignored by the natives.

While in general agreement about the existence of the buffalo, Mormons are having none of the above anthropology about the Spanish origins of horses and cattle. In Mormon-American Dreamtime, horses and cattle have been roped, branded, traded, and sold in the Americas since 2700 B.C.—not A.D. 1500—when a *Book of Mormon* tribe known as the "Jaredites" landed in eight watertight barges somewhere in Central America. Thus when Old World met New in Mormon Dreaming, the continent was already abundantly blessed with sheep, oxen, elephants, and two other odd beasts—"cureloms and cumoms"—unidentifiable, like all the others, in any American fossil record covering that period.

But for true believers, the only record needed is writ large in the pages of *The Book of Mormon*, where the story of the Jaredites is contained in an internal chapter known as the Book of Ether, which, incidentally, put Mark Twain under faster than the real stuff. The Jaredites lived in "a land northward"—presumably above the Isthmus of Panama—and Ether was an oscitant descendant of a fabled or imaginary chap named "Coriantor," the son of Moron who lived in a land of the same name. No matter. The New World beasts of burden described by the Jaredites were "useful unto man," it says in the book, "especially the cumons"—excuse me, "cumoms." Real or not likely, the Jaredites are said to have prospered in the New World, having "all manner" of Old World animals abounding, including "horses and asses"—especially, as Twain might say, the latter.

Something new began stirring in me on the Nevens Ranch—a vague awakening—simmering all day as I'd walked the hills toward Vera's sumptuous dinner. When I came across the bleached remains of a steer, I plunged Roadmaker's tip into the sandy soil, hoisted the skull, and balanced it on top of the shaft, draping my soggy shirt across it. In the grass a few feet away, I put the camera on a heap of sand, set its timer, and took a photo of myself with the gaunt, bleached skull staring over my shoulder. There's a quality to that photo that haunts me—a femur curve of hills in the background, bone-bleached clouds in a streaky blue sky, and that pale skull staring over my shoulder like a ghostly amanuensis, its vacant sockets looking west toward some mystery: my favorite photo of the trip. A stunning temporality hangs over it that brings into context the scant days that make up a life. I am a stranger in the photograph now, a mere reflection of the person I've become, and I'm solaced by the frailty of my existence—an image in which life is not perilous, but precious.

. . .

For two days, the Mormon vanguard camped three miles east of the present-day Sillasen house. They'd had hard going on May 13 and 14, laboring over sandy ridges that squeezed the road too close to the river. In his journal, Clayton uses the word *bluffs* twenty-four times in three days. On the 15th, after double-teaming the wagons, they found a patch of ground close to the water, barely making five miles before packing it in for the night. Clayton grumbled again, complaining that Appleton Harmon was taking all the credit for having "invented the machinery to tell the distance we travel, which makes me think less of him than I formerly did"—a conflict that simmered between the two for weeks. (Harmon is silent on the subject, his own journal having suddenly run dry on May 8.) Since there was "no timber . . . in sight," the camp scattered to gather more dung, "which abounds everywhere." So that evening's warmth and well-being, fostered by hot coffee and fresh buffalo steaks (harvested that day and the next), once again came down to well-aged bison scat.

Reading in the comfort of the Sillasen's guest bedroom, floating uncertainly on a plump brass bed, it struck me as curious that while the Mormons drank coffee and whiskey in both Nauvoo and Winter Quarters, no mention of either is made in Clayton's journal, as if the entire camp had suddenly gone cold turkey. In fact, most published journals of the Camp of Israel are generally bone dry on the subject—a suspect deletion, especially since there was booze in Brigham's buckboard. In 1856, six tons of tobacco, rum, whiskey, brandy, tea, and coffee were freighted by Caleb Green across the plains to Brigham who, by then, not only controlled the Utah liquor trade, but sent two rival Mormon brewers on extended "missions" so he could keep them out of the suds business and get a head on his own brew.

By 1867, realizing that the railroad and readily available eastern sour mash was cutting into profits from his locally distilled spar varnish, Young revived Joseph Smith's nearly obscure "Word of Wisdom" prohibiting spirituous tippling, "hot drinks," and tobacco. When the faithful complained that sudden abstinence might be linked to early death, Young replied, "Then die, but die in the faith." He also took umbrage with the "ambeer" slops on the Mormon Tabernacle floor: "It is an imposition for gentlemen to spit tobacco juice around, or leave their quids on the floor," he railed. "We therefore request all gentlemen attending conference to omit tobacco chewing while here."

Brigham wasn't much for ecumenical behavior. Mormon exclusivity was his goal from the beginning, and like a whole chicken in a Mason jar, Mormons were an oddity to the rest of the nation, a coagulation of believers stewing in their own juices. Despising most Gentiles, Brigham found it difficult to put up with many, a recipe that boiled over when other persuasions entered Utah. Considering the battering the Mormons took in Missouri and Illinois, it isn't difficult to understand his feelings, but the fact is, Brigham designed and ruled Utah as a kingdom and managed it that way until he died from "apoplexy" in 1877. For thirty years, Brigham tended to his own like Jim Sillasen tends hybrid cattle, rounding up the defective and, by some accounts, putting a few out of their misery while giving the yo-heave-ho to any Mormon or Gentile who hadn't the teeth to graze in the appointed fields of the Lord. Of a Presbyterian minister arrived in Zion, Brigham thundered, "He has no business here. The Lord has given me these valleys, and to those who I choose to have occupy them."

• • •

Sixty years after Brigham passed the site of Keystone, an unusual ecumenism caught hold of families ranching in the area. Christians of various denominations built a white clapboard church on their wide blanket of grass and shared it—the only combined Catholic and Protestant church in the nation and a more tasteful image of Dream. Mindful of common Christian roots, and respectful of each other's peculiarities, they built two altars—one facing west, the other east, and hinged the hard backs of the benched pews so they could be flipped to face the altar of choice. Dedicated on August 8, 1908, Little Church is no longer used, but wandering pilgrims like myself occasionally stop by for a look—a reminder of a better community.

"The trail runs north of town," Lorna Wendt told me when I showed up in Keystone. The guardian of local words was cleaning the burg's dusty and minuscule library, her hair tucked under a red kerchief, looking warily at me through glasses the thickness of pop bottles. "From the air, you can see it plain. It's greener along the old trace. It got a lot of manure in its day. Any other information you're after, we've likely got it . . . at least stuff about Keystone."

I nosed around for a few minutes, then went looking for the old greener trail, but at ground level it all looked greener to me.

• • •

Two miles later, the green ran out and the trail turned wet. Two million acre-feet wet. I'd come upon the ugliest and most woebegone place in the Platte Valley—"Big Mac," as the locals call it. Behind Kingsley Dam (the world's second-largest hydrologic fill) the Platte River is backed up to form Lake McConaughy—35,000 surface acres of water that feeds and fuels the Central Nebraska Public Power and Irrigation District, the state's largest reservoir and the main reason why Nebraska is the only state in the USA totally served by public power.

It was a hell of a fight. In 1933, the Nebraska Enabling Act gave a green light for public utilities to compete with private power companies. Both sides came out swinging, and observers recall "batteries of high-powered eastern attorneys operating around the hotels and capitol corridors" in Lincoln while die-hard supporters tried to "ward off the stultifying hand of eastern control and eastern piracy, once more reaching out." In the heat of battle, "there were stories of millions floating loose for anyone able and willing to deliver the state."

But public power won and the Platte Valley was changed forever. Greed and high-priced lawyers argued all the way to the Supreme Court, which ruled that public power projects were right up Roosevelt's New Deal alley. Senator George Norris, who drummed up federal support for the project saw both light *and* water at the end of his tunnel. Trying to ward off the badly broken Dream of life beyond the 100th meridian, he complained, "It was not such a haven as I had thought. There came the hot winds, the dry weather, lack of rain. I saw farms . . . burned to a crisp. . . . I saw the disappointment that came over the faces of these people and I could see the despair that was in their hearts." Charged up, he saw to it that light bulbs beyond the dry line were turned on at maximum wattage.

• • •

In 1913, the idea of several reservoirs along the Platte was Dreamed up by two tough sodbusters, C. W. McConaughy and George Kingsley, although neither considered a dam on the main Platte River. Their idea was to dam its tributary streams, but that idea was flushed down the tube when Major C. R. Olberg, an irrigation guru and watermonger, came up with the idea for one very large bathtub. Completed in 1943, Kingsley Dam has spun off fifty-nine years of Platte River irrigation and power projects, and western Nebraska's once-dry cup is half full or half empty. Take your pick.

But there's an irony in the dam's history: C. W. McConaughy, for whom the lake is named, bitterly opposed its construction and carried that ire to his grave—a fact I gleaned in the Keystone library under the watchful eye of Lorna Wendt. Later, when I mentioned this disparity in a chophouse to a senior Nebraskan with political connections in Keith County, and something of the same point of view as C. W., he cupped a hand around his mouth as if to cut off communication with the rest of restaurant.

"Wherever C. W. is these days . . . heaven or hell . . . he's still hot under the collar," he said. "If he's got turn-around room in his coffin, right now he'd be spinning at twelve thousand rpm and burning his main bearings."

The same spin I took on the Kingsley—damn!

25

I heard them . . . trying to make out what sort of man I could be. A woman took my part: "I dare say he is a gentleman." Another contradicted her because I had come on foot.
                                            KARL PHILIPP MORITZ,
                        JOURNEYS OF A GERMAN IN ENGLAND, 1782

Rain still continues to pour down heavily and this has been the most uncomfortable day we have had and the hardest on our teams. . . . The ox teams are improving in their condition, but the horses do not stand it as well.   WILLIAM CLAYTON,
                                                      MAY 19, 1847

Midmorning on May 17, 1847, the Mormons went underwater. Midafternoon on the 19th, they resurfaced. The geography of the march for the next two days, as described by Clayton, now lies under Lake McConaughy. The ground they crossed was "soft and springy," and when the prophet's horse mired in a slough, it had to be roped and dragged out. Altogether, Clayton mentions ten "shoal" streams, four springs, and "many ponds"—hydrology that helps explain why Kingsley Dam was well sited, however ugly a scar on the land.

But the difficulty was less swamp than "bluffs" that continued to choke the trail, forcing Brigham to double-team wagons to get across. On the morning of the 18th, his temper flared and he dressed down his captains for Mormon excesses. Having butchered too many buffalo, the Camp of Israel refused anything but the choicest cuts. Raising his legendary BTUs, Brigham denounced "a disposition in this camp to slaughter everything before them. Yea, if all the buffalo on our route were brought together . . . there are some who would never cease until they had destroyed the whole." Unintended, I'm sure, Brigham critiqued the despoiling edge of American Dreaming that, within forty years, led to a "disposition to slaughter everything" so widespread that the great herds were all but wiped out on the plains. To his credit, he put a stop to it among the Mormons—perhaps the first American Dreamer to get the conservation message.

That night, three miles west of a recognizable landmark on Frémont's map—Cedar Bluffs—Willard Richards took the "Great Pathfinder's" early Rand McNally and waylaid Clayton and Orson Pratt to "enter into arrangements for making a map of our route." Since they'd been traveling by seat-of-the-pants, the idea of creating an up-to-date *road* map—the first in the West—was a good idea. Pratt's obsessive stargazing and Clayton's compulsive need to measure accurate mileage made a natural fit between two would-be cartographers. But it didn't turn out.

Having watched a wagon wheel go around for several days, Clayton likely realized he was the one to be saddled with the drudge work, so when he and Orson Pratt hiked back to Heber Kimball's wagon "to commence operations," the wily scribe casually mentioned that Frémont's "map does not agree with my scale or elder Pratt's observations," which, as he probably hoped, put Pratt off his feed. Clayton suggested they wait until after the trip when they could compare and collaborate on their data. As Pratt was the empiricist-in-residence, any errors would likely prove embarrassing, so he agreed to the delay. But the subject never came up again. Eventually, Clayton put out a Mormon Trail guidebook of his own that did brisk business among emigrants. Stuck with Frémont's map, next day the Mormons crossed six miles "of the worst road we have had from Winter Quarters." Haunted by wolves and rattlesnakes, they gave those names to two creeks.

FOLLOWING THE WRONG GOD HOME

My day started overcast and soon turned as "gloomy," not from cold or rain but from spoiled geography. Plains Nebraska ended and Nebraska's unnatural "lake district" began. Turns out C. W. McConaughy was right. When he resigned in protest from the Central Nebraska Public Power and Irrigation Board, he struck a blow for common sense. Assuming he has living relatives and any of them read this, go down to the nearest courthouse and file a loco-motion to get your ancestor's name off the water. I'm certain he'll rest in peace.

I took the road north of the dam, heading toward Lewellen, and ran into Tacky Town instead—a strip of tourist drive-ins peddling candy, soda pop, beer, junk food, bait, and fishing tackle. One opportunist had removed an old Union Pacific depot and hauled it to its new home on "Big Mac" where he rented wet suits, tanks, underwater spears, and related out-of-geography scuba paraphernalia. Its owner turned out to be a West Coast beach bum, suntanned an artificial copper, and hoping to cash in on a Lake McConaughy micro-wave. I bought two frozen burritos, heated in the only microwave Mr. Suntan would catch in mid-Nebraska, and barely lived to regret it.

"It'll be a zoo," he told me, rubbing his palms together like Scrooge before Marley's ghost showed up. "Memorial Day weekend's coming up. The Greenies are pouring in. Enjoy those burritos!" He didn't say what the "Greenies" were and I didn't ask, but some of them were in the burritos.

I poisoned myself out front, washing the microbes down with a can of grapefruit juice and wandering over to Bill's Marine to gaze with an enraptured couple at aluminum and fiberglass boats with names like Starcraft and Aqua Patio. Make-believe seaside fops wore boat shoes, and people in shorts and alligator polo shirts were loading up on six packs, most wearing sunglasses that looked like modern art, one pair with sequined trim on a buxom, bedazzled redhead. Away from home too long, she made my knees wobbly.

When Cubby Myer at Big Mac Scuba and Sail (wind surfing was in season) told me, "the national spear fishing tournament will be held here next year," I sat down from shock—a horror unprepared for, a nightmare that I hadn't counted on. I'd walked into another story, onto another set. "It's a big draw," he said, trying to cheer me up. "A lot of sportsmen come here to hunt the bays." I closed my eyes and should have put both hands over my ears, but Cubby went on—and on—about such things as "white sand bottoms" and "perfectly clear water" in a voice that . . . well . . . babbled.

Half an hour later, I walked off the highway and down to the water, imagining 148 people, wagons, oxen, and horses disappearing into McConaughy's pale green. The "bluffs" they struggled to cross were now sand beaches, honeycombed with inlets, and I had an absurd image of wagons surfacing like dolphins, only to plunge underwater again. I imagined Brigham on an Aqua Patio, Clayton on a Starcraft, and grieved over how the changes would stun them. On a sand spit a hundred yards away, three girls were topless, lazily sunning themselves. When I focused my Pentax binoculars, they turned, waved, and tugged halter tops over ice-white breasts. Like meat inspectors, they examined themselves, their voices carrying across the water.

"You don't have any tan on 'em."

"Yes, I do."

"Well, I'm browner than you?"

"I guess. But you're not bigger."

"Browner though."

"Yeah, browner."

They ratcheted up a boom box that kicked acid rock across the water. Then I got sick.

It came on fast, swelling my throat until I flopped down in the sand, retching. At first, I thought it was heatstroke. I stripped down to a T-shirt, hydrated myself, sat back, and waited for the nausea to pass. It didn't. Back on the highway, I vomited what was left of tainted burritos and rested. Five miles outside Lewellen, I gave up. Chills took over. Ted Ramos knew it and stopped. "Need a lift?" he asked.

• • •

For two days and nights, I toughed it out in the campground of Ash Hollow, one of the more famous sites on the Oregon Trail. Ted Ramos, good Samaritan, ferried me across the river with the anxiousness of a mother.

"You sure you're gonna be OK?"

"I'll be fine," I lied. I felt like hell.

When I arrived, the campground was empty, so I staked out a spot under a shady cottonwood where I could fight back heat and fever. The tree-lined hollow still contains a spring that watered overland travelers, but it was now a pond posted with acrimonious warnings: "Don't drink the water! No Fishing Allowed!" Getting the tent up was an intermission between puking and making a bum's rush (no pun intended) to the nearest facilities where my bowels emptied. I retched with wave after wave of dry heaves. Before sunset, I stirred out of the tent. Two wary people—a man and a woman—watched me from their perch at a picnic table.

• • •

"Buddy" and "Babe" Brisco were on a weekend tour from Torrington, Wyoming, and Buddy was packing a piece. In the photo I took of them, twilight filters through the trees, and the red notebook (in front of me as I write this) is open on a ruddy picnic table, the black pen like an exclamation point, and all of it—the evening, Buddy, Babe, lengthening shadows, and the random articles a walk is made of—is renewed again. Buddy and Babe Brisco are a handsome couple, weathered and retired, with the shared familiarity that wears itself onto the faces of those who have lived together for a long time and enjoyed it. When I asked Buddy about the gun, he said, "It's a personal thing. But if you mess with me, that's your problem."

Turns out the first straight-shooting leftover of cowboy culture who didn't shoot blanks that I met was a retired mail handler, a genuine rail rider, a man who sorted first-class and magazines in a moving boxcar on an eight-hour run from Omaha to Cheyenne—and a lifelong member of the National Rifle Association. If you got *Time* or a letter from your sister in Oregon, California, Nebraska, Wyoming, or Nevada, chances are it had Buddy's fingerprints on it. "It was all work on your feet," Buddy told me. "Old-timers could tell where they were by the feel of the rails."

Buddy was a sociable conservative of the New West—a trim, straight-ahead version of the late Barry Goldwater. A true believer in the Second Amendment and a man whose right to bear arms couldn't be abridged even after this long-time opponent of the NRA had a go at him, he said, "If the government oppresses us, we can go wherever the hell it is and take it by force of arms. I got my Dad's guns, my Granddad's guns, my own guns . . . and some antique guns." When I asked about the effect of his .22 High Standard nine shot on the U.S. arsenal in case he was oppressed, Babe jumped in to mediate our gentle fracas.

"When Buddy gets on these subjects, people think he sounds like a radical. But he goes out of his way to avoid trouble. He's a peace-loving man and always has been."

Buddy blustered a little at this, as if Babe was accusing him of *not* sticking to his gun. He let on that as a member of the NRA *and* the Wyoming Shooting Association, he was willing to defend even a Canadian's "right to the death to say what you want . . . even if I don't agree with it."

"I'm an adopted liberal Democrat," I said. He kept both hands on the table, although one hand twitched. Feeling less secure, I said goodnight.

I slept on and off for sixteen hours, rising only to heave in the grass or pee. Midafternoon next day, I came around and so did Jim Amos in a silver Ford Econoline van. The *National Geographic* photographer heard about a man in midlife crisis walking the Mormon Trail and tracked me down, mainly because his magazine was planning an article on the Oregon Trail, a geography that wasn't, I told him politely, on my agenda that spring. "I'm stuck with the Mormons for the time being," I said.

Jim's face registered respectful solemnity or sympathy, I'm not sure which, but when I added, "After that I'm taking up drinking again," he perked up, tapped the table with an index finger and grinned.

Amos is a solid man, with winged salt-and-pepper hair parted almost in the middle and pulled back in a way that leaves you with the impression that he's either faced into a six-point gale or is big into hair spray. His face is square, his smile fetching, and his teeth exceptionally white, like a man who's never missed a checkup. I found him infectiously good-natured and sane with a shirt pocket full of ballpoint pens, a book of maps, and a weight of questions, some of which I could answer. His van had a platform built on top, complete with camera mounts and a ladder, where a photographer could stand to get a better angle on his subject. Inside the van was more camera equipment than you'd find in a Forty-second Street discount shop, and that day Jim was using an "experimental" film that Kodak hadn't yet put on the market. We talked for an hour before he cranked the silver van into life and headed for his next photo-op—but we agreed to meet again down the road.

• • •

"More than anything else, polygamy ruined the Mormons," Dennis Shimmin confided next morning. The superintendent of Ash Hollow State Park was in a rush that day, trying to get ready for a long weekend onslaught of "Greenies" heading for the lake. He set me straight: "Greenies," he said, "is anybody from Colorado." License plates in the Centennial State, I discovered, are colored shamrock. Dennis seemed a shade sour when I told him I was walking the Mormon Trail across the river, but with the park opening and things to supervise, he had his hands full, I expect.

"I got things to run and people to fire," he said, "and I don't get all the time I'd like to do history."

• • •

Ash Hollow was one of the most important watering holes on the overland trails. As many as 200,000 emigrants camped there on the long road to California or Oregon. Wheels first rolled into the hollow in 1827 when William Ashley's fur trading company lowered a cannon down a treacherous slope known as Windlass Hill—a drop of 150 feet in 100 yards. The first steep grade on the Oregon Trail—"no little portion of it at an angle of 45 degrees," by Madison Berry's 1850 account—trail buff Gregory Franzwa called it an "angry wash." Nearby was a snug canyon fruited with gooseberries, chokecherries, raspberries, and wild roses. In 1852, on his way to survey Great Salt Lake, Howard Stansbury camped there and found "great traces of the tide of emigration."

Although there was an "Ash Creek" on Frémont's map, on May 20, 1847, the Saints were uncertain whether a "grove of trees" across the Platte River was Ash Creek or not. "We have already discovered that his map is not altogether correct," Clayton wrote, "particularly in showing the windings of the river and the distance of the bluffs from it." There's a simple explanation for this inaccuracy: the Platte scoured new channels every year, moving back and forth across the sand-bottomed valley to suit itself. To check his bearings, Brigham ordered a scouting party across the river, one of whom was John Brown who had "traveled on that road to near (Fort) Laramie last season and knew the place perfectly well." Brown, in fact, would cross the plains thirteen times, earning him a reputation as a first-rate frontiersman. The word "road" is telling since, by 1847, the route on the south side of the river was an already established pike to Oregon and California. Brown came back with sprigs of wild cherry and welcome news: the Mormons were passing a second known Oregon Trail landmark.

· · ·

Ash Hollow is lined with emigrant graves; how many, no one is certain, but big and little expectations died there and most of the people who envisioned them are unknown. Of the known dead at Ash Hollow, at least one Mormon is buried there—Mrs. William Hawk. Killed in a stampede in 1849, she lies among strangers, a mile across the water from the overland trail of her heritage and righteous journey.

On the evening of May 18, 1849, pretty Rachel Pattison—a bride of three months—camped with her husband in the hollow French trappers named Coules des Frères. "The Draw of the Ash Trees" was a long-familiar resting place. On his way east, after discovering South Pass in 1813 (the key piece in the jigsaw that opened the road west), Robert Stuart and a company of trappers rested there for a night. An employee of John Jacob Astor's empire of fur, Stuart trudged to the junction of Ash Creek and the Platte and saw "innumerable numbers of Geese, Brants, a few Swans and an endless variety of ducks."

It had been a wildlife sanctuary for millennia. Rhinos, mammoths, and mastodons sheltered there before the ice age, their bones entombed in the Pliocene Ash Hollow Formation. The Dismal River People—ancestors of the Apache—lived in its cool recesses, disappearing a century or more before the white man discovered the hollow's shelter. Dwarf cedars familiar to the emigrants are still there, but the ash trees have long since disappeared, replaced now by cottonwoods along the creek.

Rachel Pattison would have found the hollow crowded in May, but without gooseberries to sweeten her evening meal. Already tired and aching, she drank from the spring and went to bed. Next morning, she awoke feeling giddy with a ringing in her ears. Likely she prepared breakfast for her husband, already at work with the oxen. Maybe she ate a little, but by eight or nine that morning she felt anxious, uneasiness fluttering in the pit of her stomach and a constriction like a weight around her slim waist. Not long after, she sought the privacy of the cedar shrub and there defecated the partially digested food she'd eaten that morning.

By now she was becoming frightened, a prickly sensation in her arms and legs that extended to her fingers and toes. Her hands and feet turned damp and clammy, her pulse sluggish in her breast and her head beginning to throb. On the way back to her wagon, a weakness overtook her and she crouched in the grass, vomiting until her body, racked by dry heaves, had nothing more to give up. A second uncontrollable diarrhea struck, soiling her undergarments and leaving her terrified. Possibly her husband found her in that condition and carried her to the wagon.

Rachel's vomiting and diarrhea went on for three hours, her defecation producing a cloudy liquid with tiny white fragments. The fragments, known in medical textbooks as "rice water motions," were actually pieces of the wall of her intestines flaking away. No doubt she was treated with any of several "specifics" from the camp's meager supply of medicines—calomel, whiskey, mercury, weak lye, mustard, a few grains of opium or sulfur mixed with cayenne pepper and charcoal, the last given in three doses, one every half hour.

By early afternoon the cramps began, violent and relentless, moving up her limbs and into her chest. She threw herself back and forth in her sodden bed in the wagon, her skin now turning blue or black, her body completely dehydrated, "wizened and dried up to the appearance of a monkey," as some accounts have it. In her agony, she rolled herself into a constricting ball from which even death could not fully release her. Yet she remained perfectly conscious. By late afternoon, she lapsed into sudden unconsciousness; by six at the latest she died. By seven or eight that night they buried her, perhaps in her wedding dress, two hundred yards from where I lay puking and sweating.

. . .

Rachel Pattison died because two ships of German emigrants docked in New Orleans in the fall of 1848. Carrying their cargo of hope to a new world, they also carried the comma bacillus, a pathogenic vibrio, "a sort of small incurvated bacillus." Hence its name. In eight years, the comma bacillus spread from India to central Asia to Russia and from there via trade routes to Europe and America. Arrived in New Orleans, it booked passage up the Mississippi spreading death via steamboat. Early in 1849, it reached the frontier town of Independence on the Missouri River and from there hitched a ride in pioneer wagons heading west along the Oregon Trail. Common medical nostrums—sweating the sick under bedclothes raised on hoops while pouring vinegar on hot rocks between the legs, bleeding the epigastric arteries, feeding the abdomen, or blistering the body with mustard plasters—were useless quackeries.

An earlier wave of the illness had washed ashore in 1832 in the Americas, carried by a boatload of Irish emigrants to Quebec, where it followed the Saint Lawrence River, the Great Lakes, and inland waterways into the heartland. When it reached Philadelphia, handcarts were hauled through the streets to the chant: "Bring out your dead." At Miami University of Ohio, a professor called it "God's Scourge for the Chastisement of Nations." (Today, the Christian Right proclaims AIDS a similar Godly visitation.) It spread like prairie fire across Illinois, jumping the Mississippi into Iowa and Missouri. By July, every family had fled the swampy hamlet of Chicago, "gone in different directions to escape this malignant disease." It drifted south on the Father of Waters, reaching New Orleans by September, its wave consuming thousands. By the time it reached the Gulf of Mexico, it was given a name forever synonymous with death.

Cholera.

By 1835, the first visitation passed, but in the spring of 1848, when Rachel Pattison died, the second was scouring the Oregon Trail, passed along in water or food contaminated by feces. So commonplace was cholera between 1848 and 1852 that few emigrant journals omit references to the disease; it stalked the roads west like a specter, every harmless illness spreading alarm among the emigrants. In 1850, Franklin Landworthy claimed that over a thousand died on the trails, "the principal part . . . victims to that dreadful scourge." At Ash Hollow Creek, where Madison Moorman called the water "a beverage prepared by God himself," the vibrio leached into the common trough, carried from washing soiled linen or by hands besmeared with feces. When it reached the spring, Rachel had but to dip her cup.

. . .

Before recrossing the Platte, I rested at Rachel Pattison's grave in Ash Hollow Cemetery, her crude headstone now protected under glass—another reminder of Dream gone bad. Looking back, I tried to imagine Ash Hollow in 1848—bawling animals, rings of fire in the night, the lowing of a mother to her child, a man bone-weary from the struggle down Windlass Hill huddling over a scant supper, the cloying odor of fresh scat, and a young bride dipping a tin cup into a lethal spring. But Rachel's Dream was now filling with the detritus of ours—three pick-ups with camper tops, pop cans on a picnic table, an RV, and a young woman in a halter top and shorts idly reading in a lawn chair under a cottonwood. She was pretty, like Rachel perhaps. I'd passed her on the way out and knew what she was reading—a romance novel.

In Lewellen, I ate poached eggs, toast, coffee, and juice, nursing my gut until I was sure breakfast would stay down. Outside, the parking lot was crowded with rolling stock of modern "pioneers"—Argosy, Airstream, Vagabond. Dream machines. Music pumped from one as I headed out: Willie Nelson's "On the Road Again." "Jist can't wait . . ."

26

In walking more than in most things, it is each man according to his taste.   MORRIS MARPLES, *SHANKS'S PONY*

Luke Johnson & I went to the top of "Observation Bluff." . . . On the very top of the bluff, a rattle snake challenged for battle. . . . Luke put his rifle to his Shoulder, & wong went the Snake's head.   THOMAS BULLOCK, MAY 23, 1847

"I hate cocksuckers, sons-of-bitches, and bankers," Ellis Countryman said. I didn't doubt it. The man "who was all bunged up" with a colostomy and a steel plate in his head scrambled out of his pickup and met me midroad. "I'm an old bachelor. You must be too, runnin' around the country like you do."

That morning Ellis looked like a hand-me-down denim disaster, a plug fedora on his head and his overalls and shirt months from the laundry. I stood upwind while he talked, trying to ignore a blister and a tooth—in trouble again. Ellis was a man who needed conversation badly, eyeballing the breakdown lane for a chance to get windy. "Got to piss in a pouch," he said.

"Really."

"Twenty years. Cable broke on a stack mower and threw a clamp into my guts. I would'a been OK but I got the gangrene. You think I'm jokin' don'tcha?" Without waiting for an answer, he pulled half his shirt out of his overalls and showed me the scar. It ran around his abdomen like a blue snake, twisting out of sight below his navel.

"That's something," I ventured.

"Got a plate in my skull, too. Stacker broke. Got clipped with a clevis. Damn near cut off my arm, but they sewed it back on. Hell, I'm patched from one end to the other." He took off the fedora, tapped his skull with a grimy finger and put the hat back on, so fast I could barely get a glimpse of dead white pate. "You could see what I mean?" he said.

"Just barely." What a "clevis" was, I didn't know and didn't ask at the time, but *Webster's* defines it as "a U-shaped metal piece with holes in each end through which a pin or bolt is run, used for attaching a drawbar to a plow." At high velocity, think of it as shrapnel.

The oddity about Ellis was that I couldn't get rid of him and didn't want to. He hung on full of wild tales, homilies, and barbed observations about life, lawmen, and lesser mortals, most apocryphal but appealing nonetheless. Proud that an ancestor of his, Nicholas Countryman, had coughed up "forty thousand" to fund one of George Washington's Revolutionary War campaigns, Ellis was a living testimonial that big government hadn't got the best of the family's revolutionary spirit, especially after his heifers came down with brucellosis, a virulent infection in cattle.

"They tried to put me in the state pen for neglect. I kicked the vet's ass. They said I struck a state officer," he fumed, shunting gravel with the toe of his boot. "I'm not a cooperative person . . . an' them state people are as com'nist as they come."

More ornery than a threat to the peace, Ellis Countryman did have run-ins with Garden County officials—a long-standing feud, to hear him tell it. From wrestling lawmen to the ground and taking their guns and badges (his version) to tearing out a cattle guard to keep the highway patrol from using his property for setting up speed traps, Ellis raises hell with city hall. "I give a quitclaim deed—seventeen and a half acres—to the Indians if they'd run off the Nebraska Game

Commission. If they kilt one or two, that wouldn't hurt nothin' would it? You think I'm jokin' dont'cha?"

I said I didn't know but I'd take his word for it.

. . .

How best to describe a man with so democratic a name? Equal parts eccentric, bucolic, hermetic, melancholic, and derelict come to mind. The son of a High Plains mother (she was blind) and a rancher father, Ellis with his bleached belly, scarred sunken forehead ("Had surgery on m'brain"), and an audible creak in one shoulder ("Got busted up") soon came out with the essential sadness in his life. As we drove back to his place to look at his now uninfected cattle and hay meadows, he kept hinting at it, letting it out in half-hearted bursts of verbal angst, working up to a story but choking it off at the last minute. "Ain't it peaceful down there?" he asked. "Ain't them cattle peaceful?"

When I agreed on "peaceful," looking askance at the battered and peeling two-story yellow house with abandoned and rusted farm machinery out back, he finally coughed it up. His sister "came down with the cancer" and put her three children up for adoption. "I went and got 'em," he said. "Kept 'em for eight years."

"What happened?"

"Sister got better. Came and took 'em back." His voice tailed off, dropped to a whisper. "Ain't it peaceful down there?" he asked again.

"Yes. Peaceful."

"You get to like 'em," he said. "Maybe they ain't good for nothin', but you get to like 'em. I offered her my checkbook for those kids. There was words between us. Told her husband what I thought of him. Ain't seen him since."

"How come her husband didn't take the children when your sister took sick?"

Ellis grunted and stared at his boots, avoiding another unpleasant memory. "All I know is that I got 'em," he said.

Faint ruts of the Mormon Trail ran through Ellis's back forty. That afternoon, history lingered like a staggered breath, while Ellis, his arms atop a fence post, came down to the essential hope and loss in his life. Family. His ramshackle house was empty of it, a weathered cairn, chipped away, like Ellis, by nature's flying shards. When he pointed out a shallow stream that drifted lazily in the same direction as the Dream, it seemed named for him.

"Lost Crick," he said. "That's the way them Mormons went. They watered stock along here. But the crick's dyin'. The state drilled an artesian well up above and knocked this crick in the head. Flows no more than a third of what it used to."

I asked him what happened to the kids.

FOLLOWING THE WRONG GOD HOME

"They come out once in a while. One of 'em's a lieutenant colonel just put in to retire. Only forty. Listen," he said, "you want a lift? I'm goin' about a mile in your direction."

"Sure," I said. Some miles are meant for sympathy and it took a load off my left foot. Neither coot nor codger, Ellis was a genuine "countryman"—a reminder of eccentric individualism that so becomes the American Snooze.

"You could see what I mean," as Ellis would say.

• • •

That night, air conditioner on full whoosh in the Shady Rest Motel in Oshkosh, I got a call. The *National Geographic* photographer with the toothpaste smile had tracked me down and wanted to meet somewhere on the road next day to put me in his picture. "OK," I said, also agreeing to swap stories with a *Geographic* writer over breakfast, providing he paid for it. Low on cash, I was in a no-man's-land for my "American Excess" card. Before I turned out the bedside light, I consulted a Gideon Bible to make sure I was spiritually on the right track, opening it at random to a passage that seemed an omen against temptations of rustling, Deuteronomy 22:1: "Thou shalt not see thy brother's ox or his sheep go astray, and hide thyself from them. Thou shalt in any case bring them again to thy brother." It seemed to me that the ox and sheep were safe enough, but the ass in bed was in trouble.

• • •

Boyd Gibbons was a West Coast boy, medium-sized in his late thirties or early forties, with brown hair peppered gray—a former lawyer who had worked for the Feds, written a book on Maryland's Wye Island, and was redeemed from his legal sins by landing a job as a staff writer for *National Geographic*. In jeans, blue work shirt, and Codura rough-out boots, he looked overly familiar with an Eddie Bauer catalog. Over chow at the C&S Café, he seemed freshly scrubbed—glowing, in fact. "Born in California," he said. "Attended a private college in Utah."

There are two private colleges in the Beehive State, Westminster College and Brigham Young University. Which one Boyd attended, I didn't ask. The first is a liberal arts school with the emphasis on *liberal*, and the second is closer in spirit to Bob Jones University. At Westminster a student can get by with a malt liquor T-shirt, a ring in her nose, and a shaved head. At BYU you can't get by with much of anything.

Boyd, who spent time punching cattle on a ranch in the Bitterroot Mountains of Montana, later moved to small-town Utah with its "vacant streets." Naturally, I wasn't part of any Oregon Trail story that morning. For starters, I was on the wrong side of the Platte and his *Geographic* assignment wasn't part of that scenario; but he was snooping, as all good writers do, for other people's stories. Our conversation was polite, his curiosity quickly satisfied when I let loose a barrage of anecdotal dullness, but he listened for half an hour before picking up the tab. Later, when I dug up a copy of his book, I found it to be a tightly crafted account of the struggle between developers and environmentalists on Maryland's Eastern Shore. I thank Boyd for breakfast and book, especially for a line in *Wye Island* that captures absolutely the sense of life in Utah: "The line between insiders and outsiders, between the excluded and the excluders, is a fluid one at best."

· · ·

That night, I slept in a basement, musing on the love life of hogs. Earlier, I'd been forced to cower under yet another bridge as a tsunami of water came in on the wind. I was damp, hobbling, and throbbing of tooth when Richard and Nancy Dunn took pity on me, slopping me along with the other porkers on their farm and offering me snug harbor below the waterline: most of the night it rained, beating a tattoo against the basement windows.

The Dunns raise 2,400 porkers each year, keeping 150 young gilts for propagating pork chops and 12 boars to do the grunt work. Dick told me the average sow is good for five litters (2.3 litters per year on a 114-day cycle) before she goes home as bacon from a supermarket. Litters run about 50/50 gilts (female) to boars (male); gilts are saved for breeding and the boars are . . . well . . . deboared in seven days, after which they're called "barrows," which sounded bad to me and caused me some uneasiness in the night. Breeding gilts are selected for their good looks—dainty feet, bone structure, and porcine curves in all the right places. Most hog matches aren't made in heaven, but occasionally a boar falls in love. "It's true," Dick said, "so help me." Dick is a Presbyterian so I know he wouldn't lie.

Like people, hogs have a defined social order and an active sex life. Too many in a pen causes problems—tail biting and gang wars, for example. But "the subtle nuances of hogritude," says Bill Hedgepeth in *The Hog Book*, "are nowhere more evident than in sexual patterns, protocols, and procedures as they unfold and transpire between consenting adult swine or in the rare case of group sex." For Bill the last is "a brief, horny conga line of humping hogs." But everybody knows a randy old bore is a randy old boar. Every family has one.

Forced into overuse at a tender age, even a randy boar's drive dwindles. Overusing your boar at any age carries with it certain dangers (this is from *The Hog Book*): "Injury from copulation . . . hitting the ground with the penis . . . or getting (it) caught in the fence"—which, as far as I'm concerned, is the origin of the term "going hog wild." Unlike humans, hogs make love in the "parlor" with friends around, "the females without the coyness of women or the practice of little frauds and fascinations to inflame the lust of their mates," says one expert, probably divorced. Boars are more in the mood after a full breakfast. Such uninhibited social life, wrote a dedicated hog man in 1855, makes the hog "the perfect cosmopolite."

About 360,000 hogs are butchered in the United States every day—roughly four per second—some of which add to Dick and Nancy's cash flow, which is why the University of Nebraska-educated engineer got to Dreaming about hogs.

"Ever miss it . . . engineering, I mean?"

"I think about it," he answered, looking into his cup.

"Why did you choose hoggriculture?" I asked.

His laugh was soft. "Oh . . . for all the money I thought I'd make. I graduated in 1972 in a class of twenty-five. Two of us got jobs that year."

I asked Nancy, a Lincoln girl, how she adjusted from engineering to hog farming. She looked at Richard and offered a coy, inflaming smile. "Have some more sausage," she said.

I did, but it was hard to accept that my pork links were someone's dearly beloved.

But hog lore wasn't high on my list that morning, mainly because hog farming is a pungent business requiring nasal amnesia and high-topped rubber boots. Down on a hog farm, mucking out and hosing down took up a large part of Dick's rubber-booted day. He nudged a half-eaten sausage with his fork and finally came to the point: his sister went to BYU and married a Mormon.

"Caused a lot of pain to my folks," he said. "They couldn't go to the wedding since it was in the temple."

• • •

Under an ecumenical magnifying glass, Dick's sister's marriage in a Mormon temple must have seemed like a dagger in the heart to her upstanding Presbyterian mother who wasn't invited inside. "Sacred not secret," Mormons call their marriage or "sealing" ceremony. All the same, for many it has the same ring to it as slamming the gate or trying to attend a meeting of the Moose Lodge. For the true believer, a Mormon temple is sanctum sanctorum and the "endowments" received inside are nitty-gritty essentials for salvation, although some Mormons appear to be more "endowed" than others. It's a spiritually sensitive issue.

The purpose of Mormon temples is unequivocally posted over their doors—"Holiness to the Lord"—a slogan with which few, if any, could disagree. Temples center the lives of Mormons from birth to death, and those who enter must carry a legitimate pass (which looks vaguely like my alien registration card and serves the same purpose—to weed out riffraff and those who don't pay tithes), as well as a suitcase containing formal ensemble that differs from that of Catholics, for example, who can get into any cathedral with blue jeans, sandals, and a Michelob T-shirt.

Anyone who's traveled the beltway around Washington, D.C., and ogled the Oz-like architecture of the local Mormon temple, can't help but be struck by extraterrestrial allure, which makes for a lot of speculation among flying-saucer enthusiasts about the life forms inside. Rites performed in an LDS temple, like those in a Masonic temple, are elaborate and private, including some serious dressing up. When Joseph Smith toppled into history from the second floor of the Carthage jail, his last words were, "Will no one help the widow's son," a Masonic code for "Help!" Any Odd Fellow or Mason would get the idea of a Mormon temple in a handshake.

· · ·

Mormons were far more clandestine about their temple interiors until 1911, when Max Florence, a Salt Lake City self-promoter, smuggled a disaffected Mormon with a bulky camera into the Salt Lake Temple. Gisbert Bossard took sixty-eight "flashlight pictures of the magnificent paintings, altars, furnishings and other adornments of that most magnificent structure into which no one but a devout Mormon is supposed to have set foot since the formal dedication." Using "magnificent" twice in one sentence demonstrates the awe attributed to the event in Utah. The *Salt Lake Tribune* called Bossard's photos "the greatest sensation in Mormon church circles." Max Florence skipped town for New York where he tried to hawk his purloined photos for "hundreds of thousands of dollars," proving how easy it was even in those days to overestimate an eastern audience for anything from Utah.

Recognizing a scoundrel, church leaders refused blackmail, instead ordering the inside of the temple to be photographed by one of their own—Ralph Savage. The results cut into Max's Dream of easy profits and improved the quality of the photos, which—to their credit—church leaders promptly made public. With no takers in the Big Apple and even better photos coming out of Utah for free, Max complained long distance to the *Tribune*, grousing that if the Mormon prophet "made me any madder . . . I'd come back there and steal the Angel Moroni off the main steeple." Max did attract attention, however, when a flamboyant New York showman contacted him about opening a movie studio in Salt Lake City. Max declined—so Cecil B. DeMille invented Hollywood instead.

FOLLOWING THE WRONG GOD HOME

A mile or two from the Dunn farm, Nebraska begins its slow burn into the West. Broken outcroppings begin; erosional forms like stacks of pancakes signal windblown landscapes. Near Lisco, still high on Dunn's hog, I crossed Coldwater Creek, its narrow channel of clear water gliding over a flecked, sandy bottom. Nearby, I ran into the only person who claimed to have arrived in a covered wagon to settle 460 acres.

Lanky Bill Heldt rode under a canvas top to his future in 1906 when he was two years old. In his early eighties, with high cheekbones and a face sandblasted and ragged as the hills, he stopped his pickup and accosted me with the pure curiosity that folks in large spaces carry to strangers. Bill still had a touch of wanderlust in him, as if he were drifting toward unsettled ground on air from a slow leak. Under a lowering sky near the Cobble Hills (formations named by William Clayton), he talked about a gadabout woman he'd met six years before who was walking "the Gold Rush Trail."

"Barbara Moister," he said. "That's a name I'll remember."

When he drove off, I wondered if he'd remember mine.

• • •

Babe Ruth once stepped down off a UP train and ate lunch at the local one-horse hotel in Lisco, Nebraska—the only piece of interesting information I gleaned over lunch in the place, which I ate on the curb in front of a local store. By late afternoon, when I limped into Broadwater and Kep's Café, the conversation shriveled as if an unexpected hot spell had sucked the place dry. Right away, I knew it was my "short pants." Even the waitress looked embarrassed by my bare legs. But when I asked who won Indy, the ice broke. I could hear it crack.

"Why, Sullivan did," an aging rancher bellowed.

"But them Buick engines was short starters. Blew an oil gasket or somethin'," his sidekick trumped. "There was a lot of talk about them engines . . . about speed on the straightaways."

"Hell, boy, they just fizzled."

In the middle of my hamburger, Jim Amos walked in wearing a plaid shirt, tan chinos, and a shoe with the toe cut out. A lumpy sock stuck out from the hole in the shoe, his great toe swaddled. "Chain saw," he said, answering my glance. "Clipped the big one."

He smiled through his mouthful of ivories, as if cutting a chunk out of his big toe was a ticket for a good time.

"That makes two of us with blown feet."

"I'm ready any time you are," he said.

Minutes later, we headed east, Jim's van shushing on warm asphalt, him with his ghostly white smile, and me with my godawful toothache and fire at the heel.

. . .

To the west, darkness gathered like gray paint and spread itself across a canvas-colored sky. Atop the Ancient Bluff Ruins—the same mesa Thomas Bullock called "Observation Bluff"—we stood on an island eroded from the same moraines that formed Scotts Bluff and the Pawnee Buttes of Colorado, all rising from the short-grass prairies like teats on the belly of a rolling dun- colored mare. On May 23, 1847, Brigham planted a buffalo skull where we stood with the names of "the quorum of twelve" inscribed on it. John Brown, the first-rate frontiersman, tacked his name on for good measure.

It was a snake of a day all round for the Mormons, Clayton having gone to view an "adder" George Billings captured and Nathaniel Fairbanks having been bitten in the calf by a rattler on a ledge I'd clambered across seconds before. By the time Fairbanks made it to camp, his "tongue and hands pricked and felt numb." The Brethren slapped a hot poultice concocted from tobacco juice and turpentine on his swollen leg, then prayed over him, dosed him with lobelia to make him vomit, and gave him a double shot of whiskey. In a rare reference to Mormon alcohol in his daily journal, Tom Bullock disguises the booze as "No. 6." Nat's eyes "dimmed" some, but he survived the encounter and the emetic.

Winded, Jim Amos scrabbled up after me with a satchel of cameras, staring toward the leaden horizon as lightning tongued down in the distance and a slow freight of thunder growled across the plains. Behind me, Jim's camera stuttered, its power drive whirring. Camera shy, I turned immediately to stone, a condition that the Osage carps about every time his lens turns in my direction. "A camera can't steal a Canadian's spirit," he once shouted, contradicting his Native American wisdom.

"Loosen up," Jim said, kindly.

"I was never loose to begin with."

"Well, try," he admonished.

Gripped by terminal stone-face, I faced the lens like a profile emerging from Mount Rushmore or stared resolutely into the west trying to look casual but heroic. In twenty minutes, Kodak's experimental film and Jim's talent failed to erode my Canadian geology. As lightning flickered closer, the automatic drive kept up its whirr as Jim tried, in vain, to capture me against a spike of electricity. Only a direct hit would have loosened me up.

FOLLOWING THE WRONG GOD HOME

But electricity was faster than reflex. In three photos he sent later, I'm frozen against a pewter sky, stiff as Lenin in Red Square. We watched the storm slide to the southeast like engine oil spilling from a tipped pan, leaving a thin wafer of sunlight below the black, so beautiful it seemed a Constable painting, artful not real. The same light that drove Thomas Moran to gross exaggeration when he painted the American West filtered over the horizon and touched the river. A dull, dark pencil mark across a crumpled page, the water picked it up and carried it toward us like a burning fuse. To the southwest, across the Platte, a slant of dying sun picked out the stubbed finger of Chimney Rock, a major landmark on the Oregon Trail. For an instant, it stood illuminated—Dreamscape.

• • •

Shortly after noon on May 22, 1847, Porter Rockwell relayed the news to Brigham Young that Chimney Rock was in sight. As they crossed a landscape of "petrified bones" and "tremendous storms," the sense of heavenly turmoil only added to a growing sense of awe. Brigham was anxious to sight Chimney Rock to test the accuracy of Frémont's map, and, in spite of sore feet, William Clayton climbed the Ancient Bluff Ruins and saw it, as I did on the same spot, "plainly with the naked eye." Taller when the Mormons passed by (the top was blown off by cannon-crazy American dragoons), Chimney Rock was the first important geological aberration on the road west—the equivalent of a national monument to folks heading to Oregon or California.

"Americans attach great value to the souvenirs of their history," penned Camille Pisani, an aide-de-camp to Prince Napoleon Paul, on a visit to the United States in 1861. In his travels, Pisani disliked the American penchant for "altars to . . . patriotic ideals." Unimpressed, he counted them all as "pious collections" that "date from yesterday," too recent to be "venerable." For Pisani, the United States was a pretentious young nation fit to ridicule; to Americans it was theirs to praise as they pleased, and Americans of the mid-nineteenth century had little against which to reference their political and social experience except a shared enthusiasm for individual freedom. Monuments to "liberty"—artificial or natural—were bookmarks on a common page of a text hardly begun, and, as George Will reminds us, the country was less a government than an "American project." To Pisani, Americans were compelled to explain "their mysteries to foreigners," since they were busily "preparing material for a legend." He was right, of course, but Pisan-u all the same.

• • •

Back in Broadwater, Jim headed out and I headed toward the Lazy U Motel, the only pit stop in town.

Later, I made a telephone call to Missouri.

"Two days," I said. "Bridgeport."

27

One should never underestimate the pedestrian mind. It's walking slowly that gives you the best view of the countryside.

REGINALD HILL, PICTURES OF PERFECTION

At 5:30 we discovered a party of Indians on the opposite side of the river moving west. . . . Some of the brethren went to meet them carrying a white flag. . . . Some of them began to sing and their chief held up a U.S. flag. . . . They are all well dressed and very noble looking. WILLIAM CLAYTON, MAY 24, 1847

At the Lazy U Motel in Broadwater (no water in sight), I tucked in for another troubled night; the climb up the Ancient Bluff Ruins with Jim Amos shredded the soggy ball of my foot. I felt like George Borrow who, at fifty-one, trekked across "wild Wales" with a notebook and a small leather satchel, his feet "bleeding from the sharp points of the rock, which cut through my boots like razors." Coming upon a stone wall, Borrow flung himself beside it, thinking that he would "give up the ghost." I flung myself on the bed and gave out. When I woke after midnight and limped outside into the cool night air, a yellow waste basket nudged the door, in it Epsom salts, foot powder, and Band-Aids—a gift from the Lazy U's owners, Elfriede and "Pepper" Martin, who reckoned, as Elfriede said next morning, that I was "not much better than hobbled."

For ten bucks plus tax in Broadwater, I got a comfortable bed, Elfriede's shoulder to cry on, an offer to do my laundry next morning, newspapers and magazines to explore, and a promise from "Pepper"—who stole his Gas House Gang moniker from the famed 1930s St. Louis Cardinals center fielder—for a "tour" of Broadwater and vicinity next morning. I read late, night hanging over the two-acre downtown like a sooty poncho while storms brewed in the west only to scud east, pressing me under cones of thunder.

FOLLOWING THE WRONG GOD HOME

Over breakfast at Kep's Café, I sussed out that tornadoes had carried through Banner and Cheyenne Counties again in the night, golf-ball hail in their wakes flattening crops and spewing power lines over the roads: Highway 71 was closed from Gering (a burg I passed flatfooted next day) to Kimball, fifty miles south. In France, at Saint-Symphorien, some enterprising yahoo had cooked up an omelet of 42,470 eggs (Scottsbluff-Gering *Star Herald*), that made the runny yokes on my plate enfeebled by comparison, and the coffee, as usual, tasted the same because it was. After a whirlwind tour with "Pepper," I offset my earlier indigestion with lunch at a competing village eatery, the Broadwater Café, where the home cooking of Opal Lanbhere, who cans many ingredients fresh from the garden, revived my faith. In Opal's larder that spring, 834 quarts of peaches, tomatoes, relishes, jellies, corn, green beans, applesauce, and pickles were making their way toward the tummies of a fortunate few.

"I'm not supposed to do my own canning," Opal said, "so I open 'em in the back room and put 'em in the pot."

"There's a reward for breaking rules," I said, slurping comfortably in a corner.

"Been doing it twenty-three years. No complaints."

What sparked my appetite was a condiment from Opal's larder (Country Bob Edson's All-Purpose Sauce) that took my tongue and twisted it "right good," as Kenneth Loxtercamp defined its sensation—a hefty fellow at the next table who was using it more or less as mouthwash. One of fourteen so named in the USA, Loxtercamp had a pot much larger than the one Opal was stirring, no doubt the result of frequent trips to the Broadwater Café. I took a photo of Kenneth bulked up under his Master Mix Feeds cap and another of buxom Opal wearing a rainbow turban as she fixed chicken and noodles for the next wave of the fortunate starving (about a hen per serving), then collected my laundry from Elfriede, thanked her and "Pepper" for services above and beyond the call, and limped west burping Country Bob. Across the river to the southwest, Courthouse, Jail, and Chimney Rocks wriggled in waves of humidity. Dampness seeped into my shirt, dripped from my hair, rimed my crotch and armpits until—my engine all but stalled—the afternoon turned into a tedious crawl.

• • •

The Z-T Bar Ranch is full of bull, of which its owners are unnaturally proud. It had more semen in its freezers than a cryogenic fertility clinic, all of it from upper-crust Gelbvieh stock and all of it for sale. Fact is, the Z-T Bar runs a fancy stud service without having to send over a stud. What passes for "stud" is fetched in a test tube so far below zero that parts of my anatomy threatened to turn into BB's thinking about it. In fact, Gelbvieh-in-a-jar is frozen stiff—not *sharp, brisk,* or *keen,* but more like *arctic, glacial,* or *polar.* I tried not to think of the sensation something that Siberian would give to one of Jim Sillasen's heifers on a fall morning but relaxed when they told me Daddy-under-glass got thawed in a beaker first. A Gelbvieh bull is an astonishingly handsome animal, which probably accounts for why they send his precious bodily fluids instead of sending him; heifers would go crazy and commit crimes of passion against each other, which wouldn't be good for the cattle business.

Pauline Winnifred McManis Cunningham, whose grandfather picked up the only Sioux survivor among those left on the killing fields of Wounded Knee, looked across the holdings of the Z-T Bar Ranch before letting her eyes rest on me. She sized me up as we stood in her front yard, and once she took her hands off her hips and relaxed, I figured I'd passed the test. I'd come down the lane looking for water to kill a thirst and possibly to wash down whatever history she might give me, third-hand, about the killing at Pine Ridge, South Dakota, on December 29, 1890. ("Pepper" Martin had alerted me to Cunningham family history.) Above us, soggy clouds drifted harmlessly as a slant of sun pushed shadows across the fields—as far from the desolation of the South Dakota killing fields as time and sanity allows.

"You might as well meet Mother," Pauline said. "She's advanced."

"Advanced" sounded queer to me, as if unnatural intelligence had grabbed the matriarch of the McManis-Cunningham clan, but what Pauline meant was that her mother was "up in years." She led the way into a ranch house, set under a cool ceiling of cottonwoods. The inside was cluttered with papers skewed over two tables and a desk—a condition reflecting hard work rather than sloppiness, since both living and family business were carried out under one roof.

Propped up in bed, Fern Minnie Wilkinson McManis had wrinkles like a crumpled hundred dollar bill, the kind that had "advanced" so long that age has no meaning, but her eyes cracked open with a faint glow. Against a pile of pillows, she looked wizened, wise, and ageless as a seer.

"Mother likes a visitor now and then," Pauline explained.

"Who is he?" Fern Minnie asked in a voice with a thread of high-tensil wire running through it.

"He wants to know about Grandfather Wilkinson," Pauline said. "He's from back East. New York."

Mrs. McManis's eyes narrowed as if her last experience with someone from "back East" aroused permanent suspicions. Focused on me, smiling now—too sweetly I thought—she seemed to be examining the possibilities of what to do with a vagrant. Rope, brand, or ride him off the property came to mind. Instead, she fired a slug of condensed family history memorized for state occasions.

"Came down here in Nineteen-Ten," she said. "Homesteading. August thirteen we got here. Elmer Campbell and his people made fourteen in our party. Brought cattle and horses with us. Dad got a load of lumber . . . foot-wide boards . . . and built a place." She spread her hands in a generous measure of twelve inches and moved them above her head, signing vertical. "Stood them big boards up on end. Been here ever since."

Her voice scratched like an Edison waxed-cylinder recording, but from the way she looked at me, as if centuries were nothing to a McManis, I suspected she would last at least until the centennial of the homestead.

• • •

Fern Minnie's father, Byron Wilkinson, crossed into dryline Nebraska when the land was as empty as a Montana sky is reputedly wide. Unsettled in his early years, he eventually got a leg up on his future by hauling government supplies to the Sioux on the Pine Ridge Reservation in South Dakota, which gave him plenty of time outdoors, weathered his skin to the consistency of tanned buckskin, and made him hope for better tomorrows, especially since there wasn't much future in watching road apples tumble, steaming and fetid, from the rear ends of his forward locomotion. According to Pauline and Fern Minnie, Byron Wilkinson "was friends with the Indians."

"They liked my grandmother's bread," Fern Minnie said, implying, I thought, that home baking was the secret to better relations with Native Americans, a point I was keen to pass on to the Osage. "He tried to teach them to build houses. When they got a house built, they still took their clothes out back to dress."

I mentioned that I'd been dressing out back of my own house off and on for a good part of two months, since a nylon tent has things in common with a tipi—low overhead and portability. For a people on the move with the seasons and not settled to life on limited acreage, houses were strange to the Sioux, just as a people without permanent roots were strange to whites. The old cliché, "A man's home is his castle," is white to the bone and, in balance, must have seemed off the wall to the Wind People. When the Ghost Dance swept through destitute western tribes, promising that the buffalo would return in glory, it made Washington twitch—especially after Custer's rout at the Little Bighorn in 1876, which disrupted the centennial hymn to progress that Congress was loudly singing that summer. Ordered to give up the Ghost Dance, the Sioux stoutly refused and a dry tinder of hate was set smoldering—a last gasp that led to Wounded Knee. Whether the Sioux or the U.S. Cavalry opened fire is disputed, but the bloodbath decimated and savaged the natives.

A period photo of Byron Wilkinson shows him standing next to a wagon full of frozen Sioux corpses at Wounded Knee. He stares into the camera, fixed in that awful time, a thin, rugged man with a mustache, trapped in the carnage—a frontiersman who, in the next frames of the picture, would throw corpses into a common pit. Soon after, Wilkinson married, started a family, settled down, and homesteaded on the Platte.

Later in the afternoon, Mrs. Cunningham and I walked down to the river bottoms. "As long as you've come this far, you might just as well have a look at some wagon train graves," she said. "They're all over this country."

What Pauline Cunningham said to me that afternoon came as close to defining the lingering separation accorded Mormon Dreams and other American Dreams as I've ever heard. Spoken within spitting distance of ground Brigham and company had crossed, her words were poignant, truthful, and guileless. Cloud shadows drifted over her meadows like ghosts on the land. She waved an arm across the alfalfa, pointing at a vague spot in the green.

"There's three graves out there," she said. "Two Mormons and a pioneer."

. . .

In his delightful, if dark, book *Grave Matters*, Nigel Barley explores death in multiple cultures. "For the West," he writes, "the problem of death centers on maintaining individual existence beyond the grave. For Buddhists it's a matter of getting rid of individual existence, for the headhunters of South America the problem is one of reassigning it, and for many Africans it is one of dismantling existence and recycling its various components." To summarize in inverse order: 1. break it up and use what's left (Africans), 2. turn it into a personal promotion (headhunters), 3. dump it (Buddhists), or 4. keep it intact and in the first-person singular (Christians). Overall, Western civilization prefers to keep "I" or "me" intact; once off the mortal twig, a personal existence goes on in "spirit." I'm with the Africans. Anything left over is up for grabs. For Mormons, however, life after death comes with an added attraction—an opportunity to move on, not merely in "spirit," but with all body parts intact. (As Gene Wilder says in *Young Frankenstein*, "You can't keep a good monster down.")

Turns out, Mormons are really with the headhunters. Like headhunters, they're big into "reassignment." A lot of folks are rounded up to become Mormons after they die—certainly many more in death than when they were kicking, screaming, or making stump speeches. George Washington and Thomas Jefferson, for example, which might give Washington or Jefferson an ugly turn come any resurrection. Deceased U.S. presidents and other notables are regularly gathered into the Mormon fold, many by a distant Mormon relative who discovered a "family" connection through ardent genealogical research. Catholics, Protestants, and assorted what-have-you's are reclaimed by the thousands to be baptized in absentia and rigor mortis in Mormon temples—by proxy, of course. Think of it as tidying up loose ends.

"Baptism for the Dead" is less a ghoulish than a sacred Mormon ritual to preserve continuity of families in this life and the next. It purports to give people, whether they like it or not, a second chance to sign on with Joseph Smith. In an odd slice of American Dream pie, Mormons believe that if they gather their ancestors (or any others who are handy) into the fold using proxy baptisms for the deceased, the dead have a chance to end up in an afterlife with body parts "reassigned." Otherwise, they've got to take a more difficult route—something equivalent to climbing Mount Everest on one's hands or solo swimming the Atlantic. But for all its generosity, it's an offer that leaves some people, myself among them ... well ... cold.

Frankly, Mormons are a trifle presumptuous about my welfare. I'm touched, of course, as they are, and relieved to know that someone other than Mom has an interest in how I turn out in the long run. But frankly, I wish they'd ask me first. Besides, it's human *imperfection* that makes life or death interesting. In one of his novels, Reginald Hill lets a character speak of the dangers of lusting for *perfection:* "Don't be too hot for perfection, Caddy. It is, in human terms, a form of stasis, the inevitable precursor of decay. Wherefore resist it, distrust it, if necessary destroy it."

Recently, the Jewish Anti-Defamation League sued the LDS Church to stop it from baptizing dead Jews. (Sigmund Freud became a Mormon over his dead body and was only recently struck off the LDS rolls because of negative publicity.) Mormons reluctantly agreed to remove the father of psychoanalysis and other Jews, thus assuring that the Found Tribes of Israel will remain, in Mormon eyes, forever Lost. As Sparky Anderson said, "We can always say it's silly, but if there's one thing we know for sure, it'll get sillier down the road. That's the American way."

"Riding circle" on dead folks has become as much a Mormon practice in the New West as a cattle roundup in the Old—a "peculiar" instinct to corral as many stray jackasses as possible and brand them for eternity. With great respect, I say Mormons have jackasses of their own and don't need to trouble with mine.

28

On foot, weighted down with a heavy burden on his back, Chris-
tian falls in with Mr. Worldy Wise.   MILES JEBB,
                                                     QUOTING *PILGRIM'S PROGRESS*

I consider our view this morning more sublime than any other.
Chimney Rock lies southeast, opposite detached bluffs of various
shapes and sizes. To the southwest, Scott's Bluffs look majestic and
sublime. The prairie over which our route lies is very level and
green as far as we can see. WILLIAM CLAYTON, MAY 27, 1847

By five-thirty next afternoon, a wind moved along the streets of downtown Bridgeport. For the second time, I crossed the Platte River, settled into a motel (the Delux), this time to wait. By six, wind was rising, fast drying out the topsoil, and a skim of dust wafted through the alleys, spilling onto the pavements and ruffling up my pant leg as I headed into burg central. I dropped into Carl's Beer & Pool, sucked down a wet one, and wandered into the loo to bleed the lizard. A sign on the wall read: "In case of a tornado, hide in the urinal. It's never been hit."

• • •

All evening wind sucked at Nebraska, stirring things up, flecking debris against the window, dragging out the day and sumping moisture out of the fields. The Scottsbluff-Gering *Star Herald* reported "crop damage in the millions" from hail the night before; Arlo Jones, a Federal Crop Insurance Corporation agent in Sidney, estimated that "as many as sixty farmers" in Cheyenne County suffered "one hundred percent losses." Describing the storm, he groped for a simile. "Like a lawnmower at its lowest setting," he offered glumly.

Freaky food was in the news again. Frostburg State College served up a mile-long wiener; slices of the 5,280-foot hotdog were eaten by frost-for-brains students along with 9,000 rolls, 27 gallons of mustard, and 20 gallons of ketchup. At an average serving of six inches, enough wiener was left over from the initial circumcision to fit into 4,000 rolls (roughly 2,347 feet by my reckoning), all of which was given to local charities. Whether the charities lopped off chunks, three hundred feet at a whack, wasn't clear, but the article raised enough gastronomic interest that when I read it to the bartender, the guy two stools down ordered two pickled eggs before I realized the subliminal effects of reading food news aloud in a beer bar.

About nine, impatient with waiting, I ventured outside. By now wind was nipping my heels, but in the lee of buildings I was able to shuffle along, although cannonades from the spaces between twice carried me into the street. Twenty minutes later, I was back at Carl's, the place now smoky, cramped, and full of talk about bad weather and belly-up. I took a stool near the window. The same newspaper was parked on the counter, this time with more ketchup on it, but I took it up again. In Casper, Wyoming, Gerald Lenhart, 57—a World War II vet—was run over in a cemetery during Memorial Day ceremonies by Iona Ridgeway, 83. Betty Puettman, who saw the whole thing, claimed that the matronly perp "was frozen at the wheel" and didn't stop until she broadsided another car. As for Mr. Lenhart, Betty said, "He rolled. Several times I saw his face come up."

A face came up for me too, sidling past the bar in a burgundy Honda—an owl's face in the night, two caliginous eyes blinking through a husk of graying beard. When it passed out of the frame, I hustled outside and waved, but the car drifted slowly on. Back inside I ordered two bottles of the cheapest beer, a White Owl cigar, and a book of matches. When he finally walked in, I was halfway through the cigar and condensation was drying on the bottles. We shook hands.

"Well, Chisholm," the Osage said, "you've made it halfway."

• • •

Of all my friends, the Osage is the most infuriating—a man who gathers details like a pack rat gathers glitter and, like a pack rat, he hoards. He's so good at what he does that a person with aspirations to the same occupation suffers depression on reading a few of his crafted pages. Unlike Bill Bryson, whose first rule of travel is "never go to a place with a name that sounds like a medical condition," the Osage actively seeks them out. Several times a year he can be found in towns with names like Toejam, Itchenut, or Pinkeye. Usually these are in some state where inbreeding is considered "local color" and the inhabitants bear a resemblance to Alfred E. Newman. Not infrequently, as he's studying some analeptic destination—say, Runninghole, Kentucky—he explodes for no apparent reason.

In the two days I spent with the Osage probing the nether regions of Scotts Bluff County, Nebraska, he was blown over by high plains wind at Courthouse Rock, visited a Mormon grave at midnight (next to the Burlington and Northern main line), and stepped in some very smelly scatlike stuff on a back street, all normal activities for a man whose next destination is, perhaps, Pfeces, Wyoming. Fussy about dress, even his jeans are pressed. *Tidy* is a word that comes readily to mind, although *compulsive* would do. Glancing at the Osage in the smoky hole of Carl's bar, I recalled Charlie Roemer's last words to me as he left Omaha.

"Charlie told me you bet on some other guy," I said.

He grinned, showing well-formed nuggets of white teeth, swept his thick, silvering hair with a slender hand, and ogled his beer. "My round," he said, tipping the last of his beer back, ignoring my comment, and sliding cash across the counter. It barely registered that the wind had died down. What did register was that my eyetooth was throbbing again.

· · ·

I didn't get much sleep that night. Pain focused my attention, drawing me into a tangle of semi-snooze. By morning, wind clawed at the window again. Outdoors, the sky was scoured by whirling dust; acres of Scotts Bluff County were airborne. Soaring particulates shrouded the town, smearing the air dun in its passage, thick enough to consider planting a crop.

"There goes the county," the Osage said. "A high-velocity move." He had the look of an out-of-sorts badger, the lines around his eyes hatched into webs.

Downtown turned decidedly Stephen King. Grimy-lipped zombies appeared out of the dust, lumbering along the sidewalks with Frankenstein clones, body parts skewed by wind as if only recently attached. We made it to the local library where a prim librarian was noisily prying dust from her nose with what looked like a polka-dot Kleenex. She tucked the tissue under a book when she spotted us, her eyes sad and seepy.

"Can I help you," she said. "You" sounded derogatory. Her look was a rebuke, knowing full well we were using her sanctuary as a storm shelter. A corpulent woman blew in, also seeking refuge from high velocity, clothes akimbo, hanging onto the door as if it were a raft in a wild ocean. "Good Lord," she said. "It's awful out there!"

"Shut the door," the librarian snapped, her eyes following a tongue of dust licking into the temple of words.

· · ·

Next to a bookstore, a library is the safest harbor to shelter the Osage from unpleasant elements. He finds havens among books and tucks into them, reading glasses tipped on the end of his nose and his eyes following lines of prose to the most devious conclusions. In bookstores where there's real money to spend, he forages like a tropical monkey. A rapid once-over-the-titles man myself (a "shelf plunger," he calls me), I miss the good stuff while the Osage nitpicks his way to treasures. Such disciplined snoopery makes me feel a bibliophilic failure, especially the time when I fell backward down the stairs of a bookshop in Sussex, England, tripped by a tome. From his wheezy laughter, you'd have thought I was doing a pratfall in a suit of armor. Sadly, the Bridgeport library contained no treasures, and he emerged from the stacks looking unsatisfied as a eunuch in a bordello.

"It's out of town for us, Bud."

. . .

For two days, we did what most emigrants did in 1847—gaped and gawked. At Courthouse and Jail Rocks, he wrangled his Honda up a sandy track where we observed up close two natural monuments to Dream on the Oregon-California Trail. Most of Scotts Bluff County had blown east, gusting winds carrying only occasional grains of its geology. When I exited the car, the wind flattened me against the side and, spilling over to the driver's side, staggered the Osage like a blow from a truncheon. Later, snooping around the spike of Chimney Rock, my Karloffs anchored me in the wind like diver's boots, but the cheap sneakers the Osage wore ("On three continents," he boasted) made him floppy as a sheet of windblown papyrus. In one photo, he leans into the blast, arms extended like a tightrope walker's balancing pole, wedged into the slipstream to make a sixty-five degree angle. With his mane slightly duck-tailed out behind him, he looks like a hood ornament on a 1950 Pontiac.

"Pretty good country around here," he yelled, borrowing a line from a character he'd met. My tooth was stabbing big time, and I was overdosing myself with painkillers.

Later, atop Scotts Bluff National Monument, where an edge of desiccated West spread out below us and we could see deep into Wyoming along traces of the Oregon Trail, he gave a fulsome lecture on landscape and the American mind— a "Mr. Worldly Wise" disquisition punctuated by references to his travels—typical Osageiana, which I enjoy in the way a man enjoys watching a dog catching Frisbees. Once, in a part of southern Illinois called Little Egypt, he pointed to the road ahead and said, "Bud, this is the longest curve in Illinois."

"What curve?" The road was plank straight.

He pointed to a compass on the dash of his van, his finger jabbing a silent rebuke, and truth be told, the thing rotated ever so slowly from due south to due east without losing the illusion of straight. A man with a neurotic love of detail like his is dangerous, but the pleasure of his eccentricities more than makes up for his occasional on-the-road tantrums.

Now, on a Nebraska street after dark, he was about to explode. Up ahead, a fetid mass had turned slowly saprogenic under an afternoon sun. When he stepped in it at ten minutes past 10 P.M., lecturing now on the medicinal benefits of certain foods after a fire-breathing Mexican dinner, and extracted his shoe from the mephitic sludge, he misidentified the stuff—one of the few times a detail's escaped him. "Oh, shit!"

It was rank, but it wasn't that kind of fertilizer. Still, it was joyous to see him so nimble, like a tap-dancing amputee high stepping around the addled pile.

"Rotten potatoes," he said.

"Sugar beets," I corrected, clearing up his second factual confusion and feeling really good about it.

That did it. He went up like a NASA rocket, blowing smoke, trailing flame, thundering at the heavens, belching torrid language—creative, I admit—into the Nebraska night, a seldom-heard "scatawatami" dialect of native Missouri Osage. When he fizzled out in front of a local bank, a spent lump smoldering in the dark, he searched out a hose and washed off the offense, but a hint of stench remained embedded in the nylon webbing of his "three continent" running shoe and held his attention like a foreclosure notice. He was putting his damp, odoriferous shoe back on when I mentioned a grave I wanted to see. The coals of his eyes blazed for an instant, then winked out. He grew cool and curious.

. . .

After midnight, as we stumbled east along the Burlington and Northern Railroad tracks, we found it. When they put Rebecca Winters in the ground in 1852, she was fifty and had dragged her lingering cholera five hundred miles from the Missouri River before giving up the ghost three and a half miles from what became Scottsbluff. For years, her grave was almost unknown, marked only by an iron wagon rim on which a friend, William Reynolds, chiseled her name and age. As the tale goes, surveyors for the Burlington and Northern came across the site and in a gesture of respect diverted the main line. Eventually, Rebecca's story ran to poetry:

> "Boys," said the leader, "we'll turn aside,
> Here, close by the trail, her grave shall stay,
> For she came first in this desert wide,
> Rebecca . . . holds the right of way."

Not by much. Rebecca lies eight feet from the drive wheels of today's big diesels—so close that draft from a passing freight would cause her living kin to jump back. If the ground trembled and tossed me like a rag doll when I slept thirty feet from the Union Pacific tracks near Fremont, the Burlington and Northern rattles Rebecca's bones whenever a freight rumbles past.

Unlike so many of the faded gravestones along the western trails, Rebecca's is now marked by a hefty granite slab placed at the site by her "numerous descendants in Utah." One of her brood, a daughter—Huldah—became the wife of the seventh prophet of the Mormon faith, Heber Jeddy Grant. She bore him a single child.

By 1902, Heber J. Grant was established in the Mormon hierarchy, which may have had something to do with kindling his interest in Rebecca's grave that summer. A jittery sort, he led the LDS Church for twenty-seven years (1918–45), causing occasional speculation about his "relaxed golf games and trips to California resorts," medical excursions to ward off the shakes from a nervous breakdown. What role his second wife played in his meltdown is unclear, but with a first name like Huldah you've got to wonder.

Close by Rebecca's grave stands a cast-iron hand pump, as attentive as an undertaker. Next to that is a wooden storage box serving as both mourner's bench and chest for the tools to tend the site. A rusting bucket sits to one side so visitors can limber up the pump handle, suck up a quart of liquid Nebraska, and water the flowers. On the night we arrived, there weren't any. Rebecca's memory was littered with detritus from the recent big blow—tumbleweed, snags of paper, even a plastic bag. The grave looked forlorn and abandoned.

· · ·

To say the Osage is sentimental is like saying an Irishman doesn't drink at a funeral. Although sentiment creeps over him from time to time like a fog over deep water, it's an emotion reserved for relationships more central to his life, especially India Pale Ale on tap at his favorite Missouri watering hole. If anything, he's word-drunk. The precise, the exact, and the cleverly arranged haunt his language and his life. Which is why, come to think of it, he acted in character at a moment when I thought he was acting out of it. Compulsively, he began cleaning rubbish off Rebecca Winters's grave.

"Look at this crap," he complained. "Can't Mormons do better than this?"

Although bellyaching creeps over him like an occasional cloud over a full moon, it was more lament than diatribe. Not a bemoaning sort, his nature is best revealed in a Show-Me voice edged as fine-grain sandpaper.

"Why am I doing this?" he groused. "Cleaning garbage off a dead Mormon's grave?"

"To settle old scores," I answered. "Atoning for sins against Mormon missionaries. Like that time in Missouri . . ."

But he looked at me warily, as if I'd caught him in a sentimental act, as if there was a lump in my varnish that he'd prefer to sand down. "Something wrong with you?"

Truth is, I'd slipped into the sentimental myself, missing sentiment entirely. He wouldn't understand, of course. But at that moment, he seemed as grand a friend as any errant Canadian could have and, more than that, a friend to Rebecca Winters and to her kind.

"My tooth is killing me," I answered, trying to get us both out of a swamp.

29

With the vogue [of walking] came special vocabularies. . . . The regular rounds came to be known as "grinds," . . . implying some self-discipline. MORRIS MARPLES, *SHANKS'S PONY*

President Young and Brother Kimball have been privately exhorting some of the brethren to forsake an excess of mirthfulness and indulging in plays, dances, sham trials, etc., which have been carried to excess. APPLETON MILO HARMON,
MAY 28, 1847

Steven L. Combs, DDS, lifted my upper lip and pressed his finger into my gum. Pain sprouted into my sinuses and my left ear. Young, svelte, handsome with chestnut hair and a slim furze of mustache, he tapped my incisor with the heavy end of his dental pick. Agony. "How long has this been going on?" he asked, as if my relationship with a raucous tooth was a song title.

"A fu wks."

"How many weeks?"

"Fee m'be fo."

He took his nimble rubber-sheathed finger away, smoothed my lip back in place, and shook his head twice. "Abscessed. Puss. Nobody wants a root canal."

Since I'd paid up front using the Osage's MasterCard (they didn't take "American Excess"), I responded with a touch of pique. "Except the dentist," I said.

He ignored the jab, but lifted my lip and sledged the tooth again. "How do you do on novocaine?"

"Ptty gd."

"Let's start with a topical," he said, putting a saturated cotton-tipped swab the size of a vaulter's pole between my lip and gum while he assembled instruments of torture. For a second, I thought he'd said, "let's start with a topic," as if the test of whether or not he'd get down to business was scintillating conversation. I spluttered an expletive. Tooth pain puts you out of sorts, as it did William Clayton in the spring of 1847; his chalky English teeth were eroding as fast as the white cliffs of Dover.

Removing the swab, Doctor Combs punctured my sore gum in front, between and behind the tooth with an anesthetizing needle that required two fingers and one thumb to maintain a steady grip—the same grip pitchers use on a split-fingered fastball. Tears gathered, followed by delirious relief as the nagging in the sickened tooth died away. "How's that?" he asked, rubbing my gum, padding it with cotton.

"Fn."

"Now comes the easy part."

Since it was after working hours when he finished, Dr. Combs generously gave me a lift to a motel, a prescription for pain killers (we filled it on the way), and, unexpectedly, his family history. Turns out, his great-grandparents were Mormons who settled in Utah but whose descendants got really religious about the sugar-beet business near Scottsbluff. Although there's no way of telling, the Osage's odoriferous episode might have had a distant Combs' family connection. Made me smile. On doctor's orders, I took two painkillers, crawled between the sheets, and floated into a deep, delicious sleep. Somewhere on the plains, the Osage was heading toward another scorbutic destination—maybe Soretuth, North Dakota.

· · ·

Come morning, minus toothache, I put Scottsbluff behind me, stopping briefly to get a haircut. Two months shaggy when I hit the Scissor Wizards Salon & Sun-Tana, pretty Lori Gowan cut away the offending thatch and, like the Osage raking litter off Rebecca Winters's grave, made me respectable to receive visitors. The "trim," as she kindly put it, was the Osage's suggestion, but I turned down the Sun-Tana part of the deal. No need looking like a beach bum.

By ten, I headed toward the Wyoming state line. Under full steam, the eroding island of Scotts Bluff National Monument slid away and a scabbed landscape loomed ahead, crusty with undersized buttes and rusty under a swollen sun. Towns now dwindled and distances stretched out as the country opened and population shrank. I felt uneasy, a fish out of water.

· · ·

On May 27, 1847, the day the Mormons passed Scotts Bluff, Clayton noted in his journal that "northernmost peak of Scott's Bluffs" was "19 3/4 miles from the meridian of Chimney Rock." He rode part of that rainy day in Luke Johnson's wagon reading aloud to Heber Kimball from the New York potter's own journal—a daily revelation to Heber, I'm sure, because the journal was written by Clayton. The fact that Kimball was short-changed in the reading and writing department didn't prevent him from using Clayton as a ghostwriter. Clayton, as it turns out, simply cribbed from his own journal to keep Kimball's up to date. They crossed Spotted Tail Creek, found the water "very good and cold," but lamented the poor feed. "Vast quantities . . . of prickly pear grow on these sandy prairies where there is no grass," Clayton mentioned.

Hard cases Tom Brown and Porter Rockwell, out hunting, saw "five or six" Indians that sent them hotfooting it back to camp. Now entering lands populated by Blackfoot, Arapaho, Cheyenne, and Crow, the Mormons covered thirteen dreary miles before making camp and, next day, wallowing through another nine hard miles before stalling—wet, cold, out of sorts—almost on today's Wyoming state line. Under a drizzle, Clayton complained, "I went to writing and wrote in Heber's journal till nearly eleven o'clock." Kimball couldn't have been dictating, since he was busy in another wagon "where some boys were playing cards," exhorting them "to be sober and wise." They ignored him.

· · ·

Beyond Scotts Bluff, Brigham Young saw his known world coming to an end. Up ahead lay a landscape where strange or startling images festered the horizon. Entering an altered geography, his mood tipped toward discipline—a gut response, I suspect, to his growing anxiety. Whatever, he resorted to blackmail and threats of murder. Before morning coffee took the chill off the Saints, he ordered "each captain of ten to lead out his company." Platoon formation. Quick time. The clerk read the roll. Too sick to stand, Elijah Newman and Nathaniel Fairbanks answered muster from their wagons. Joseph Hancock and Andrew Gibbons, "absent hunting," and thus accounted for, missed out on one of the most incendiary and revealing moments in Mormon history.

Mounting a wagon box, Brigham's square-jawed demeanor stiffened. "This morning I feel like preaching a little," he began, "and shall take for my text, 'That as to pursuing our journey with this company with the spirit they possess, I am about to revolt against it.'" One imagines a sudden rustling of wet feet, a stuttering alarm in the eyes, an uncertain guilt suffusing the faces of those called onto the soggy carpet of the plains. Riding a hobbyhorse of indignation, Brigham thundered, "I know that you are a ruined people and will be destroyed . . . unless there is a change and different course of conduct. . . . I have let the brethren dance and fiddle and act the nigger night after night to see what they will do . . . if suffered to go as far as they would"—which, as he saw it, was straight to hell. (Acting "the nigger" may have grated on the handful of blacks in the group, but there's no telling. A *Godly* segregation in Mormon life existed for well over a hundred years until the civil rights movement cornered the LDS Church and a "revelation" reversed its all-too-obvious discrimination of blacks.)

Next, the prophet outright lied: "Nobody has told me what has been going on in camp, but I have known it all the while."

Nonsense. Imagining Brigham without informers is like imagining a Mormon prophet having a sex change. Always privy to insider accounts and what he liked to call "intelligence" (for years the Salt Lake post office was in his home), his hand-picked factotums scoured the Camp of Israel sussing out contrariness. Hadn't Heber Kimball tried to shut down a card game the night before? Didn't he warn the backsliders against "profane language frequently uttered by some"? Wasn't he Brigham's right-hand man? Sent to reconnoiter bad apples in a barrel, Heber likely returned bearing rotten news.

In Appleton Milo Harmon's version of the dressing down, Brigham himself was busy "exhorting" the offending brethren "in private" the night before, but in Clayton's account it was Kimball who admonished the cardsharps and backsliders. Not having been present at the time (he was ghostwriting for Heber at the time, you remember), the version that made its way into Clayton's journal could only have come on the wings of Heber's after-the-fact report. As for the Camp of Israel, Brigham had been "watching its movements, its influence, its effects," and was now rising to hammer its shortcomings.

Something in Brigham's harangue that morning smacks of outright staging. If not, the Camp of Israel had gone to hell in a handbasket in six days. A week earlier, after a night of dancing "spent very joyfully among the brethren," Brigham had "expressed himself satisfied with the conduct of the camp in general" and "pleased to see so much union and disposition to obey counsel among the brethren." The two key words in this account are "counsel" and "brethren."

Obeying *counsel* or, more precisely, failure to obey among the *brethren* (*counsel* is a Mormon euphemism for follow-the-leader or there's hell to pay), has always been a burr under the saddle of Mormon prophets. Doing the prophet's bidding, few questions asked, if any, became a dictum that spread easily across Utah's Saints like jam over warm toast, and it was definitely on Brigham's plate on that damp May morning.

Having taken the stump with guile aforethought, Brigham roasted the lot for an "excess of dancing, froliking, playing cards, dice dominoes, and checkers," evils that could run "to neglect of duties, to carelessness, to recklessness, to quarrels, divisions, sin and death." He demanded an on-the-spot "covenant to reform, cease levity, pray diligently, set good examples, and serve God." They had given up "everything," he reminded the slackers: "We had to leave our homes, our houses, our land." Sounding the familiar cry of "persecutions against the Church in consequence of the doctrines of eternal truth," he outlined the Mormon Dream: "Before we left Winter Quarters it was told to the brethren that we were going to look out a home for the Saints where they would be free from persecution by gentiles, where we could dwell in peace and serve God according to the Holy Priesthood, where we could build up the kingdom so that nations would begin to flock to our standard."

Although fear of Gentiles festers less in Mormon minds today, they were always to blame in Brigham's mind. Unwilling to condemn his own outright that morning, Brigham laid the blame at the doors of the handful of non-Mormons in the camp, first blackmailing them with a Hobson's choice (stay and obey or go it alone) and then offering a homicidal cheap shot: "If they . . . introduce iniquity into this camp . . . I swear to them, they shall never go back to tell the tale." Lock-stepped with his prophet's *counsel*, Heber Kimball reinforced the threat, claiming he "would never rest satisfied until his family [was] liberated from the gentiles."

Done thundering, Brigham offered an olive branch to the threatened minority, telling them "they should be protected in their rights and privileges" if they didn't seek "to trample on the priesthood nor blaspheme the name of God." Then, having stewed them in the juices of sin, he put the matter to a vote, all eagerly yea-saying. What other choice did they have? Chastised and downcast, blasphemers and Mormons headed on.

· · ·

The thumb of Laramie Peak began to show itself, dark as a licorice gumdrop, its isolation in the plains often confusing emigrants who thought they'd reached the Rockies. Glued to the asphalt, I soon crossed Spotted Tail Creek where the land was clotted with prickly pear in yellow bloom and the grasses of Nebraska began falling away. Geologically, I walked above a platform of Cenozoic rock, the surface having its origin in volcanic debris carried eastward by prehistoric rivers. Unlike in the more easterly plains with their monotonous repetition, the horizon now seemed broken into scarps and buttes, its features jagged and raw.

On the outskirts of Mitchell (the redbrick old-folks home was once a dormitory for German POWs in World War II), I fell in with Steve Senteny, thirty-five, a part-time painter whose passion is long-distance biking. Balding with wispy blond hair, he had the grainy look of someone who'd been sandpapered, and he looked at me through troubled eyes—one red and one milky. "When things get cloudy," he said, pointing at his faulty eyeballs, "I go to Denver in a hurry."

Steve's problems (three corneal transplants) kept him from getting a driver's license, although he mentioned, "I see well enough to have a motorcycle license," which seemed to me analogous to having the state of Nebraska say, "OK. Let's give the boy a beginner's missile and see how it goes." At his invitation, I rested at Steve's house, cool under a shady porch, drinking a generously offered soft drink while shooting the breeze. His conversation was filled with good humor, as if he'd been waiting for someone to come along to relieve the tedium.

Steve Senteny was the last person to invite me home in Nebraska, and a comfort to have along for an hour or two. He walked three miles with me, his chatter keeping pace with my increasingly ragged footsteps. Unpretentious, curious, and interested about life beyond Mitchell, Steve seemed Cornhusker content, a child of what the Tao master Hua-Ching Ni gleaned to be true: "The highest spiritual life is the ordinary life." But I don't suppose he knew it at the time any more than I did.

· · ·

In Morrill, I gave out. My jaw ached, my feet were cooked, and my will collapsed like a rotted roof. I missed the recent good life with the Osage—food, beverage, conversation, his quirks of companionship. My exchange with Dr. Steven Combs mocked me, as if time in his dentist's chair, like time with the Osage or Steve, was time better spent than shunting over hot tar. Enfeebled by lack of resolve, I wound up in the Bridge Café, shoring up its profits with six cups of "Fraternal Sons of the Soil." My fat backpack drew attention.

"What farm are you runnin' away from?" grumbled a farmer. He looked beat, trapped by weather or depression.

"I'm from New York," I answered.

Turning to his buddy, a woebegone bulk squeezed into jeans, he said too loudly to suit, "Harve, this man's runnin' away from a farm in New York."

"Where's he heading?" asked Harve, showing a line of thin, nicotine-stained teeth. His eyes had slight epicanthic folds and what you could see of them through the cigarette smoke were the color of ash.

"West," I answered. "I'm walking the Mormon Trail."

Harve shoved his coffee away, laced big fingers into a knot on the table. "You're too far north. Your missing all them ruts and graves. Got two graves on my place. Five miles south."

"South of the river?"

"Yup."

Deja vu. "That's the Oregon Trail," I said. "The Mormons traveled north of the river."

"You don't say."

"I do."

· · ·

Around 7:00 P.M., a burden to the café's owner, I ordered two hamburgers, a mound of well-larded French fries, and a Coke, all under the frequent gaze of curious customers—two farmhands in from the fields, three aging couples dressed as if by a contrary wind, and a fistful of the town's better-known stragglers. When two leggy teenagers came in sporting short shorts, the farmhands stopped mid-chew, poked each other on the arms, and mouthed silent whistles. The nymphettes ordered orange juice, hanging around just long enough to raise the testosterone level. When they left with their assets packed into less-than-subtle advertising packages, a large but agreeable woman in a plaid jumper gave the girls' retreating legs a long, wistful look—the kind that made me want to tell my own sad middle-aged story to someone, maybe her. So I did. She persuaded the owner's wife to call a local authority on my behalf, but the news from inner Morrill was thinner than the teenagers' legs. No camping allowed in the town park. She apologized on behalf of the locals.

"There's a lodge back a ways," she said, meaning a wreck of a motel I'd passed outside of town.

"It's bad luck to go backward when you're trying to get ahead, " I said, philosophically.

"Well, if you head toward the Wyoming line, I'm sure you'll find some place to camp. There's lots of open ground out there."

On the way out, I discovered I wasn't the only one lost. Sarah Ann Rairdon was MISSING. It said so in big letters on all four sides of the poster. Her photo stared at me as if she'd known all along she was doomed to disappear—a thirteen-year-old kid, four years younger than my own daughter. Thinking about her parents' agony dragged me out of my cesspit of self-inflicted fortunes. I could sleep in a ditch if I had to; but for Sarah's parents, there was no shelter, no rest, and perhaps no news of her for the rest of their lives.

At the edge of town, a cop stopped me, checking up on a stranger. Young and taciturn as a zombie, when he looked at my driver's license, I asked him about Sarah. "One of hundreds," he said, suddenly taking pity on a man old enough to be his father. "Go ahead and camp in the town park, Scott. Any trouble, let me know." I gave him a parental blessing, split for bed ground, and packed it in, listening to the hum of a transformer from the electrical substation across the street. But there was too much light in the night and the tent was raked by moving shadows—perhaps the ghosts of lost children.

PART 3

Over the Great Divide

30

*And the moral of my whole story is that walking . . . gives an
intimacy with the sacred things and the primal things of earth
that are not revealed to those who rush by on wheels.*

JOHN FINLEY, "TRAVELING AFOOT"

*I feel quite unwell yet and have been sick all night. At a quarter
past eight we proceeded onward, found good level traveling, the
day cool. . . . We soon struck a wagon trail which evidently leads
direct to Fort Laramie.*   WILLIAM CLAYTON, MAY 31, 1848

Squinting hard into my future, I made out a sign. It hung on two rusty chains
from a wooden crossbar, its bottom edges chained horizontally to anchoring
posts. The silhouette of a cowboy on a bucking bronco, one hand on the cinch
rope and the other waving his hat against a background of snow-crested mountains and a giant orange sun, reminded me less of a welcome than an invitation
to a rodeo. "Howdy," the sign enthused. "You're in Big Wyoming." And then I was.
June 6, 1985. 2:30 P.M. Fifty days on the road.

Beyond Scottsbluff, the North Platte River thins to a trickle. Towns fall away
and land stretches out, forcing the eye to function as a wide-angled lens. Even
humor is "dry"; in high desert towns, only laughter seems liquid and what little
there is seems measured, as if one mouthful too many might deprive others of
their full share. Such desolation is partly illusion, since people do live there, but
living seems as dehydrated as the land, and it requires a leap of faith to imagine
how American Dreams could get started in so fractured a landscape. Less barren
than when Brigham passed by, the land still gave off a forlorn aura so unfamiliar
that I grounded myself under an overpass for half an hour. Outside its shade, a

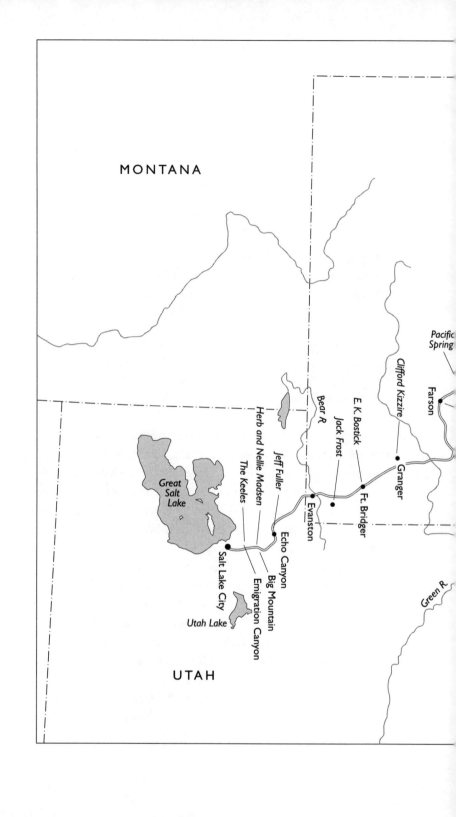

MONTANA

Pacific
Spring

Farson

Clifford Kizzire

Bear R.

E. K. Bostick

Jack Frost

Granger

Great
Salt
Lake

Herb and Nellie Madsen

Jeff Fuller

The Keeles

Ft. Bridger

Evanston

Green R.

Echo Canyon

Big Mountain

Salt Lake City

Emigration Canyon

Utah Lake

UTAH

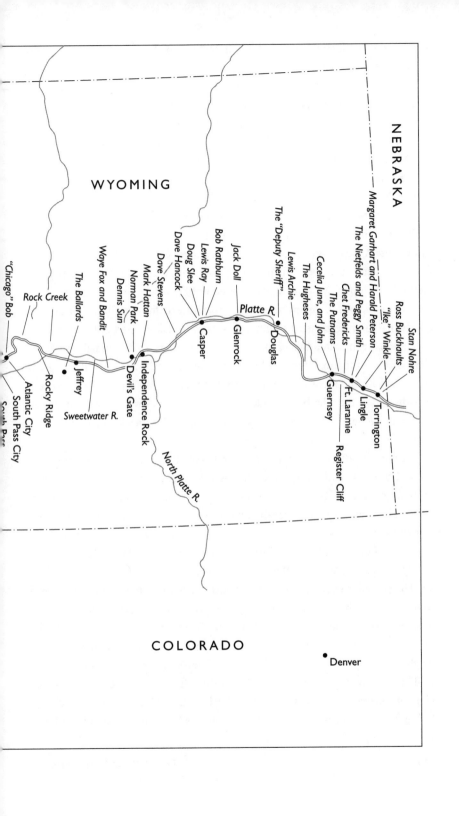

NEBRASKA

WYOMING

Stan Nohre
Ross Buckhaults
"Ike" Winkle
Margaret Garhart and Harold Peterson
The Nietfelds and Peggy Smith
Chet Fredericks
The Putnams
Cecelia June, and John
The Hugheses
Lewis Archie
The "Deputy Sheriff"

Torrington
Lingle
Ft. Laramie
Guernsey
Register Cliff

Jack Doll
Bob Rathburn
Lewis Ray
Doug Slee
Dave Hancock
Dave Stevens
Mark Hattan
Norman Park
Dennis Sun
Waye Fox and Bandit
The Ballards
"Chicago" Bob
Rock Creek

Platte R.

Glenrock
Douglas

Casper

Devil's Gate
Independence Rock

Jeffrey
Rocky Ridge

Atlantic City
South Pass City
South Pass

Sweetwater R.

North Platte R.

COLORADO

• Denver

scattering of lank trees struggled like desert prospectors down to sucking on stones. Ninety degrees.

Reminders of Dream's uneasy past soon showed up. I passed the Horse Creek Treaty Grounds where Sioux, Cheyenne, Arapaho, Crow, Arikara, Assiniboin, Mandan, Gros Ventre, and Shoshone met in 1851 to parlay a "New Deal" with Uncle Sam. The grandest and most colorful Indian council to ever assemble in the West, it was called to set "firm" tribal boundaries. On September 8, a cannon belched and the council convened.

For three weeks, the tribes haggled over details of their new homelands, finally negotiating the Treaty of Fort Laramie (the council was held thirty-five miles east of the fort where grass was more plentiful), but Congress didn't ratify the treaty since white Americans insisted on making changes to their advantage. So-called firm boundaries became "infirm," falling away with each new load of settlers. In spite of this duplicity, a general peace lasted until 1864 when settlers, having broken their word one too many times by encroaching on the boundaries Uncle Sam had sworn to protect, tasted a wrath of their own making, part of the same acid cocktail that eliminated Custer on the eve of the American centennial. Cut Nose, chief of the Arapaho, lamented both hope and promise broken: "It is a good earth, and I hope there will be no more fighting. . . . We have to live on these streams and in the hills, but I would be glad if the whites would pick out a place for themselves and not come through our country." But they kept coming.

· · ·

Legal justification for taking Indian lands was always "a knotty problem," says Harry Chrisman, and deserves mention here, because it applies as much to Mormons as to any other American Dreamers in the West: Mormons don't have clean hands, although they did better than most in their dealings with native peoples. Struggles over lands in Cache Valley, Utah—the tribal hunting grounds of the Northern Shoshone—led to the Bear River massacre in 1863. With Mormon complicity and guided by Porter Rockwell, U.S. troops stationed in the Salt Lake Valley slaughtered over two hundred fifty Shoshone men, women, and children in a frigid winter ambush, many as they slept, a despicable action characterized in the *Utah History Encyclopedia* as a move to "chastise some . . . Indians who had been raiding emigrant trains." Butchery pure and simple, it was undertaken to preserve Brigham's self-proclaimed "right" to occupy Utah's valleys as he pleased.

The case for the takeover of native lands was first made in 1823 (*Johnson and Graham's Lessee v. William McIntosh*) with Chief Justice John Marshall presiding. Ruling for the white man and Christianity, Justice Marshall carved out a dubious and Dreamy loco-logic: "However extravagant the pretensions of the discovery of an uninhabited country into conquest may appear, if the principle has been asserted in the first instance, and afterward sustained; if a country has been acquired and held under it; if the property of the great mass of community originates in it; it becomes The Law of the Land and cannot be questioned." The flaw, of course, is that America wasn't uninhabited. Marshall's decision is "Might Makes Right."

Adolf Hitler took a keen interest in similar fictions of the American West, gobbling up the novels of Karl May. A hack writer, May forged an Aryan hero in Old Shatterhand whose dark-skinned nemeses were the fictional "Ogalla" Indians. White supremacy, however unintentional, ran through May's Wild West like cholera through a wagon train. By one account, Der Führer took the swastika from "an ancient Hindu symbol" for the sun. But there's another speculation: Der Führer stole an American Indian glyph for his genodical cause—a totem once used as a cattle brand in the Nebraska Sandhills. A native sign for "Good Luck," Hitler made the swastika bad luck in spades for millions of European Jews.

•   •   •

Torrington, Wyoming, is a farm-and-cattle town getting bigger and doing a bad job of it. Grumpy as usual, I ordered a coke at the local Pizza Hut and sat outside, sipping slowly and taking in the local ruins. After discovering South Pass, the gateway to the far West, Robert Stuart and his Astorians wintered nearby in 1812, holing up in hastily built log cabins. Riding a sugar high, I holed up in the Blue Lantern Motel but ate dinner at a pricey restaurant. A hog late to the trough, my only choice was the "cold plate," which featured a plate correctly advertised and food partly identifiable, one lump disguised as "chicken." The Holy Roman Emperor Henry IV (1040–1106) said, "I wish there was not a peasant so poor . . . who would not have a chicken in his pot on Sunday." Not this chicken, Henry. Not this pot. But Henry's regal sentiment survives, having floated the Atlantic where it washed up on the democratic shores of Dream. First used by Herbert Hoover as a slogan to jump-start Republican voters in the wake of the Great Depression, "a chicken in every pot" drifted in another direction to become, more or less, the "good times" message in the bottle of Franklin Roosevelt's New Deal.

Back at the Blue Lantern, I thumbed through a copy of a local tabloid, its news as cold as my dinner. Larry Bird and the Boston Celtics were in a shooting slump; Gillette, Wyoming, was making shaky plans for Jell-O wrestling; two deputy county attorneys had been indicted on drug charges; and the Bureau of Indian Affairs was calling for a meeting of the Arapaho since the tribe wanted to hire better legal eagles, something they didn't have at Horse Creek a century earlier. Other than a clutch of ads, those tepid stories were the best hard news the *Torrington Telegraph* could tap out that day—about as much as a fingerless man on a telegraph key.

I cranked up the air conditioner, doused the light, and fell into a cool, drowned sleep.

• • •

"I'm a full-blooded Norwegian," Stan Nohre told me. He made Norh-WEE-Jun sound as Scandinavian as any refugee from Min-Eh-SO-Tah, which he was. An advertising sales whiz, Stan was the closest to a basset hound in disposition and temperament of any human I'd met before or since, a condition abetted by bad luck and religion, which gave me the best two lines on the walk.

"My wife ran off with her minister," he said. "I still miss him something awful."

Under his expensive tan suit and open-collared shirt, Stan radiated dustyard casualness. A pair of black-rimmed specs made his eyes woefully large, and his face, hound handsome, folded into deep-set lines. His mouth was large, his lips well formed, his chin firm, and his voice throaty. So likable and loose is Stan that when his prize Ford Mustang was stolen, a local newspaper ran this headline: "Red Mustang Stolen, Ad Man Discos."

Stan spends parts of his winters in Guadalajara, his springs in Las Vegas, occasional summers fishing on Chantry Inlet on the Arctic Circle, and what's left over on the road for his Norco Advertising Agency in Dickinson, South Dakota. When I met him in the motel parking lot, he was planning to make a late-morning sales call on the Valli High Supper Club, which, neatly etched on the card Stan gave me, was "south of Torrington on the Valli High Road." He offered me a "Dinner of the Month Membership," but I declined since I wasn't planning a long stay. To tell the truth, even if I had been, I wasn't keen on dining in a chophouse where there was a better-than-average chance that someone would sing mutant show tunes from *South Pacific*.

Wolfing sunny-side-up eggs and toast like a man uncertain of his next meal, Stan explained his life as a Las Vegas low roller. "Mormons run Vegas," he explained. "They don't gamble, so they're reliable. Howard Hughes hired them by the busload." His voice squeezed itself into a narrower bandwidth and came out thin and high like an old Edison gramophone recording. "Hell, I make money without ever handling the dice." Avarice looked over my shoulder and Stan's magnified left eye began to water. He pushed a thick finger under his glasses and brushed a bead of sweat away; the folds in his face lifted into a wry smile. "When the house wins, I win," he said smugly.

"It's supposed to be the other way around."

"Not at craps. See, I bet with the house against the player. If he rolls seven or eleven, I lose. But the odds favor the house. Most times a player doesn't make point. So I double the amount on the next player." Now his voice turned soft as a basset's ear. "There's only one time the house wins and I don't . . . if the roll comes up twelve. You don't lose your money, but you don't win either." He leaned toward me. "Between you and me, I learned it from Kid Kalin and Abe Rosenblum."

"Sounds like a punch-drunk fighter and his manager," I ventured. Stan bared his teeth and looked as if he'd go for a mailman's ankle, but I wagered a small side bet, asking him what he remembered best about gambling on the strip. Highs. Lows.

"I hit a royal flush and a straight flush at the California Club in half an hour."

"Big bucks?"

He looked hangdog. "Nah. The total winnings from both hands was about ten bucks. But it was good times. I once played poker fifteen hours without eating. Stayed twenty-seven days in Vegas that year and it cost me nineteen bucks and change."

We parted in downtown Torrington, what was left of it, and he gave me a parting shot, baying velvety as a wandering hound. "If you play on your money, don't tip. But if you come up a winner, always tip. It's called the 'Nevada Law,' but it works for me anytime."

Later, I realized that Stan Nohre left *me* a tip. High finance or low life, Stan's "Nevada Law" seems to work—win, lose, or draw.

· · ·

Torrington advertises itself as "Wyoming's cleanest and friendliest city." *Clean* is easy to understand since anything not tied down exits the city limits in a high wind. When I dropped into the state brand inspector's office on the west edge of town, I managed to interrupt three pairs of feet up on two desks. Otherwise, their owners were having a good day. Both desks were littered with paperwork and a window-mounted air conditioner whined in the background.

Knowing nothing about brands, I let loose a stream of questions that Ross Buckhaults did his best to answer with a straight face. Ross had a blue one-size-fits-all baseball cap with "Brand Inspector" on an embroidered patch, not unlike those worn by a SWAT team. Close-cropped dark hair sprouted from under it. With oversized glasses, he looked vaguely nerdy.

Buckhaults's office is tacked on to the Wyoming Livestock Commission Company where every Wednesday "load lots" of cattle are sold to the highest bidder at

Wyoming's "Largest Livestock Auction." Ross makes sure there's no funny business when the gavel falls on a load lot—no doctored letters, numerals, symbols, monograms, or combinations on any critter's flank that shouldn't be there, since a brand is a rancher's trademark.

Seared into a cow's hide in the spring, branding came to be known as "ironing the calf crop," and the person who did the burning was, naturally, "the iron man." A good iron man learned never to risk a "hair fire" with a too hot iron, since "fire brands" don't take well. A brand artist wouldn't use a forge or coal fire to heat his irons either, but stuck to wood.

A skilled iron man knew that if a brand wasn't burned deep enough, it would peel off or "fade." If it was burned too deeply, it would cook the flesh and "blot" the mark. So he rocked the hot iron from side to side to let air under it and uniformly sizzle the hide. Otherwise it causes "warting," a scaly growth that catches a steer's tail when the tail flicks against it. On the other side of the law, a talented but crooked iron man could alter almost any brand to make it look "long on the hide."

Brands are read from top to bottom, Ross told me, and a cowboy can read most of them from a distance. Triangles, bells, pots, kettles, tools, spurs, hearts, and God knows how many other symbols are used in brands. An "open brand" is any capital letter not "boxed," that is, with nothing around it.

Learning brand language is essential to a cowman. In a "bench brand"—say, one using a heart—the heart rests on a downward curved bracket; a "flying brand" is a figure with wings; a "forked brand" is one with a V-shaped prong; and a "connected brand" runs two or more symbols together. A round "O" is the "circle brand;" somewhat flattened it's a "goose egg"; a small "O" inside a large "O" is a "doughnut." John Chisum of New Mexico used the "running brand"—a single seared line running from shoulder to tail, also known as the "fence rail." A letter or figure "too tired to stand up and laying on its side is a 'lazy brand.'" A diamond brand with an "A" inside is a "Diamond A." If it sits above a straight line or "slash," it's called a "Diamond A Bar." Tipped on its side, it's a "Lazy Diamond A Bar." Real cowboys know this stuff. They can tell an "R Lazy Two" from an "O Bar O" and a "Y Four Connected" any day. Some of this material I dredged up from Manfred Wolfenstine's *The Manual of Brands and Marks*, mostly to save face with Ross if he ever reads this.

• • •

When I walked into Buckhaults's cluttered office, three dusty pickups were lined up out front like winded nags loosely roped to a hitching rail. Inside, dust motes floated like satellites where sunlight filtered around the edges of the drawn blinds. The whole place was an embodied sigh.

"About rustling . . ." I ventured.

"What about it?"

"Well . . . does it still go on?" I almost added "in these here parts," but it sounded tinhorn.

Buckhaults scratched a sideburn, looked pleadingly at the two other occupants of the room who so far hadn't paid much attention to the dude in short pants, because I was standing at a counter and they were sitting on the other side. One looked at me suspiciously. One picked up a wad of newspaper and smacked at a fly. They ignored Ross too, going back to their low-drone conversation about iffy cattle prices.

"Sure, rustling goes on, but not much these days," Ross said. "Mostly it's mix-ups on open range. One rancher's steer mixes in with another rancher's herd and gets branded over. When they get shipped here, we try to sort things out."

"Anybody ever steal a herd?"

His eyes rolled. "Only in the movies," he said.

Any brand too complicated to read is called a "fool's brand," but Ross knew I wasn't that complex. To him, I was a "Brand You Can Read By Moonlight," as seasoned cattlemen call anything oversized or out of place. From the expression on his face as I headed for the door, I could tell he'd pegged me as "Jackass Bar None."

. . .

To understand Wyoming, a person first has to understand that it was Dreamed up on anthems of opportunity and a gospel of grass. In 1847, east of Laramie Peak, the North Platte Basin contained 8 million acres of grassland. Beyond Laramie Peak and South Dakota's Black Hills lay another 40 million. Having crossed the first, I was now entering the second—a region where streams like the Horse, Slate, Sheet, Sweetwater, Pumpkin, Big and Little Laramie, Ash, Deer, and Chugwater are thin ribbons draining a whole lot of nothing and less rain. But it was everything to a would-be cattleman. Cattle and grass abundant are a stockman's first religion and, beginning in 1870, God's earthly promise was "open range." In 1985 an estimated 150 million cattle were fattening up on American Dreams.

The cattleman's Genesis was written by Hiram Latham, whose book *Trans-Missouri Stock Raising* caused an exodus to the High Plains. Latham's graze-to-the-ground prophecies (he told the Colorado Stockmen's Association to "never cease" until "every acre of grass in Colorado is eaten annually") became a ticket to the pastures of the Lord, which is why the Union Pacific Railroad laid hands on him and ordained him its high priest. In 1871, two years after the Union Pacific and Central Pacific joined rails near Promontory, Utah, there was grazing land aplenty to sell along the right-of-way through Nebraska and Wyoming. The Union Pacific invited Latham into their holy-of-holies, overprinted copies of his gospel of grass, and gave them away by the boxcar load back East. Another "American" sacred text, it started things rolling.

Latham used the oldest scam in a missionary's bag of tricks—testimony—filling his Good Book with letters from the newly converted. The Honorable William H. Hooper, five times Utah's territorial delegate to Congress, joined in the hymn to heavenly fodder. Even L. P. Bradley, brevet brigadier general of the U.S. Army, foamed at the mouth over Latham's scripture: "I believe all the flocks and herds of the world could find ample pasturage on these unoccupied plains and the mountain slopes beyond. The largest herds and flocks in the world will be found right here where the grass grows and ripens untouched from one year's end to another."

In 1871, the Union Pacific began selling off its land—the twenty miles on either side of the track from Ames, Nebraska, to the Rockies that enterprising Clark Ames had swindled from Uncle Sam. A decade later, needing more priestly assistance where Latham came from, they reached out and offered the mantle of prophet to General James S. Brisbin. Palming silver, Brisbin obliged. Brisbin's book *The Beef Bonanza* had even more wide-ranging appeal—a Newer Testament replaced Latham's Old. "The growth of this West of ours has been the miracle of the nineteenth century," Brisbin preached, selling a vision that offered an alternative to "the overcrowded East and the tyranny of moneyed aristocracy"—well-known American Dream themes.

Latham's *Trans-Missouri Stock Raising* and Brisbin's *The Beef Bonanza* were to the gospel of grass what *The Book of Mormon* is to the gospel of Joseph Smith—part prophecy, part religious conviction, part hallucination. For many Americans it became a gateway to broke; for others it became a restoration of earthly promise. From Brisbin and Latham, Americans took the epic of man against land, the myth of the cowboy, vigilante justice, and the legacy of the National Rifle Association. Backed by Union Pacific cash, *The Beef Bonanza* became the West *as advertised*, and Brisbin's subtitle *(How to Get Rich on the Plains)*, a lyric from a dayDream. Today, the plains are still flushing out people headed for somewhere else. In 1955, when Charles Towne and Edward Wentworth wrote *Cattle & Men*, they borrowed a line from the Apocrypha to describe American cattlemen:

"Their discourse is the stock of bulls." "Bulls" should be singular. The western horse opera isn't yet over, but as I walked deeper into "Big Wyoming," I imagined a fat lady singing.

31

Six hundred miles I (very neere) have footed,
And all that time was neither sho'd nor booted;
But in light buskins I performed this travell,
O're hill and dale, through dust, dirt, flint or gravell.

JOHN TAYLOR, THE "WATER POET," 1649

I continued with a great deal of Fever through the day . . . having
on our right very Sandy Bluffs and Rocks. . . . Continued our route
and in a short time heard the cry of "I see Fort Laramie," when all
were anxious to see an habitation once more.

THOMAS BULLOCK, JUNE 1, 1847

Three miles west of Torrington, a blue station wagon squealed, made a U-turn, and cut me off. A woman in a blue-and-pink flowered blouse got out and in my face. Dust from her fast brake boiled off the shoulder, drifting in whorls. She whacked at it to clear the air, dark eyes masking grim determination.

"You don't look like an ordinary tourist," she said, sizing me up, hands on her hips. "Let's have a talk."

"What about?"

"Get in the car. I'll drive you back."

"Back where?"

"To the station."

"Why?"

"Because that's what I get paid for."

"You don't have anything to do with the state brand inspector's office? If you do, I apologize . . ."

"I'm with KGOS," she said, studying my confusion intently. "Radio. You're my feature of the day. For tomorrow."

Being a "feature of the day" for tomorrow on KGOS AM made it clear how desperate small towns are for "color commentary," and plucky Donna Anderson, who skillfully groped for anything interesting or substantive, pummeled me with questions for the better part of an hour. As nearly as I remember, the topic was "Freaky Tourist Visits Our Town." Ad-libbing, I tried to sound pleasant and refreshing, offering windy observations like this:

"If Mormons walked on asphalt highways in 1847, they would have caved in early. Zion would be somewhere in mid-Nebraska . . . not further than the Wyoming state line."

An "expert" is anyone fifty miles from home, Mark Twain said. Good enough for me. But the real story, as I saw it, was that Donna Anderson had nothing whatever to do with the Wyoming State Brand Association.

• • •

In Lingle, Harold J. "Ike" Winkle, formerly of Wyncote—a town that no longer exists except in memory—drove me around in a 1962 Comet, which he hand-painted pink and yellow with a four- inch latex paint brush. "Looks pretty good," I told him, "and it's got a nice texture."

"When I painted it, I took some ribbing," Ike allowed. "'You made an awful mistake,' one fella said. 'You don't dare rob a bank in a car like that.'"

We were chuffing along a back road in Big Pink, looking for the PF Ranch, the closest thing to a historical landmark in Lingle. Never a careless driver and not a fast one, Ike was watching the scenery crawl past when Pink's engine began to lug. I drew Ike's attention to it.

"Well, I guess it is," he said. "One thing these cars don't like is too slow. I better put it in intermediate."

"Does it ever go into high?"

He furled his lip, whuffing so I could see the breeze startle his gray mustache. "Not on a day like this."

The PF Ranch was purchased at the height of the cattle boom (1879) by James Pratt and Cornelius Ferris, bigwigs at the Marshall Field Company in Chicago. Squat, one story, built of native stone, the house (1890) stands on naked ground, and except for a fringe of trees, a shady pillared side porch, and a dustyard dog, it looked like a helluva place to live—though Ike had lived there as a boy of four-teen. How old he was when we met, I didn't ask, but he'd lived sixty-one years in a neat white-frame cottage in town where he nursed his mother through her last illness (she died thirty years earlier) and hung on in its cool interior. The dining room table was still set for company, its china covered with a large cloth as they used to do in midwestern farm homes during "fly season." Stocky, broad-shouldered, and terminally pleasant under a panama hat, Ike snagged his nom de plume as a skinny kid from a literature lesson on Washington Irving's "Legend of Sleepy Hollow" when a teacher dubbed him "Ichabod," which he later shortened to "Ike" to avoid the childhood tag "Ikky," which "sounded disrespectful." Indeed, there was a literary quality about him, a gentleness of habit, and a distinctiveness of speech, as when he said of a chore needing to be done, "I have a man well recommended to me."

Ike's life was so rooted in the sleepy hollow of Lingle (he'd been once to Chicago, Milwaukee, and Spokane) that my evening with him was shaded with colors of a quiet life well lived with no hint of ill will or confinement. If he hadn't traveled beyond Chicago, his mind had. "The railroad brought lots of foreigners to Lingle," he told me. "Some of 'em was from Pennsylvania."

A bachelor, Ike holds a degree in chemistry from Hastings College. After he kindly let me wash up at his kitchen sink, I noticed the diploma hanging on the wall of his living room. Outside, my tent was pitched on Ike's lawn, the pack tucked inside out of sight. I'd made it to Lingle late in the afternoon, drenched in sweat and worn ragged with heat. Now, freshened up, I was looking at another man's history. I asked Ike if the college degree had done him any good. I thought he might, like Richard Dunn, the Nebraska hog farmer, have a nugget of regret in him. Not so.

"I still read articles on chemistry and know what they're talking about," he answered. "The basics haven't changed much."

Ike's ambition was to become a doctor. "I was nineteen when an accredited high school opened," he said. Three months shy of twenty-three when he graduated, his mother insisted he go on to college. At Hastings State, he completed his requirements for medical school, but the family had no money. When he managed to save some, "the Depression put an end to that."

Afterward, he moved from one job to another—farmhand, filling-station attendant, road construction, lumberyard foreman, interviewer for a federal relief agency, three years in the county treasurer's office—the last a political job. "You know how those things are," he said, chuckling. "When the next election came up, I was out of work." Then he had a stroke. Unable to work, living on Social Security disability, he took up local history, remaking himself once again from his interest in shards of the past, particularly in keeping a daily diary, which he began in 1970.

Nothing on the walk thus far seemed so poignant as my conversation with Ike that day. Humble and considerate, he nursed a stranger as he had his mother, happy to be able to meet my needs for water, shelter, conversation; his generosity was nowhere more evident than when I asked him if he felt the American Dream had passed him by.

"No, I don't," he said. "This is personal, I guess, but I call at the hospital every Sunday. There's always something to give back . . . and I've lived a full life."

I invited him to join me for dinner at Lira's, a Mexican café he'd recommended just off the highway. He begged off, eager to study my trail journal under a dim light at a small table set against the wall, curiosity gathering on his face, like moths to a flame. He broke off long enough to confuse me.

"They usually have three or four entries at Lira's," he said, leaving me with the impression that Lira's would be a safe place to chow down for a man running from the law. But I got it wrong, as usual. "They list the entries on the menu," Ike went on. "Good food. Good people. Make you feel right at home."

I spent $7.13 on two entrées, including chips and salsa, burritos smothered in green pork chili, and two bottles of beer. The place was jammed. Dark-eyed Mexican waitresses managed to raise a faint lust in me in proportion to the pepper in their salsa. Out front, a man and his wife were nearly killed. A blue sedan (eastbound) crossed the yellow line, tempted too soon by Lira's home cooking; a blue pickup (westbound) slammed into it nearly head-on. Between mouthfuls of burritos, people rushed to the windows. In less time than it took to say "hot sauce," a local cop was on the scene. Minutes later an ambulance. The trauma team laid a body on a gurney, strapped it down; then the ambulance screamed away toward Torrington, fading like a last breath. The driver of the pickup leaned against his shattered cab, waving off a policeman who put his arm out to steady him. As I exited, he shook himself loose and walked toward the café, visibly shaking in his faded green work shirt and blue jeans, running his hand through salt-and-pepper hair, eyes foggy.

"They tuk one out'a that car," he said, looking at me but seeing something else. A tow truck was already at the scene, moving the crushed sedan whose windshield was cracked into a spider's web where a head had smashed against it. A woman in shock huddled in the back seat of a police car.

"How many were in it?"

"The ol' fella they tuk away an' one other." He looked back at his shattered truck dripping green radiator fluid onto the asphalt. "I drove that heap sixteen years. Maybe I ought'a gone fishin'."

Next morning, over a fat-filled breakfast at the Stagecoach Café, I asked Ike if I could look at his diaries.

"No reason why not," he answered, "but I've got a little side trip planned. After we eat."

Finished with eggs and bacon, Ike drove southwest, ending up in a sugar-beet field among lines of Mexican laborers hoeing the rows, most under wide-brimmed straw hats, runnels of sweat staining their shirts. Already on its way into the mid-nineties, the cloudless morning steamed under a pale, watery sky. Among all the new agriculture was a red granite marker about six feet tall.

"Mormon history," Ike said.

Turns out, it was a monument to a stolen cow and an ignoramus. The cow belonged to a Mormon emigrant headed for Utah, and the ignoramus was Lieutenant John Grattan. Fresh out of West Point, Grattan rode from Fort Laramie to an Indian village (now the beet field) to confront the accused. The Sioux chief refused to give him up, but promised to deliver the thief to Fort Laramie next day. Stupidly underestimating the danger, Grattan was intent on showing who was boss. Warned by the chief that he had, at best, a toehold on mortality, the lieutenant ordered his men to fire. Grattan died instantly in the answering volley. Minus their commanding officer, soldiers broke ranks, only to be hunted down. All told, twenty-nine troops were killed in the fight (described on the monument as a "massacre") along with several Sioux. Next day, the dead were buried in a common pit.

The Bordeaux Trading Post was situated near the Sioux village, and, on August 19, 1854, spectators watched the killing from its roof. Seth Ward, one of the traders, later claimed Grattan's interpreter was drunk and couldn't translate the conversation with the Sioux chief. Maybe so, but the Historical Landmark Association of Wyoming was also under the influence when it erected the monument in 1953. No mention is made of the stupidity of the commanding officer.

Ike asked me what I thought of it.

"It's too small," I said.

Fact is, I'd like to live in a country where heroes are buried in unmarked graves. That way, we'd have to keep their stories alive, retelling them to remind ourselves of what's best in all of us. Nincompoops like Grattan should have blockbuster public monuments to remind us that the line between *cupidity* and *stupidity* is thin, at best. When I asked Ike what the Mexican laborers were doing, he replied, "blocking and thinning the beets."

"Maybe they'll do some blocking over the blockhead," I said.

• • •

A person could forecast weather from Ike Winkle's diaries. Sun, rain, sleet, snow, hail, and wind appear in them regularly as the equinoxes come into rotation. Written in a compulsively neat hand, they are stuffed with commentary about people who make up a life. They cluster in its corners like friends at a church social or a barn dance, alive again as fragments, small pieces of their history flaking off, a word painting removed but intimate in the mind. "Jack mowed the lawn this afternoon" or "Walter Elmore's in intensive care" make up most of the day-to-day. "5-2-65 Went with Bob and Fay to Guernsey and then up to the old Chicago iron mines. 1st we went to the north side and looked over some old house foundations etc . . . drove upon the old railroad right of way and got clear up to the mine. Saw two old shafts and other interesting things had chicken dinner."

Ike's diary is filled with the dearly departed, his hand releasing anecdotes onto the paper, scraps that only he can make whole. He saves clippings, obituaries, notes that interest him, and writes alongside them moments he's saved up.

> Ray "Shorty" Walker, 72. I've known Ray or Shorty since 1933
> or 1934. He lived on his mother's homestead . . . Sec 10-25, 5
> or 5 1/2 miles south of Fort Laramie.
>
> Anne Phelps 5-17-85. My family got acquainted . . . just after
> they moved onto their homestead.
>
> Effie Watkins 101. I knew Effie at the center in Torrington. She
> was short and always walked with a spry gait. She sat at the
> table in front.

Sitting at Ike's table, I was taken by the richness of the small. Ike led an open life. A western flycatcher rose from a wire, swooped into an umbrella of shade under Ike's trees, splayed his wings, and glided into the darker recesses of the branches. "Got him his dinner," Ike said. "Oh, I enjoy that."

So did I. When we parted company standing in his shady yard, I wondered why it was I liked so many extraordinary Americans like Ike when I couldn't get a handle on their Dream.

I passed the band shell on my way out of town, still gaudy in its red, white, and blue stars and stripes nine years after the hoopla of the 1976 bicentennial. On Main Street, I passed the U.S. Male Barbershop and stopped to look over "Injun Joe" who sat in a worn chair in front of Wagon Wheel Western Wear, deaf and

FOLLOWING THE WRONG GOD HOME

dumb, holding this sign: "Injun Joe says these gotta go." Constructed life-sized of rubber, he looked whacked-out on joy juice, the stereotypical grinning Indian drunk. Evidence of a mindset that dies hard in the West, it made me think of Nekiia and my beery evening in the Odessa Bar. I took a look at what had to go—moon boots. Jesus, I thought, I am in another world.

. . .

Brigham camped near Lingle on May 31, 1847. Crossing "barren country," Thomas Bullock was taken sick with "Auge and Fever," perhaps because the night before he'd eaten some prickly pears "stew'd" in sugar; a toxic experiment concocted by J. C. Little. He was given a strong "composition tea" in the afternoon and later dosed with an emetic (lobelia), but even after inducing the pukes he was fevered for two days and was carried in Willard Richards's wagon. Orson Pratt mentions "muddy, yellow" streams and the "monotony of landscape."

On June 1, a day "fine but cool," the Mormons passed four bodies of Indians "tied up in Skins and fastened to the Trees." An hour and a half into the afternoon march, a cry went up: "I see Fort Laramie!" Across the Platte, four miles to the southwest and forty-eight days after leaving Winter Quarters, the Camp of Israel was again in sight of white-man's habitation. Brigham and Heber Kimball climbed a bluff to take in the view where they "offered up . . . prayers together." Whether of thanks or trepidation isn't clear; some of both, I'd guess, since they were about to cross the Platte and join up with the Missouri "pukes," the Illinois "suckers," and all other Americans on a common road west. From Fort Laramie to Fort Bridger, they entered the American mainstream for the last time in the century.

. . .

In the summer of 1849, another dogged walker arrived at Fort Laramie: "The last arrival from the frontiers is a solitary foot traveler, who says he has come all the way from Maine without the assistance of either railroad, stage, [or] steamboat. He is accompanied by a savage looking bull dog, has a long rifle over his shoulder, on the end of which he carries his baggage, consisting of a small bundle the size of your hat. He has no provisions but gets along pretty well by sponging on his fellow travelers."

Minus the bulldog, I arrived in much the same way, although I was in a "savage" humor when I walked into Margaret's Café. From Lingle, the road was squeezed between sugar-beet and corn fields, the highway choked with traffic, and a stream of RVs towing boats with watery destinations in mind. One towed a twenty-foot cabin cruiser named *SUM FUN II*. Drafting past, I gave it the finger, sincerely hoping that *SUM FUN I* had been holed and sunk by the idiot who was looking for water in a desert. But I waved like an old friend at the other idiots who followed. Someone, no doubt as grumpy as I was, returned an Italian salute.

Margaret Garhart, who owned the café, knew a walking thirst when she saw one and came over, unasked, with a large glass of iced tea. "Make you feel better in no time," she said. Behind her was a fair-skinned, balding man in an orange shirt who offered me his card—"Harald Peterson, Margaret's Café, Fort Laramie, Wyoming, 82212." I accepted it and was about to tell him I already had plenty of insurance, thank you anyway, when I noticed that Harald was ... different.

"Harald keeps a guest book," Margaret said. "He's wondering if you'd like to sign it."

I did and counted it an honor.

· · ·

Harald Peterson was abandoned by his mother in a farmhouse near Laramie when he was nine months old. A law officer with the incongruous name of Missies Smith found him squalling the next morning. Harald's father—an intinerant ranch hand—was seldom home off the range, but he came back on weekends after that and eventually remarried, again to the wrong woman. His stepmother "beat Harald with a piece of stove wood," Margaret told me. The baby was paralyzed, and the stepmother was sent "to a girl's home in Sheridan for eight months."

Aunt Margaret Garhart took Harald into her home and heart when he was eighteen months old and raised him as her own, but he never got over the paralysis completely. One arm was still useless.

"After a year, he was up and hobblin' around," Margaret said. "One leg shorter than the other."

Margaret saw him through a series of "handicap schools" and rehabilitations, but the child was brain damaged. Doctors said he would always remain a two-year-old in his mind, but Harald had beaten some of that as well, serving up food and friendship in Margaret's café, which she'd owned for twenty-three years. He became a fixture and a friend to everyone—an industrious, gentle man with a smile like a candle in the dark. When I signed his guest book, I noticed signatures from all over the globe, including Walt and Evelyn Connor from Painted Post, New York, my neck of the woods. Gerhard Froll from the Black Forest, West Germany, wrote: "My family and I together have been here to visit old Fort Laramie." In 1982, a kindred spirit had written, "Say it ain't so, Harald. Rock'n'Roll is here to stay."

It is but I wasn't. I ate a hearty meal, Margaret's cooking fine by me. When I left, I photographed them, side by side outside the front door, below a faded Pepsi sign. Harald is gently pot-bellied, and Margaret stares into my history in a sleeveless dress splashed with large flowers such as a child might paint. I never mentioned the Dream to Margaret or Harald because I knew I was as close to it as I was likely to come.

32

We walk for a thousand reasons, because we are tired of sitting,
because we cannot rest.　　　　　　　　　EDWARD THOMAS,
　　　　　　　　　　　　　　　　　　　　　　THE ICKNIELD WAY

J. B. [J. Bordeaux] remarked . . . that there never had passed Fort
Laramie such a company as this. . . . When Ex Governor Boggs
passed thro . . . railing about the Mormons . . . he was told that the
Mormons could not be worse than [his] company, for they were
fighting . . . every other night.　　THOMAS BULLOCK, JUNE 4, 1847

A way station on the road west with a history like a well-worn tapestry, Fort Laramie has been talked about, written about, and lied about extensively. Important to the early fur trade, several forts were assembled at or near the junction of the Laramie and North Platte Rivers, beginning with Fort William, Fort Platte, and Fort John. As each unraveled, another sprung up. None of the names took, and by 1841 the Laramie River lent its name to the most recent adobe structure. The river took its name from Jacques La Ramie who, so goes the story, was murdered by Indians near its banks.

Traders and trappers bargained in its shadow; Indians traded pelts for trinkets and blankets. By 1849, when the fur trade gave way to emigrant throngs and expansionist Dreams, the army took it over and eventually rebuilt it, but the entire overland traffic on the Oregon, California, and Mormon Trails stopped at its door.

The far West begins at Fort Laramie. Five hundred miles beyond the Missouri frontier, it was a magnet of last-chance civilization where outbound Americans huddled before moving on into terra incognita and across the Great Divide. Old Fort Laramie no longer exists, and the fort built by the U.S. Army after 1849 is mostly in ruins, fragments of its barracks standing like tombstones along a ridge.

Its most famous barrack, "Old Bedlam," has been restored, but today the fort's only purpose is to recreate military history as designed by the National Park Service; but even with black-powder cannons, a summer make-believe encampment, actors in nineteenth-century costume, and big booms from period artillery, it's less history than show time. In the tourist crowd, I heard none of the mixed tongues and dialects (Yankee, Southern Cracker, French Canadian, Mexican, Native American) that made for whoop and holler when the place was booming in the 1840s.

In 1847 prices at the fort were outrageous—five-cent tobacco at a dollar fifty, flour at twenty-five cents a pound. "Taos Lightning," was in plentiful supply, semi-lethal rotgut used by trappers to fuel Indians and relieve them of their pelts. "Broken Hand" Fitzpatrick, mountain man turned part-owner of the fort, once confiscated several barrels of "Taos special" and dumped them into the Laramie River, worried that unscrupulous traders would use it to distill a drunken uprising. Like Fitzpatrick, Brigham also fretted about an uprising: worried about the safety of the Latter-day Saints in a stockade full of Gentiles, and angst-ridden lest there be trouble, he ordered a scouting party to cross the river, himself taking the lead.

• • •

For two summers, trouble had festered all along the overland trails. In 1846 the historian Francis Parkman wandered the western plains and, at a fort at the junction of the Arkansas River and Fountain Creek (the Pueblo), he encountered a party of Mormons planning to head west on the Oregon Trail that summer. Recently arrived from Mississippi, they had no idea they were a year ahead of their Prophet, Seer, and Revelator. Parkman was barely out of the saddle when they "began earnestly to discuss points of theology." The Boston Brahmin listened for an hour to Mormon complaints about "Gentiles" before remounting and spurring his horse, "happy that the settlements had been delivered from . . . blind and desperate fanatics." Rumors of Mormons with "ten brass field pieces," all "armed with a rifle, a bowie knife, and a brace of large revolving pistols" fissioned along the Oregon Trail in 1846. Rumors of equally hostile Gentiles harried the Mormons as Brigham was crossing Iowa's mud before the Saints holed up at Winter Quarters. "No one could predict what would be the result when armed bodies of these fanatics should encounter . . . their old enemies on the prairie," Parkman wrote.

But by the summer of 1847, things had cooled. At the fort, Brigham was "shown up a flight of stairs into a large room" where he met the "principal man, J. Bordeaux" who "answered all questions put to him." Satisfied that the Mormons

FOLLOWING THE WRONG GOD HOME

weren't in danger, Brigham hired the fort's "flat boat" and, without incident, the Camp of Israel crossed the North Platte on June 3, 1847. People at the fort were so impressed with the Mormons, wrote Thomas Bullock, that they "several times expressed their great pleasure at seeing us . . . & stated their intention of visiting us when we get settled."

The day after the Mormons crossed the North Platte—almost a year after the discussion of "theology" with Francis Parkman on the Arkansas River—the "Advance Guard of the Mississippi Saints" caught up with Brigham at Fort Laramie, swelling the original group: 10 men, 8 women, and 5 children were added to the Camp of Israel. Now halfway to the Salt Lake Valley, and 161 strong (only 4 dropouts), they traveled with 79 wagons, 96 horses, 51 mules, 90 oxen, 43 cows, 9 calves, 3 bulls, 16 dogs (they'd lost one), and 16 chickens.

• • •

I crossed the Laramie River after lunch at Margaret's. There were two bridges: one closed to traffic and sanctified by a historical marker (Crook headed for the Little Bighorn across it), and a newer one sanctified by entrance fees courtesy the National Park Service. I paid for sanitized history and walked to the visitors center. Arrived on the same site in 1847, William Clayton and Thomas Bullock immediately fell to work measuring the fort with a "tape line," outside *and* in. Turns out Fort Laramie was lopsided—eleven inches out of whack in length and five inches in width, details that made it into Bullock's journal. Minus Bullock's compulsive accuracy to the inch, Fort Laramie was 167 feet long and 121 feet wide.

Why would Clayton and Bullock measure the place? Aside from the Mormon obsession with record keeping, one idea comes to mind: the stockade was important to Brigham's plans. Halfway from the Missouri to the Salt Lake Valley, it was a possible takeover opportunity waiting to happen, perhaps as a way station to Zion—a strategy that Brigham carried out a few years later at Fort Bridger. With his compulsive need for detail and what he called "intelligence," the Mormon prophet could easily have coveted a lopsided fort, although nothing the Mormons ever built themselves was that far out of plumb or extravagant. No offense, but as an old friend once quipped, "If a Mormon had been present at the Last Supper, he'd have asked for a separate check."

• • •

I came across Peggy Smith in the first stages of culture shock. A fellow Canadian, she was pretending to mend a period cavalry jacket under the shade of an army tent (circa 1876), and her costume for the day—a full-length red gingham skirt and bodice, white apron, and a matching bonnet—hinted at the nineteenth century but didn't confirm it. The tents were too clean, the iron beds too neat, and the trunks at the foot too recently painted. With all the stage props, including Peggy, an air of make-believe suffused the place. Besides, there were no Indians around: the "Laramie Loafers," as Native Americans were disparaged in 1876, had disappeared.

Peggy hailed from Windsor, Ontario (opposite Detroit). A young, dark-haired, apple-cheeked woman, she'd endured a thirty-three-hour bus trip to take a volunteer job with the park's "living history" program. When she passed through Cheyenne on her way to "living" at Fort Laramie, she came down with shock and was not yet recovered.

"I just about died," she told me. "Hills I expected, but there were absolutely . . . absolutely . . . no trees there. The only things I knew about the American West was from stuff on television." On brief experience (she'd been there a week), Peggy allowed that "the West would have been a great adventure."

When I mentioned that settlers weren't allowed into Canada's western territories until the Royal Canadian Mounted Police first brokered treaties with the natives, she looked askance. "What thrill is there in the Mounties going first and the settlers following?"

Thrill had that all-American joyride sound to it. "Don't you feel like you're in a movie out here?" I asked.

"Sure, sometimes . . . and I get nervous," she answered. "When they find out I'm from Canada, they always ask me about hunting . . . and guns. They don't know much about Canada. They know a lot about hunting and guns."

"Canadians have plenty of guns."

"They don't talk about them."

"The West wouldn't be 'wild' without guns," I said. "It's part of the *thrill.*" I can be nasty at times. "That must have been part of your training."

She looked at me as if I was belittling what she'd traveled thirty-three hours to impersonate. Turns out her education on how to be a "historical interpreter" was the *National Parks Service Manual* and a book called *Glittering Misery: Dependents of the Indian Fighting Army*, by Patricia Stallard. The latter I was never able to find, although its main title, I thought, nicely summed up Manifest Destiny. Peggy dutifully consulted them. "I had to be on the job the next morning," she said. "I haven't had much time to read since."

The fort's cannon belched suddenly and an acrid smell of black powder drifted in on the breeze along with the nervous clapping of tourists. A knot of visitors walked toward us, trailing children and exhaustion, all hoping, I suspected, that the admission price would lead to some fun after all.

"Why should Americans care about Canada?" Peggy asked, watching them close in. "They don't have to worry, do they?"

"Why?"

"They're rich."

Christ, I thought, she's already singing Dreamsong.

In Graham Greene's *The Confidential Agent*, there's a question that parallels what was running through my mind while Peggy tugged at her gingham dress and nervously watched the cluster of tourists descending on her tent: "If we lived in a world . . . which guarantees a happy ending, should we be as long discovering it?"

• • •

When Mormons crossed the Platte in 1847, they joined up with the mainstream of Americans—a concern for Brigham, since Gentiles and Mormons usually mixed like oil and water. Leaving Fort Laramie, the Latter-day Saints and all others followed a common road as far as Fort Bridger, where the trails split for Utah, California, or Oregon. Having crossed the Platte River into the mainstream trail as they had, I was now faced with a more diverse American Dream to think about—a reverie hinted at by James Hutchings on June 21, 1849. A non-Mormon, Hutchings made this entry in his diary when, as a forty-niner, he headed for the gold fields of California: "Fort Laramie. We see some of the results of starting on this journey without a good knowledge of your traveling companions. Few agree; all seem reckless; and few, who were known as good men at home, are good on the journey. There are no social influences to restrain natural impulses."

It was not Brigham's communal "home for the Saints" but Hutchings's good men turned "reckless" that came to define the West in popular imagination as rough and ready self-interest. Rugged you-know-what. For the next three hundred miles, my journey was in all-American tracks, crossing a common path that shared Yankee *individualism* and Mormon *community*. If my left foot walked in one extreme of Dream and my right foot in another, I was no longer free to think of the Mormon's trek as a discrete historical or religious exodus on a road less traveled, as they tend to think of it. Beyond Fort Laramie, it was everybody's common road.

With former enemies before and behind them trailing dust and old hatreds, Mormon diary entries betray both nervousness and uncertainty, especially toward the dreaded "pukes." Movements of "the Missourians" are carefully noted, and, while Mormons fired up their forges to aid in resetting wagon wheels for some of the Show Me State travelers—at a price, of course—they were wary and competitive, often making an early start "so as to pass . . . and get the best chance for feed at night." Like the mainstream today, it was every man or company for himself or itself. Brigham's objective was to save his own. Period.

• • •

That night, I slept alongside the Laramie River, isolated from government show time, courtesy of Albert and Marjory Nietfeld, an elderly couple, who had graduated from Fort Laramie's one-room schoolhouse in 1915. Mr. Nietfeld was separated by a foot in height from his silver-haired wife and walked with the aid of a stick, but even stooped he was a tall, imposing man. When the fort's buildings were auctioned off in 1890 (locals still call it the "Abandonment"), Mr. Nietfeld's father purchased the Long Porch Barracks, which he turned into a store, a hotel, a dance hall, and a saloon, the last of which I could have used before turning in.

Albert Nietfeld was a bear for local history. But he wasn't sold on PhDs. "Some of them educated boys get carried away," he told me. "One of 'em found a big earth ring near here. Saw it from the air. Had a whole page in the local paper about how the cavalry exercised their horses on it." A grin burned across his face, his eyes tearing up.

"What happened was this," he said, trying to plug a laugh with his fist, but it spilled around the edges before he got it under control. "One day in about nineteen twenty-seven or eight, I was goin' to town. Dwight Walker . . . he ran the county road grader . . . was settin' in the middle of the field . . . 'en he motioned me. So I come on over."

The laughter started again, surfacing like an artesian well. He capped it off after a gallon or two leaked out. "'Dwight,' I says, 'What the hell are you doin' with the county road grader in the middle of this field?'"

Albert tottered on the concrete stoop of his home, shaking from telling it. His wife, now infected, sniggered while her husband replayed the tape of long-ago tomfoolery, hand across his tummy as if you could rub away a belly laugh. "'Albert,' Dwight says, 'I'm supposed to be makin' a racetrack because they's goin' to have a rodeo. Albert, how do you build a racetrack?'"

By now I was as far gone as the Nietfelds, chortling like a Buick with a blown head gasket.

"So . . . so I says, 'Well, Dwight it's kind of an oval with banked corners.' So he says, 'Albert, you stand out here an' I'll run a circle around you.' Don't you know, we graded us the ugliest damn racetrack in Goshen County. But if that ol' boy from the State University wants it to be the field where the cavalry trained their horses, he can have it. It'll sure get Dwight out of a bind."

33

Talking tends to make men aware of their differences; walking rests on their identity.　　A. H. SIDGWICK, *WALKING ESSAYS*

Traveled four miles and then mounted the bluff in a gradual winding pass and then down a steep hill. . . . We have passed a very rough road this day.　　APPLETON MILO HARMON, JUNE 4, 1847

We traveled ten miles to Warm Springs which are out of the rock and warm enough to wash.　　MARY STUART BAILY, JUNE 23, 1852

Register Cliff looms a few yards south of the Platte River near Guernsey, Wyoming. To reach it, those headed for California, Oregon, or Utah took the same road I did next morning, dropping toward the Platte River on a bone-rattling descent called "Mexican Hill." Briefly, I stopped to look at the grave of Mary Homesley (1852), whose name carved on a fieldstone is now encased under glass in a white-washed obelisk a few yards off the trail. The next day, June 10, marked the 133rd anniversary of her death.

Situated on the Fredericks Ranch, Register Cliff was once the site of Nine Mile Station, a pit stop for the Pony Express. "Chet" Fredericks, a man with a face weathered as the cliff's sandstone, told me his family deeded "the face of the rock and about two foot of ground to the state for preservation in 1932." They tossed in "a pioneer cemetery to clinch the deal. Unknown graves," Chet called the small plot, taking off his hat and swabbing his forehead, after which he contradicted himself. "The fella who manned Nine Mile Station, his kids got the smallpox and died. They're the ones buried over there."

No one knows for sure how many people visit Register Cliff every year to ogle the hundreds of pioneer initials carved into its face, but it struck me less as historical reliquary than a monument to fear of anonymity. Travelers have carved images on rocks for millennia to ward off impending or impersonal darkness. Graffiti on the pyramids dates at least to the thirteenth century B.C. when "Hadnakhte, scribe of the treasury, came to make an excursion and amuse himself." By the second century A.D., the paws of the Sphinx were covered with similar messages. At Register Cliff, the vanishing initials scrawled in its soft sandstone looked like type spilled and scattered on a printer's floor.

"My sister copied all of 'em off the rock at one time," Chet said, replacing his hat with the care of a man laying concrete block. "Don't know what ever happened to 'em."

A cave in the cliff's face had eradicated the names of God knows how many, and the names and initials that remained—faded, obscure, some vandalized—announced a vanished presence, like notices in small-town newspapers yellowing in an attic in which one might read, "Mrs. Wilbur Thompson had an unexpected visit from her cousin Jack Teagarden on Thursday last. Jack dropped in from his home in Ohio while on a trip to California."

But it was Chet's account of the cave's origin that got my attention that afternoon. "A point of some argument," he called it, politely, unfolding yet another anecdote of the delusions that overcome Dream makers. Seems Chet had once quibbled with "a fella from Alliance," Nebraska, about the cave's history.

"He was givin' a talk out here one day on how Indians built that cave. Now, it's true there's Indian graves up on top, but the way he was tellin' it, that hole in the wall was special . . . religious, y'might say. The ol' boy was way off target. Hell, he missed it by a mile."

Chet took his hat off again and rubbed a fist across his forehead in a straight line above his eyes, erasing beads of sweat. A few yards away, the braid of the North Platte caught an edge of breeze and riffled in the heat.

"Here's the truth," he chuckled. "When we moved up to this place in 1926, we had an old Swede who liked to play with dynamite. My dad said, 'Swede, go up there and shoot a hole in the cliff.' Damned if he didn't do it. Dad used it to store potatoes. I thought about usin' it as a bomb shelter in the sixties, but it got wet back in there."

I had no sentimentality in my baggage, but I made a discovery at Register Cliff that gave me goose bumps. Barely legible on the sandstone was carved "J. C. Little for Utah." J. C., you'll remember, was the Mormon who stewed up the prickly pears that gave Thomas Bullock the pukes. At last, I'd come face-to-face with a faint human trace of the people whose "community" I'd been following for two months. That I was now on an all-American road, there was no doubt, since J. C.'s initials commingled with those of other Americans laying claim to Dream on the "register" of the new democracy—both "Saints" and sinners. I didn't linger at Register Cliff. Other than J. C. Little, many of its written notes seemed discordant; I was searching for a melody that, as it turned out, I didn't find.

• • •

When I left Chet Fredericks, a question fretted in my mind: What was the rest of the United States like in 1847? Thinking it deserved a closer look, I later snooped out a handful of details. For example:

In 1847, the United States had no more than 20 million people (17,063,355 by the 1840 census), of which 2.5 million were slaves. Its newest state was Iowa, admitted to the Union in December 1846, ten months after the Mormons had crossed it outbound from Nauvoo. New York, Philadelphia, Baltimore, and New Orleans were its largest cities, none with more than 380,000 (New York), and New Orleans bringing up the rear with 102,193. Americans heading west that year were leaving behind a depression, while famine and political unrest in Europe had loosed a tide. When Brigham and the Mormons left Winter Quarters in April, 27,000 emigrants had already landed in New York; by July, when they reached the Great Salt Lake Valley, 81,000 emigrants had made America their new home. The roads west were choked with the down-and-out, among them the Mormons.

In 1847 the U.S. Post Office issued its first adhesive-backed stamps, bearing the likenesses of George Washington (10 cents) and Benjamin Franklin (5 cents). A savvy person could cut a ten-cent stamp in half and use it as a five. The cornerstone of the Smithsonian Institution was laid in Washington. That spring, Edgar Allan Poe was in "the depths of wild misery," since his wife, Virginia, had died in January. At Walden Pond, Thoreau was busy writing *A Week on the Concord and Merrimack Rivers*, and William Prescott published *History of the Conquest of Peru*. Prescott's earlier *History of the Conquest of Mexico* (1843) stirred wide interest in America's long-vanished cultures, especially among Mormons who believed that ruins in the New World were evidence of lost civilizations mentioned in *The Book of Mormon*. No sooner had Prescott published *History of the Conquest of Peru* than the infamous literary hack Ned Buntline, of dime novel fame, rushed into print with *Virgin of the Sun: A Historical Romance of the Last Revolution in Peru*. The great American soap opera was catching on.

While J. C. Little and the Mormons were carving their initials into Register Cliff, another utopian American experiment was ending in West Roxbury, Massachusetts. Brook Farm was down for the count. One more venture with its roots, like Mormonism, in nineteenth-century visions of perfect "community," its on-and-off residents included Ralph Waldo Emerson, Margaret Fuller, William Ellery Channing, and Nathaniel Hawthorne. "A perpetual picnic," Emerson called it, "a French Revolution in small, an age of reason in a patty-pan." Another "American attitude" added to an already overworked pot, the farm combined "idealism, mysticism, and a dislike . . . of unaesthetic manifestations of industrialism" (factories were ugly) with "a forthright insistence on the importance of the individual"—all in all, a Mulligan stew that's still being stirred today. Brook Farm lasted from 1840 to 1847, roughly the same amount of time it took for the bustling Mormon city of Nauvoo to wink on and off in its Illinois backwater.

But neither the intellectual Brook Farmers nor godly Mormons could bake up an altogether successful American pie: Mormon "community" experiments consistently failed as well. Unable to fully meet the demands of Brook Farm's utopian lifestyle in a "patty pan," Nathaniel Hawthorne walked out because he couldn't reconcile the "individual"—namely, himself—with the "community" need to shovel shit from the horse barns. The last Mormon communal experiment ended at Orderville, Utah (a tidy name), where it fell apart because one "individual" preferred to buy his jeans in another town from an eastern manufacturer, probably named Levi Strauss. Ironically, a handful of Brook Farm survivors made their way to abandoned Nauvoo where they bought the ruins of the Mormon temple and tried fabricating yet another utopian American Dream on the banks of the Mississippi. Fourierism winked on and out as well.

• • •

A mile outside of Guernsey, the evening before I hooked up with Chet Fredericks, Glenn Putnam and his wife, Jean, offered me a hefty slice of watermelon, a soft drink, a comfortable respite in their back yard, bed and breakfast, plenty of interesting conversation, and another footnote to Mormon history.

Glenn's great-grandfather, Green Marion Putnam, was a Mormon in Nauvoo in the days when Joseph Smith was courting "the Principle." To hear Glenn tell it in his well-lubricated voice (he worked for Marathon Oil Company), his great-granddad was perfectly comfortable with his wife, Mary, who was equally comfortable with Green Marion. "But the Mormons kept pressuring him to take another wife. He didn't want any of it. They kept it up. They came to the farmhouse three times. The last time they said, 'Brother Putnam, you're going to take another wife.'"

Glenn sank back into the lawn chair and took a pull at his soft drink, eyes bright as newly minted dimes. Jean sat next to him, her arm hooked in his as if to hold down his enthusiasm. Glenn's great-grandmother, Mary, understood her husband's needs perfectly—or else—and resisted, just as Emma Smith understood Joseph's when she beat Fanny Alger out of their home and gave her brother-in-law, Hyrum, the boot when Joseph sent him to break the news of his revelation on plural connubial bliss.

"Well, he and Mary got out two trunks, took what little possessions they could carry in a wagon, put themselves on a flatboat, and sailed down the Mississippi to Keokuk," Glenn continued. "They crossed into Iowa and out of Mormon territory and settled there."

Tales like Glenn's sound incredible today, and polygamy is still the darker side of Mormon life, erupting into daylight with predictable regularity—most recently before the 2002 Winter Olympics with the highly publicized trial and conviction of Tom Green who was sentenced to five years (about nine months for each of his seven wives), and who had made the talk-show circuit discussing his polygamous lifestyle, thus drawing attention to himself and exposing what Mormon church leaders fear most—Utah's uncomfortable past. A Mormon fundamentalist whose polygamy is not in any way condoned by the LDS Church today, Green also made a habit of marrying child brides, one of them at thirteen. Personally, I believe consenting *adults* should be free to make fools of themselves any way they please so long as they pay taxes and don't drink whiskey through a straw; but having opened a Pandora's box, Mormons are having a hard time closing it again. "Shades of Nephi!" Mark Twain has Brigham say in *Roughing It.* "My friend, take an old man's advice, and *don't* encumber yourself with a large family . . . ten or eleven wives is all you need."

• • •

Known as "Deep Rut Hill" to old timers, the "Guernsey Ruts" are indented on a shallow slope just south of the town of Guernsey, Wyoming. Famous to any overland trail buff, they display the grinding power of iron-shod wagon wheels—an unintentional memorial to people on the path of empire. When wagon axles began to scrape as the ruts deepened, settlers would scab off enough sandstone between the wheels (Mormons were the first to do so) to allow the axles clearance. In time, rolling stock cut a trench six feet deep through the Arikaree sandstone of the White River Formation. Just above the often-photographed ruts is the grave of Lucindy Rollins, who died in 1849. During eleven days in 1850, 933 wagons with 6,900 oxen, 1,465 horses, 1,988 cows, 544 mules, 2,817 men, 393 children, and 242 women left Fort Laramie and passed through the trench. Musing on so evident a history, I fell in with Marge McClain and Lou Dextraze, a romantic couple from Colorado Springs planning full-time monogamy who happened along to view the site. "This is great," Marge said. "What'ja think?"

I thought Marge and Lou were terminally friendly and suited for each other, but I answered, "Well, it's a big surprise. History in the West is usually piled high, not deep."

· · ·

Under a clear sky, an uneasy thunder rolled in the distance. Sergeant Gary Wellington and Private Pedro Negrete stared me down over a perimeter wire. With the Mexican War of 1847 long over, the descendants of former combatants had joined forces against a Canadian. Dressed in fatigues, sporting loaded M-something rifles and solemn dispositions, the National Guardsmen were touchy about anyone crossing land on which they were playing war. They bobbed up from under a dugout in a sandbank, rifles at chest level, and gave me a feeble "halt" as if it were a courtesy salute extended to oddballs out of uniform.

Challenged, I lied. I told Negrete and Wellington I was a reporter on assignment to do a story on the "Emigrants' Laundry Tub," a site up ahead where I planned to spend the night.

"Nocandoo," Private Negrete said. "Hey, we're on graded maneuvers."

Sergeant Wellington shuffled army issue boots on the sandy track, pulled himself up to nearly six feet. He had what kids of my generation used to call a walky-talky. "I could get the CO," he said, overruling his subordinate. "But he might not like it . . . you wanting to cross, I mean."

"Do it," I said, "please."

Denver boys, young as my own former marine, they looked at each other as if their dad had just ordered them to stand down. Wellington clicked the squawk box, walked out of hearing distance, and started pleading quietly, like a man not anxious to give away his position to a sniper. When he turned back, I knew things would work out quickstep.

So Private Pedro Negrete marched me across a half mile of enemy territory, little suspecting I was a Canadian spy. "You can cross," he said, "but you can't write nothin' about what you see goin' on. Orders from the CO." Since I didn't see anything or anyone, although I suspect plenty saw me, there wasn't much to write about anyway. I should have told Pedro I was on "graded maneuvers" myself, still rising eight inches to the mile in the Land of Hope and Glory.

· · ·

I defended my own patch of ground that night against an invasion of cattle. I'd put the tent up on a protuberance of rock three feet above running water at the

Emigrants' Laundry Tub—as close to Warm Springs as a human could get without taking a bath. "Three hundred gallons a minute," a rancher told me. "So warm that flowers bloom in December."

Being there, alone, gave me the heebie-jeebies since as many as 300,000 people had camped on the spot between 1845 and 1870, and the place was rumored to be littered with graves. Cattle I hadn't expected. Half asleep when they splashed in for a drink, I was rousted in a second, their great necks and dumb eyes craned in my direction while they sucked at the warm teat of plenty.

Joel Palmer came across Warm Springs on June 28, 1845. The springs were well known long before that, but Palmer recognized a good place to take a bath. Although the water was too warm to be potable (70 degrees Fahrenheit), he found it just right for a good scrubbing, as did most settlers who laundered clothes in it. At Warm Springs, Lieutenant John Charles Frémont ate lunch on the return trip from his 1842 exploring tour to the Wind River Mountains. "Here I am sitting with my book and compass . . . at the shore of Warm Springs," his cartographer, Charles Preuss, wrote, observing Frémont's preparations for a triumphant return to Fort Laramie; but in Frémont's windy account of his travels that year, the "Great Pathfinder" makes no mention of the springs, noting only that when he arrived at Fort Laramie, "the fort saluted us with repeated discharges of a single piece, which we returned with scattered volleys of our small arms." It was fart for fart. He'd been gone forty-two days and never run out of natural gas.

"A young lieutenant is always a strange creature," Preuss scribbled, "on the old as well as the new continent."

• • •

One by one, the cows straggled away, pissing in the source of their refreshment. Asleep, I tossed in the half-remembered dreams older men get on uncertain nights, waxing and waning like unfamiliar moons.

34

Walking is a natural recreation for a man who desires not
absolutely to suppress his intellect but to turn it out for a season.
LESLIE STEPHEN, "IN PRAISE OF WALKING"

*I have put up two guide boards today. One at 10 and the other at
20 miles from Fort John or Laramie. . . . The gentile camp is a little east of us.*　　　　　　　　　　WILLIAM CLAYTON, JUNE 5, 1847

*We are now among the Black Hills and grass is scarce. . . . The road
today has been up and down hills, yet with a good hard bottom.*
　　　　　　　　　　　　　　JAMES M. HUTCHINGS, JULY 22, 1849

Thunder worried me again, fetching me in and out of sleep. I woke before dawn, opened the tent fly, and looked up at a perfection of stars, not a cloud in sight, the hills beyond the cattle wallow pale and ghostly. I rolled back in, but the continued rumbling unnerved me until I gave up, crawling out before 6:00 A.M., cattle again sucking at the spring.

I packed quickly and headed out, my back to a feeble sun, only a hint of a track ahead. Digging the compass from my pack, I turned its bezel and sighted due west. Here the land took on an even more ravaged look with swags of sand hung below brittle sandstone ridges. Stunted conifers clung to ridge tops, and by mid-morning, when the sky began to carry a sheen of high silver, unnerving thunder rumbled again from the cloudless east.

Near Warm Springs, the Oregon and Mormon Trails angle northwest. Leaving behind a northerly bend of the North Platte River, Utah- and Oregon-bound settlers bisected the shortest distance between two points, making do with a cross-hatching of lesser creeks (Wagon Hound, Horse, La Bonte, La Prele) before rejoining the main river near Glenrock, Wyoming.

Truth is, I was uncertain of myself in this raw country, a condition that ate into my resolve the deeper I got into it—an uncertainty that harried the Mormons as well. As the East died away, the unfamiliar haunted me. At Fort Laramie, my mail contained a packet of maps from a popular Oregon Trail guide, but the details ran together and the scale was too small to get the big picture. "What I need," I complained, "is a Wyoming road map"—which, of course, I didn't have.

When I picked up one in Glendo next day, I saw the state laid out in full color like a satellite view, greenly lush where mountains tumbled skyward, yellowing where topography favored grassland basins, and faded peach where desolations sprawled from Worland to Ten Sleep and from Rawlins to Rock Springs.

Topping a ridge, I sprawled myself on a warm outcrop to watch Wyoming spread out, taking in a sweep of geography, no sign of a house and nothing for me to do but drink in rising sun. When a jeep track opened up, I followed it, angling northwest until I crossed U.S. 26 where two leftover hippies were huddled over a rusted Coup DeVille, its hood gaping like a toothless alligator. Its rear window ledge was choked with religious tracts, its trunk lashed down over a load of unrecognizable artifacts, its back seat removed and tied on the roof along with a much battered wooden chest, and its dash crammed from side to side with hand-picked wildflowers. A scrawled message on the glass read "Remember to Keep Holy the Sabbath." The two stranded pilgrims—a man and woman—looked up, startled.

"Troubles?"

"No, brother," the man said. "Praise Jesus we're alive."

When he handed me a religious tract, *Breaking One Means Breaking Ten*, I knew I was in trouble.

The girl looked eighteen at most, with hair the color of crude oil. She looked me up and down as if I was a potential convert—the kind of look Mormon missionaries give someone who's invited them inside.

"Praise Jesus," she said. "Are you saved?"

Her shaggy partner in the throes of zealotry reminded me of Charlie Manson with his dark, fanatic eyes. "Been here seven hours," he said. "From California heading for Heaven."

He pressed a card into my hand with the enthusiasm of a TV evangelist. On it were two names—"Cecilia June and John"—and a wholly speculative address, "77 Orion Way, New Jerusalem, Heaven." Minus a surname, they were headed "east." Cecilia June was more specific. "New Jersey," she said. "Praise Jesus."

Having spent time in Newark, it didn't seem to me a state for which to praise Our Lord.

John wore ratty blue chinos and an immense hooded sweatshirt with a brown knitted watch cap; hair shot out from under its edges as if he'd been caught in a sudden updraft. Cecilia June sported an ankle-length denim skirt, a wool sweater, and moon boots. Stuffed with detritus of hit-the-road-in-a-hurry, the Cadillac had settled on its rear springs like a failing horse. Fast-food cartons were tossed onto a gray mattress in the back seat. Grass stained, it told me they'd been "sleeping rough," as the British put it, looking up each night toward their new address.

A yellow pickup stopped, and a lanky man with a face worn smooth as a well-thumbed coin slid out and drifted over. Another would-be Samaritan, W. W. McClain claimed to be the great-great-grandson of Jesse James's grandmother, an admission that seemed at least as interesting as Cecilia June and John's address. Since W. W. had once farmed near Saint Joseph, Missouri, where Jesse was fatally plugged, I took his word for it. Lean, hardened, dressed in denim, with gnarly, callused hands, W. W. did Christian things under the hood, asking John to "turn 'er over" and "pump the peddle," for which John praised Jesus before each crank. It wheezed but couldn't breathe, its starter motor grinding down to irascible clicks, tics, and, finally, nix. Old Paint had died (she had a Nevada license plate), and there was nothing to be done.

"Gotta be towed," W. W. prophesied.

I was beginning to sweat in the fast-rising heat. Under heavy-weight togs, the heaven-bound couple looked unshakably cool. W. W. in his denim looked as composed as an experienced bank robber. I felt like I was mixed up with a gallery of outlaws or, if things turned out better, a misfits reunion.

"Praise Jesus," Cecilia June said again, as if towing were a blessed sacrament. While W. W. dusted off his hands and looked around as if he'd just spotted a promising small town bank with a lone teller, I peeked into *Breaking One Means Breaking Ten* and realized I was going to an address other than the one on John's card.

John allowed how he'd "been truly blessed by the delay," since he'd gotten to read "all of the Acts of the Apostles" in the breakdown lane. Cecilia June allowed that God worked in "mysterious ways" since engine failure had given her a chance to share "God's message." As if to get us all back on the right road, W. W. allowed that he occasionally read the Bible but the main revelation he had in mind was getting a tow truck to haul the Caddy into Glendo. I allowed the Coup DeVille might rise again, although I half expected W. W. to walk back to his pickup, take down a rifle hanging in his rear window, and pump a round through the radiator to put old General Motor out of its misery.

But John also allowed that he couldn't lock the doors of his heavenly wheels, which struck me as truthful since all of its once-fitted parts seemed sprung. He picked at his collar, tucked his updraft hair under his watch cap, and fumbled with the keys. His eyes kept shifting, anywhere but at W. W., Samaritan of the hour.

"I'd better stay," he said. "Sister Cecilia June can go."

"I'll go," she said, meekly in the voice of one often called by John.

When I asked to take a photo of the outlaws, there was an awkward moment and stuttered approval, but at the instant I pressed the shutter, John held a magazine over his face. Would an apostle do that? Developed, it turned out even more bizarre—W. W. with his hands stuffed into his denim jacket, silvering hair wafting on a breeze, Sister Cecilia June arms locked with John and peering joyfully at him—her personal savior—and John hidden behind a Christian magazine with a headline message for backsliders: "There's Still Time!" Only the broken-down Caddy seems normal.

. . .

Dwyer Junction's center had a wind-scrubbed shack passing itself off as a quick stop. A few sparse cottonwoods drooped in mourning. Three lopsided Texaco gas pumps stood outside—white, green, and red. The shack had the peeled paint of despair one sees on abandoned farms. A door the color of dried pea soup was set between two out-of-plumb windows with the same color trim, and a lopsided sign above the entrance had lost four big letters to inclement weather. Someone had stenciled "BEER" over a faded advertisement and over that a second, less alcoholic invitation, "POP," in midnight black. Above that, in even smaller uppercase, was "DWYER JUNCTION."

Of all the woebegone down-in-the-dumps I'd come across, this was the worst. Inside was brooding darkness, stale smells, and a rattrap interior of capitulation and make-do. After stumbling into its dimness, I bought a POP (no BEER in sight) and was promptly ordered off the property since the couple who willingly accepted my fifty-five cents were closing up pronto. I drank my Mountain Dew sitting on the concrete base of the red gasoline pump, pondering the familiar Texaco fireman's hat and hoping an arsonist would show up, "Well recommended to me," as Ike Winkle phrased things. It wasn't hard to understand why Dwyer Junction was junked. Practically at its back door, Interstate 25 carried traffic north from Denver and south from Sheridan in a long, continuous whine, shooting past without so much as a fare-thee-well.

. . .

Laramie Peak now bulked large to the southwest, and I turned northwest on the first leg of an arc that would eventually take me to Casper. To avoid the stench of the interstate, I crossed a fence line and headed into the hills, stopping at a stock tank to pump water through my filter and into my dry canteen. Dipping my head and arms to the shoulder in the tank, I shook loose a shower of water and climbed, dripping, toward a ridge of low-clumped pines. The further I mounted, the more optimistic I became. Near dusk, I came across a sheltered wedge of ground overhung by pines and away from the yammering interstate.

Before dark, I crested a ridge to get a wide-angled view of the sunset, rose and gold leaking between the clouds, splaying shafts of color over an all but empty land. I thought of Cecilia June and John, her apostle, pushing their rust bucket from Lotus Land to "77 Orion Way, New Jerusalem, Heaven." What, I wondered, had turned them so eccentrically "other-worldly"?

Watching the pyrotechnics of a Wyoming sunset, abundant and breathtaking, I realized that walking toward a dying light was more appealing than walking toward a sunrise. Once, on Maine's Mount Katahdin, I'd watched rising sun touch America for the first time in a new day. Sunrise announced itself slowly and weakly, rising from the ash gray of early morning to crawl over earth's rim, its first faint gleam on my face, then breaking in ever widening waves over the land. But sunrise veils the universe, cuts off the cold mystery of limitless, unimaginable creation. Sunset in Wyoming, especially, was satisfying, holding my eye in a grip of majesty, opening a naked universe to wonder. Watching Wyoming's swollen, dying sun dragging up stars, I wanted to believe, like John, that "There's Still Time." And space.

· · ·

"People in Wyoming have got wilderness stuck up to their eyebrows," Glenn Putnam had told me the day before. Too polite to use the A-word, which disappointed a Canadian, he groused, "We don't want no more wilderness. Alaska didn't want any more wilderness either. The Sierra Club fights anything that contributes to American energy—oil, gas, coal development."

In 1985 James Watt (secretary of the interior under Ronald Reagan) was yammering for a "multiple use" policy of federal lands in the West, which meant, more or less, that in addition to "public use," huge federal tracts (including wilderness-designated areas) would be opened to "extraction industries." Glenn Putnam was an oil man, so I gave him his point.

"Take Basin Electric," he complained. "The Sierra Club held up that project for three years. Cost billions. It all came down to the whooping crane."

"What about cranes?" I asked. "Important or not?"

Glenn ruffled his body as if a cold breeze had shot up under his loose shirt, eyes burning like pine knots. A plume of silvering hair hung over his forehead like the misplaced beard of an Airedale. I'd liked him immediately, a kind and considerate pup who, when he nipped at you, was gentle about it. Now we were straying into each other's back yards, facing off at the fence line. I gave him my Scottish terrier face, ears alert, eyes hot with suspicion, nostrils flared, and mouth stubbornly down-turned through a flare of whiskers.

"Basin Electric offered to give enough water to meet Nebraska's needs to maintain marshes and flyways," he growled. "The Sierra Club said it wasn't good enough. Basin Electric put up millions to maintain habitat. Still wasn't good enough. It wouldn't ever have been good enough. Dinosaurs once roamed all over Wyoming. Some species die out in this world."

FOLLOWING THE WRONG GOD HOME

"You're a species," I snapped. "Would you want to go?"

"Species adjust to change . . . but Wyoming has got to expand industry and energy. Today, we got more antelope and elk than ever before."

Around us, oil was boosting in from Wyoming, Montana, North Dakota, and South Dakota, filling Marathon tanks to fuel America. U.S. Data had computerized Marathon's operations at the pumping station, and hard-muscled "techs" were fast being replaced by computer "techs," both volume and flow computerized to cut costs. Marathon's big white tanks held "sweet crude," a high specific-gravity oil used for gasoline and jet fuel; others held "general sour," a lower grade high in asphalt, hydrogen sulfide, and sulfur. In Glenn's bark I heard "general sour."

"Economic growth means more humans," I said. "Could the Putnams adjust?"

Jean Putnam tendered Glenn a fake punch on the arm, giving things a lighter touch. "A true Wyomingite doesn't want more population," she said, "but they want more jobs."

"A contradiction," I said. "How do you answer that?"

"No answer," Glenn said.

And that's the problem with Dream. It's tough to have things both ways.

35

Every walk is a sort of crusade, preached by some Peter the Hermit in us, to go forth and reconquer this Holy Land from the hands of the Infidels.   HENRY DAVID THOREAU, "WALKING"

On this camp ground is one of the clearest and largest springs of water. . . . Elder Kimball having discovered it, he calls it his spring or Heber's spring.   WILLIAM CLAYTON, JUNE 7, 1847

I witnessed a fine scene in these hills this morning. It was like a large city upon a mountain—immense buildings one above the other, and interspersed with stunted pines. What I would have given for a good Daguerian instrument!

JAMES M. HUTCHINGS, JULY 23, 1849

"Heber Springs," Lewis Archie said.

It looked suspiciously like a galvanized stock tank to me, its water placid as a glass eye. I blinked at it, but no history blinked back and, for one awful moment, another myth shrank and rattled inside me—dried beans in a bucket. This landmark on the Mormon Trail, named for Heber C. Kimball, appeared painfully dehydrated—if, that is, it was Heber Springs at all.

I'd spent a day looking for the site, following suspect maps and getting nowhere, taking advantage of the sympathy of fine people like Lewis Archie and, before that, Jim and Florence Hughes near Glendo who, after I walked onto their ranch, listened politely to all my excuses for trespassing before Jim asked, "Have you had lunch?"

Praise Jesus, as Cecilia June would say. Florence led me into the cool interior of their home and set a spread so tasty that I ate with the abandon of a slopped hog—lemonade, potatoes with sour cream dressing, hamburger patties, fresh baked bread, stewed tomatoes, cottage cheese, ice cream, and angel food cake. All this for a stranger they'd met thirty minutes before.

Jim Hughes is a heavyset, open-faced man with a cabbage head, withdrawing dark hair, a belly that precedes him, and a missing left arm. Shelling corn in a hammer mill one fall, his arm fell victim to a tractor belt that snaked around his left wrist, pulling "half of it off." With little medical help and most of that some distance away, the doctor who got to him first tried to save the stump, but as Jim put it, "the gangrene set in and they took it off at the shoulder."

Occasionally, Jim gets a word twisted around his tongue as if a memory of the snaking belt settled into his speech. "They *forged* that river," he said, talking about a pioneer crossing on the Platte, and mentioned that a one-armed rancher faced more "diffigulties" than the two-armed variety. Florence, who'd grown to look a lot like her husband, wore her silver hair in a fuzzy perm and beamed through large, oval glasses that lent accent to her matronly features. After lunch, we sat on the covered front porch of their white ranch house in yellow cushioned chairs, lounging with feet stretched out on a carpeting of shamrock-colored AstroTurf, swapping yawns and doing our best not to nod off from Florence's belly-blitz and eighty-five degrees in the shade.

· · ·

I admit that I would never have found Heber Springs without Lewis Archie. I would have stuck to Highway 26, following what's left of the old "Yellowstone Highway"—parts of it now replaced by Interstate 25—and Highway 319, north and west toward Glenrock; but one mention of the springs and Jim hustled up

Lewis who changed all that. Lewis showed up in no time and, like a good omen, set me back on course.

"The springs are on my ranch," he told me. "I'll take you out there."

Lewis is a trim, fit, toughened rancher of indeterminate age with a rawhide complexion. Under a broad-brimmed Stetson held up by elegant ears, he negotiated roads I never could have found on my own, dust-deviling his pickup into the back country west of Glendo past roadside stands of purple phlox and surface deposits of russet dirt (the "Red Hills") until we zigzagged our way onto his spread and pulled up to the alleged water hole where the Mormons camped on June 7, 1847. The tank—eight feet in diameter—was surrounded with a two by six triangular rough-sawn plank fence. I dipped a tin cup into the cool water and tipped one back in honor of Heber. At 2.5 gallons a minute (Lewis had it recorded by the state), it seemed short of William Clayton's description as "one of the . . . largest springs of water I have seen for a long time." Of course, "large" is a relative term and Clayton could have been thirsty.

Brigham's right-hand man once lived in Mendon, New York, only a few miles from my home, and this natural memorial bearing his name deserved a toast, although I would have preferred a spot of old "No. 6" with my branch water. But I expect Heber knew the medicinal value of old "No. 6," since he had forty-three wives and sixty-five children and probably needed something to settle his nerves each night before making a decision. As first counselor to Brigham, he also had a hand in the "valley tan" distilling business, selling Utah-made moonshine "at $6.00 a gallon" to miners on the road to the California gold fields.

After the celebration, Lewis drove me to his place where I holed up for the night in comfortable quarters on his back porch, talking late into the evening over dinner and finally slumbering deeply on a camp cot. Mrs. Archie was away for the evening and my showing up offered Lewis an opportunity to "visit."

The Archie ranch house with its rough, brown clapboard exterior nestles in a valley close to Horseshoe Creek, a tributary that's mentioned again and again in the diaries of overland travelers. As a young man with ambition, Lewis moved onto the ranch, originally known as the 4T, in 1955. He built the house around an 1890s cabin with a wizardry both sumptuous and appealing. Cool and comfortable in a shelter of cottonwoods, heated in winter by solar panels, the house is lined with burnished pine walls and filled with sturdy furniture—restored rockers, lamps made from wagon hubs, hand-built kitchen cabinets, and antique desks— all western themes that, for once, suited the landscape, including a sculpture of a cowboy, hat raised on a bucking bronco, that reminded me immediately of the Cowboy State logo.

"It's some kind of plaster," Lewis said, apologetically. "My wife knew I liked it and got it for me. Could never afford a bronze one."

What Lewis could afford, however, was to part with his house, which he tried to give to his son, but the boy "thought he needed something more up to date, so he built himself a new log cabin." There was lingering melancholy in Lewis's voice, but he compensated. "He's got a great view of Laramie Peak."

Lewis's tone was less melancholy over being turned down than concern about his son's motivation for new real estate. I thought I knew why. There was nothing magnificent about the Archie place except this: a person could feel centered under its roof, as if hand-worked timber, hard work, and solitude made it a finer place than any other, an uncommon house where "a great view" is what other people yearn for at greater expense and much less reward. Offered to me, I would have moved in that week.

Like many other Americans bedeviled by death and taxes, passing a legacy on to his children worried Lewis, surfacing like a shark in the waters of our conversation, most of it carried on through mouthfuls of steak, carrot wedges, green onions, bread, vanilla ice cream, and scalding coffee. Estate taxes were on his mind, of course, and his retirement, which would be financed, I suspected, from the sale of his land.

"Sometime I've gotta figure out how to leave this ranch to my kids. But at today's prices, they can't afford it. We're family, and that means we gotta look after our own . . . make something good happen for them."

Looking after kids and making something good happen was a job the Archies were accomplished at. Besides their own two, they'd helped raise several foster children, mostly boys from troubled homes, including a Denver kid who became an actor, working in television (*Doctor Kildare, Hawaii Five-O*), and in movies (*The Andromeda Strain*). That spring, he was on location in Texas, working on a movie with Willie Nelson.

"Mark never made his fortune," Lewis said, "but he makes a good living."

The boys bedded down in the bunkhouse along with Ross, Lewis's son. "On the ranch they just learned how to work," Lewis said. "We made sure they got to play a lot . . . fishin' and swimmin'."

He talked with pride about a young Hispanic, Candelaria "Candy" Martinez, and, with deep regret, about two Native American teenage brothers—who later hanged themselves while in state custody. "If we could'a had 'em longer, those kids would'a turned out all right. But their Momma . . . a nice looking woman who got jobs as a . . . mistress . . . took 'em back when she got a real job. She loved those kids and tried her best to take care of 'em. Didn't work out."

That evening was the first time I felt that what I was up to might work out. It wasn't hope that came over me so much as admiration of a fine man on a good place—a generous human being with an attachment to his land, his children, and other people's children. Not only did Lewis harbor a "Manifest Kindness," but he also harbored few illusions about the frailty of the human condition. Unpretentious and unaffected by a windy Canadian, he talked of Dreams plain-style, offering occasional homilies on human nature.

Talking late into the Wyoming evening with Lewis was, for want of a better word, a *conservative* moment that untangled the skeins of my eastern knee-jerk liberalism, since his commentary on the good, the bad, and the ugly was not right wing: it was "right placed"—what you'd expect from someone who lived, worked, and deeply considered his life in the process. Lewis was as close as I came to Tom Jefferson's ideal "agrarian" citizen—a strong man rooted to the land, nurtured by it, steeped in it, and accepting of it as the basis of his wealth, worth, and happiness. If he wasn't entirely happy, he was in hot pursuit.

"When do you like to get goin'?" he asked. A chill settled in, making the night air cool as a blade.

"Whenever you do."

"I'm usually up by six. At it by seven."

So was I.

• • •

Most historians and trail buffs never see the high plateau between Heber Springs and La Bonte Creek where the West rose to meet the Mormons. Like others who crossed the long finger of high, treeless ground known simply as "the Ridge," the Mormons came face-to-face with their first awesome hint of the land of their inheritance. Off the beaten track, I wouldn't have been struck numb by it either except for Lewis who set my foot on the right path. Hanging precariously on the drop edge of Dream, I crossed an emotional and psychological divide next day that stirred my imagination as nothing else had so far.

William Clayton's description of the vista is understated, as if he were holding his breath at the time, afraid in Mormon reticence to give it full measure: "While traveling on top the wind blew very strong from the west. . . . The road over was indeed very crooked but mostly bending to the north. We could see a long distance from the top. The country to the north looks more even but south and southwest very hilly and broken."

To the south, Laramie Peak looms in dark glory. To the west, Clayton's view of "a long distance" badly serves reality. The eye does not see "out" so much as the landscape swarms "in." I'd stepped onto an artist's palette mounded with colors—ocher, rouge, rusts, mauves—waiting to be dipped and smeared on an immense sweep of blue canvas, and I *discovered* (there's no other word for it) that the voyagers who crossed this immensity gave up the last vestiges of their former existence and entered a geography of illusions in which their lives and that of the nation were redefined. I crossed it with mixed emotions of fear and awe, engaging it like a voyeur. By day's end, I'd walked twenty-seven miles of blistering country that gave me a new appreciation for that excellent western word *tenderfoot*.

• • •

Horseshoe Creek and Heber Springs were the last sources of good water for nearly thirty miles. From Heber Springs to La Bonte Creek in Converse County, Wyoming, the arched spine of the plateau was and remains a dry crossing. Formed from the Hartville Uplift, which divides the Denver Basin from the Powder River Basin, a trained geologist's eye can scan Precambrian, Paleozoic, and Mesozoic remnants from the Laramide Orogeny, the upthrust that produced the Rockies. Cenozoic sediments cover the plateau, as they do further east near Glendo.

On the push up to the ridge, I came across Jay Gruwell, thirty, at the old stage stop known as Elkhorn Crossing, a site that for a brief time became Foxton, Wyoming. Foxton has long vanished, but the stage stop hotel still stands, a three-gabled white-framed building with peeling red trim looking forlorn and abandoned in old age—a long-widowed matron clinging to vague memories. Doing some "fix-up," Jay was in well-worn jeans and a sleeveless T-shirt. He tugged a bill cap down over his eyes, took off his work gloves. I asked about the trail. "You get many folks who cross this stretch?"

"Not many," he said. "Some ride it on horses . . . like for the Bicentennial. One lady got bucked off up that hill and had to be rushed to the hospital with a concussion."

Used tires were strewn on the widow's-peak gables like coins on a dead man's eyes. I asked about those as well.

"It's to keep the roof from rattling," he answered.

Dry bones.

On my delirious crossing of "the Ridge," I met nobody, although in 1847, the road was crowded as the exodus from "the States" headed toward Dream or nightmare. Of this stretch over high ground, trail historian Gregory Franzwa writes: "This area cannot be probed efficiently; one would have to penetrate many miles over poor roads to find so much as a mile of the trail and it simply isn't worth it." Franzwa missed the bus, the train, and the boat; it was the most magnificent day of the walk. The trail is so obvious it could be followed by any near-sighted wanderer.

Inscribed along the ridge's spine, the trail couldn't have varied more than a hundred feet. At a U.S. Geological Survey marker where I stopped to rest (5,825 feet above sea level), I encountered my first and only violence on the walk— attacked by a prairie chicken. Bursting from cover, she circled me with a thrum of indignation, piping and wheeping at my legs as her yellow fluff of chicks scattered into the sage. Later, a red granite Oregon Trail marker hugged the original road as it began a slow descent toward water, exactly as described in overland journals.

On their crossing of this stretch, the Mormons met up with "four Missourians"; one of the dreaded "pukes" was recognized from the bitter days in the Show Me State. Tension lingered in the air. Harriet Crow, one of the Mississippi Saints, "got run over by one of their wagons" and "screamed and appeared in great agony." Her foot and thigh were badly bruised, and she had to be doctored with camphor before they "proceeded on." At ten minutes past six, the Mormons crossed "a stream about thirty feet wide and nearly two feet deep with a very swift current . . . named on Fremont's map as La Bonte river." As for the Missouri "pukes," Clayton wrote, tongue in cheek, "They seem . . . not fond of our company."

Almost to the same minute, I reached La Bonte Creek, pausing at the ranch house on the site to ask permission to camp, but nobody was home. I crossed the water and chose a sheltered spot out of sight among the chokecherry and willow greenery on its far bank, set up my tent, waded into the water, and washed my badly mauled feet. Along with salami, from which I cut chunks and gorged, my Glendo supplies included two cheese sticks (limp), peanut butter, two chocolate bars (melted), a can of tuna, a grapefruit, and several dry tortillas. A receipt for $14.67 was in the bag. I ate everything but the tuna, two tortillas, and the butt end of the salami. In the night, I awoke to breezes in the scrub willows, listened to the past roll by, alone again on the edge of yet another strange country.

36

*Nothing educates an eye for the features of a landscape so well as
the practice of measuring it by your own legs.*

LESLIE STEPHEN, "IN PRAISE OF WALKING"

*Our road lay over a kind of red earth. . . . It affected my eyes much
from its brightness and strange appearance.*

WILLIAM CLAYTON, JUNE 9, 1847

*The country around is broken and singular and uninviting: hills,
red sand, and sage bushes . . . no hope of camping. We kept on . . .
winding our way till past midnight, traveling by starlight.*

JAMES HUTCHINGS, JUNE 27, 1849

The sheriff's deputy said, "You put God number one in your life and you'll make
it. Before I accepted Jesus as my personal Savior, I said, 'Thank you, God, for letting me be born in Wyoming and not some com'nist country.'"

He sported cinnamon cowboy boots, dark nutmeg pants, a curry-colored shirt
with chestnut pocket flaps, a wide belt with a sage-colored buckle the size of a
saucer, a gleaming badge over his heart, ginger-hued shoulder patches, and a
black sidearm that could drop a moose. He watched me warily over the top of his
sunglasses, down so far on the bridge of his nose that his wispy mustache seemed
part of the frames. Lurching north toward Douglas, Wyoming, in a county-
mounty Ford Bronco, he ran a check on my driver's license, reminding me in
minutes that my criminal record—one arrest on suspicion of illegal border crossing and another for misdemeanor trespass—had followed me from Nebraska
where I'd last been hassled.

"Otherwise, you're clean," he said.

I was nursing blown feet from the long haul over "the Ridge" and wouldn't
have minded much if he'd jailed me; doing time could at least get my ten little
piggies right with God. Before leaving La Bonte Creek, I'd put a double insole in
my boots hoping to get shuck of the agony of frayed skin, but it hadn't worked.
Crabbing my way along the asphalt of Highway 94, I passed what seemed a litany
of misery—Poison Lake Road, Knob Hill, Bed Tick Station, Wagon Hound Creek,
the last with a bridge near the spot where the Mormons had crossed. The day so

far was memorable for condensed excitements—a coiled bull snake behind my tent that made me leap, throwing off my aim so I peed down my leg; the caroling of a western meadowlark; and three antelope grazing on a grassy creek bottom, the first I'd seen. Other than that, it was an asphalt pain in my lassitude.

Aside from outlining long-term benefits of fundamentalist religion and his brief discussion of my arrest record, the topics in the Bronco ran as follows:

On gun laws: "I was in the Philippines when they declared martial law. Took everyone's guns away. When they take our guns away, we'll all be slaves."

On the agenda of the National Park Service and Bureau of Land Management: "I've been around enough to see com'nist countries up close. I can spot a pre-arranged program."

Between diatribes, his gnarled fists tightened on the wheel as if he were choking the combined personnel of the West's two most despised federal agencies, but as far as I could make out, the deputy's ire focused that day on the burning of abandoned log cabins.

"The Park Service and the Bureau of Land Management made a pact. Whenever you find an old cabin, burn it down."

He looked at me knowingly, nodding as if the deception of legalized pyromania was plain to see. "It's all part of a prearranged program to deny people refuge."

"Refuge? From what?"

"You don't get it, do you?"

"You mean burning abandoned cabins is a communist activity?"

"Burning them cabins is a conspiracy to deny survivors a place of refuge."

"What survivors?"

"Patriots," he said.

Remembering Buddy Brisco at Ash Hollow packing a .22 High Standard and urging me, politely, not to mess with him, I reconsidered saying aloud, "Bullshit." Alone in the Ford Bronco with my duly sworn county protector, I felt a sudden need to be armed and dangerous myself. On the outskirts of Douglas, a town with the appeal of an IRS audit, I asked to be dropped at a motel. When he pulled up at a Super 8, I scrambled out.

"One last thing," he said. "Keep out'a trouble. Keep your powder dry. Put God number one in your life."

• • •

Fort Fetterman on the old Bozeman Trail is a hop, skip, and jump from Douglas, and on the day I checked into the Super 8, it was holding an imitation "rendezvous"—the kind of event where otherwise sane people dress in early-nineteenth-century costume and pretend to be trappers, mountain men, or other early American indigents. Oddly enough, it was the Red Alert deputy who suggested I take it in, and he even swung by the motel an hour later and offered to give me a lift. On the ride, he seemed to have taken a controlled substance, since anti-Soviet inclinations or "prearranged programs" never came up. By the time we got to the hoopla, he seemed perfectly normal.

At a western rendezvous, the dancing Indians are usually real, although they seem confused by all the whites in wacky costumes. I have friends who are make-believe mountain men, including a respected financial advisor, but I remind John Unice that he takes a shower every day, supports a brand-name soap company, brushes his teeth frequently and visits his dentist, scrubs his selected bodily orifices, and generally believes that cleanliness is next to Godliness—something the roughcuts he imitates seldom did, which is one good reason why he has paying clients and mountain men had crabs. One other point: his buckskins don't stink.

But when I mentioned this to one of the fake mountain men who had just erected his tipi and was preparing to cook dinner in a cast-iron pot, he gave me an unfriendly glare and gestured, I thought, toward his "authentic replica" Indian lance, which was displayed menacingly in front of his industrial canvas digs. I commented on the lance's fine beadwork, rabbit fur, and rawhide bindings and moved downwind out of range.

A book I consulted on Fort Fetterman (*The Encyclopedia of the Central West*) claims the reconstruction of the place "preserves the post which was once an important supply point for the army." The last half is true. But old Fort Fetterman doesn't exist, and except for a make-believe barracks on the site, a flagpole, a contemporary American flag, a sprinkling of spiked period cannons, and a dizzy view across treeless, open territory, any sign of its real history had vamoosed; although when one of the costumed participants stripped down to a Speedo, unable to take the ninety-degree heat, exposing a bleached belly that would have done "Old Bill" Williams proud, I caught a faint whiff of authenticity. Back at the motel after dinner, I wasn't surprised to see the same "mountain man," sans buckskins, making his way toward a comfortable air-conditioned room. He recognized me too and looked as if he'd flubbed his lines.

· · ·

Born as a railroad town, Douglas, Wyoming (formerly "Tent City"), is known by the locals as "Jackalope City." Because of its interest in comic mammals with large, floppy ears, "Jackass City" might suit it better. A "jackalope"—the invention of a mentally unstable western taxidermist—is a jackrabbit's head fitted with miniature antlers, usually taken from a deer or antelope after hunting season. This cranial adornment gives an otherwise ordinary stuffed rabbit's head and glass eyes a fierce mammalian dignity, as if it woke up one morning to find evolution had expedited the survival of the floppy-footed and chosen it for the trial run. Having a jackalope on the wall (there's one in almost every Wyoming restaurant) is to hope some eastern stooge will actually fall for the ruse and perhaps inquire how, when, and where they can be hunted in season. In Douglas, you can even buy a jackalope license, yuk, yuk.

From Douglas on, I encountered jackalopes daily on the walls of eating emporiums—hulk-headed jackalopes, bantam-brained jackalopes, imperious or august jackalopes, jug-eared jackalopes. By the time I exited Wyoming, I'd abandoned conservationist principles and considered the "species" worthy of extinction. An insult to rabbits and an affront to antelope, it wasn't until I was over the state line that I realized what was actually going on—a "prearranged program" to deny wall space to velvet paintings. I considered placing a call to the Douglas County sheriff's department, but I was flat out of change. Besides, I was certain one of their deputies had figured it out already.

. . .

Douglas did clear up my lingering mystery of thunder on a clear day. Dan Hymore, a six-year veteran of the National Guard, Third Battalion, Forty-ninth Field Artillery, set me straight about the unusual rumblings I'd heard in the night at Warm Springs and on the Hughes ranch.

"Howitzers with a twenty-eight mile trajectory," he said. "Summer maneuvers on the Guernsey Range."

Self-propelled, the tanklike guns are backed by M548 cargo carriers, each carrying sixty shells, and rain destruction on the Wyoming landscape at regular intervals during the summer, thundering at painted pylons and other targets.

"One year we set up a Cadillac at 1500 meters . . . a little under a mile," he said. "Scored a direct hit. The hood went up eighty yards, and when it come down it was drove three feet into the ground."

I admired the precision with which Dan gave the exact feet of the hood's rise, fall, and interment. I wondered if the blown- up Caddy might be the one Cecilia June and John had purchased cheap for their journey to "77 Orion Way, New Jerusalem, Heaven."

. . .

My next-to-last stop before leaving town next day was the Wyoming Pioneer Memorial Museum where I talked with its director. Blond and attractive, she accounted for most of my interest in prolonging the conversation. Having been away from home for several weeks, I sympathized that the "badly underfunded" museum needed a leg up on unavailable resources—as I did.

"Legislators who control the purse strings don't comprehend a small museum's needs," she said as I comprehended mine. "They're all cowboys in the statehouse."

In a region where the word "pioneer" has the significance of holy writ, the museum's focus is supposed to be history; but as she put it, "We've got a lot of 'pioneer' stuff and not enough of the 'history.'"

"Too much of Uncle Bill and Aunt Belle's leftovers," I said, remembering cluttered county museums I'd wandered through hoping for threads of a story, but finding most crammed more with debris than artifacts.

"Got it in one," she said.

I found two exhibits of interest to me in the Douglas County pioneer museum. Turns out Charles Starkweather and Caril Fugate, two midwesterners who went on a Bonnie-and-Clyde-style killing spree in 1958, were captured in Douglas where, rumor has it, the local Keystones owned no handcuffs at the time. A soft-drink bottle (black cherry), now labeled "Property of Charles Starkweather," was found in their stolen Packard when the deadly duo were captured on January 29, 1958. Unsettling in the way mundane objects associated with violence can sometimes be, it vaulted me back to my senior year at an Iowa college when headlines of the duo's killings made it sound too close to home. Now I was staring at something tangible connected to those deadly events; a thirty-year-old horror resurfaced with startling vividness. Starkweather was executed. Caril Fugate served a lengthy jail term. Who drank the black cherry soda isn't known, but if Miss Fugate did, the exhibit is mislabeled.

The second item—actually items—was a collection of "brass checks" used as a medium of exchange in what the director called, euphemistically, "parlor houses." One and a half times as large as a silver dollar, these curious mementos are reminders of high old times in such palaces as Denver's Silver Dollar Hotel, Swede's Saloon in Yuma, the Hog Ranch in Fort Laramie, the Diamond Lil' in San Francisco, and the Adobe Concert Hall in Goldfield, Nevada. Each bears a different "pioneer" inscription— "Good for a Screw, a Stogie and a Whiskey"; "Good for One Piece"; "Good for a $2.00 Piece"; "Good for One Screw, Madame Ruth Jacobs, Prop"; and "Good for One First Class Lay."

• • •

Before leaving Douglas behind, I did some last-minute laundry. In the Laundromat, I begged a cup of soap from a middle-aged woman from Glendo. Ruth

Gatto was originally from New Jersey, but she'd moved west to join her daughter at the "Lone Tree Bible Ranch," an outpost for troubled kids where therapy included daily doses of Bible readings and occasional tramps along the Oregon Trail. Ruth wasn't pushy about her faith, but in three days I'd come up against a hefty measure of Wyoming redemption—first with Cecilia June and John, next with the conspiracy-ridden sheriff's deputy who'd accepted Jesus as his personal savior, and now with Ruth whose own kids, she confided, had attended only institutions of higher learning where salvation was on the curriculum—Bob Jones University (BJU) and the Word of Life Bible Institute in New York. Ruth's husband, Charles, took early retirement from his job to move to Glendo and "serve the Lord," a condition that seemed endemic to the Cowboy State. There was good reason to save folks in Wyoming; the deeper I got into it, the more it looked like Hell.

Ruth told me that her family ran two outposts specializing in Good Book therapy, one managed by a daughter and son-in-law in Glendo and another by a daughter and son-in-law in New Mexico, where Ruth and Charles wintered. I was glad Ruth was doing good work as she understood it, which made me think more Christian-like toward the deputy sheriff, except that he was paranoid, armed, and dangerous where Ruth was gentle, forgiving, and nurturing.

. . .

Glenrock, Wyoming, lies at the junction of Deer Creek and the North Platte, where the Mormons camped "in a large grove of timber" on June 11, 1847. I holed up at the Higgins Hotel, a grand place with a restaurant called The Paisley Shawl. Jack Doll, the owner, made me welcome in no time flat. He rented me a big, airy, room on the second floor at back, a wide front porch to have a "set-to" on, and sold me a meal that turned me as somnambulant as a well-fed mouse in a cheese factory.

The Mormon, Oregon, and California Trails collapsed in Glenrock—the truth, so help me. The ground was sturdy enough when the Mormons passed by, but by the turn of the century when John Higgins, a local tycoon, built his small but opulent hotel, things turned shaky. Higgins began tunneling for coal, hit several rich veins (Thomas Bullock mentions "Bright Black Coal" and William Clayton "stone coal" as they passed), but undermined the town, except, of course, for the ground on which his hotel stood.

"Fifth Street, hell, it just caved in one day. Right where the trails ran," Jack said. "You could'a lost a wagon train in that hole. They filled it back in, but it took time to get it level again. Hell of a mess."

A tall man with a trim mustache and an expressive face with folds like wet plaster, Jack Doll chain-smoked Marlboro Lights. His polyester pants were a shade of blue that I hadn't seen before and he wore them sans belt. When he bought the place, he realized opportunity in the offing and milked it for its history.

"Higgins was a friend of Buffalo Bill. Bill stayed here a couple of times. Claimed it was the finest hostelry north of Denver. Last year, we got it on the National Historic Register."

"Beats any hotel I've stayed in so far," I said, which was the truth since I hadn't stayed in any. As for motels, there's no danger of a Super 8 standing long enough to make the National Historic Register.

"Higgins's wife was an Italian of social prominence," Jack said. "She furnished the dining room with the finest of crystal. It all disappeared. She got furnishings from Chicago . . . a European influence."

I'd never thought of Chicago as a "European influence," except, perhaps, for white-coated waiters at the Berghoff. It's always been a Democrat's town. Still, there was a cosmopolitan air in Jack's speech, surfacing in words and phrases like "hostelry," "a woman of social prominence," and "the finest of crystal." I arrived on the afternoon of Jack's thirty-seventh anniversary, and his red-headed wife, Margaret, came into the bar to celebrate. "I'll have a Manhattan," she said, perhaps to encourage a cosmopolitan sense in me. It worked: I ordered a round in honor of the occasion.

"What happened to Higgins?" I asked, sipping urbanely, tucked up to the bar like a citizen of the world.

"Killed by an Apperson Jack Rabbit."

Momentarily nonplussed, I thought it sounded like a "jackalope" hit and run.

"The Apperson Jack Rabbit was an automobile," Jack said. "Actually, it was Higgins's car. A rollover. Him and his wife both died."

Next morning, there were more exciting revelations about Glenrock, the most unsettling of which was that Jack and Margaret's "bed and breakfast" served no breakfast. In a local eatery, where I loaded up on huevos rancheros, I discovered that the Higgins Hotel was known for many years as the "Higgins Estate Hotel" because, when the Apperson Jack Rabbit took its fatal hop, John Higgins and his wife died childless. Higgins left everything to the state, who ran it, naturally, into the ground.

Back at the hotel to pay the bill (pricey but worth it), I learned another tidbit of interest: Margaret's grandfather was once the champion quoits player of the world, a wily Scot who took on all comers and eventually changed his name from

FOLLOWING THE WRONG GOD HOME

George Walkinshaw to George Ferguson (his wife's maiden name) when the supply of rubes who hadn't heard of him dwindled. Quoits is a form of that old favorite horseshoes and takes place on a level "pitch" using flat rings of iron or rope to circle a stake. George's infamy began in Scotland, moved to Canada, and onto Williamsburg, Colorado (now Cripple Creek), where quoits fanciers were financially crippled by the time he fleeced them. In his old age, after his quoits arm was gone, he moved to Glenrock to work in the coal mines.

. . .

Outside Glenrock, on the road to Casper, I came across the grave of Ada McGill, who died heading for sundown in July 1864. Her stone is another of those so precisely astride the trail that the railroad had to adjust its right-of-way to accommodate her. Three thousand feet below Ada McGill's bones lies one of the sources of John Higgins's wealth—the oil-bearing sands of the Big Muddy Field, "one of the richest deposits of Black Gold in the West," as Gregory Franzwa frames the cliché. On this ugliest of all routes, steel oil jacks go through their nodding rituals like Muslims at prayer, extracting what's left in the greasy subsoil that gave America the age of the automobile, the Rockefellers, and the political scandal of Teapot Dome, which, incidentally, is nearby.

Pausing for water at a Conoco pumping station, I met Jack Brown, a senior research technologist out of Oklahoma. Jack took off oil-stained gloves, wiping his hands on streaky coveralls. Sixty-two, he had the tanned, lined face of a fifty-year-old and the muscled arms of a man in his forties, and was, he told me, "kind of winding down with ninety days to go to retirement." From Jack I learned about "R&D"—research and development—on an oil field that was winding down itself. "This field's got fifteen . . . maybe twenty years left in it," he said. Maybe the two of them would wink out together, I thought.

"It's all downhill from here," Jack said, speaking of the oil field but, possibly, of himself.

As I understood it, Conoco had adopted the Maxwell House Coffee slogan for the Big Muddy Field—"Good to the Last Drop." When I showed up to fill my canteen, Conoco was pumping water into the wells, followed by what Jack called "a polymer surfactant," otherwise known as "detergent." Since detergents separate oil molecules from surfaces in the same way that Palmolive Liquid slides grease off a dinner plate, polymer surfactants clean oil out of sand and lift it to the surface.

"Polymer has high viscosity," Jack explained, "which means that it stays behind the oil while moving it to the producing wells. On the surface, we get a mixture of water and oil and separate them. So far we spent thirty million on the project."

"How much oil did you recover?"

"Hell, we only got about ten million back. But that's R&D for you. You learn something. That's why we did it."

. . .

Crossing this most ugly stretch of ground, Mormons took to grousing. Thomas Bullock got into a shouting match and fistfight with George Brown, who accused him of "idling & fooling" his time away. Umbrage taken, Bullock replied, "O Good God, what a lie . . ." and the dustup commenced. Brown struck Bullock "with his Whip . . . ready for a fight," but nimble Tom evaded two punches. It ended in a draw. Wrote Bullock, "George Brown has lied to and about the Lord's anointed. . . . He has now struck me with his Whip and I now pray that the Lord God of Israel may reward him according to his evil deeds & punish him until he repent & forsake his evil ways." They'd been on the road a long time and probably needed a "brass check."

37

I am constantly thrown back upon my old plan to make hand-carts, and let the emigration foot it. BRIGHAM YOUNG

At about half past four the encampment was formed on the banks of the river. . . . Two of the Missourian companies arrived about the same time. . . . It was now contemplated to leave a company of brethren . . . to ferry over the gentiles. WILLIAM CLAYTON,
JUNE 12, 16, 1847

At this point the Mormons had established a blacksmith shop and ferry . . . for filthy lucre to be obtained from the Gentiles. Contrary to expectation . . . we found those in charge of respectable appearance, well informed, polite, and in every way agreeable.
WM. G. JOHNSON, JUNE 3–4, 1849

Casper was named for a fallen hero (Caspar W. Collins, lieutenant, Eleventh Ohio Cavalry) but it's best known in Wyoming history for misspelling the hero's name (a telegrapher's error) and its notorious whorehouses along "the Sandbar." Almost from its beginnings, illicit sex was carried on in the city with a commercial pragmatism that Republicans would admire. A mainstay moneymaker when the Wyoming oil fields went into production, the skin trade kept on pumping through the Depression. Except for the Natrona County Courthouse with its handsome bas-reliefs on themes of western settlement, Casper's architecture is about as interesting as the Omaha stockyards. Its history, on the other hand, raised my interest.

The Sandbar was originally an island in the middle of the North Platte River. Prone to spring floods, the river alternately erased and exposed the island until one of its channels permanently dried up, leaving the "bar" high and dry. To its shifty sands came prostitutes' "cribs" where the destitute, drunken, and driven soon crowded in—working stiffs and city fathers with unmet needs. It served all comers for three-quarters of a century and was the lone piece of local color, so far as I could tell from my brief stay in town, which gave me a tingle.

Casper's "boom" started in 1895 when the Pennsylvania Oil and Gas Company opened a refinery to process the high-grade crude pouring from the recently tapped Salt Creek Oil Field. Until then, the Sandbar had been used as a tenting ground, a place for sheepherders and their wagons to winter over, even the town dump. Earlier, in 1889, a civic decree was adopted that made it unlawful for any woman "to use . . . vile, profane, or indecent language, or to act in a boisterous or lewd manner, or to smoke any cigar, cigarette, or pipe on Casper's streets." Nor was she "to frequent or remain in the barroom of any saloon . . . between the hours of 7 A.M. and 10 P.M."—which left the rest of the night wide open for raising hell.

In no time, a railroad showed up and with it the ragtag of roughs and toughs needed for the oil boom, along with more women who saw the wee hours as their golden opportunity. By one period account, "Casper was spinning headlong into undreamed of wealth." In 1914, when the Burlington Railroad constructed a spur to get its railroad cars to the Standard Oil refinery, it built a levy that cut off the low-water channel between the Sandbar's east bank and the town—a move, you might say, that put the island and town in bed together.

By 1918, "painted ladies, tinhorn gamblers, bootleggers, and criminals on the lam," had taken over the treeless wasteland. More rows of ramshackle frame "cribs" were built along West B Street, single windows facing the street so customers could size up the goods. The Sandbar had its own "Queen," Virginia Cawley, who, with her husband, "Big Boy," became outspoken, defiant, and notorious. Killings were common, beatings routine, and a "dozen houses of ill fame," supporting the less public needs of the town's leading citizens, became watering holes on a street still known to old-timers, affectionately, as "the Line." When local matrons grew indignant or suspicious of their husbands, the cribs and "parlor houses" were raided and the girls flushed out of town, but they always drifted back to the legendary outposts of vice—Southern Mansion, Palace Hotel, Jazz-land Theater, Columbia Billiard Parlor, Texas Lunch, Canyon Hotel. During the Great Depression, the "cribs" along West B Street were razed, only to be replaced years later by the Laurel Gardens Senior Citizen Housing Project, where, no doubt, some of its residents carry memories of a youth misspent on the site.

· · ·

Before the Sandbar was a twinkle in a roughneck oilman's Saturday night, Brigham Young had sussed out the entrepreneurial possibilities of the Casper site. Arrived three miles east of there on June 12, 1847, he constructed "pole rafts" to ferry Mormon wagons across the Platte. Recognizing the buildup of Manifest Destiny behind him, he reasoned a Mormon profit could be made off Manifest Cash and, with an unwavering eye for business, founded a ferry service. At a buck fifty per wagon, payable in cash or goods, the "Mormon Ferry" floated Missouri "pukes" and all others over troubled waters, in the process restocking the Saint's badly depleted financial larder—"As much of a miracle to me as it [was] to see the children of Israel fed with manna in the Wilderness," said Wilford Woodruff.

Turns out that Brigham's entrepreneurial "Mormon Ferry" was a metaphor for the Saints' future and set Mormons on the road to welding American capitalism to the articles of faith, perhaps their greatest achievement. Although the Mormon Church has faced bankruptcy or financial hard times at least twice—once in the 1890s when the U.S. government threatened to confiscate church properties as an incentive for them to give up polygamy, and again in the 1980s when the bottom temporarily fell out of the stock market—by the 1950s the church was spreading "faith in business" hand in glove with "faith in the gospel." Brigham's Manifest Business was picked up and expanded by subsequent presidents and prophets and, more than any other American-born faith, the LDS Church is a financial empire with corporate and controlling interests in real estate, industry, agriculture, and telecommunications, among others. Today, its prophets are as well versed in *fortune* as some think they are at *fortune-telling*. The faithful pay a flat 10 percent of gross income (most of it invested) into the church coffers: those who don't are called annually to settle accounts and, failing to divvy up, are denied access to LDS temples. Hell-bent on building a separate theocratic "kingdom," Brigham invented the 1040 short and long forms over half a century before the IRS. Worldwide, even a Mormon widow is expected to pay up her mite.

FOLLOWING THE WRONG GOD HOME

Beyond the North Platte the Mormons crossed a sixty-mile stretch of waste-land rife with stinking chemical seeps and choking alkali beds before reaching the Sweetwater River and water abundant—a long haul known as the "Poison Spider Route." By 1985, it hadn't changed much, and the two-day haul was as "poison" to me as it had been to them. Utah was thirty-six days in Brigham's future when he started for the Sweetwater, but as each day slid away, the Mormons saw more and more traces of the weakening resolve of other Dreamers heading toward Promised Land, especially on this stretch of ground. In uncharacteristic ferocity, William Clayton wrote, "One of the most horrid, swampy, stinking places I ever saw."

As Dreams shrank, emigrants of all stripes began tossing off anything cum-bersome, particularly when fetid alkali "sinks" shimmered in the distance. Litter along the trail bespoke Dream's future inheritance—a "disposable" culture. Three years later, James Hutchings noted: "Here, as in many other places, useless articles had been abandoned, boxes, barrels, ironwork of all kinds, etc. . . . trunks, boxes, clothes, tools, chains lying around!" Among the debris, the British-born emigrant saw "the skull of a man who had parts of him taken away . . . an arm here and a leg there, tendons showing where the flesh had been gnawed off," but arrived at the Sweetwater, he penned a line revealing a numbing indifference to the day's horrors: "Today we found gooseberries."

• • •

Of the geography I crossed between Nebraska and Salt Lake City, the sixty miles between Casper and the Sweetwater River were the most daunting. Apprehension gripped me, tightening into a knot of foreboding. Potable water on the route was scarce, the only source supposed to be at Willow Springs, halfway across, so I tele-phoned the Bureau of Land Management and asked for confirmation.

"Yep, there's water at the spring," I was told.

But I wasn't comforted. The deputy sheriff back in Douglas had succeeded in undermining the BLM's reputation: although I wouldn't go so far as to call a gov-ernment agency "com'nist," I felt the information was unreliable, since my informant had to search for someone in the office who'd been "out that way in the last month."

Seeking more reassurance, I headed toward the Sandbar, where information was perhaps more up to date and local history more interesting. No shots were fired on the day I was there, although shoot-'em-ups were plenty in the old days. ("Queen" Cawley once pumped five rounds at "Big Boy," later claiming she "only wanted to scare him.") When I hit upon Ray's Taxidermy Studio with its window full of the snuffed and stuffed, and the motto, "Moose or Mouse, Just Drag It to Our House," I figured I was at the right place. When I walked in, Lewis Ray met me at the door.

A big man, over six feet (three feet across the shoulders), Lewis Ray wore five large rings (two on his right hand, three on his left) and a watchband with combined silver and semiprecious stones that must have weighed in at over a pound. His red T-shirt, stretched over a sizable midriff, and shoulder-length hair parted in the middle, gave him a touch of out-of-place distinction, as if a distilled remnant of hippiedom had arrived in town, unannounced, to "age" quietly in Casper's barrel. His mustache was salt-and-pepper and his beard so flecked with silver that he seemed an understudy for the role of St. Nick. I asked if he knew if there was water at Willow Springs. I told him I needed a second opinion. Pronto.

Doug Slee, who worked for Ray, yawed a gat-toothed grin. He had unevenly cropped blond hair, blue eyes, and a frequent manner of pushing his hair up on his forehead as if he were fighting gale force winds, but his manic grin was unsettling.

"Been over to the BLM?" Ray asked.

"Yes."

"What do they say?"

"They say there's water."

"Shit," he said. "Those assholes will say anything."

By then, I was looking over his shoulder at a pair of very large bronzed work boots nailed to a sign that read: These boots kicked the ass of Deputy Sheriff Dennis Kelleher." If Kelleher had hemorrhoids at the time, he was in big trouble.

Rumor had it that Kelleher came west from Boston to hunt "the hub of antelope country" and stayed on, eventually settling into a job with the uniformed constabulary of Natrona County. Lewis Ray did all his taxidermy work until (Lewis's version), after shooting a "big Powder River buck," Kelleher took his trophy kill to a competing taxidermist for "a ten percent discount."

"That did it," Ray said. "After all I done for him. I got down a gun scabbard and whipped him."

"The sign says you kicked his ass."

"I did that, too."

This was more like it, I thought. Sandbar flavor.

"What happened to Kelleher?"

"Left town. Couldn't take the embarrassment," Doug Slee said, talking right through his smile, like a ventriloquist's dummy.

The Kelleher dustup must have put Lewis in full kick mode because he had a separate "Ass Kicking List" done up on plywood. Kelleher was on it, but he'd been crossed off and "done" painted to one side. But two other guys and the competing taxidermist were waiting their turn.

During a lengthy discussion of what mayhem he had in mind for the remaining three, Lewis gave me his business card. The front was straightforward enough with Ray's name above a bellowing elk, but on the back was a list of avian taxidermy he'd do "FREE": "Short-tailed Bed Thrasher," "Horney-Headed Legpincher," "Ruffled Spouse," "Extra-Marital Lark," "Gimlet-Eyed Titwatcher," "Morning After Grouse," and the "Hairy Chested Nutscratcher." I qualified tenth on the list—"Bald Old Coot"—and made for the door, but not before he fastened a ham fist on my shoulder and guided me into a back room to "visit" his collection of rattlesnakes—six, all told, in a glass aquarium tank. I allowed as they were as fine a half-dozen rattlers as I had ever seen. Lewis was so pleased I liked his venomous friends that he gave me a box of twenty-four chocolate-covered Moon-Pies as a parting gift "for the road." On the way out, I leaned down to stroke the house cat, Ol' Poacher, who, Lewis told me "lost his teeth, his nuts, and his tail in one month."

· · ·

I took Lewis Ray's advice and headed deeper into the Sandbar searching out the War Surplus Store. A man like Lewis Ray couldn't be wrong about the BLM, I reckoned, since he seemed so religious about his personal convictions. Besides, Doug Slee's sly smile was on my mind; few things make a westerner smile more maniacally than thinking they know the truth about the BLM.

Dave Hancock, the surplus store's owner—who served in both the U.S. Navy and the Army Air Corps in World War II, flying Stearmans and B-25 bombers—had finally gotten his motorcycle license. Crowding sixty, he was as flushed as a teenager after his first bungee jump.

"I need some canteens," I said.

"What size?"

"Enough for two or three gallons."

Taking no chances with the Bureau of Land Management or its sympathizers, I'd secretly developed a scheme to get the weight off my back while carrying enough water to cross the Poison Spider with a dash of Mormon authenticity thrown in for good measure: I planned to simulate a Mormon handcart, pulling my possessions behind me—except I didn't have a handcart. Yet.

• • •

Mormon historian LeRoy Hafen once defined the Mormon handcart experience as "the most remarkable travel experiment in the history of Western America." There's hyperbole in Hafen's claim (surely Lewis and Clark's jaunt to the Pacific qualifies as "remarkable"), although his enthusiasm is relieved by the word "experiment." By 1849, with many of its members scattered and living hand-to-mouth in the upper Midwest, Mormons in Utah incorporated a Perpetual Emigrating Fund Company to help out. Known as the PEF, its president was Brigham.

A nuts-and-bolts operation to assist refugees left behind after the troubles in Nauvoo and Europe's newly converted, the new company floated loans to help with migration to Salt Lake. Repayment of loans, with interest, was intended to make the fund "perpetual," thereby assisting even more Saints to "gather" to Salt Lake City. As Hafen observes: "For nearly forty years it was to assist in the removal of fifty thousand individuals over land and sea to Utah." One of the assisted was his grandmother, six years old at the time.

Problem was, only 30 percent repaid their loans in full. Many worked off their debt as laborers on church building projects, a third came up with partial repayments, and "the rest paid nothing." By 1856, the PEF was broke and Brigham needed less expensive options to get newly converted Saints "home" to Zion. His motive is obvious: he needed warm bodies to shore up the Mormon kingdom.

It was Brigham's idea to let Mormons hoof it. Strapped for cash, the church couldn't afford horses, oxen, wagons, or too many attending personnel. In 1855, he'd written to his son-in-law in England. Savvy, if never a dab hand at spelling, he laid out his idea deftly.

> We are very ancios to have a company got up in England to cros the planes with hancarts. I due beleve that I could bring a company across, without a team and beet eny ox trane if I could be there myself. Would you like to try it? If we can have our emegration come to the eastern citys and the northan rout, it will be much relieve our Brethrern from sickness and deth. . . . There is a raleway from New Yourk City to Iowa City and will cost onley 8 dollars for the pasedge. Then take hancarts and there little luggedge with a fue good milk cowes and com on til they are met with teams from this place.

Between 1856 and 1860, about 3,000 Saints labored from Iowa City, Iowa, to the Great Salt Lake, with 650 vehicles that looked like pushcarts in reverse, each cart hauled across 1,400 miles of rutted roads, ridges, sand tracks, and salt flats—a feet-first enterprise of great hardship that later ballooned into one of the most heroic myths of Mormon death and endurance against the odds.

For all that, it also contains a tale of bad judgment, false promises, and desperation as much as hope, faith, and salvation. Handcarts were often made with unseasoned wood that cracked under high desert conditions. Each cart carried up to 500 pounds, mostly foodstuffs. Adults were allowed 17 pounds of "baggage," children 10—five people per cart. Ten companies crossed the plains, and one who made the long haul, J. Rogerson, left this description of a handcart: "The open handcart was made of Iowa hickory or oak, the shafts and sides of the same material, but the axles generally of hickory. In length, the side pieces and shafts were about six or seven feet, with three or four binding cross bars from the back part to the fore part of the body of the cart; then two or three feet space from the latter bar to the front bar or singletree for the lead horse or lead man, woman or boy of the team."

As an "experiment," Hafen is right. As a good idea, it's unsettling. Franklin Richards, president of the European Mission, advertised it "as a plan of inspiration," selling it to new converts like a contemporary cruise agent. "When we allow our imaginations to wander into the future and paint scenes that will transpire on the prairies next summer," he said, "they partake largely of the romantic." Overeager Saints were willing to leave everything "and toddle off with a few things in their pocket handkerchief." Brigham advised, "They should only bring a change of clothing."

Brigham seems to have been high on large doses of the "romantic" himself, confidently predicting "fifteen miles a day" for the average daily walk. At that pace, he predicted, "this will bring them through in 70 days, and after they get accustomed to it, they will travel 20, 25, and even 30 with all ease, and no danger of giving out." He'd forgotten, perhaps, that even with wagons, horses, and oxen to do the grunt work, his own average on the 1,032-mile trek from Winter Quarters was 9.3 miles per day, not counting blisters. At fifty dollars a head, it seemed a "win-win" proposition; but in the history of Mormon overland travel, it became the only time the Saints were hit with truly gruesome fatalities. Today, Mormons see it as a chapter in their history that speaks to the power of faith and people's endurance. Maybe so. But viewed wide-awake and less Dreamy, it was a scheme that oversold the goods with fatal consequences.

· · ·

My own handcart revelation came at the Fort Caspar Museum where a model of a Mormon handcart (think of a child's sandbox on two wagon wheels) was on display. It wasn't for sale and I couldn't have pulled it anyway, but I suggested to Dave Hancock at the War Surplus store that he might give me a few alternative ideas on rolling stock for history's sake. Straightening the pens in the plastic holder in the pocket of his I've-seen-better-days blue shirt, he considered the problem as he might have considered a bombing run over Germany. We discussed the tactical advantages of a single-wheeled elk cart (requires two pilots), a grocery cart (wheels too small), and finally a golf cart, which, he implied, was about as much use a Cessna in a dogfight but better than nothing. Dave called the country club, and they promptly offered a used cart for twenty-five bucks, cash and carry—anything to help a stranger and, as it turned out, to get a lemon off their hands. I agreed to pick it up next morning. Next, Dave laid out a battle plan that included several bungee cords to secure my pack and worldly goods to the cart's frame, including the four two-quart canteens I'd purchased, along with a wide-brimmed straw hat foisted on me "for good measure."

Across the street, Daylight Donuts was having a grand opening, offering free coffee-colored hot water for anyone willing to pay for greasy delights. Dave pointed to a half-hidden gate beside the doughnut shop. "They called the girls 'pigeons' in the old days. There's six pigeon holes still back there," he said, "but the birds all flew the coop. They should'a saved somethin' from the old Sandbar," he complained. "They should'a remodeled the Southern Mansion. It had a fine staircase, long hallways, a dance hall and a piano. But they didn't save nothin' but two damn trees."

· · ·

Over dinner, I tumbled into conversation with a casualty of the road—call him Dooley—whose face resembled a heap of broken glass. Only duct tape or a pricey plastic surgeon could have improved his profile. Long-winded, Dooley spent time on the road as a sales rep, and his interest in Sandbar history was less historical than libidinous. He claimed firsthand experience of "pigeons" in six states and was adamant that Utah women were as adept at paid performance, if not better, than anything Casper had to offer in its prime.

But even windbags have a tale to interest a traveler.

"There was a madam up in Lusk. She ran the only legal whorehouse in Wyoming. The town tried to shut her down. Next thing they knew, the lights went out all over town." He stopped, going for his apple pie like a cowboy for a hooker's garter.

"I don't get it," I said.

He chortled, spewing piecrust across the table. "She owned the utilities company. It was only after she died they managed to close her place down."

The tale proved true—most of it, at least. When I called sparky Twyla Barnette, director of Lusk's Stagecoach Museum, she not only knew of the madam, "Del" Burke, but the ill-reputed house in question, The Yellow Hotel. Turns out, Del Burke did have a "heart of gold." When Lusk was down on its luck, she invested her profits and bought the power company, saving some of her customers from moving and the city from a big overdraft. Del Burke's new "civic" virtue kept a lot of people working hard, including the ladies at the Yellow Hotel. When the hotel was threatened with closure, she turned the power off, but it came back on in no time at all.

Dooley was a gent who knew something about everything and said so—frequently. But he didn't know this: as part of another American Dream, Philip Syng Physick (1768–1837), a Philadelphian, invented an artificial anus. Dooley, on the other hand, was the real thing.

38

Arise, take up thy bed, and walk.
JESUS OF NAZARETH, MARK 2:9

We . . . arrived at "Willow Spring" where we halted a little to water. This spring is about two foot wide and the water . . . perfectly clear, cold as ice water and of very good taste.
HEBER KIMBALL, JUNE 20, 1847

Pursued our way over hills and dales, scorched with heat; came to a copse of small willows, from which issued excellent springs of water.
JOHN BIDWELL, JULY 4, 1841

Next morning, I took a taxi to the country club, paid the golf shop with a check, and, back at the motel, bungeed my pack and two gallons of water to its aluminum frame. The wheels splayed on either side from the unexpected weight, but at eighteen inches in diameter, they appeared up to navigating dirt roads. When

I hoofed out of town, a few of Casper's citizens looked at me as if I carried the placard: "Outpatient, State Mental Hospital."

From Casper, the "Poison Spider Route" crosses tortuous ground, its drab monotony punctuated only by an occasionally changing sky and tails of hot wind that tug at the shirtsleeves and suck at resolve. Platte and Slater's *Travelers' Guide across the Plains* (1852) offered this grim warning: "You will find no good water for 22 miles. . . . You will find some which is very poisonous, on account of the immense amount of alkali in this region." As if to punctuate the land's venomous nature, the Rattlesnake Range hovers in the distance.

The toll on people and animals was staggering. Driven by thirst and desperation to drink bad water, cattle, mules, oxen, and horses keeled over. By one account, "thousands of cattle and horses have died here from drinking the stinking water," and the stench of rotting animal flesh was oppressive. James Hutchings saw "thirty dead oxen" when he crossed the Poison Spider and J. Goldsborough Bruff noted "five yoke of dead oxen . . . fallen in geer." Overland travelers choked on wind-driven alkali dust. In the "vestiges of camps," Bruff saw "clothes, boots, shoes, hats, lead, iron, tin-ware, trunks, meat, wheels, axles, wagon-beds, mining tools" and passed them all by. He promptly "dismembered" one "very handsome and new *Gothic Bookcase*" to boil his coffee. But he also noted a marked change in his fellow travelers: "Their true character is shown, untrammeled, unvarnished (with) selfishness, hypocrisy. . . . Some, whom at home were thought gentlemen, are totally unprincipled."

When I reached Willow Springs, I prayed Lewis Ray would kick the ass of the regional director of the BLM. There was water all right, but the "springs" were a font of urine and cow dung, rank as an outhouse in August. Walleyed cattle waded through the manure, stupidly watching me stupidly watching them. I made my way through a field of excrement to the so-called spring house; it was full of stinking antelope bones. This was the oasis Clayton called "one of the loveliest camping spots I have seen on the journey," where springs, "ten inches deep, perfectly clear, cold as ice water, and very good tasting" soothed dusty Mormons.

While I rested in the shade of a urine-nourished cottonwood, a steer arched its neck over the fence and plucked off my straw hat, shredding it with slow, maddening, bovine contentment. With no decent place to camp and no possibility of a refreshing wash, I pressed on, facing a four-hundred-foot climb across the divide between the Platte and Sweetwater drainages. Worse, the light was beginning to go. As I began the climb, a white 4×4 Chevy truck lumbered along. A swarthy, mustached man was driving, his eyes opaque as tar pits, with two women perched like songbirds beside him, warbling to each other. Bold lettering on the truck's door read: "Manager: Rattlesnake Grazing Association."

"What's going on here?" he asked. The songbirds stopped twittering.

"I'm walking the Mormon Trail."

He scowled down at me and said, curtly, "This here's RGA land. With things as they are, I'd just as soon you stick to the road. Understand me?"

I hadn't the foggiest about "things as they are" and didn't give a damn anyway. "What's ahead?" I asked.

He was already cranking up his window. "More dust," he answered and rumbled the big diesel up the steep hill.

. . .

Willow Springs sits at the base of one of the most notorious climbs on the Oregon-California-Mormon Trail. In its heyday, "Prospect Hill" was both the graveyard and junkyard of the trails west—a vertical Dreamkiller. Like others before him, Howard Stansbury saw on its slopes the frailty of Manifest Destiny in "the relics of seventeen wagons" and in "the carcasses of twenty-seven dead oxen," eight "in one heap." Tossed aside as emigrants' prospects dimmed were "bar-iron and steel, large blacksmith's anvils and bellows, crow-bars, drills, augers, gold-washers, chisels, axes, lead, trunks, spades, ploughs, large grindstones, baking-ovens, cooking stoves without number, kegs, barrels, harness, clothing, bacon, and beans," strewn in a feverish abandon as animals and people struggled to cross the divide. Stansbury recognized a few names on the abandoned trunks as belonging to settlers who earlier "had accompanied me from St. Louis to Kansas."

At the summit, a fast-moving darkness rose in the northwest, blanket-heavy and thicker than steel wool. A wind came with it, cruel and moaning, carrying flecks of moisture and memories of winter. At first, it blew grit and dust, but soon it blew menace and fear; atop the plateau, a cruel landscape spread out in every direction, raw and foreboding. Then the rain came, the first wave striking hard and heavy. Quickly wet to the skin, I stripped the tent from the pack, walked ten feet off the road, and fought to lock its bendable aluminum rods into place. Spread out, it acted like a sail, taking on wind and dragging me after it. Fighting back, I pinned it down in the middle with the golf cart and piled rocks on its corners. When I tried to stake it down, the ground was concrete. A plastic tent stake snapped while I was hammering at it with a fist-sized boulder: I swore long and loudly, cursing, among other things, the Douglas County deputy sheriff's "personal savior."

Soaked through and shivering, I finally got a grip on myself, realizing that ranting would get me nothing but high blood pressure, hypothermia, or both.

Heaving the backpack inside the tent as an anchor, I managed to get the tent's aluminum exterior frame up, but with wind sailing under its corners, it behaved like a wounded goose trying to get off troubled water. To hold it down, I gathered rocks, ingeniously (so I thought at the time) placing them *inside* the tent to anchor each corner.

By now rain lashed in horizontal, wind-driven bursts. In the open, I stripped to the skin, crawled inside, dragging my soggy clothes after me. Numb, worrying for real about hypothermia, I dug out my silk T-shirt, a pair of undershorts, a fresh pair of socks, and my surviving pair of zip-off-legs hiking pants, damp but serviceable. Finally, I took out the GoreTex rain suit at the bottom of the pack and contorted myself into it. Once my self-inflating mattress was spread out (the only thing I didn't have to do to aid in my survival), I rolled out the down sleeping bag, wriggled inside, pulled it over my head, and tightened the drawstrings. Slowly warming, I prepared to ride out the storm.

Rain hammered at the tent. Wind, often screaming, bowed a tent wall in. By ten o'clock, the wash of rain gave way to intermittent slapping, which I took to be slush. By ten-thirty the ground under the tent was turning to gumbo. By eleven, the wind shifted more directly to the west, luffing the tent like a spinnaker. Lifted by gusts under the floor, the rocks in one corner toppled into the other and my nylon house of cards came down, half of it yawing over. I hung on for another half hour, tugging the rocks back into place, but it was obvious I had a night's work ahead. Near midnight, there was a skim of water on the floor, driven up under the rain fly by the wind. By two o'clock the slap, slap of tacky slush gave way to a softer brushing. I unzipped and peeked outside. Snow. At dawn, the wind broke. Sensing calm, I fell asleep. When I next looked out, the world beyond my tent flap was thick with fog.

Evening went and morning came, the first day. The Lord, I like to think, looked around and saw that it was bad. The fog lingered until midmorning when pallid sun broke through streaky sheets of cloud. In early afternoon, I ventured out into a ruined world; three inches of snow had fallen and melted as easily as it had come, but walking was impossible: sodden clay balled under my boots, filling the cleats, hanging off the soles in loaf-sized globs. As I was steeling for another night and praying for a warm, drying wind, the earth moved in a heaving, shuddering, grumbling sigh.

• • •

Dave Stevens drives a fifty-ton hydraulic crane over the back roads of Natrona County. The crane is mounted on a mobile transporter of staggering size and tonnage. There are two single-person cabs—one on the transporter and the other on the crane, which sits atop eight wheels, four in front, four in back. To keep an erect crane from toppling over, the rear of the crane bed is laden with tons of floating weight attached to its cab. Dave's behemoth—the C2—was owned by Getter Trucking, Inc., which specializes in monster machines from corporate offices in Billings, Montana, and Lufkin, Texas.

Mud-fouled in jeans and jacket, Dave looked down at an idiot from atop his monster.

"Anything I can do for you?" he called.

"Can you get me down off this mountain?"

"Sure as hell try," he said.

It took fifteen minutes (with Dave's help) to pack up. The golf cart and backpack were dumped on the exposed deck of the crane and I mounted into its cab, high above Dave. When the transporter moved, it shuddered—a dinosaur heaving awake—then it crawled to life, grumbling, and lumbered on, churning gutters of mud beneath its wheels.

That day, I discovered two things: nothing had changed on Prospect Hill since 1847, and a man alone isn't worth much crossing it without "community" to help out. That Mormons had got it better than most Americans on the trails west, I had no doubt, but looking back, I questioned Brigham's judgment. Atop Prospect Hill, the prophet remarked on its "romantic beauty," confessing "what a splendid place it would be for a summer mansion or a tavern." By then, I expect, he was running low on water, cutting his dust with Colonel Kane's brandy and without the benefit of reading Mark Twain.

"All saints can do miracles," the prickly Missourian observed, "but few of them can keep a hotel."

·   ·   ·

Dave turned left onto a side road, stopped his juddering monster, and waved me down from the crane cab.

"Far as I go," he apologized. "If you're on the road later on, I'll pick you up."

I offered to kiss his boots and vowed to light a votive candle in his honor if and when I turned religious. With much shaking and groaning, the leviathan lumbered east on another godforsaken stretch of dung-colored track, grumbling until it became a faint speck of yellow on the skyline, its diesel garbling in the distance before dipping over a crest—gone. Fixed to the gumbo, my feet held fast like the flukes of an anchor. I moored there for several minutes, awed by the sealike surface of sage, the road drifting in and over groundswells of faded green like a ship's wake. When I weighed anchor myself and turned into the wind, its music was mournful.

On slightly drier ground, I managed to drag the golf cart, stopping every hundred yards or so to clear its spokes of sludge; its complaining wheels toed further and further inward under the weight, not unlike Edward Oliver's green wooden axle in Nebraska. Overhead, the sky narrowed to a graphite sheen—low, brooding, unforgiving. I managed about three miles, one in damp, one in drip, one in drizzle while summoning courage for another one-night stand with Mother Nature. When a 4×4, mud-besotted pickup growled slowly alongside and braked, it turned out to be Dave with a roughneck from an oil crew.

"You're one lucky SOB," Dave said through a crack in the window. "The crane got stuck, goddam it."

Inside, two damp and drying bodies fogged the windows, the defroster at full throttle. The driver—Glenn, Slim, or Phlegm, I forget which—gave a lumpy, wet laugh. He had the darting, manic eyes of someone marooned too long on a desert island and whose best friends, lots of them, were himself. I heaved my "handcart" onto the truck bed, rattling empty beer cans, and squeezed myself, dripping, into the cab. "No beer for hitchhikers. But you can have a Pepsi," Phlegm offered.

Drinking a Coors Light, he winked and coughed up something chewy which he ejected onto the driver's side of the road, looking at it as if to see whether or not it was edible and he'd made a mistake. Then he gunned the engine, whipping sideways until the wheels caught and slithered forward, driving with road-warrior insanity, fisting the wheel, now and then turning an incisor-missing smile in my direction, and jabbing his finger at the ice chest under my boots. Dutifully, I plucked a Pepsi out of his cooler, digging for it among silver cans of Colorado Kool-Aid. With Phlegm at the throttle and Dave white-knuckled, we crossed the last miles of the Poison Spider Route. I tumbled out on Highway 220, rubber-legged as a greenhorn exiting a roller coaster. "Safe journey," Dave said—enviously, as if he knew his own chances for survival were all but blown riding shotgun with his designated driver.

Phlegm raised an arm in a mock salute, showed me a missing bicuspid, pressed his tongue into its empty socket, and backhanded an empty Coors can over the cab into the truck bed where it clattered among several dozen dead soldiers. In a crisp follow-through motion, his right arm reached for the cooler, snapped it open, and plucked out another Coors. "Good luck, buddy." He snapped the cap and punched the gas.

Lunging east in a high-throttled whine, the truck skidded once on the mud clinging to its wheels, corrected, and shook itself back on course, Dave's arm waving a frantic farewell. I headed west along the highway, relieved to be moving away

FOLLOWING THE WRONG GOD HOME

from the wired chauffeur whose DNA had sprouted a triple helix. Half an hour later, in sight of Independence Rock, a wheel caterwauled off the golf cart, tottered drunkenly on the asphalt, and keeled over on the shoulder. On cue, another cold rain came down, hissing on the highway with the relentless rhythm of a steel whisk beating an egg. I gave up, climbed a fence, and sheltered under a concrete highway culvert where half the steers in Wyoming had hung out long enough to evacuate their lower intestines. Overhead, eighteen-wheelers drafted long wings of water in sheets that washed over both ends. I could have wept, but instead made a decision I should have made earlier, even if it meant staying the course with Dave.

I emptied what water remained in my canteens, stripped away the bungee cords from the cart, gave it last rites, and flung its flimsy aluminum remains under the culvert into a slurry of well-digested Wyoming before hoisting the pack and climbing back to the highway where I stuck out a thumb. Another roustabout named Bob Hehn from Montpelier, Idaho, picked me up. His wife, Connie, did-n't mind sharing the cab of the pickup.

"You looked a sight back there," she said.

"I stink," I said, water pooling under my feet. "I'm sorry."

Bob sniffed, "Just as a matter of curiosity, what the hell have you been up to?"

"Bob," I began, "you can't trust an American-made handcart these days."

An hour later, I was back in Casper, holed up in a Super 8 Motel, defeated. Outside my window, snow clung to the hills. "Six inches in South Pass," a waitress told me over dinner. With my Canadian arrogance drained, I put myself to bed early, beaten but besotted with admiration for all those who accomplished what I hadn't on the Poison Spider. Over the years, I've wondered what happened to the golf cart, especially the innocent who might have stumbled across it under a Wyoming culvert—perhaps a motorist desperate for a pee or a rancher checking fresh plops for traces of his lost herd. Whatever they thought of the oddity, I know the truth and nothing but: I abandoned it on the eighteenth shit hole.

39

I will walk into the southwest or west. Eastward I go only by force;
but westward I go free. HENRY DAVID THOREAU,
"WALKING"

OVER THE GREAT DIVIDE 283

Arrived at the noted Rock Independence . . . there are hundreds of names of persons who have visited it . . . painted on the projecting surfaces. . . . The brethren put up a board opposite to the Rock with this inscription on it . . . Pioneers, June 21, 1847.

HEBER J. KIMBALL

This morning rote my name on the Rock called Independence.

SAMUEL PARKER, JULY 4, 1845

After breakfast, Bob Rathburn drove me back to where I'd ditched the golf cart. The manager of the Super 8 Motel took pity on a stranger. Slender in washed-out blue jeans and checkered shirt, Bob talked my head off about his off-the-job religion—windmills and barbed wire. A devoted student of the *"Bobbed" Wire Bible*, Bob's prophet of barb was the book's publisher, Jack Glover from Sunset, Texas. "Everybody trades wire by Glover's numbers," he told me, his graying hair tussled by draft from an open window. Whether a strand of Kelly's Diamond Point, H. H. Frye's Twist, E. Havenhill Y Barb, Billings Four Point, or Reynolds "Necktie," Bob knows Glover's *Bible* chapter and verse. Back at the motel, displayed against walnut-framed yellow backboards, I'd counted 113 strands of wire, each eighteen inches long, all different but each with a similar barbed intent—to keep what's out from getting in and what's in from getting out.

Each strand had at one time marked a boundary in someone's Dream—113 metaphors for *how* and *why* the West was carved up, and for how unexamined Dreams cordon off far more than our tidy back yards, often contrarily so, by keeping out anything that might trouble the prevailing mirage. In so lonely and expansive a land as the American West, to be "fenced in" is psychologically comforting, shrinking horizons to a manageable territory of defined lines. To be "fenced out" is to come face-to-face with someone else's self-imposed limitations and, stepping across the line, to be barbed or bled for crossing it. Across "Big Wyoming," even in its more remote sections, I was more often troubled by "fenced out" than "fenced in"—"No Trespassing"; "Trespassers Will Be Prosecuted to the Full Extent of the Law"; "Keep Out, No Exceptions"; "Protected by Smith & Wesson." Most boundaries I ignored, but they still left me vexed or uneasy.

• • •

Bob Rathburn also spoke a second tongue unfamiliar to a Canadian—a language of American wind. From him, I discovered the secret of the "Nebraska Spread," that low-to-the-ground windmill I'd seen near Fullerton, Nebraska. "High

FOLLOWING THE WRONG GOD HOME

water table," he said. "You could scratch the ground there and get a drink. Nebraska's full of water."

Whether it's a Plattner-Yale, Currie, Dempster, or Aermotor, before you can say "Bob," Bob will give you its history and statistics. Back in Scottsbluff, I'd passed a collection of windmills owned by Don Hanley, all striking to see, each a history of American breeze, all graceful as they caught the slightest draft. Under Bob's tutelage, even creaky octogenarian windmills I'd seen pumping stock water in Wyoming became comely in spite of broken blades or rusted vanes.

"I don't want to offend John Wayne or the movies," Bob said, "but it wasn't the gun and the plow that settled the West. It was barbed wire and windmills. Made sure a Kansas farmer or a Wyoming rancher got a cool drink. Made sure his stock did too. The wind always ran on Mondays. It drove the old rocker-type washing machines for the farmer's wife."

Windmills made it possible for the aquifers of the Great Plains to be tapped, and the resulting drink of water, used or abused, opened already "open spaces" to other American Dreamers. The exquisite Plattner-Yale has wooden fins that unfurl like a tulip to catch the air. The "poor man's windmill," the Currie, cost fourteen dollars in 1914. By the summer of 1950, the same model sold for seventeen bucks and change.

"After World War Two, the Rural Electric Association came in and everybody went to submerged pumps. That did it for the windmills." Bob sighed. "There's not many of us freaks left."

"I'm with the freaks," I volunteered.

"The biggest freak of all is L. T. Baker," Bob said. "If Jack Glover wrote the *"Bobbed" Wire Bible*, L. T. wrote the Good Book on windmills."

What I remember most vividly that morning was Bob's ardor for implements of western life, a contagion for the mechanics of wire and wind. I thanked him for it when he dropped me off, shook hands firmly as a westerner expects, and caught a fresh breeze of my own.

. . .

On the summit of Independence Rock in 1843, Matt Field "got mellow." James Nesmith nearly swooned, "having the satisfaction of putting the names of Miss Mary Zachary and Miss Jane Mills on the Southeast point"—a timid ménage à trois. Three years later, Henry Tappan "had the pleasure of a game of cards" on its surface. By 1853 Maria Parson Belshaw "felt very dizzy" on reaching the top. When I arrived on its dome, I sympathized with Orange Gaylord who, on June 15, 1850, remarked in his journal, "Had a snowstorm this morning," a discouragement we'd both experienced almost to the day but not the century. So famous a symbol of American pluck and promise did Independence Rock become that during the summer that Maria "felt dizzy," Stephen Forsdick wrote home: "I had seen pictures of this rock in London and I readily recognized it."

To travelers on the trails west, Independence Rock was one of the greatest curiosities on the road. It looked alternately like "a huge tombstone," an "unshapen pile," a "turtle shell," and "an egg divided lengthwise." Richard August Keen reckoned it "a freak of nature." Almost everybody who passed it scratched or painted a name onto its surface. Said Richard Burton of *Arabian Nights* fame: "Prairie travelers and emigrants expect to be followed by their friends, and leave, in their vermilion outfit, or their white house-paint or their brownish-black tar . . . a homely but hearty word of love or direction." Even buffalo skulls were made "to do duty at this *Poste Restante*."

Some believed the rock was named by J. C. Frémont, John Sublette, even Lewis and Clark, but who gave it its name remains a mystery. "Broken Hand" Fitzpatrick could have named it on July 4, 1824. In a fit of enthusiasm, James Mason in 1850 gave the credit to "American trappers who chanced to pass that way upon the 4th of July. Wishing to be Americans even in that secluded region of Aboriginal barbarism they proceeded to celebrate that great day which gave birth to human liberty." Manifest Destiny at its most pompous. This much is accurate: emigrants needed to reach Independence Rock by July 4 or shortly after if they were to make it safely to Oregon or California before winter.

• • •

Geologically, Independence Rock is a rounded monolith of granite cooked up in the depths of the earth where metamorphic origins are measured in billions of years. In spite of immense surrounding pressures, it reached the earth's surface, breaking through a veneer of sedimentary sandstone like a fist through Jell-O, and its surface peeled off like an onion, producing its rounded dome, a process known in geology as "exfoliation." Windblown sand and silt—not, as some believe, glacial polishing—gave the rock its deep grooves. So famous was the rock, emigrants were often disappointed (as was I) on coming across it for the first time, having expected, as Vincent Geiger did in 1849, "a spire, a pyramid, or a shot tower." James Evans wrote: "It appeared so insignificant that I scarcely noticed it at all," but he couldn't help noticing the Sweetwater flowing past its flank and the meadow crowded with pioneer wagons.

In his diary, Evans renders the river's name as two words—"Sweet Water"—a cleavage that more accurately describes its importance and promise. The "Sweet

Water" was the hydrous charm that shattered the dry hex on westward travel to Utah, Oregon, and California. In the early flow of Manifest Destiny, its abundance was discovered in the right place at the right time (1812), spilling off the flanks of the Wind River Mountains. Named because errant trappers supposedly spilled a sack of sugar in it—a myth—this last, long drink of water flowing toward the Mississippi carried Americans to the edge of "Oregon Territory" where Mormons, Presbyterians, Baptists, Catholics, Whigs, Democrats, do-gooders, and up-to-no-gooders crossed South Pass and took their first drink from a spring that flowed to the Pacific.

Fabled as "the Great Register of the Desert," Independence Rock was a geological PO where folks stopped to send out a final brief message before entering outer space. Perhaps the most tattooed piece of granite in America, it signified the last-ditch outpost between East and West—a geological semaphore of good-bye to all that. Religion and politics frequently visited the rock, as did Mormon free enterprise. Frémont was so moved by its spirit that he "engraved on this rock of the Far West a symbol of the Christian faith . . . the impression of a large cross." When the Mormons arrived on June 17, 1847, Brigham put his name on it. Always interested in "ready" business, Mormons with stone-carving tools were back on the site in 1850, willing to carve out your niche in history, cash up front at $1 to $5 a head. In election years, it was used as a political billboard. In 1843 Matt Field found "Henry Clay" painted "on this remarkable rock." When he returned later in the summer, he discovered "Martin Van Buren" had been added. In 1834 William Marshall confessed in his journal: "if our union and independence coexisted with it, it would have the brevet of immortality." Rock solid.

• • •

I was having a one-way chat with Milo J. Ayer on top of "Rock Independence," as it was frequently recorded in pioneer journals, when Mark Hattan came along. Milo hadn't said a word during my attempt at conversation, and when later visited by Jim Amos of *National Geographic* (I put Jim up to it), a photo of his name made the magazine. From Rochester, New York, Milo passed the rock in 1849, pausing to carve his name and age (27) on the cusp of a natural stone basin that was, on the afternoon I visited, full of recent snowmelt. I'd stopped to visit with Milo because he seemed more determined than others to send his message, having carved it painstakingly on a lip of that ghost-ridden granite before disappearing into the unknown.

Mark Hattan seemed much as I imagined Milo, a gritty and resolute young man, heading in the same direction. Biking from Washington, D.C., to Portland,

Oregon, following the route his great-great-grandfather took in 1846, he plotted his long-distance ride from a copy of his ancestor's handwritten account of his continental crossing. At the end of Mark's road was the Hattan Family Picnic, an annual blowout held on the Clackamas River. An actor, Mark worked out of New York City doing "eight-week gigs . . . four in rehearsal and four on the road" in towns like Richmond, Springfield, and Indianapolis. He'd also appeared in television commercials, once in his underwear for Fruit of the Loom, but also in lip-smacker roles for Minute Rice, Dry Sack sherry, and Oreo cookies. Mark gave me insider's dope on how Dreams are marketed these days.

"Mostly, it's how you hold the product, look into the camera, and say, 'MMMM, this is good!'" he said. "You're pampered on the set because they can't afford for you to get it wrong. There's a lot of time and money riding on retakes."

I asked him what his journey had taught him so far.

"I've relearned conversation," he said. "You sit down in a restaurant and people want to talk."

Mark was anything but sanguine. Sadly, there was no mail awaiting him at the PO of "Rock Independence"; he searched in vain for his great-great-grandfather's initials on the surface, but they had likely worn away as had so many others, leaving him adrift in sepia-tinted family memories.

"It was a long shot," he said, disconsolately. "I wanted to believe his initials were still there."

"Don't we all," I said.

Listening to wind carrying whatever faint echo was left of Milo J. Ayer's voice, I watched Mark Hattan pedal disappointment west, growing smaller in the distance until he vanished. With a raised finger, I traced the Sweetwater's liquid hope to the horizon, watching its untangling ribbon of silver. I was sitting, I realized, on a shard of Dream from which I kept a Canadian's watchful, fascinated, distance. When I looked down at Milo's desperate name on the rock, I realized my journey was inward all along.

• • •

There were no dumbbells on the Dumbbell Ranch when I dropped in to beg for a place to camp. A few hundred feet east of Devil's Gate—another famous trail site—I was "well received," as Ike Winkle might say. Norman Park was on crutches, hobbled from a fall from his horse. A hired hand told me he'd been bucked off and "broke a hip." A soft-spoken man, Norman was naturally reticent about details, no doubt because taking the plunge was embarrassing after long years firmly in the saddle.

FOLLOWING THE WRONG GOD HOME

I crossed the river and made camp where Mormons and thousands of foot-loose Americans had camped before me, their fires winking in the dark like fire-flies in summer, subdued talk and laughter mingling with lowing cattle, restless oxen, and barking dogs, with the sun having sunk over the "Sweetwater Rocks" through which the river had cut a famous gorge 330 feet deep and 1,500 feet long. An "alternated and perpendicular strata of gray granite and scoriated trap rock," the Mormon scientist, Orson Pratt, called it in 1847. To James Mather in 1849, it was "the most interesting sight . . . on our journey." Four years later Rebecca Ketcham described it as "wild indeed." Rebecca was closest to the mark.

Although Devil's Gate is easily climbed from its south end, few settlers could steel themselves to look over the rim. In the 1860s, four women made the climb, and eighteen-year-old Caroline Todd plunged over, was killed and buried in the gorge. No marker survives. A violent, gloomy place during high water, in 1843 Fré-mont considered its name "quite new." But whatever it was called early on—Hell Gate, Devil's Gap—it was always associated with death along the Sweetwater.

Not far away, Ella "Cattle Kate" Watson and her "husband," Jim Averill, were hanged in 1889. "Cattle Kate," who operated a lively "hog ranch," had a well-developed habit of "ironing" stray calves with her own brand. Worse, she fenced a piece of open range, causing a slow burn among local cattlemen. Jim, who ran the saloon, was adept at flushing "range pay" from cowboys, pouring watered-down shots of tanglefoot at elevated prices. After a wild night, "Averell usually had their money and Kate . . . had her brand on from one to half a dozen calves. In a few months Kate's fenced-in pasture held a herd of questionable origin." All hell broke loose when ranchers resorted to "drastic action." A vigilante band dragged "Cattle Kate" and her man to Spring Creek—a tributary of the Sweetwater—and strung up the pair on the limbs of a scrub pine. No indictments were ever returned.

In 1943 Irene Paden called the Sweetwater and Devil's Gate "a regular gangster of a river shouting defiance down its own dark alley." With enough light left to see by, I entered Paden's "dark alley," shouted my own defiance, and was "pleased with the reverberation" as J. Goldsborough Bruff had been in 1849. The echo set in flight a blossoming of swallows, swooping and diving in the evening air, only to return to their stately mud-daubed nests and settle into stillness. Unnatural cool-ness lingered between its walls, like the temperature in an icehouse, while the river flowed in twilight the color of green tea.

I studied irrigation flumes used to divert the Sweetwater to thirsty ranches and took my ease on a nearby ledge, listening to what hell sounded like. Contrary to what I'd been told, it was serene, as it must have been for William Lutton in 1860.

He'd lingered long enough to carve his name on the canyon wall a few feet away. Entranced by shadow and silence, I stayed until a rising bloody moon and swarming mosquitoes drove me toward my tent. Two young antelope on stick legs grazed close by, bounding into the sage as I approached. I slept easily at the Devil's Gate. Old Scratch didn't seem to be around after all.

40

The thought you cannot escape is that you have to walk this view, and this is the barest fraction of what you will traverse before you've finished.   BILL BRYSON, *A WALK IN THE WOODS*

President Young, Kimball and others went to view the north side of Devil's Gate and returning reported that the devils would not let them pass.   WILLIAM CLAYTON, JUNE 21, 1847

En route we . . . passed by the Devil's Gate, one of the great curiosities of this line of travel. It is the beau ideal of a kanyon; our portal opening upon the threshold of the Rocky Mountains.   RICHARD BURTON, AUGUST 17, 1860

Next morning Norman Park informed me that the only visitors he let onto the Dumbbell Ranch to view Devil's Gate were those "who have the common decency to ask." Turns out he'd been kicked by a horse and hadn't been bucked out of the saddle—a point he was anxious to clear up to avoid any misunderstandings. With a gold inlaid tooth and a poker face, he reminded me of a saloon-style gambler, although I suspect he seldom shuffled a deck or drank much red-eye. What made Norman wobble on his crutches that morning was unpleasant memories of the National Park Service and the state of Wyoming. "A concerted effort by a bunch of do-gooders to turn Independence Rock into a tourist trap," he groused.

Right up my alley, I thought, lending an ear with the attentiveness of a cub reporter. Around us, heat was gathering fast and the faded sky was as oppressive as a hot towel.

FOLLOWING THE WRONG GOD HOME

"Independence Rock was always open access," Norman told me. "It was part of the Dumbbell and the Hub and Spoke Ranches until the Bicentennial came along." With it came renewed interest in historical preservation, and the rock, after all, was aptly named for the occasion. "The do-gooders started sniffing around," Norman continued, acidly. "They wanted to build a motel down there . . . a big damn development. But ranchers got hot about it. Y'see, if the state comes in, they want 'easements.' If a rancher wants to make changes on his ranch afterward, he can't do it without a lot of government red tape. No way in hell can you run a cattle or sheep operation that way."

Eventually, in the interests of history or patriotism, the Dumbbell and the Hub and Spoke Ranches gifted Independence Rock to the state, but not until the ranchers had a legal showdown with the bureaucrats who, as Norman put it, "came to their senses and danced to a different tune. Now they own the Rock and a small perimeter around it. But we wrote a provision in the deal that no commercial or fancy development can take place at or near it or the title will revert."

No dumbbell there.

• • •

On the west side of Devil's Gate, the Tom Sun Ranch was getting its first wash of morning sun. Officially on the books as the Hub and Spoke Ranch, it's most often spoken of using its founder's name, Tom Sun, Sr., who got his hands on it in 1872. Born Thomas de Soleil, the migrating French Canadian said to hell with Old World charm and Americanized it to Tom Sun. Besides, a name like de Soleil seems effeminate in a neighborhood where names run to more matter-of-fact syllables. Imagine saying, "Let's ride on over to Thomas de Soleil's place" or "That's a Thomas de Soleil brand on them critters."

The Dominion of Canada was five years old when Tom packed up and left Quebec, possibly under the impression that things had gone south when "New France" joined the Dominion in 1867. Tom's American Dream was space where a man can remake himself—right down to his name.

Tom's great-grandson, Dennis Sun, was the man to talk with that morning, especially since I intended crossing the Hub and Spoke with an eye on Split Rock, seventeen miles away. Visible for miles and resembling a gun sight, Split Rock is part of the Granite Mountains—pink igneous outcroppings (Independence Rock is one) that litter the Sweetwater Valley. Locals call them the "Sweetwater Rocks." At 7,305 feet, Split Rock is among the highest, and the river runs around it. Mormons and all others followed the river, aiming at Split Rock.

"It's your hide," Dennis Sun said when he gave me the go-ahead. "You can burn the hell out of it any way you please on the Sun Ranch, so long as you don't start any fires."

I assured him I wouldn't unless winter set in before I got off his spread, a possibility since Sun Ranch properties eat up a whole lot of Wyoming. We talked under the overhang of the original ranch house, a long bunkhouse-looking affair whose most commendable scenery was a view from the front door over Devil's Gate and the Sweetwater. The view out the back door was bleak at best, and I was about to walk into it. I told Dennis I'd give the old route a go, sunburn or not.

"Suit yourself," he said. "It's a hot, dry stretch between here and Jeffrey City . . . thirty miles if you take the highway."

• • •

Near Devil's Gate in 1856, death stalked Mormons heading for Zion—a frozen November hell that carried them off in droves—the first awful legacy of Brigham's handcart economies. When I passed Martin's Cove (another nautical name, like Windlass Hill, laid on a sea of sand and sage), I paused to pay my respects but did not sail in. West of the Sun Ranch, the historical marker told the story—"rescued in perishing condition," "delayed in starting," "inferior carts," "overtaken by an early winter," "insufficient food." They died from exhaustion, hypothermia, and freezing, less a triumph of endurance than a testament to bad planning, poor equipment, and a too-eager reliance on Mormon Dreams. In Europe, missionaries were instructed in Dreamspeak: "Tell them to flee to Zion. . . . Should any ask 'where is Zion' tell them in America." For Mormons, "every hope of the future" was to "gather to the land of America." In Britain, elder Orson Spencer exulted, "The channel of the Saint's emigration to the land of Zion is now opened. The resting place of Israel has at last been discovered."

Of the ten handcart companies to cross from the Missouri River to Utah in 1856–60, the Martin Handcart Company was the fifth. It left Winter Quarters on August 27, 1856, which, at the earliest, would have put it in the Salt Lake Valley in late November. By the time it reached the last crossing of the Platte, near Casper, the river was mushy with "snow and ice." Women and children waded across, exposure creating "temporary dementia." No sooner was the company across than it was "visited by a tremendous storm of snow, hail, sand, and fierce winds." Earlier, as desperation deepened about approaching winter, their load was lightened—cut to ten pounds for each adult and five for children. Blankets, bedding, and clothing were thrown away in a fit of uncompromising stupidity. Halfway across the Poison Spider Route, where I had been hit with mid-June snow, the dying commenced. Snow fell for three days; before the company reached Willow Springs it was snowed in. People died "lying side by side, their hands entwined." Some snuffed out sitting by a fire or singing hymns. Fifty-six were dead when the company's captain, Edward Martin, stood guard over their shallow graves, "shotgun in hand, firing at intervals to keep the crows and buzzards from hovering around in mid-air."

Yet the company straggled on. When help arrived from Salt Lake City, it was too little, too late. Daniel Jones, one of the rescuers wrote: "There were old men pulling and tugging their carts . . . women pulling along sick husbands . . . little children six to eight years old struggling through the mud and snow." I knew about that mud, how it balled under the feet, sucking at resolve. It froze on their clothing and shoes. "What could we do?" asked Jones. Very little, it turned out.

They made it by degrees of death to Devil's Gate and, beyond that, to the cove that bears the ill-fated name of the company captain. Eighteen inches of snow was now on the ground, so deep that the Saints had "to shovel away with their frying pans, or tin plates . . . before they could pitch their tents," the ground "so frozen . . . that it was almost impossible to drive the tent pegs into it." They prayed "without ceasing," less than a third able to walk. When a full rescue party arrived from Salt Lake City on November 12, the death toll stood at 147, nearly 20 percent of the 546 who entered "the channel . . . to the land of Zion." Ahead of the Martin company that November, 13 members of the Willie Handcart Company froze to death near South Pass. Of its 500 members, 67 perished.

But it was the Saints' "godly" endurance, not the naïveté of the 1856 project and its leaders, that blossomed into myth. After her husband died with his boots frozen to his feet, twenty-nine-year-old Elizabeth Jackson, widowed and a mother of three, wrote from the safe harbor of the Salt Lake Valley: "I will not attempt to describe my feelings at finding myself a widow with three children, under such excruciating circumstances. But I believe the Recording Angel has inscribed [it] in the archives above, and that my suffering for the Gospel's sake will be sanctified unto me for my own good." Ignoring the culpability of her prophet, Elizabeth is uttering more Dreamspeak, as if her husband's freezing to death was divinely ordained and her suffering, along with her children's, a righteous responsibility.

On November 16, 1857, Brigham rose in the Salt Lake tabernacle to assess the disasters. In spite of the death toll, he intoned, "We are not the least discouraged about the handcart method of traveling. This season's operations have demonstrated that the Saints being filled with faith and the Holy Ghost can walk across the plains. . . . The experience of this season will, of course, help us to improve future operations." It did. But a Mormon prophet's judgment in matters of life and death goes unquestioned. LeRoy Hafen, Latter-day Saint and historian, could summon only this feeble rebuke: "The optimism of Brigham led him to simplify the vicissitudes."

Eight handcart companies safely crossed to Utah between 1856 and 1860, as much a triumph for reduced overheads as for Brigham's "faith and the Holy Ghost." Five handcart companies had struggled through in 1856, the first leaving the Missouri River on July 20, the Willie and Martin companies unwisely departing in late August per Brigham's instructions. Only two companies crossed the plains in 1857, another in 1859, and two in 1860. Of the final five to cross, the latest left the Missouri River on July 7. Four departed in early June.

But handcart history could be read like this:

Faced with the need to expand and solidify his hold on Utah and a tenuous Mormon theocracy, Brigham acted out of character, careless and overenthusiastic. "We want men," Brigham's refrain went. "Brethren, come from the States, from the nations, come! Help us grow . . . until the valleys of Ephraim are full."

They did, putting aside worldly goods and marching west. Instructed to suffer for the Lord—indeed, appointed to suffer for their beliefs as had Joseph Smith—they came, many blindly, at their prophet's call. When the handcart companies began their long haul to Dreamland, J. D. T. McAllister equally simplified "the vicissitudes" when he composed words to an old Mormon favorite, "The Handcart Song."

> Some must push and some must pull
> As we go marching up the hill,
> And merrily on the way we go
> Until we reach the valley, oh.

That morning, I kept well away from the ghosts in Martin's Cove, holy or otherwise. Not inclined to think of the place as a triumph of faith or virtue as Margaret Jackson had, the memory of its once frozen dead stuffed in crevices in the rock didn't make it an inviting spot for a picnic lunch. Instead, I followed their pain toward Split Rock, stopping once to splash Sweetwater on my head and filter Adam's Ale from its supply. I made it to U.S. 287 by late in the afternoon, sweat-soaked and grumbling, still well short of Jeffrey City and sulking about it. Now I stuck to the asphalt. When my stomach began making serious protests and depression was setting in, a three-quarter-ton truck pulled up beside me and a dog named Bandit looked down from the passenger seat, panting in the heat.

"Need a lift?" said his master.

"How far to Jeffrey City?" I asked.

"Eight or nine miles."

I looked at the black ribbon of highway running through more and more desolation, at early shadows beginning their tedious crawl among the "Sweetwater
Rocks," and calculated an answer by way of my stomach. "Sure," I said. "Maybe I
could buy you dinner if you know a good place."

Wayne Fox and Bandit took me up on it.

"This is my back yard," Wayne said.

. . .

Jeffrey City is a narrowing in the road on U.S. 287 that, as often happens in
America, sold its distinction to the highest bidder. It was originally known as
"Home on the Range," which George Stewart in *American Place-Names* called "a
sentimental, commendatory naming, from the refrain . . . of a popular song."
Sometime after 1950 the romance of the place collapsed. A boom or bust town, it
most recently boomed when uranium speculations turned up deposits in the
nearby hills. Like other dusty western towns hoping to cash in on fissionable materials, Jeffrey City took up uranium mining with the fervor of a Douglas County
deputy sheriff. Born again, it was caught up in Dreams of salvation.

In 1955 the radioactive illusion—as revealed by Kathleen Bruÿn in *Uranium
Country*—went like this: "The ancient alchemists dreamed of transmuting base
into precious metals. Today's chemists and physicists have put the dream to shame
and have, moreover, learned how to release the tiny, invisible atom power tran-
scending the heights of human imagination—power capable of driving gigantic
machines, providing abundant light and inexhaustible fuel, ridding the world of
diseases that have scourged man from time immemorial."

Bruÿn's hymn to radioactivity sounds suspiciously like Hiram Latham's hymn
to grass, supported to the max by those with vested interests. As Bruÿn puts it,
uranium turned towns like Jeffrey City into a "three-ring circus"; it was capable
of converting any dusty burg into "a Mecca for fortune hunters with uranium
fever." In the 1950s, uranium fever raged in Salt Lake City, its stock market bal-
looning with news of each new strike.

In Moab, Utah, "Charlie" Steen hit it big in 1952. "At thirty-three, Steen is already
a legendary figure," Bruÿn gushed. "His success story is a genuine American saga
embodying those things which are especially dear to the heart of a democratic people." Ms. Bruÿn wields every cliché in the Big Snooze: "formidable odds," "courage,"
"tenacity of purpose," "dared to discard accepted ideas," "grassroots individual

whose dream of empire . . . included the good of the common, everyday people whose strengths and weaknesses he came to know." Last but not least, "He is now fabulously rich."

Any "saga" (which means a long-winded narrative, by the way) is an open invitation to deflation—particularly Bruÿn's take on "Charlie" Steen. "Fabulously rich" or not, Steen was first a geologist. Second, geology was his life's work. Third, he practiced it daily. Fourth, it was a task he did willingly, diligently, and he probably enjoyed it. Fifth, he found what he was looking for. Last but not least, it wasn't a Dream. It was a discovery.

Jeffrey City went belly-up on uranium as did Moab, although Moab resuscitated itself as a red rock biker's paradise in the 1980s, becoming a tourist town riddled with motels, gift shops, tepid upscale saloons, overpriced restaurants, and pretentious art galleries. No such luck for Jeffrey City, although in Moab uranium left behind a cesspit of radioactive poisons leaching into the groundwater. Meantime, the climate of the nation changed. Workers in the uranium industry died at unusually high rates from cancer. Three Mile Island nearly melted down. Chernobyl blew up.

Uranium has a long history in America—too long to tell here. But radioactive minerals were thought to be a fountain of youth. Early in the century, a gent named Thomas Curran created "Ferr-Vanadium" pills, a radium-laced patent medicine to "promote good health and vitality." White-haired codgers past their prime dosed themselves with his "radium water." Folklore has it (Bruÿn again) that a Mormon octogenarian and his wife dosed themselves liberally and "found themselves expectant parents."

·   ·   ·

Wayne, Bandit, and I ate at the Split Rock Bar and Café—a dinner of halibut steak, soup, homemade rolls, fresh vegetables, pie, and ice cream. For all three (Bandit had a hamburger), it set me back $12.40, including coffee. We washed it down with two beers, courtesy of Wayne. When I mentioned a motel, Wayne said, "You can bunk at my place."

After dinner, Wayne took me on a tour of his "back yard." Twenty-six, he'd lived all but one year in Jeffrey City. Young, personable, mustached, and single (he never once mentioned a girl), he sensed my need to see parts of the trail I'd missed from the highway, so he headed back toward Split Rock and turned off on a side road. On the edge of lands controlled by the Nuclear Regulatory Commission, near the site of an abandoned nuclear processing plant, we were dead on the track of the Mormons. An unwelcoming sign barred our way.

"Can't get in," Wayne said. "It's off-limits now . . . radioactivity or somethin'. The mine's closed."

And the damage done, I thought.

Stretched out in the front parlor of Wayne's house trailer with Bandit occupying the space next to my feet, I slept lightly. Both of us awoke in the night, and when I scratched Bandit's ears he gave that whimper dogs do when good times may not last.

• • •

At the Jeffrey City Café, where Wayne and I ate breakfast next morning, I ran into "Timberjack Joe," an honest-to-God mountain man who made his living trapping skunks, badgers, and whatever else he could lay his traps on. He lived "over to Dubois," he told me. With a pickup full of yapping dogs (tools of his trade) and a horse trailer minus horse, he came in for coffee wearing a fur hat with feathers, fringed buckskins, and decorative beadwork and smelled as if he'd been hard at skunk trapping all week. As he was leaving, a chiseled gent in a cowboy hat, jeans, and boots dropped by our table with a bad case of the shakes. He nodded.

"Howdy, Wayne."

"Howdy, Thad."

"How you been, Wayne."

"OK, Thad. How'r yew?"

"Not too bad. But the undertaker got after me."

"What'cha do, Thad. Outrun him?"

"I done shook him off."

I shook off Jeffrey City. No offense to Wayne, Bandit, the undertaker, or the gent with the tremors.

41

Then, should we fall to work, with a general impression of Ghosts being about, and of pictures . . . that of a certainty came out of their frames and walked. CHARLES DICKENS,
THE UNCOMMERCIAL TRAVELER

At 3:30 we tarried a little south from the road and formed our encampment in a line so as to enclose a bend in the river, having traveled seventeen and three quarters miles. . . . The feed here is very good and plenty of willow bushes for fuel.

WILLIAM CLAYTON, JUNE 24, 1847

In the afternoon we cross the Sweetwater 3 times, through romantic rocks embellished with the names of individuals who had passed that way. GEORGE TEASDALE, SEPTEMBER 6, 1861

The trail to South Pass leaves U.S. 287 midway between Jeffrey City and Sweetwater Station near a spot where a natural phenomenon had a chilling effect on westering Americans. At a nearby "slough," an exploring hand reaching below its boggy surface could bring up chunks of ice in the middle of August. "A bason surrounded by sand plains," as James Pritchard described the famous "Ice Slough" in 1849; he took an "Ax" and cut out "Squar blocks" to fill his water bucket. "As clear ice as I ever saw," William Clayton noted two years earlier, "and good tasting."

Preserved by insulating layers of grasses and peatlike soil, the slough became the mountain man's icehouse, the emigrant's curiosity, and, today, a Wyoming historical site. Mentioned in most overland journals, its bounty was used to cool meat, make a cold compress, or "to enjoy an occasional whiskey on the rocks." In 1849 Henry Tappan concocted "a good julep" beside it. Four years later, George Belshaw "made some lemonade for dinner." Today, it's a pull-over for an occasional tourist, but three hundred thousand Americans once passed by and stopped for a cold one. Thrusting my hand into what was left of it, it came up chilled but ice-free.

An unnatural day from the beginning—hot too early, cool too late, a barbecue in-between—the morning unfolded with stunning monotony. Beyond the slough, the trail gradually climbs, settling west toward Sweeney Basin through rough country, opening onto a rolling expanse of sand and sage that stretched to the horizon— the beginning of a seventy-mile stretch through rough country that leaves all roads and towns behind until it crosses South Pass. If you took a 3" by 5" card, drew a line across the middle, colored the top half a washed-out blue, the bottom half beige, and painted a thin smear of white two inches from the right edge of the card along the line between blue and beige, it would be close to accurate. The thin opalescence is the snow cap of the Wind River Range making its appearance on the horizon—

"perpetual snows," Orson Pratt called it, "which, glittering in the sunbeams, resemble white fleecy clouds."

Even with clear tracings of a track, I crossed Sweeney Basin by intuition, two quarts away from dehydration. Beginning the longest sustained walk between towns I'd faced so far, I was fully burdened with supplies, my backpack choked with foodstuffs—nearly the original weight with which I'd left New York. The road ahead was grim; dead cattle lay among the sage, hide and hair dried over their skeletons, flesh rotted away from the inside. Every mile or so, I took a photograph of the road ahead, each a spitting image of the next. When the track turned sharply south, following the 1854 route of the Oregon Trail's Seminoe Cutoff (an alternate route south of the river named for Basil LaJeunesse, who was known to the Shoshone as "Seminoe"), I aligned my compass northwest and walked overland through dense sage. By noon, I was dizzy with heat, my two quarts down to two cups—but the willowy line of the Sweetwater was bound to show up and by midafternoon it did, drawn across the emptiness like a slash of viridescent eyeliner.

With the trail narrowing as the river squeezed against a redrock scarp, I searched for a crossing, finally coming to a thirty-foot weir with a spillway churning water downstream. Too "deep & swift" to wade, as the river was for the Mormons (they raised their wagon boxes), I stripped naked, stuffed the clothes into a waterproof sack, and tested my sea legs on the ten-inch narrow spillway. Roiling water crashed over my ankles midcalf deep, threatening to topple me. On hands and knees, I made it across and back, Wind River meltwater lapping at thighs, stomach, and chest, contracting my family jewels to the size of chickpeas. Ferrying goods to the far bank like a neutered hermit crab, one waterproof sack at a time looped across my back, I was thoroughly chilled, making a last crossing with the nearly empty backpack strapped on. Dressed again, I clambered up a ridge past an abandoned cabin, considered the desolation ahead, and began searching for my compass. Gone. Back at the weir, it stared at me from the opposite bank, dangling by its scarlet lanyard from willow brush, its glassy eye fixed on true north. Cursing, I stripped again, crawled back over the chilling flow, and retrieved it, carrying it in my teeth to make the return trip.

Security in hand, I headed through deeply rutted country, the river a quarter of a mile to the left. In ten minutes or less, I was sweating runnels again, sun now in my face, the river hidden by bluffs. Faced with "hills more numerous and rolling" (Orson Pratt) but scarcely less barren, I ticked off a litany of the Mormon scientist's geological colorings: "bluish limestone," "white marl," "red mineral clay," "fine grained sandstone"—the last a form of "gritstone" from which, he deduced, could be fashioned "excellent millstones." His colors were true.

I boiled through a long afternoon, head down, stolidly trudging, stupidly wandering away from the river by a half mile and having to backtrack to find it again before dark. I found what looked like a trace of old ruts leading to the river and walked down into a splendid campsite. Without knowing it, I'd walked from the middle-of-nowhere to the center-of-everything and into an astonishing personal denouement I hadn't intended.

. . .

It seems odd to speak of my camp that night as being in a "desert." American deserts—the Chihuahuan, Sonoran, Mojave, the Painted, and the Great Basin—are less "dry" than "occasionally moist." Even Death Valley has its river (the Amargosa), several seasonal creeks (Furnace Creek is one), and a watering hole named Stove Pipe Wells. So the Sweetwater was not so much a long drink of water to me as a condiment, as it must have been to Robert Stuart and the Astorians when they discovered it in 1812 and the same to westering Americans who seasoned their hopes with its waters while heading toward South Pass.

Before setting up my tent, I tested a notion that Bob Rathburn, the manager of the Super 8 Motel, had put in my head back in Casper and stirred the ground with the metal ferule of Roadmaker. Bob's voice had an edge of experience when he talked of barbed wire and windmills, so when he mentioned "fire rings," I paid close attention. As he explained it, the "rings are leftover traces of pioneer campfires on the bed grounds along the river. You can find 'em all along that stretch," he emphasized. "They're everywhere."

Two inches down, I hit carbon traces. In fifteen minutes, I'd turned up the remains of seven fire rings within thirty feet, the deepest at about four inches. Filtering traces of charcoal and sand through my fingers, history was both palpable and unnerving; others had slept here before me.

I made a sorry supper of canned salmon, peanut butter, and bread topped off with a Hershey bar, then waded in for a more relaxed dunking. Water in a nearby shallow was warmer than the icing I'd taken crossing the weir and, buttocks to gravel, I scrubbed away the day's discomforts, soaking as the shadows lengthened and three antelope huddled downstream at river's edge to drink. Dusk's breeze cascaded from the ridges and moved along the river, furling willows and speaking a language that Bob Rathburn would recognize.

As earth fell toward darkness, I entered twilight with a begloomed sensation that a curtain was coming down: a moon, ghostly rising, lit up the panoply of space, pale at first, enlarging in splendor as it climbed higher across an arc of blossoming stars. On this section of the western stage, the original props hadn't changed much, but the footlights had long dimmed on the fabled road show, its cast of thousands long faded. Hovering everywhere, these vanished players took asylum in my imagination.

Close by, on the night of June 24, 1847, Brigham Young lost his best horse, "accidentally shot" when John Holman, carrying a primed rifle, caught the cocking mechanism in his clothes and blew "quite a large hole" in the animal's belly. Reading about it in Clayton's journal by penlight, I was stunned by a distant gunshot that caromed off the darkness like the sound of a broken bat in the cavern of a ballpark, punctuating my reading with unnerving reality. Young's horse died slowly and painfully, nobody in the Camp of Israel willing to put it out of its misery. When it crossed the Styx next morning, the "brethren" were "sorrowful"—Brigham foremost, since it was his second horse to go belly-up on the trip.

But the gunshot jittered me (I wasn't alone after all), as if I'd treaded too deeply on the past and heard its murmur. Drip-drying, watching shadows crawl up nearby formations, a fret of sudden isolation gripped me, forcing me into the tent. I lay naked on the sleeping bag, head outside as stars at last blinked on in full majesty. Except for three nights in the Northwest Territories in my twenties, I'd lived largely unaware of such spectacle—stars and planets splendid in their isolation, strung on invisible threads of gravity and motion. I hung by the same threads, rotating west with the night as Brigham had done, trying to find a way toward a new morning, another beginning.

Cold and implacable, a spellbinding space filled me as constellations eased across the sky's rim. I drifted into them or them into me with clarity only the awareness of immensities can bring. Four years later, I experienced a similar night with the Osage on the Kansas prairie; a night, he wrote, when "a meteor, the slowest falling one I ever saw, dropped right across the Great Bear like a thrown spear." We were following a trail of Native American design at the time, and I asked him, "Would you say we've found the old track?"

"No," he answered. "Blindly crossed it, yes. Often, I think. We've been entangled in its lines the whole way."

For the Osage that Kansas night, a "circle seemed to loosen." For me, alone on the Sweetwater, something more like entanglement lifted and, with it, the blindness to what I'd crossed: I disappeared into the strangely benevolent cosmos. Dreaming was impossible. To *imagine*, yes. To *understand*, in eons, perhaps, but to Dream, no—not with new suns being born and old suns dying out, the starbursts of their beginnings and endings telescoped across space in billions of light years. I was never so wide-awake.

The Osage once described me as a man who "had lived in this country longer than in Canada and liked the United States but wouldn't admit . . . that the U.S. is a place no Canadian could ever love." Truth is, he fingered me rightly for having contracted a nightmare.

> In 1975 he built a two-story log house in the hills west of Canandaigua Lake, the "thumb" of the Finger Lakes. Chisholm drilled a well and hit sweet water at thirty-five feet. It produced six gallons a minute. Even though a human being needs only a pint of water a day to survive, Chisholm decided his family couldn't live on 8,640 gallons a day. So he drilled to sixty-eight feet and got fourteen gallons a minute—fourteen gallons of gassy, sulphurous stuff. Probably the most American thing he ever did.

Chastened, I both laughed and smarted at his jibe. He was right, of course. But now, untangling myself, I knew this: folks who believe they've got Dream by the tail have a fistful of trouble. If they keep on believing, they contract cultural narcolepsy.

I shook off a chill, got up, and walked into the night, almost a shadow about to step through a ripple between earth and sky. Names floated in the darkness— Jedediah Smith, Jim Bridger, John Charles Frémont, Kit Carson, Marcus and Narcissa Whitman. Each had passed this way. Each had slept nearby, listening to the wash of the river. Deep in the Antelope Hills, a band of coyotes made hauntingly beautiful music, consuming the night in tiny oval mouthfuls of near crystal sound. Around me, the warmth of the day seeped out of the earth, while, above me, a turpentine odor of sage drifted on a thin stream of cool night air. Dead center on the bedding ground of an older American Dreaming, I was a century and a half deep in the time machine that invented the West. Moonlight dappled the Sweetwater—silver dollars spilling from a sack of night. The coyotes hesitated briefly, perhaps troubled by an alien presence, but turned splendidly hymnal again. Ringing night away, I joined them. Howling myself awake. Waking up for good.

42

Afoot and light-hearted I take to the open road,
Healthy, free, the world before me,
The long brown path . . . leading wherever I choose.

WALT WHITMAN

Severe frost in the night. Ice in the buckets of water. A pail of milk
in Brother Rockwood's Wagon frozen solid. . . . On a sudden come
to the Sweetwater in a deep ravine with many Willows & Scrubs
on its banks. THOMAS BULLOCK, JUNE 26, 1847

We now begin to ascend the mountains. Traveled six or seven
miles on the roughest road we have seen on this trip. . . . It is so cold
that a man has to wear an overcoat to keep comfortable.

THOMAS CHRISTY, JUNE 13, 1850

It was, of course, an exorcism—my walk—although in April when I began hoofing I couldn't admit it. But that night on the Sweetwater, a burden lifted. Two ogres had been sitting on my shoulder for twenty-five years, but I'd never faced them down and, truth be told, I'd taken to the road aware of my fatal attractions. Getting shuck of the American Dream, as I did that night, was difficult enough after thirty years of living in the United States, but all advertising is about turning wants into needs and possibilities into promises, however false. Like the Dream, automobiles are sold against a backdrop of open road, obscuring any dead ends.

It was not the same, I'll admit, for young Annie Moore, the first to cross the threshold of Ellis Island on January 1, 1892, where, as the Irish Tenors sing of her:

> Courage is the passport
> When your old world disappears
> 'cos there's no future in the past
> when you're fifteen years.

For Annie—and for the seventeen million who followed her until it closed in 1943—Ellis Island was an "Isle of hope, Isle of tears, Isle of freedom, Isle of fears," with no turning back once she took a ferry to New York City and stepped onto the vast continent where Dreams were being invented larger than life. What happened to Annie Moore is anybody's guess because, as happens to so many to whom we assign a Dream, the American landscape swallowed her. Annie arrived from Ireland's hunger not seeking Dreams but *sanctuary*, and for her and me, an "isle of home was always on my mind." After all, one has *roots* in culture and homeland in the same way we inherit genetic codes.

Still, there was more to it than that.

Confused by my own failures and small successes, tainted by an uneasy experience as a stranger in a strange land, another demon drifted in and out of my adult consciousness, persistent as a consumptive's cough. My wife and the Osage long sensed its presence and effect on my life, even in my denials, the Osage taunting me toward exorcism ("If there's enough Canadian left in you to do it"), and Linda all but pushing me out the door ("Hit the road!")

Still, exorcisms are difficult, coming as they do with no little anxiety. Even when appearing benign, one's personal ogres turn succubus or siren, and to rid yourself of demons, however benign they appear, is no easy task. In my case, the second ogre was as much about getting rid of a disease as a demon. Purging it required fancy footwork, and that was what I was actually doing. Unlike a wallflower at the prom, I was dancing toward the center of the floor hoping for a cure.

· · ·

But for a Frenchman, André Siegfried, I would never have considered my grandmother's legacy a "disease." A monograph of his, published in 1959, aided the diagnosis. Touted as "a small work on an unusual theme," Siegfried claims (*Routes of Contagion*) that ideas are *infections* and the "degree of contamination between one region and another is in proportion to progress in communications." In a word, *catching*. Traveling across borders, intermingling with other fevers of the mind, ideas infect our permeable world one person at a time like any other pestilence. No matter if it's Black Death along Asian trade routes, sniffles on a plane from New York to Chicago, or a fever in Boston harbor for freedom and independence, there's always a *carrier* and a *host*. In the case of my grandmother's disease, the carrier was John J. Cornish.

As I write this, petite, blue-eyed Abby Burley Alderson stares at me from a hand-tinted photograph on the wall of my study—the only image ever taken of her. In 1912, twenty-four years before I was born, she died of uterine cancer, and her daughter, Laura, nine at the time, raised Abby's seven remaining children—

FOLLOWING THE WRONG GOD HOME

three sisters and four brothers. In my grandmother, I recognize my own features and in Laura, my mother, an often frightened determination.

My maternal grandparents settled on the shores of Lake Huron, holing up in Stokes Bay—a mosquito-infested, shallow draft harbor with a weedy river traversing shifty sands. Both Abigail Burley and Allen Alderson, my grandfather, like their families before them, were familiar with the distemper of an empty purse. Both Burleys and Aldersons traced their lineage back to the American Revolution when, banking on the fortunes of King George, they'd pulled up stakes and left Virginia. Floating on a tide of the frequently displaced, they eventually arrived on Ontario's Bruce Peninsula as itinerant loggers come to strip its wealth of hardwood and pine. Burley and Alderson men lived in the "bush" over long, harsh winters, feeding from a common camp kitchen, while their women and all-too-numerous children lived hand-to-mouth in nearby log cabins, making do on meager earnings. They suffered from diphtheria, measles, chicken pox, scarlet fever, tuberculosis, and rattlesnakes. Few of their children attended school, none beyond sixth grade. Highly susceptible hosts, they were given to religious afflictions.

. . .

John J. Cornish, born on October 17, 1854, in Usborne Township, Huron County, Canada, remembered the country as "practically raw, partially settled . . . heavily timbered with beech, ash, sugar maple, oak, basswood, elm, hickory, and cedar," a country of rude clearings in which "few had more than one to five acres." Houses were "log shanties, mostly low," the "sitting room, kitchen, dining room, bedroom, and pantry being all one room," and floors were made of split basswood logs, round side down, with roofs the same. When John's mother died (he was nine), the boy was "bound out" by his drunken father, "Rattling Jack," as an indentured servant to an ill-tempered and violent man named J. J. Vail. When John asked Vail's wife where parents go when they die, she replied in a thick Devonshire accent, "Oh, h'up in a 'ome beyond the sky, h'and they'll put wings h'on us, h'and we can fly h'all around h'and be 'appy h'all the time."

At "twelve or thirteen," Johnny Cornish bolted from the field he was working, leaving horse and plow midfurrow, striking overland on the run to find a new life. Vail tracked him for days, but young Cornish had better wind and stronger legs. For the next few years, John worked off and on as a farmhand and mill worker, but by the end of his life in 1937, he'd lived another of Mrs. Vail's Devonshire-laden sentiments: "Praise God from whom h'all blessings flow . . . day h'in and day h'out, through countless h'ages of h'eternity." Struck by "the light," Cornish became a preacher. When he hit the road on his Maker's behalf, the Canadian clearings were ripe for the harvest. The "light" had crossed the U.S. border into Canada without tariffs or taxes and found a ready-made proponent in the young man who caught its gleam in 1871 while on a visit to an uncle near Bothwell, Ontario, where he was warned away from his kith and kin by a well-intentioned, if bemused, neighbor.

"Well, sir," the neighbor said, when John asked directions to his uncle's farm, "Taylor has joined the Mormons."

"What are the Mormons?" Cornish asked.

"Why sir, they're a devilish sect."

Turns out John's uncle hadn't hitched his star to "a devilish sect," but to a non-polygamous faith stemming from the fever of Joseph Smith's Mormon-American Dream. Smith himself had preached near Toronto in the early, fruitless days of his New York years before moving west into harm's way.

Cornish was infected in 1873 by two fervent carriers from south of the border, John Lake and Joseph Snively. After debating "the fine points of the gospel," he seems to have had a sense of impending peril: "I went to bed and thought I was all right," he later wrote. But he quickly succumbed. Elder Arthur Leverton told him, "I'll baptize you, John Cornish; but if you don't live right to the gospel ordinances, we'll pull you out again." On February 22, 1874, Cornish was immersed through a hole cut in the ice of Ontario's Thames River, had his sins "remitted," and was welcomed into the Reorganized Church of Jesus Christ of Latter Day Saints—the same group that Alice Howell had mistaken for "reformed" Mormons back in Kearney, Nebraska.

In 1874 the *Reorganized* Church had recently reassembled the disaffected remnants of Mormon Nauvoo—Smith's Found Tribe of Israel having fractured over issues of leadership and doctrine. Emma Smith, Joseph's occasionally balky wife, believed the mantle of prophet should fall on the shoulders of her Lincolnesque older son (it eventually did), a teenager at the time of his father's murder. After all, that had been Joseph's wish, and Emma detested Brigham Young. Strong in her Mormon faith but weak on the "Lion of the Lord," she considered Brigham little better than an opportunist and whoremonger; it was Young, she insisted, who introduced the "abominable heresies" of "baptism for the dead" and "spiritual wifery" into her husband's homegrown religion. In Emma's mind, no blame for polygamy attached to her husband, a bald-faced fiction that persisted among the RLDS for a century until an accumulated tonnage of irrefutable evidence toppled it. By 1874, when Cornish was baptized, the RLDS Church had 8,300 "reformed" members worldwide, of which 160 were Canadian. By the end of his life, John

Cornish changed all that, infecting over 2,000 Canadians, the first his future brother-in-law.

In his memoirs, Cornish reveals a remarkable similarity to events in the life of his martyred prophet. Taking himself into Ontario's woods as Smith took to his "sacred grove" near Palmyra, New York, to inquire direction of the Lord regarding which church to join ("None of them," the Lord replied, launching Smith on his road to martyrdom), John "prayed earnestly that . . . God would speak through Myron Haskins in tongues, and tell me that the work is true." Myron obliged that very evening, and Cornish admitted he "did not understand a word." Haskins himself had to interpret: "Oh, thou son of man, inasmuch as you have inquired of me this day to know the truthfulness of the gospel, I now reveal it unto you. . . ." And so on, etc.

But there were other signs and portents of God's favor, several accompanied by troubled atmospheres. Of his chilly baptism, John wrote, "the Holy Spirit came upon my head like a rushing wind. . . . I heard, up in the air, a sound like the rumbling of a railroad train coming nearer and nearer." (His rumblings show the influence of the iron horse, only recently blazing its trail to the Canadian West.) Thankful for his deliverance, he swore off playing cards.

But his unusual wind returned when Sarah Lively and Mary Taylor "offered themselves for baptism." Predictably, they'd been "persecuted" beforehand—the most common Mormon theme well into the twentieth century—and John led them to the nearest river: "The moment my foot touched the water there came a sound from heaven as of a terrible rushing wind and with it came a very bright light, more bright than I had ever before seen. The light came down from heaven and it was a circle, and it was large enough to take in thirty people, and also a part of the river, just that part where I baptized and it was as dark one foot from the outer edge of it as it was ten rods away."

By 1876 he was under full missionary steam, sending words, staccato, back to the States for insertion in the church magazine, the *Herald*: "January 8, baptized two; January 9, two; January 12, two; February 5, one; February 6, four; February 7, two; February 9, three; February 16, two; February 20, three; February 26, one; and March 1, one."

John showed up in the vicinity of "the Queen's Bush"—an unfortunate name for my Canadian neck-of-the-woods, but there you have it—in the 1880s. Contagious as whooping cough, his virus passed from one person to the next, overwhelming weakened immune systems. God would provide, Cornish assured his converts, so long as they remained faithful, studied *The Book of Mormon*, and paid heed to Smith's revelations, collected in a thin volume called *Doctrine and Covenants*. When his message reached Bruce County, it swept into dismal backwaters and hamlets, infecting Burleys and Aldersons.

Having contracted the "bug," Abby passed it to my mother, who passed it along to me, my sister, and eventually to my Presbyterian father who died four years after his distemper set in. (Faith didn't kill him, but the effects of mustard gas he'd breathed during World War I.) My uncle Aubrey Mason, a convert and redeemed alcoholic whom I remember with the greatest affection, stood barely five foot four behind the pulpit of our local RLDS meetinghouse, remonstrating a flock of decent farmers and townsfolk, often with eclectic visions, some obviously related to Joseph Smith's teachings but many of his own colorful devising. My beloved Aunt May Mason, frequently as off-key as my mother, raised her voice in RLDS favorites while Margaret Smith, ringing out a conflagration of notes on the upright piano—perhaps in the hope that the Alderson sisters would at last stumble on-key—accompanied the congregation in Mormon hymnody as they loudly and joyously sang:

> The Kingdom of God like a fire is burning.
> The Latter Day glory begins to come forth.
> Visions and blessings of old returning.
> Angels are coming to visit the earth.

Like them, I steamed, I cried, I testified, and I believed . . . well . . . I wanted to anyway.

• • •

But the Latter Day glory never fully manifested itself in this Canadian. Yet so virulent is any strain of Mormonism, so engaging its obsessive attention to otherworldly doctrine that, to this day, I'm trying to shake my grandmother's lingering infection. Doubt—that most robust antibiotic—was for me the outgrowth of the very absolutes and certainties that Mormon life offered. Skepticism followed, and on its heels, abandonment. Only the Mormon-American Dream of community lingers. As Rebecca Solnit puts it in her book *Wanderlust*, "Walking, I realized long ago in another desert, is how the body measures itself against the earth." For me, the measurement was exorcism, but even under Wyoming desert stars, where Dreams yet have dangers, there's still nothing so perilous as an unquestioning belief.

43

I mustn't be sentimental about the loss of my former attachments;
I must forge ahead. Walk off the cliff with your eyes open.
DEBORAH TALL, *THE ISLAND OF THE WHITE COW*

This creek is very clear and cold. Its banks are well lined with wil-
lows and about a mile below the camp there is a grove of white
poplar. . . . There are also some strawberry roots.
WILLIAM CLAYTON, JUNE 25, 1847

Drove fifteen miles to strawberry creek.   HENRY M. JUDSON,
JULY 16, 1862

Morning crawled to life over the hills, peeling away shadows and gilding the leaves of scrub willows. Up early, I rinsed myself in the river, its chilly water stinging my forehead and eyelids; then Helios was up, showing no inclination for mercy. By nine, it laved in waves over the sage, distorting distances and siphoning the Sweetwater with its powerful evaporative pull.

Nothing vexed me that day, neither Wyoming's emptiness nor anything of earth, air, water, or fire. I fell easily into a blisterless stride, placid of spirit as a tramp in springtime. Soon I passed a rough-hewn log ranch house plumped a few yards south of the river. Brown from years of unforgiving weathers, the ground around it was worn, as if a forlorn pacing had formed its perimeters. When I sashayed in for a closer look, I was met in the yard by three men and a fetching woman who came bounding out of the cabin, each kicking at dust and worrying as if they'd seen a plane crash and expected a corpse to deliver a eulogy.

Turns out, I was crossing the million-acre Yellowstone Ranch, owned (temporarily at least) by the John Hancock Insurance Company, which had signed the deed in triplicate when the ranch was auctioned off for back taxes on the courthouse steps in Lander. Since John Hancock held the original mortgage, its own "insurance" was to make sure it had the only out-of-reach bid in town. The ranch's former owners, strapped for cash or business smarts, were forced into unseemly foreclosure but had been given a last-minute reprieve—nine months to redeem themselves or, so to speak, take out another policy. Wyoming Governor Ed Herschler, I was told, had a financial stake in the ranch. Crossing Ed's interest in the million acres, if true, I never saw a single gubernatorial steer. I never knew when I walked onto the ranch or where I walked out of it.

Ken and Donna Ballard and their sons, Duane and Les, live on the Yellowstone Ranch in summer, watching over the 3,000 whiteface cattle that Ken assured me roam God-only-knows-where across open range, roughly 334 acres per every four hooves. Square jawed, well muscled, and over six feet, Ken was a shade heftier than his sons, but all three were obviously related bodies, sporting faded jeans with belt buckles the size of beer cans. Both boys were trying on mustaches that summer and, like father like son, hooked their thumbs in the corners of their pockets, legs apart, leaving their fingers loose in the way gunfighters look in spaghetti Westerns. Mrs. Ballard, a shoulder-length blonde with an indelible smile, a splashy pink shirt, and denim slacks, stood amid her menfolk looking well protected and proud.

Ken Ballard is the kind of man who makes a greenhorn look like he should—seriously out of place. There was a gentleness in him that overshadowed tough-ness and inner strength—something I wouldn't have suspected if I hadn't spent part of an afternoon with him in a truck with a bad case of metal fatigue hammering over Wyoming's Antelope Hills. Ken turned Robert Frost's most famous dictum on its butt. When he let it drop that good fences don't always make good neighbors in Wyoming, I felt constrained to ask why and got virtually the same answer Susie Oldfather had given me on the plains above Fullerton, Nebraska.

"Build a fence, create a corner," Ken said. "Cattle gather in corners, and once the BLM spots them, they call it overgrazing. Usually it is."

Slapping at his dungarees with a dusty hat, he climbed into the truck's cab, wheezing its engine to life. "A fence is no management tool. Cattle come to natural water on open range. With fences, they get boxed up and, being stupid to begin with, they can't figure out how to get from there to a drink. Leave things open and they'll make out OK."

About noon, when we set out on the "dry tour," as Ken called it, the sky turned porphyry, its glare more glazed and its dome burnished nearly white with a scattering of darkening clouds high enough to pose no threat, except to make open space gloomy as an ocean under a forlorn scud. We stopped at the remains of the St. Mary's Stage Station, a place where Mark Twain stepped down on his way to Nevada and fame. But it was death that drew us across the river, searching out a grave near "Mormon Springs," spotting it at last in the ocean of sage.

When she died of cholera on June 29, 1849, Sarah Thomas was twenty-nine years old and well short of South Pass from which she might have gazed into her future. Her gravestone, carved by a grieving husband, is remote and seldom visited. A poor speller, her husband inscribed an illiterate's pain.

Saraha Thomas
DJun.29.54
10.10.24
Dog.um
Colic

As I'd done at all the forlorn monuments to Dream's dead—Ada Magill, 6; Joel Hembry, 9; Rachel Pattison, 18; Rebeccah Winters, 50—I pondered on loss, despair, grief, and failure. Each had gone underground under the influence of Manifest Destiny, each denied the end of their rainbow. For their survivors, most had come too far to turn back, their bridges burned, but on the route ahead there had to be places where a circle in the sand, perhaps at a grave like Sarah's, marked a turning back in the fragile landscape of human hopes.

"Six, maybe seven years ago, somebody dug in the Sarah Thomas grave," Bob said, anger sprouting across his forehead. He scuffed the ground, toed the broken stone as if to mend it again or to put its rent parts right and undo a nightmare. Sensing even deeper water in Bob's well that needed pumping out, I kept silent. He scuffed at the stone again, letting his anger gush. "I found her bones scattered all over the place! No skull! They took it! I put the rest of 'em back in, covered 'em up and lay the headstone down flat so you wouldn't see it. But they broke that too! What the hell have we come to? What?"

Bob's was a question I can't answer; but when I looked more closely at the halved stone, I saw two fragments of Sarah's pale bones, one later identifiable in Gray's Anatomy as a metacarpus or phalange of the dorsal surface of her hand, the other fractured and splintered beyond recognition. Pondering human remnants of Manifest Destiny, I picked up the fragments, placed them on her headstone, and photographed the ravages of moral decay. Of the 206 bones in the body, those single fragments of a lost American remain the most poignant memory of my journey; in them, I'd touched a fatal shard of Dream.

· · ·

The grim stone flank known as "Rocky Ridge" rises near rough-cut palisades known as "Sweetwater Narrows," a spot where the river is wedged into a gorge making wagon travel impossible. Mormons were forced to higher ground, flanking around the "Narrows." As late as 1981, Oregon Trail historian Gregory Franzwa called this stretch of misery a "remote and dangerous area." To William Clayton, these were "rough, rocky ridges—dangerous to wagons . . . to be crossed with care." A "high stone hill," J. Goldsborough Bruff called them in 1849, "very stony and rough, requiring care of the teamsters."

The highest and most godawful stretch on the Mormon Trail (7,900 feet), Rocky Ridge was and remains a mixed bag of desperation and despair to any person on foot. It lacks water, shelter, or comforts, exposing travelers to walls of battering wind (hot and cold), rain, sleet, or snow in their seasons, which is any month excluding July and August. At its eastern foot, Rocky Ridge ascends through a valley that marks the farthest point reached by the ill-fated, snowbound Martin Handcart Company before it was rescued in the late fall of 1856. Frostbitten and walking in worn-out shoes, those rescued referred ever after to the ridge as the "Trail of Blood." Walking its history, lamentation was my constant companion. Two Mormon historical markers tell its tale along the route—the first a reminder of the hell suffered by the Martin Handcart Company and the second announcing the summit of Rocky Ridge.

Rocky Ridge was an eighteen-hour scrabble over broken, jagged protrusions made more poignant by its bone-rattling geology. The climb is steady and tedious as the ground crumbles beneath your feet, first into sand and rock shard, next into ankle-threatening small boulders, and finally—crowning its high point—slabs of rock tumbled like tombstones, all of it with less a sense of Creation than of vandalism. Nearby, I was told later, a prospector found the largest platinum nugget ever discovered in the United States, now on display at the Smithsonian Institution.

• • •

(In late September 2000, three days after a foot-deep snowfall following unseasonably hot weather, I crossed "the ridge" again on foot, this time with a British friend and fellow rambler, Brian Knox-Peebles. Even with his splendid company, a phantom of dread lingered around us. For two days we lived off meltwaters, squirreling into our bivvy sacks at last light, Brian listening for unfamiliars in the dark— not an uncommon concern for someone who lives in London's West End and who finds himself in Wyoming on what appears to be the surface of the moon. Nights were clear; stars majestic, but the wind moaned unending. On Rocky Ridge, there are few Dreams left.)

• • •

Late afternoon next day, I stopped at Rock Creek to take in a third monument. During a single October night in 1853, fifteen Mormons froze and were buried beside its banks. Three days ahead of the equally ill-fated Martin Handcart Company, early snows swallowed them. Citing James Chislet's on-the-spot account, Ray B. West writes: "They died . . . like lamps whose oil had been depleted, whose wicks grew gradually dimmer, until they expired."

When they were yet glowing lamps in the darkness, the Mormon apostle F. D. Richards overtook them on the Platte River with an "outfit of light carriages and wagons" heading for Salt Lake. Richards preached from his carriage to the newly arrived converts in the Willie Handcart Company—English, Scots, Scandinavians, and "a few Germans." Winding down, he prophesied "in the name of Israel's God that 'though it might storm on your right and on your left,' the Lord will keep open your way before you and get you to Zion in safety." Either Richards was wrong or God wasn't listening. Of the seventy-seven persons who died in the Willie company, fifteen are buried by the banks of Rock Creek. A resting place in near desolation, like the grave of Sarah Thomas, there was nothing to hold me there, not even grief. My brief visit was abetted by a heat-relieving cloud, an infrequent joy not to be had during the sweaty march of a long afternoon. On a table of raised fieldstone, a bronze plaque was laden with a plain prose of misery surrounded by signs of neglect, as if enough history had been expended in the text but not in upkeep, suggesting that when the past is well away from the common path, it's difficult to find a way back.

· · ·

(Fifteen years after I'd first stopped by, in early October 2000, Brian Knox-Peebles and I ate lunch on Rock Creek, a few yards below the gravesite. When we hiked in, everything had changed. Gone were any signs of neglect. In its place had risen a shrine. A new, expansive road had been bulldozed into the site and a once grassy area along the creek transformed into campgrounds (suitably wide-gated to allow an influx of RVs) complete with toilets and showers. A pint-sized information kiosk greeted visitors; an impressive American flag flew eaglelike on a beetling white pole. An amphitheater of log benches circled, cathedral-like, an open altar near the grave, and a granite marker proclaimed the message: "To the People of the Second Rescue, REMEMBER." Carved into the stone were the names of the Mormon top brass who had ordered up memory like a plate of fish. Unmitigated overkill.

The sole improvement was the addition of a tasteful ground-level granite marker with the names of those buried on the site between October 24 and 25, 1856. Names, writ small, made the story poignant. Ranging in age from nine (Bodil Mortensen) to sixty-seven (James Gibb), they included three children and twelve adults. British and Scandinavians, new American Dreamers all. The flagstone monument I paused beside in 1985 still stands, its tabletop bronze marker (Number 27, Utah Pioneer Trails and Landmarks Association, Erected 1933) telling its story of misery and death with unassuming dignity; but it now looks out of place in the unctuous and sentimental shrine, and seems to be grieving for its lost solitude.)

* * *

I crossed Rock Creek to keep water between me and the ghosts of the Willie Handcart Company, walking steadily into deep twilight. Where I camped that night, I have no fixed idea, except I crossed another stream and set up my tent under pinpoint lights in the vault of dark, watching the Milky Way, like a streak of faded whitewash, edge across sky's rafters, the moon festooned as a carved marble boss on a cathedral ceiling. Next morning, when I eased out of the tent, two moose (a cow and her calf) and the grandeur of the Wind River Mountains greeted me—the first sentinels of passage into old Oregon.

Midmorning, I passed Pete Petry tending fence, replacing eighty-year-old wood with new metal posts. He lived, he said, "on a crick at the Carpenter place." Muscled tough, Pete was averaging "about a mile a day," working out of a rusted four-wheel drive, but his winter occupation was trapping, sleeping out in snow caves (two down sleeping bags required) and running trap lines along "Rock and Willow creeks, the Little and Big Beaver and Deep Gulch." The winter before, he'd trapped 82 beaver, 17 bobcats, 17 martin, and 33 coyote, hauling their pelts back home on an army packboard. That season, beaver fetched $22.50, Bobcat $205, Martin $32.00, and coyote $52.50. Sold by the pelt, Pete's winter takings were $7,600, give or take a couple of bucks.

As we talked, a light airplane came in low over the sage, seemed to stall, and slipped over a ridge. "That guy's gonna crash," I said.

"Nah," Pete said, cupping a gloved hand over his eyes. "Government men. Shooting coyotes. They cut the prop so they don't shoot into it. That's about all the sense the sons-of-bitches got. A government man gets maybe three hundred coyotes a year. They're my competition."

The engine throttled back to life, its echo sputtering over the hills as it rose on a slipstream of high octane, banked hard to the left, and disappeared in a rising whine.

* * *

At Burnt Ranch, I met up again with the Sweetwater River. Ignoring No Trespassing signs, I holed up in a down-on-its-luck ranch truck while pollywog-sized rain plocked in the dust (the last rain on my walk), its dampness freshening the air and the breeze carrying the sickly, sweet scent of sage. I dozed on and off to a less than easeful tump-tump-tumping of rain on the truck's steel roof. Variously known as Gilbert's Station, Upper Sweetwater Station, and South Pass Station, what's left of Burnt Ranch—one usable cabin, an outhouse, a pole barn, and corral—stands at the ninth and last crossing of the Sweetwater River. (By the fall of 2000, the buildings were much improved, the main cabin showing signs of a child in residence.) In 1862 Henry Herr wrote: "Indians here are bad," and by 1868 the stage and telegraph station had been burned twice. Marks of the raids are still visible on its log buildings.

Another famous emigrant road (the "Lander Cutoff") also began at Burnt Ranch—the only part of the Oregon Trail ever constructed by the U.S. government for pioneers heading to Oregon. Surveyed, graded, and built by Frederick Lander, from whom Lander, Wyoming, takes its name, its beginnings at the ranch marked an important hub on expanding roads west. A Mormon killed Lander's meteorologist, Charles Miller, at Burnt Ranch in 1858. Buried nearby in appropriately named Slaughter-House Gulch, his bones rest among graves of several unknowns.

• • •

Crossing the Sweetwater for the last time, I climbed a steep hill known as "Mormon Gulch," heading toward the broad saddle of South Pass. By nightfall, Oregon Butte showed up to the southwest, with South Pass bowed between its headland and the Wind River Range. A vestige of setting sun crept under the clouds like a gilded blade. I trudged on, hoping to come to the edge and peer like pilgrims before me into the Dream that was "Oregon."

I didn't make it. The pass stretched out-of-reach, and I put the tent down next to the trail in a concave of pitiful grass. Walking steadily for two and a half months, it doesn't matter where daylight ends. You find a place. You make do. I did.

• • •

Next day, I met John Huffstetler hauling disassembled sheep pens on a white Dodge flatbed truck. He climbed out of the cab, shook hands, and told me he worked for a local sheep rancher and was the only non-Basque on the payroll, information he volunteered almost before I could say, "Glad to meet you." Antelope shared the landscape with me that morning, but sheep and sheepherders seemed curiously absent, as if the Basque employees and their charges had decamped overnight, perhaps for Spain. When I mentioned this to John, he informed me that, given so much open space and a Basque's love of solitude, they were probably hiding. But he assured me they'd seen me.

Festooned as John was in an incandescent T-shirt advertising "Orange Crush," I asked if, by any chance, he had a can of the elixir that he might part with for cash, considering his chest was about the breadth of a billboard and the advertising had achieved its desired effect.

"I got a coupl'a Cokes," he said. "Have one on me."

I took one, sucked at it mercifully, and warmly thanked him. "Any time," he said.

• • •

"I crossed the Continental Divide at SOUTH PASS around 10:00 A.M. on the morning of July 2, 1985," I wrote in my pocket diary. The hour is tentative because I carried no watch. Below me, old "Oregon" stretched in a continuation of the utterly dismal, although the road downhill toward a distant patch of green marked the end of my 8.4-inch-per-mile "mountaineering" from the Missouri River. For half an hour, I rested by the monuments atop the pass that announce the arrival of Manifest Destiny beyond the Rocky Mountains, my back propped against a slab of black slate celebrating Narcissa Prentiss Whitman and Eliza Hart Spalding as the first white women to nudge over the edge in search of a new inheritance, appropriately on July 4, 1836.

Four months after Brigham dipped his finger in the Great Salt Lake, Narcissa and her husband, Marcus (the man who doctored a dying Joel Hembree), were killed at their mission at Waiilatpu on the Columbia River Plateau, done in by Walla Walla and Cayuse Indians who were having none of Destiny, Dream, or white man's gods.

• • •

Ezra Meeker, who first went west in a wagon in 1852, came back as an old man in 1906 to plant a red granite marker on South Pass as a labor of love. Meeker lived to be ninety-eight, taking the big leap into eternity in 1928, but in the memorial edition of *Covered-Wagon Centennial and Ox-Team Days*, published to commemorate one hundred years of the Oregon Trail's history and, in part, Ezra's lifetime devotion to it, he stares out of a photograph, face adrift in a Niagara of white hair with a nine-inch fall of snowy chin whiskers surrounding a face dignified by small, wire-rimmed specs and nimble eyes. By the 1890s Ezra was convinced that the trail had been "lost"—its geography mislaid; so he set about to "find" it again, single-handedly founding the Oregon Trail Memorial Association.

The commemorative book, however, is filled with the laud and blather of celebrants who love the trails in memory where Ezra loved it in fact and on foot: in 1906, the year he placed the granite marker on South Pass, he crossed it from west to east with an ox team and covered wagon to be feted by Teddy Roosevelt at the White House. Crossing and recrossing the trail to him was less a Dream than a lover's caress, and, to that end, I'm an Ezra Meeker fan. Coming or going, it's splendid to walk in his footsteps.

Sadly, too many folks in the Oregon Trail Memorial Association these days sound like advertising gurus. Take this blurb from a past president in the centennial hymnbook who never hauled his personal *assets* over the trail's expanse: "The old pioneer trails will be marked. Strategic spots . . . will be turned into historic shrines where young and old may linger and learn the story of America's making. . . . Artists and sculptors, poets and musicians, will cast the vibrant epic of the westward march of America into forms that will reach and hold the heart of humanity." Mythmaking as an art.

• • •

Having no Dreams to betray, I entered the lands of Zion, pausing at Pacific Springs, a mile or two downhill, which still flows aplenty from spongy ground. I took a plank path leading from terra firma to terra soggy and knelt beside clear running water, filtering a cup into my canteen. Before drinking, I toasted the thousands who'd camped by its bounty—the weary and worn, the ordinary and extraordinary, the families broken by desperate journeys across arid spaces and hard miles. No Dream in that. None at all. Like Ezra Meeker, I'd "learned to recognize the old trail by its countenance." Its countenance was mine. And his. And theirs.

PART 4

Promised Land

44

There cannot be progression without retrogression. . . . I'm a walker still, but . . . I do not feel so native to the earth as formerly.
W. H. HUDSON, *A FOOT IN ENGLAND*

It was with great difficulty that we could determine the dividing point of the land which separates the waters of the Atlantic from the Pacific. This country is called the South Pass.
ORSON PRATT, JUNE 26, 1847

Near twelve Oclock we hooked up and commenced jaunt through the Pass, passing the summit about 4 Oclock and encamped near a Spring branch. . . . This suits me, I feel very well.
DR. JOHN HUDSON WAYMAN, JUNE 22, 1852

"Whatever you do," the park ranger said, "don't get in a truck with Bob. He's crazy on wheels"—all the incentive I needed from a well-intentioned man in government employ to do the opposite. The "crazy" in question was a six-foot, leathery-skinned, tawny fellow with a ruddy face like a crushed felt hat and a magisterial nose. Single-handedly the most eccentric spectacle in view, Bob Lieberenz was more quirky than the entire summer tourist population of South Pass City that afternoon. Gussied up with fresh summer paint for the season's fret of tourists, the "city" gave off the same stale aura of synthetic history as Prairie Village in Grand Island, Nebraska. The restored mining town's tales had been so often told and retold for tourists, each time with less clarity and more imagination, that its "living history" had curdled into romance, which always unsettles me; I preferred the original—unwashed miners, fleshpots, drunks pissing in the street.

South Pass City sprang up on the heels of an 1868 gold strike along Big Hermit Creek. A town churned to life, at one time sporting "5 hotels, 13 saloons, 3 meat markets, 2 bakeries, a band, 4 law firms, a weekly newspaper, a gun store, several stamp mills, a shooting and bowling alley, a beer garden, and 2 doctors." When they weren't setting broken bones or handing out nostrums, the sawbones worked their mining claims; but quacks were outnumbered, two to one, by legal eagles. By 1870 the town touted 4,000 residents: by the 1930s the *WPA Guide* listed "50 pop." Minus tourists in July 1985, that figure seemed high.

Aside from gold, South Pass City's chief claim to fame lay in Bill Bright, a local politician harassed by an outspoken wife into introducing a bill in the territorial legislature in 1869 to grant equal voting rights to women. It passed, making Wyoming the first state in the union to do so. Next year, Esther Hobart Morris of South Pass City became the nation's first political gender bender, elected justice of the peace—an office she held for eight months.

A supporter of feminist causes, Esther "contributed regularly to *Revolution*, the organ of the Women's Suffrage Society." Miffed that a suffragette's organ had somehow helped dangle a political modifier in South Pass City, Esther's ireful predecessor refused to surrender his hold on the John Thomas of pending cases—the court docket. Esther sued to get her hands on it. Resistance was stiff. When the things got too hot to handle, Esther dismissed the case and started a new docket of her own. Defeated, her nemesis drifted into the mists of history while Esther made out and Wyoming led the way toward the feminist revolutions of the next century.

Truth be told, Esther's role as a feminist advocate in the "Equality State," which Wyoming dubbed itself for a time, and in the women's suffrage movement, as was later claimed, turns out to be a large measure of pipeDream. Elevated to feminist "heroine" during an early publicity blitz for national women's suffrage (she once attended a dinner for Susan B. Anthony), Esther as pro-fem was the creation of two political opportunists—Grace Hebard and H. G. Nickerson—who thought that "it would be nice if a woman were recognized for having something to do with Wyoming's pioneer history." The pair latched on to Esther and her eight-month tenure as a justice of the peace in South Pass City like two trout rising to the same fly.

In 1920 Hebard put up a cairn on the presumed site of Esther's South Pass City home, boldly claiming that Esther was nothing less than the coauthor of Bill Bright's equal suffrage bill. She wasn't, of course. Turns out Grace Hebard's original monument wasn't on the site of Esther's home at all, although that didn't stop the Wyoming Professional Women's Club from building a log cabin on the wrong lot in 1975–76. The phony cabin is now a state historic site.

. . .

Dan Allen, the amiable park ranger, was explaining the town's boom and bust miseries, including the Esther Hobart saga, when I spotted Bob Lieberenz outside the Clarissa Exchange—a tourist emporium with enough elk antlers hanging over its portico to send the entire Asian aphrodisiac market into a frenzy. Bob was involved in simultaneous conversations with the owner and two confused tourists. When he looked in my direction, Dan issued his on-the-spot warning. It didn't take.

Needing no further recommendation to exit town, I climbed into Bob's pickup, testing Dan's prophecy and my personal resolve. Beyond the Continental Divide, giddy with wide-awake, I was ready to shuck South Pass City, even if it meant risking all in a Canadian version of derring-do. When Bob fished a fifth of Old Forester from under his seat, swabbing its neck with a greasy hand and offering me a pull, I reconsidered. The manic gleam I'd found appealing turned out to be bottled.

Under the circumstances, a leap from a moving pickup was ill-timed and Bob had the "peddle to the metal," fishtailing out of town. He knocked back a mouthful of sour mash as if it were Seven-Up, corked the bottle, popped it back under the seat, and ground the truck into low gear to climb the ridge, tracing a northerly, if shaky, course toward Atlantic City on the other side—another mining town busted for good. Headed downslope toward a sadness misnamed for a respectable ocean, I considered that if New York Life knew what I was up to, they'd cancel my policy on the spot.

After a sojourn in high gear to get the full flavor of "the downhill special," as Bob put it, he knuckled the rattletrap pickup into low gear again, explaining to me between cursing a complaining transmission that the brakes were "not all that good, but low will sure hold her on the way down." By now, I'd noticed holes in the floorboards, each sucking dust from under the cab, which gave the inside air the color and texture of a sandstorm, which Bob, ever one-handed and nonchalant at the wheel, swatted away from his eyes like black flies in a northern Maine spring. When I ventured that we stop for refreshments at a local watering hole (the Atlantic City Mercantile), hoping to steady my nerves or enhance the thrill, I'm uncertain which, Bob let it slip that his welcome was "wore out, in that place, by God." Seemed he'd been jubilant one time too many in the local saloon, which was humping that summer for respectable tourist trade.

"You know *National Geographic*?" Bob shouted over the din, taking his eyes off the road, searching for me in the dust.

I ventured I did, yelling back that I'd recently met one of Geographic's photographers. Then I screamed, which drew his attention to the road that he'd momentarily forgotten.

"You ever read that Robert Redford piece in *Geographic* about the outlaw trails?" he hollered.

Redford's name was certainly familiar, but "No, I haven't read it," I shouted, doubting that I ever would because Bob had driven off the shoulder toward an impending ravine. When I screamed a second time, he swerved back on course, not missing a conversational beat.

"Well, Redford come over to the Atlantic City Merc. Hung around for an hour. Took four pictures inside, four out, and listened to some of Wyoming's best liars. Then he wrote up a whole lot of stuff that come right out of a bull's ass. Some of it could have been true. But it had color, I'll give it that . . . brown."

We twisted through town like a sidewinder on a sand dune, Bob forcing the truck down another dirt road even more sinister than the last, turning off sharply at a chained and padlocked green metal gate, and braking so sharply I was launched at the windshield, a choke of dust boiling from under the cab.

Gate opened, he wrangled the rust bucket up a rutted slope to a green-roofed log cabin. A freshet ran below the place and the yard was littered with odds and ends, mostly odds of well-tussled junk, some usable and all of it—truck parts, rusted oil drums, a littering of hubcaps, coil springs, iron bars, engine blocks—the collected leftovers from abandoned Dreams that made Bob's life possible. I expected him to come up with a cliché: "It ain't much, but it's home." Instead, he said, "This is my summer place."

"Where's your winter place?"

"Down in Wamsutter," he replied, as if sixty-three miles as the crow flies between two lonesome, no-account fly specks on the Wyoming map was the difference between Point Barrow, Alaska, and Palm Springs.

"What's the attraction in Wamsutter?" I asked, hoping he'd come up with the name of some faded femme fatale who persuaded him to come in from the cold and snuggle up during her winter solstice, but his straight-talk answer held no illusions of shared BTUs or passion.

"Easier to get to the liquor store," he said. "It's hell to get out'a here in winter. Hell, spring shows up in a four-wheel drive and chains. It's summer this month."

He went for the throat of Old Forester again, tipping it back with a gentleman's hand, letting amber nectar ride over his tongue like a stream of mild summer air. Eyes shut, he savored his best friend, and when they opened again they seemed like a hound's eyes, drooped and weary in the dog days and looking for a patch of shady dust next to a stoop. Bob swung the bottle at the end of one languid arm, a finger unfurling from its neck, pointing toward a stand of trees.

"There's a good spot down by the crick to set up your tent. It's yours as long as you want it." He offered me the jug and, this time, sun all but over the yardarm, I fetched fire to the belly. Then Bob shot me—well, I felt as if I'd been shot.

"John Neihardt's tree," he fired point-blank, waving to a slope above the cabin. "That's where I got it for 'im. Little jackrabbit of a fella . . . some kind'a professor from Missouri."

I took it in the gut. Once again, there was too much "coincidence clumping around a theme"—obviously Osage magic.

$$\bullet \quad \bullet \quad \bullet$$

In 1962 Bob's "little jackrabbit of a fella" was a fixture on the campus of the University of Missouri where I was studying at the time, a scrivener whose epic poem *A Cycle of the West* came as close to Dreamland (or Dreamscript) as any American writing could. A grand swath of laud, it's the Alleluia, Te Deum, and Gloria of the American West. Born in Illinois in 1881, John G. Neihardt died in Columbia, Missouri, ninety-two years later (1973) after a career that included doing time as poet laureate of Nebraska (he lived in Bancroft and is buried there), literary editor of the *St. Louis Post-Dispatch*, and poet-in-residence at the University of Missouri until 1966. His middle name, "Gneisenau," sounds like a sneeze and may have been what drove him to belle lettres, since onomatopoeia is an attraction to poets.

A quill-diver of imposing diminutive stature, Neihardt strode across Mizzou's lawns and along its chalk-scented halls with a leonine mass of silver hair flowing behind like the wake of a cabin cruiser, a demi-saint to many who took his class and an inspiration, I suspect, to the Osage, who shares the same leonine hair style. It took Neihardt thirty years to complete *A Cycle of the West* and about that long to read it in a semester.

"Feisty little bugger," Bob said, faking a couple of air-punches while enlarging on his acquaintance with John Gneisenau (Bless you!) Neihardt. "You couldn't keep a glove on 'im. I come across him in Atlantic City in . . . gimme a second . . . nineteen and sixty-three. He was writin' a book . . . him and some newspaper fella from Omaha. Wanted to dig up a South Pass pine and find somebody fool enough to take him to Pacific Springs. Nobody made an effort, so I said, 'Professor, if you can ride in my old army four-by-four, let's go.' Hell, I brought him out here an' dug up the tree with my grave robbin' shovel. It's on the University of Missouri campus. My brother's kid saw it. It says, 'A tree from old South Pass, Wyoming.'"

"But this isn't South Pass. It's Atlantic City. It's not even close. The tree's a phony."

"Hell, they don't know that in Missouri. I don't think he knew it either. Anyway, it's close enough and he didn't raise no hell about it."

"What's a grave robbing shovel?"

Bob turned sheepish. "I was up to poach a calf-moose on the cemetery road above South Pass an' I see this fella digging up a pioneer kid's grave. So instead of the moose, I took a shot at him. That fella took out'a there and bailed the fence. Didn't get the calf, but I got me a damn good shovel."

Bob had "only a day to yip with Neihardt," he said, but he did see him again. "One winter, down to Wamsutter, I was watching Johnny Carson. I heard this voice . . . some little guy in Californy sunglasses. It was him. I don't know what his book was, but I'd sure like to get a copy."

I didn't know either, but I'm sure it took at least a year to read in a semester.

• • •

After filtering water from Willow Creek and flushed from Bob's whiskey, I set up camp, dozing off while Bob rattled around among his field of leftover Dreams, doing a little of this and a little of that, much of it noisily, occasionally grunting curses. Half an hour later, he wandered down to my tent, woke me up, and suggested a hardscrabble drive on jeep trails to the site of Fort Stambaugh, one of the long-gone military palisades on the Bozeman Trail. "We could take us a watermelon," he said. "I got one in the crick."

Another drive with Bob was a health hazard I'd rather have avoided, but with a snooze and a snort under my belt and a plump, cool watermelon in the cooler he'd dug out from the rubble, I risked it anyway. He drove with the same personal denial of gravity, grinding through backcountry, tossing me around inside the cab like a tennis ball in a steel barrel, braking at last on a stretch of nothing *but* nothing. In the distance, Bob pointed out a dark spec against the sage—a cabin.

"That place is owned by a lawyer out of Lander known for ulterior motives," he said. A memorable turn of phrase.

Fort Stambaugh having long vanished, except for a few rusty tin cans and an occasional hand-forged nail, we got busy on the watermelon. No ordinary melon, I might add. In the middle of stuffing my face with sweet pink, I caught Bob's eye glinting with pleasure.

"Crick ripened," he said. "Takes five days. Recipe come to me in a dream."

Unprepared for salvation by a watermelon, I was struck by Bob's recipe, much as John J. Cornish had been struck thirdhand by Joseph Smith's aurora borealis. As I saw it—and still do—something that works in two days less than the Creation, something that comes out of nowhere in a Dream, as it did with Bob, has only one word to account for it—revelation. A very Mormon moment, there was no nay-saying that this was the most delicious damn watermelon I'd ever eaten and—praise juices—Bob led me out of darkness and in on his secret.

"I got converts," he said. "They thought I'd stripped a gear. But I'm tellin' you, mister, there's nothing better than a crick-ripened melon."

Dream or no, Bob spoke the truth and nothing but in the melon department. He didn't know it at the time, nor did I, but the true "Zion" of watermelon huddles not far away, near Utah's San Rafael Swell. Turns out, Green River, Utah, is the "Watermelon Capital of the World"—the Solomon's temple of melon worship: its crops command top dollar in the Big Apple, Windy City, and Bean Town. Even those perennial outcasts like Buffalo and Cleveland pay top dollar for Green River's annual harvest. Except for Utah's odd liquor laws, Bob might have prophesied and prospered in Green River, since he believed—and I testify—that watermelons can be saved by immersion.

Like other apostles struck dumb on a road to somewhere, I've translated Bob's basic teachings using American scripture as a reference.

> *Bob's Book of Meloni*
>
> *It came to pass there was a man who came into the land of Wyoming by way of Arkansas. "Behold a stranger," said the priests, "one who is unclean and given to too much wine. He shows no respect for our elders. Let us turn him away."*
>
> *And it came to pass that another said, "Let us not act in haste, for he may have traveled in foreign lands and has knowledge of strange customs and mysteries. Let him speak before we toss him out on his ear."*

Upon hearing this, the stranger looked to heaven and, refreshing himself from a jar of seven-year-old forest wine, said, "I am a prophet commanded to preach good news. Listen up, for what I say was revealed to me in a Dream."

"This man is a holy messenger," exclaimed a woman among them. "He comes out of the desert and thirsts not for water but for old forest wine. Surely, this is the one who was spoken of by the prophets!"

And it came to pass that the High Priest condemned the woman. "Would you claim the right of priests? This man is an imposter."

But the righteous woman fell at the stranger's feet and said, "Master, what would you have us do?"

And it came to pass that the stranger raised her up and, pointing at the High Priest and keepers of the temple, said, "Take a watermelon and put it in a flaxen sack* and take it to the river. Leave it in the water for five days. When you take it out, break it into many pieces and taste it, and you will know the truth of which I speak for it was revealed in a Dream."

At this, the High Priest was confounded. But the woman did as the stranger commanded. At the appointed hour, she did pluck it out, broke it into many pieces, anointed it with salt and eat of it. "Verily, this man speaks the truth," she said to the crowd. "Behold this is revealed in the latter days as was prophesied of old."

With that, the High Priest fell upon his knees saying, "This is he of whom our scriptures spoke. This is the one anointed. This is Meloni, the chosen one."

And it came to pass that they did leave the land of Wyoming and were led, in the fullness of time, deeper into the desert where they raised temples and an abundance of crops. There they did raise up a mighty people, favored of nations, from which they sent forth melon seeds, two by two, and these bore fruit and were named according to their many varieties, Royal Flush, Oasis, Sweet Scarlet, Sugar Baby, and StarGazer.

---

* Author's note: "flaxen sack" is a mistranslation from the original "reformed Arkansian" dialect. A better translation is "burlap bag."

FOLLOWING THE WRONG GOD HOME

45

The foot traveler need not be ashamed of his mode of journeying.
To travel on foot is to travel like Plato and Pythagoras.

AUTHOR UNKNOWN

It is three years today since our brethren Joseph and Hyrum were
taken from us ... [and] we have so far prospered in our endeav-
ors to get from under the grasp of our enemies.

WILLIAM CLAYTON, JUNE 27, 1847

As I looked down on the Pacific slope, a long vista widening in the
distance, it seemed like entering upon a new world.

BERNARD J. REID, JULY 19, 1849

At sundown, another Bob showed up hauling a camper. The two old friends backslapped and whooped it up for as long as it took for Bob #1 to get thirsty and Bob #2 to bed down on a float of Kentucky Cream. In between, the evening turned into a rigmarole of "top this" braggadocio while night cooled to a sharp edge unexpected in the heat of the afternoon. I slept in the camper that night, grateful to be off the ground.

Two Bobs in one place is like two hens on one egg, so, next morning, I sorted out the confusion by calling the original "Wyoming Bob," and his amanuensis "Chicago Bob," which, as it turned out, was actually his moniker. This arrangement seemed reasonable to both, since it defined respective pissing rights and avoided confusion. Smitten with the novelty, and not remembering my name anyway, they decided to call me "Canada Bob."

Chicago Bob showed up with a vehicle packed so full of legal firearms that, given inclination and a cause, we might have staged a civil war in Wyoming. As the owner of an army surplus store in the Windy City that rented military paraphernalia to Hollywood (his story), he was also an antique arms dealer, offering explosive wares to denizens of the fading West, mostly rawboned older men who still used words like "pardner," "showdown," and "yonder." Chicago Bob's customers were broad-shouldered cowboys familiar with frontier armaments like the Hawken, the Trap-Door Springfield, and the Hall Breechloader. I thought of

Peggy Smith at Fort Laramie who recognized westerners' unnatural love of guns, all pledging allegiance to God, the flag, muskets, flintlocks, carbines, rifles, six-shooters, and derringers. Chicago Bob's clientele were magnum fellows, several in the blunderbuss category, although most ate with a fork.

"It's great to be out of Chicago," he said over coffee next morning. "South Pass City is one hell of a town."

I agreed.

· · ·

During the Wyoming gold rush of 1867–68, James Chisholm (no relation whatsoever) wrote occasionally lurid accounts for the *Chicago Tribune* from South Pass City—pieces full of the lure of quartz-veined gulches and new strikes at the Miner's Delight, King Solomon, Caribou, and Buckeye mines, while fighting off bouts of "neuralgic agonies"—the same painful combination that eventually caused Brigham Young's left eye to droop. In the Windy City, James Chisholm had courted Mary Evelyn Garrison, the daughter of an upstanding Chicago judge, whose wife opposed any match with a newspaperman since "the wife of a man on a morning paper could expect to spend her nights alone."

Whatever his wife's concerns, Judge Garrison mortgaged his daughter's virtue, making Jim promise not to see Mary Evelyn for at least a year, which accounted for why Jim accepted the *Tribune* assignment and took his cold shower in distant Wyoming. Jim bought a ticket on the Union Pacific from Omaha to Cheyenne, "a town that was listed in the timetables before it ever appeared on the official maps," and spent some time at Green River, Wyoming, the end of the line in 1868, before arriving by wagon at South Pass City on September 12. He found "50 dwellings," most "forsaken, or . . . never inhabited" and a population "not over 50 or 60." Claims were already playing out, and most had abandoned the mines, opting for steady work laying track for the Union Pacific.

Chisholm made the best of his experiences. Recording them plain-style style in his journal, he left a record of life in the mines at a time when the West was about to be tamed by the "iron horse." A down-on-his-luck gambler visiting South Pass City detailed for him the frontier's "old familiar horrors—the flaring gambling tents, the dance houses, the eternal strumming of banjoes, the miserable females" and games of faro, three-card monte, and roulette. There were "quarrels, cursing, drinking, and the flash and bang of pistols," as well as "shameless pimps, shameless women, broken gamblers, thieves." In a word, *society*.

While away from his intended, Jim met characters like Moss Agate, Fat Jack, Mag & Moll, Crazy Jane, the Schoolmarm, and Mormon Annie, "all pioneers of

FOLLOWING THE WRONG GOD HOME

vice." Whether he was on intimate terms with any of the "pioneers" isn't recorded, but he did diddle with conjecture. "I often speculate on what will finally become of all that rolling scum which the locomotive seems to blow onward as it presses westward," he wrote. "Will they get blown clean off the continent at last into the Pacific Ocean?"

As the railroad moved on, Jim imagined "the same faces in each successive shanty town, the same gamblers, the same musicians . . . the same old tunes to the same old dance, the same females always getting a little more dilapidated." "Dilapidated" is a nice touch. At every step, he saw "a lengthening chain" of vice and asked, "What will become of them?" He imagined gandy dancers and whores wintering over in Mormon Zion, remarking tongue-in-cheek, "It seems to me the whole crowd will find themselves in a difficult fix when they get to Salt Lake, for Brigham is a highly moral prophet and will not permit gambling, nor the presence of any superfluous women . . . but his own." "Superfluous" is another nice touch.

Arriving back in Chicago, Mormon Annies behind him, Jim won over the judge and his wife, married Mary Evelyn, and settled down. But something of the "flash and bang" in the Sweetwater mines fastened on him for the rest of his life, because he turned to "dramatic criticism," earning a national reputation. His portrait hung in the foyer of Daly's Theatre in New York until the place was torn down, and he and Mary Evelyn counted as friends the likes of Lillian Russell and Isadora Duncan. Still, one can't help but see Jim stagestruck to the end by Wyoming's "old horrors" and its long-playing drama of "rolling scum" pressing westward.

· · ·

I spent the Fourth of July, 1985, Bob-Bob-Bobbing along, eating my way through the annual buffalo barbecue, celebrating the hoopla in South Pass City, taking refresher courses on tall tales while conversing with John Barleycorn, the two Bobs, and other miscreants—cowboys, befringed women on horseback, off-key musicians, and other triumphal tokens of Dream's western heritage that trooped past. To the day, 139 years earlier, Marcus and Narcissa Whitman had crossed South Pass.

Squat Johnny Gilmore was over from Jeffrey City for the annual South Pass City strut. Eye on the cowgirls, he said of one, "Hell, she must'a put them tits in a pencil sharpener to get 'em that pointy." Minstrels rolled past on a wagon, sweaty under multigallon hats with brims so wide only their chins were in the sun. The parade master bellowed through the whine of a suspect speaker system, "Folks, that boy's playin' an a-cor-deen. He's either playin' an a-cor-deen or a cabinet fell on his lap."

Conversation at the fete covered a broad swath of Dream's grievances—political shenanigans, bloated government, taxes, the rising price of smokes, as well as admonitions on how to "get a leg over a cowgirl," how to "nigger rig" an American flag on a makeshift pole (racial sensitivities hadn't made it to South Pass City), how to celebrate the Fourth with a fifth (both Bobs were big on this), and how to dress a poached sage hen after you've hoodwinked a game warden.

One game warden in particular was taking a shellacking.

"Ol' Underwood was death on hands," Wyoming Bob said. "He'd check for blood under the fingernails. We called him 'Underbrush.' He learned camouflage in the army."

"Show Canada Bob how to gut a sage hen," Chicago Bob suggested.

Wyoming Bob stood up and struck a wide-legged pose. "You wrap the wings around their head like this," he said, raising a pair of imaginary wings on each side of an imaginary sage hen's head, balling his hands around the imaginary bird for best effect. "Y'take a hard grip. Crunch the wings and head t'gether. Brace your feet good, mister, squeeze the neck, and sling the birdy off your shoulder like you was hittin' a baseball."

"I don't get it," I said.

"He's a Canadian," Chicago Bob offered by way of an apology.

"I was in the Canadian Air Force," Wyoming Bob said. (Interesting news to me.) "They're not as dumb as they look."

"Help a Canadian out," I said.

"Hell, Canada Bob, the guts, gizzard, and everythin' come right out'a the hen's bungy hole . . . all except the windpipe and you're hangin' on to that."

• • •

Some of it was true. "Wyoming Bob" did fight for king and country in the Royal Canadian Airforce, joining up at the Prince Edward Hotel in Windsor, Ontario. "I showed up in Canada in one of them Palm Beach suits," he said. "Walked across the Ambassador Bridge from Detroit . . . holes in my shoes a bullfrog could'a jumped through. I was eighteen. 'What'cha want?' the man in blue asked me. I says, 'I come to join the RCAF and waved a clipping from the Detroit newspaper. Citizenship didn't matter a damn. After that, I was a guest of the King." He shipped out to an air base near Brandon, Manitoba, eventually flying Lancaster bombers from Oxford, England, to "bomb whatever the hell we could in Europe." By 1943, running short of cannon fodder, the United States threatened him with the loss of citizenship, so Bob was honorably discharged from the RCAF and joined the U.S. Army, serving as a communications specialist in Patton's tank corps, ending the war in France.

• • •

In Bob Lieberenz, I saw shades from James Chisholm's journal—a specter of Mountain Bill Rhodes, the "lymphatic" Mr. Fry, an apparition of "Major" Gallagher drunk in the mines "under a cloud," and the spook of another "indefatigable drinker," Mr. Tappertit. Ghosts of tarantula-juice, red-eye, Jersey lightning, tanglefoot, and the Mormon's No. 6 mingled with Bob's close-at-hand Old Forester. Later, I found an insight into Bob from a Richard Stengel article in *Time:* "History is written by the victors, but what of those who called in sick that day? There are those who started a movement or hitched their wagon to an idea that never quite panned out. Or the idea succeeded, but one that makes us uncomfortable."

Bob Lieberenz was no ordinary Dreamer, if a Dreamer at all. He'd seen too many bad times, the ravages of war, too many bodies, too much Old Forester. If his Dream never quite panned out, what he settled for is something that makes many of us uncomfortable. He chose to disappear into the landscape, not to lose his identity but to gain it. No matter how much of a vested tippler, he was a man of humor, compassion, and, better than that, an amiable and honest drunk. Because of Bob's unapologetic lifestyle, I felt a need for an unapologetic humanity of my own, since no relationship can be better than one that makes you examine your own narrow view of the world.

Bob wrote to me on and off for two years after my journey. Here's an excerpt from his last letter:

> "Walkin' Stik" Scott,
>
> I decided on an Arkansas trip, so went in with "Chicago Bob" and got a '74 Ford 4×4. I came out in a blizzard, spent one night in Rock Springs. . . . Two fronts hit me all the way. . . . Hi-way patrol men looking and shaking their heads. I bought a case of Old Forester at Wamsutter, Wyoming. When I got to Fayetteville, Ark, I had four left.
>
> I helped "Chicago Bob" get out in the first 3" Snow—for NEVADA, gave him my Briggs "dry-wash" gold rig to play with. . . . His wife is trying to completely cut him out of everything. This is "confidential." . . . "Never" depend on relatives.

They sucked me in, then made life complete hell (holy rollers). I lived out of the back end of the Ford most of the time.

I got me a busted heel, broken ankle, etc. Spent last winter in a Hot Springs V.A. hospital. The workin' days are all over now, kid. I tried to prove they wasn't last summer. If I had to walk ten miles, I'd end up crawling on my belly.

I'm still going to make the hi-line trip from South Pass through to Jackson WYO by horses—interested? There's only two outlets to civilization on the way—Crow Heart (near where Washakie and a Crow Chief fought to see who would eat each other's heart). Washakie won!

Well, this is the biggest line of horse-shit I've put out since social Security. Write to me, you bugger!

Midafternoon, Bob dropped me at the Cove Bar on the highway a few miles below South Pass City. We had a fare-thee-well beer, clinking the bottles like friends will before taking separate journeys. Behind the bar was a wall plastered with money—dollars, marks, pounds, francs, pesos—all signed by the thirsty of nations who'd stopped in to cut their dust. I put a greenback of my own up, the only time I left my name anywhere on the land I crossed: "Chisholm was here. July 4, 1985." I left it for the Osage who, sooner or later, I've come to believe, will turn up just about everywhere. A woman came in, flustered, and got a big laugh from the customers. "Oh God," she said, "I been on a mission even a Mormon couldn't accomplish."

Humor like hers forewarned that I was entering Mormon country, not exactly the "new world" Bernard Reid imagined atop South Pass in 1849, but more the view of Reid's fellow traveler, Niles Searles, who thought himself "abandoning the world . . . with prospects exceedingly dubious." I hadn't abandoned the world completely; not even Bob had done that, depending as he did on what the world coughed up—a salvageable space heater here, a crankshaft there—but I shared Searles's notion of the "exceedingly dubious."

Today, when I think of the people I met on the walk, Bob's name turns up first. When he left, heading for something stronger than a bottle of Miller Lite, I turned back to see my name printed on a dollar bill posted on a Wyoming bar wall. That it wasn't a Canadian dollar with the queen's head on it made me nostalgic. But then I saw a sign hanging above it, fading Dreams written all over it: "It is unfortunate the situation you describe exists. However, we don't give a shit."

46

I can only meditate while I am walking. When I stop, I cease to think; my mind works only with my legs.

JEAN-JACQUES ROUSSEAU

The brethren commence ferrying Wagons over the River. . . . I was sick in bed from over exertion. Doctor gave me orders not to do the like again for any man, or Saint, King, Lord, or Devil. William Clayton, Ezra T. Benson . . . and others sick.

THOMAS BULLOCK, JULY 1, 1847

Having filled up our water kegs and canteens at 4:00 P.M., we left for the long drive, variously estimated, from 35 to 55 ms, without water.

J. GOLDSBOROUGH BRUFF, AUGUST 4, 1849

The trail from Farson to Fort Bridger, Wyoming, was the most desolate country I walked, at least the parts of it I did—about half—having absolutely no remorse for those stretches I didn't, counting it Canadian common sense for giving up my solitary foolishness in so ragged a geology. Unremarkable for any stark desert beauty such as one finds in the Southwest, devoid of any vestige of charm, its rivers and streams (Dry Sandy, Little Sandy, Big Sandy, the Green, Ham's and Black's Forks) run muddy and slack in season, its topography brutal and its geography unsettling.

Beyond South Pass, a footpad cuts briefly along an edge of the Red Desert before entering the Green River Basin, which falls like a stair step into Bridger Basin, a hundred miles of worry sunk among mountain ranges—Tetons to the far north, Wind Rivers to the northeast, Wasatch to the west, Uintas to the south. Think of it as three shallow bowls nesting on a Precambrian basement floor 2.5 billion years old, with each bowl, bottom to top, 570 million, 239 million, and 65 million years in the making, each a layer of sedimentary rocks formed from Mesozoic and Cenozoic seabeds with the oldest Paleozoic rocks (the bottom bowl) tipped against the edges of the mountains. Its openness is nearly unspoiled, its monotony endless.

In 1847 the distance between the Little Sandy Crossing at Farson, Wyoming, and the Green River to the south was almost a dry hole and still is—a droughty no-man's-land in which even seasonal runoffs are occasionally subterranean. Occasionally, a pool appears from an unexpected shower, but for the most part it tested the stamina and dehydrated the bodies of those who first crossed it. "Upon the old road water is not found in the dry season," Richard Burton noted, "a terrible *journada* for laden wagons and tired cattle."

At the Little Sandy Crossing in 1849, Bernard Reid found the creek bottom reeking with the "stench of dead oxen." Graves abounded, including those of the Reverend Robert Gilmore and his wife, Mary, who "Died of Cholera." Nearby, Reid found their daughter, seventeen, "her eyes . . . directed at vacancy. She seemed like one dazed or in a dream." Her younger brother was sick in the wagon. After their parents' death, both children were abandoned by the wagon train in which they'd been traveling. With Reid's help and the generosity of another company of emigrants, they survived.

In 1847 the Mormons scrabbled their way past the Dry Sandy (they found water a foot below the creek bed) heading toward the Little Sandy and, beyond that, to the Green River and Fort Bridger on Black's Fork of the Green. It was this "long drive," as J. Goldsborough Bruff put it two years later, which vexed me—the same stretch of anhydrous ground that Richard Burton called a "terrible *journada.*"

. . .

Below Pacific Springs, I put in at a roadside historical marker announcing: "The Oregon Trail / In Memory of Those Who / Passed This Way / To Win and Hold the West"—Dreamspeak of the first magnitude. Passing the Sublette Cutoff (it rearranged the road to Oregon and left Fort Bridger off Destiny's beaten path), I almost reached Farson and the Little Sandy by nightfall. In South Pass City, I'd made up my mind to walk only those sections of the trail that held historical interest—South Pass to Farson and the Little Sandy Crossing, Simpson's Hollow to Green River, and Church Butte (where the Mormons held a prayer meeting on July 4) to Fort Bridger. If I could, I'd hitch across the rest. As austere a landscape as anyone could find, everything beyond the Little Sandy—long, cheerless stretches of desert and dust away from main roads—made me anxious.

On the edge of the Green River Basin, Farson basks in butterfat glory—home of the "World's Largest Ice Cream Cone." The two-storied emporium (Farson Mercantile) was doing land office business, and I could almost hear arteries clogging as I sat on the steps outside lapping at a giant chocolate cone. A stone's throw away, the famous Little Sandy Crossing was now bridged, and, wouldn't you know it, a freshly graveled road (paved the next year) angled southwest on a beeline with the trail toward Green River, where a new bridge had been thrown across the water. The ice-cream cone was to celebrate, since I'd been having the heebie-jeebies about possibly having to ford the river.

"Where you heading?" a skinny-hipped man said, mouth full of buttery French vanilla. The license plate on his car read "Ohio." He had the forlorn look of someone badly out of place.

"Salt Lake City," I answered.

"Me, too. Never been. They say it's all Mormons. Want a lift?" He sounded hopeful, as if companionship offered him a slim chance of survival. Stating my foot-sore purpose, I declined.

By now, his cone was beginning to melt, its runoff substantial. "I can't eat this," he bitched, chucking it into a trash can. "Don't know why I bought it. Y'know, people do the damnedest things when they're on vacation. I bought me a pair of cowboy boots in Cody. What the hell do I need with a pair of cowboy boots? I'm from Cleveland." Fresh out of a box, two pointy toes stuck out from under his trousers. He'd already scraped a neat triangular wedge of hand-tooled lizard from one brown tip.

· · ·

Near the Little Sandy, Brigham had a fortuitous meeting, coming across the extraordinary mountain man Jim Bridger, who, as General Grenville Dodge later eulogized him, "was a born topographer; the whole West was mapped out in his mind, and such was his sense of locality and direction . . . that he could smell his way where he could not see it." Proprietor of the trading post that lay ahead of the Saints, Bridger was on his way to Fort Laramie and just the man to ask about Mormon prospects in the Salt Lake valley. Brigham and Bridger jawed over dinner, Jim suggesting that the valley was an unlikely Zion for too large a population of Mormon farmers. As myth has it, he offered Brigham "one thousand dollars for the first ear of corn ripened in these mountains."

Reactions to the mountain man were mixed. After a parley about the route ahead and Salt Lake Valley, Clayton wrote that "it was impossible to form a correct idea of either from the very imperfect and irregular way he gave his descriptions." Of "his appearance and conversation," Howard Egan was even less hopeful. "I should not take him to be a man of truth," he wrote. "He crossed himself a number of times." Jim was nominally Catholic, a religion Mormons couldn't abide. Wilford Woodruff, destined to become the president of the LDS Church and who would abandon polygamy for statehood, saw the mountain man in a different light: "We met in council with Mr. Bridger . . . and found him to be a great traveler, possessing an extensive knowledge of nearly all Oregon and California. . . . He spoke highly of the Great Basin for settlement . . . it was his Paradise." But Egan may have been closer to the truth—at least that day. Despite Jim's wager with Brigham, Bridger knew that corn had already been grown in the Salt Lake Valley—and kept silent about it.

. . .

Like Thomas Christy in June 1860, I filled my "water vessels for the desert," determined see if it "was as large an elephant as is represented." I began walking toward Simpson's Hollow, ten miles below Farson, daily temperatures the hottest in a decade—a long, dusty tramp from ice-cream paradise into sagebrush hell, but thanks to the ministrations of a fan of Jack Daniels weaving his way over "the new shortcut" to Kemmerer, Wyoming, the burg where J. C. Penney opened his first store, I was saved seven miles of purgatory. I asked if he knew Wyoming Bob. He didn't, and thought Bob's choice of whiskey little better than paint remover.

. . .

The Mormon history of Simpson's Hollow is a story born of hysteria. In 1857, during the tenth anniversary of their arrival in Salt Lake Valley, Mormons were stunned by news that U.S. troops were on the march to Utah on orders of an ill-advised president, James Buchanan, who was hell-bent on making sure that government in the Mormon kingdom was "civil" not "religious." Rumors of Mormon insurrections circulated in Washington, part of the endless round of enmity against the Saints and their much-discussed system of "spiritual wifery." In Washington, Mormons were castigated by Stephen Douglas, a former friend from their Illinois years, as "unscrupulous characters" and a "pestiferous, disgusting cancer" to be "cut out by the roots." They were "aliens," Douglas claimed, although his harsh comments were conditional, "if" the reports from Utah were true.

There's an uncomfortable edge of truth in Douglas's cutting remark. Having left the United States, Mormons were "aliens" by choice, seeing themselves as victims of a government whose claims of religious freedom for all had been found wanting. As Ian Pears says of his countrymen, "The English may not dress well by continental standards, but the way they dress badly is of enormous importance." Joseph Smith's religious couture, so to speak, never set the style by American standards, but, for Mormons, the peculiarities of their social, political, and religious dress in Utah were enormously important, accompanied by an unremitting fear that the church and its members would be stripped nude by hostile Yankees. Too easily given to theocracy, "until the mid-1850s the Saints had no party allegiance and usually sold their votes to the highest bidder," historian Leonard Arrington wrote. Brigham Young turned Democrat when the political climate suited

Mormon interests, something that would make his Republican successors twitch. Democrats in Utah are scarce—almost an endangered species.

On hearing the news of invasion, Brigham retorted that "priests, politicians, speculators, whoremongers, and every mean, filthy character that could be raked up" were gathering to "kill the Mormons." For five dollars a day, Jim Bridger became the U.S. Army's guide, hoping to even an old score, as we shall soon see. With Mormon bloodshed and murder by Gentiles in their past, Utah went into a frenzy, the specter of renewed persecution covering the territory like wildfire. Two weeks later, on August 4, 1857, Young wrote to his "Indian Missionary," Jacob Hamblin, asking him to make friends with the Paiutes "for they must learn that they have either got to help us or the United States will kill us both."

On the front lines, the Mormon War was bloodless. Brigham barricaded all routes into Salt Lake City, thundering threats and dire warnings. For all his bluster, Simpson's Hollow would have remained an unnamed piece of wind-swept Wyoming desert if, on October 5, 1857, U.S. Army wagon master Lew Simpson hadn't lost to a Mormon attack twenty-three wagons with supplies earmarked for the troops of General Albert Sidney Johnston's army. "On this occasion the *dux facti* was Lot Smith, a man of reputation for hard riding and general gallantry," wrote Richard Burton on passing the site ten years later on his way back to England.

Smith was a major in the Nauvoo Legion and probably a member of the feared Mormon Danites, which contained notorious hard cases and enforcers like Porter Rockwell and "Wild Bill" Hickman. By the time his night rides were over that fall, Smith had burned 72 supply wagons and 368,000 pounds of goods to support Johnston's army, thus launching guerilla warfare in the West. Arrived on the spot a decade after the flames, Burton found "two semicircles of black still charred on the ground," which he described as "a neat foundation for a structure of supersti-tion." Earlier, in Salt Lake City, he noted that Mormons "boast loudly of the achievement." On the actual spot, he wrote: "The juvenile emigrants of the creed erect dwarf graves and nameless wooden tombstones in derision of their enemies."

Simpson's Hollow is a futile monument to the myth of a "bloodless" war. Nothing, of course, survives there, although a red granite marker I rested against commemorates the event and tells a lie: "This delay of the army helped effect a peaceful settlement of the difficulties." Unwelcome, the U.S. Dragoons marched through a deserted Salt Lake City (Brigham's orders) to bivouac at Camp Floyd on the shores of Utah Lake, becoming a hated Gentile presence—no fraterniza-tion allowed with the locals.

But if the settlement was "peaceful," it was anything but "bloodless," except in Mormon fiction. An ugly tide had turned in the West, leaving real "blood" on Mormon hands. Bent on preserving Mormon theocracy and political control from without, Brigham was left to count the cost in blood from within. But the Lion of the Lord never faced up to the most notorious event in the history of Joseph Smith's "Restoration"—not the martyrdom of its prophet, but the largest slaughter of white civilians in the history of the American West—all of it at the hands of Mormon investigators.

On September 7, 1857, as hysteria spread, a band of Mormons and Paiute Indians butchered 120 Arkansas emigrants near the southern Utah outpost of Cedar City. As news of Buchanan's "invasion" spread, tensions sparked like crossed wires along the southern trails. All Gentiles came under suspicion, threats were exchanged, panic among the Mormon settlements flared, and the Arkansas outsiders—bound for California—became tinder for white-hot resentments touched off by the lingering slow-burn of Mormon memories over their treatment in Missouri and Illinois.

A fracas broke out in a hummocky Utah meadow and, giving as good as they got, the Arkansas travelers at first believed they'd been attacked by Indians. Mormons came to their rescue with offers of protection and, under a flag of truce, while walking to presumed safety beside the Mormons, the Arkansas emigrants were turned on, most shot point-blank in the head. Their bodies were buried in open pits, carelessly flung in to conceal the evidence. Only a handful of children survived what became known as the Mountain Meadows Massacre.

On whose orders the killing was undertaken isn't fully known or admitted, although many believe the truth was buried with Brigham. Theories abound, but there's little doubt it was ordered by someone in Mormon authority. Juanita Brooks, a Mormon historian who wrote in depth about the massacre at the risk of summary excommunication, concluded that Brigham's hands were clean. Her research seems impeccable. Yet she admitted to a friend that she'd destroyed papers that were too revealing. Two weeks after the massacre, Brigham Young—Utah's acting superintendent of Indian Affairs—ordered $3,500 in goods to be distributed to the Paiutes.

After two decades of "sanitizing the foul deed," Brigham's adopted son, John D. Lee, was executed by firing squad at the massacre site. A token scapegoat, he was shot in the heart to satisfy not only a fragile Utah "justice" but also an early Mormon belief in "blood atonement" for the most heinous of crimes—one reason why Utah and Idaho, both settled by Mormons, are the only states in the union in which the firing squad is a legal method of capital punishment. To this day, the LDS Church admits no responsibility for or complicity in the murders at Mountain Meadows, although the church has sought to heal the wounds, hoping, as Mormon president Gordon B. Hinckley said recently, to "let the book of the past be closed."

However, the LDS Church is "on the horns of a dilemma," claims historian Will Bagley: "It can't acknowledge its . . . involvement in mass murder and if it can't accept its accountability, it can't repent"—the predicament faced by all true believers, their Dream gone sour, who see themselves as set apart, specially chosen or elect of God. Bagley is speaking not only of Mormons but also of the larger lessons of history, the same "dilemma" of conscience Germans were forced to confront, but have not yet fully resolved, when Hitler's delusion of a pure "Aryan race" collapsed after the murder of millions, every German soldier going into battle holding up his pants with a belt buckle embossed with these words: *Gott Mit Uns*. The sad question of any Dream of special selection is always the same: If not with us, who is God with?

Mormon writer Levi Peterson puts the question bluntly: "If good Mormons committed the massacre, if prayerful leaders ordered it, if apostles and a prophet knew about it and later sacrificed John D. Lee, then the sainthood of even the modern church seems tainted. Where is the moral superiority of Mormonism, where is the assurance that God has made Mormons his new chosen people?"

In 1994 Simon and Schuster published the *Historical Atlas of Mormonism*, which, says the jacket blurb, "chronicles in meticulous detail the rise and spread of this burgeoning religion." Its three authors were professors of geography, ancient scripture, church history and doctrine at Brigham Young University. Nowhere in the *Atlas*, neither in its appendix nor in articles by its "fifty-two authors," is there a single reference to Mountain Meadows.

• • •

On Wednesday, June 30, the Mormons arrived on the banks of Green River, camping under cottonwoods with wild apple trees and roses nearby. Six days too late to commemorate the anniversary of the Mormon crossing, I paid my respects at the waters of the Green, bedding down comfortably in a roseate glow of last light.

At the crossing of the Green River, Sam Brannan, the Mormon who helped turn sleepy Yerba Buena Cove into San Francisco, arrived to meet his Prophet, Seer and Revelator. Leader of the California Mormons, Sam had earlier taken a ship of Saints around the horn to San Francisco Bay. Many of the passengers of the ship *Brooklyn* were at work in the vicinity of Sutter's Fort on the south fork of the American River, including Jim Marshall, who later plucked the first gold nugget from Sutter's millrace, and John Bigler, who recorded the event for history.

Part con artist, part entrepreneur, part visionary, Brannan opened San Francisco's first store, printed its first newspaper and book, preached its first "Protestant" sermon, officiated at its first marriage, built its first flour mill, and sold materials to John Sutter for his new mill, where the discovery of gold and all that glitters turned America on its head. Brannan opened up California's wine-growing regions and became the state's first millionaire. The son of an immigrant father who knew how to make "good Irish whisky," Sam Brannan "built railroads, opened a curative spa, opened a bank, and issued his own currency," his biographer, Louis J. Stellman, wrote.

Brannan showed up in the company of a Mr. Smith "of the firm Jackson, Heaton and Bonney, bogus snakers of Nauvoo," as Clayton described him. Neither man left a good impression in the camp. Having spent weeks on the road from California to proposition his prophet, Brannan's real interest was to sell a scheme for Mormon settlement in California, a notion that Brigham rejected on the spot, wary of lotus-land snake oil. To bolster his case, Sam announced that many of the California Mormons were now "apostates" and needed their prophet in person, but the Lion wasn't buying it. California would give the Saints at most five years of safety from Gentiles, he told Sam, but the Salt Lake Valley would be a "home" for a chosen people.

It took several days for the Mormons to cross Green River and reach Fort Bridger. On Independence Day 1847, a Sunday, they assembled at Church Rock—a nub of forsaken geology—for holy service and a faint hurrah for the birthday of the United States on which they had turned their backs. Deep in Mexican territory, they were now almost "home" free. Sam Brannan didn't linger, but sulked back to California (as I sulked past Church Rock) where he was soon declared an "apostate." Anyone with visions contrary to his wasn't tolerated by Brigham, who regularly cleaned house, frequently sending offenders on lengthy "missions." Out of sight, out of mind. Eventually, Sam Brannan lost his fortune, and when he met his maker, bankrupt, his grave was "marked by a modest headstone provided by the charity of a man who never saw him."

• • •

Next day, I crossed two-thirds of the world's supply of trona, Wyoming's third largest cash cow after petroleum and coal. Trona is a mineral that's used to make

FOLLOWING THE WRONG GOD HOME

glass, detergents, baking soda, and chemicals. Precipitated from a prehistoric lake, it covers 15,000 square miles of the Cowboy State, much of it in and around the town of Granger.

To my surprise, the U.S. mail is delivered on Sundays in Granger, Wyoming, proving that even in hell there's time for charity. However wretched, desolate, melancholic, dolorous, funereal, and bummed-out the sad burg was, I'm obligated to offer a kind word on behalf of its generosity, although I can't praise its domestic architecture—largely constructed of aluminum on wheels or up on axles.

Granger leaves the impression of a town whose citizens and their real estate are portable, ever ready to move on given the least incentive—an offer of four used tires, for example. The post office, cramped inside and made of concrete block, hinted of no permanent affection by the U.S. government. Heat, oppressive as a sun lamp in a doghouse, baked the town's surfaces to a fine ashlike grit, which blew along its dreadful thoroughfares like the whispers of preachers advising either repentance or a life doomed to Granger. No citizen walked its streets that Sunday, no dustyard dog barked, no children laughed. Even the miniscule blue mailbox outside the PO looked forlorn, as if hundreds of letters a day couldn't give it purpose.

Attached to the post office was a stucco house, one end sinking into the desert as if trying to hide from the sun. Two aluminum awnings hung over its out-of-square windows, a continuation of the town's general architectural scheme, one blocked from the inside with a full-length tinfoil insulation blanket to hold back the heat. On the door was a fading Coca-Cola sign, an invitation, I hoped. I tried the door, found it open, and walked into a jungle.

The "confectionary," as Clifford Kizzire called the sole salvation for thirst and conversation in Granger, was a converted kitchen complete with stove, refrigerator, an old-time Coca-Cola watercooler, a brass National Cash Register, a case of candy bars, soft drinks, and a three-stool bar for customers, which, when I sat down, made me one-third of a full house. When I ordered a double cheeseburger, microwaved in a cellophane envelope, and introduced myself, he said, "You're the one I've been holding mail for!"

"Could I get it?"

"Sure could."

And I did, on a Sunday no less, reading news from home and friends while convincing myself that a plastic-tasting cheeseburger could digest given a day or two, plenty of acid reflux, and an iron stomach.

Clifford had been on the job in Granger for forty-one years, a mellow post-master in his sixties with a canoe-shaped smile, trifocals, and a need to be in a much cooler environment, one preferably involving things green. The "confectionary" was awash in subconscious desires—plastic tubs of geraniums, African violets, a clock (ten-to-one) with hands ticking against the background of a cool mountain lake, snow-capped mountains, and trees high enough to give an impression of wide patches of shade. Having shut out desolation, Clifford had created a climate of deep inner desire. I couldn't help but think that after his forty-one years living in the belt buckle of trona, retirement in a meat locker would suit Clifford nicely. A dark-haired, skinny woman came in yammering for the local sheriff, full of misery. Clifford gave her his canoe smile, laid his elbow on the counter, his head against one hand, and predicted a sane lawman's future. "It's his day off. He leaves town on his day off."

I left too, knowing in my heart that if I were the local sheriff, I would as soon leave the country.

· · ·

From Granger to Lyman, Wyoming, a dirt road roughly parallels Interstate 80, dropping into a frying pan near Church Rock where the Mormons whooped it up on Independence Day, 1847, the Uinta Mountains showing up to the south, the first visible promise Brigham saw of Zion and my first promise of a way out. In a down-at-the-heels mood, I was raw-edged and sandblasted as the butte. A moonscape of eroded sediments, "Church Rock" is another failed attempt to give a wastrel chunk of geology a name suiting a forlorn imagination. Looking nothing like a church—one end having the characteristics of the Sphinx after a bombing run and the other the dreary construction of a collapsed cake—nothing at the rock inspired any feelings of worship, although I sympathized with the Mormons for making do with what little they had. Like them, I thirsted for salvation.

At a crossing of Black's Fork, it showed up in the form of Bill Jenkins, a recently indigent young bloke given to mouthfuls of odd-sounding syllables and whose teeth looked as if he'd temporarily borrowed them from someone else. Husky and sunburned, he was manhandling a large hose from the river to a tanker truck, sucking up water from Black's Fork to be used by oil and gas drilling rigs to cool augers a mile or more in the ground.

"Aloo," he said, "ts'hot."

"Which way are you heading?" I asked, prayerfully.

Turned out it was mine.

47

A kind of philosophy distills itself in the mind of the saunterer.

CHRISTOPHER MORLEY

Fort Bridger . . . grass is "knee deep, and deeper." Water very clear, excellent mill sites, Timber plenty, the Scene lovely & delightsome.

THOMAS BULLOCK, JULY 7, 1847

Broke camp this morning and passed Fort Bridger which is a rather small place. . . . I saw a Mormon to day, by the roadside he had erected a hut & sort of a blacksmith Shop & was prepared to do all the work he could get & also sold Butter, Eggs, Cheese.

MARY C. FISH, JULY 25, 1860

No sooner had I exited the cab of Bill Jenkins's tanker truck in Fort Bridger than a big hombre in a white polo shirt and jeans walked up to me and said, sourly, "Are you the guy who come by our well site looking for bones?"

I had bones of my own to pick that afternoon, but I asked, "What bones?"

"Like a big elephant."

"Mastodon," I said, taking a wild guess. I was now in the land of dinosaurs. He ignored my clarification.

"Are you the archeologist from the University of Utah?"

"Paleontologist," I corrected.

"Yeah. Are you him?"

One of the gents seated at a nearby table said, "He was from Brigham Young University."

The big guy gave him a glance as sour as the one he gave me. "Hell, they're both the same to me."

"I'm not from BYU," I confessed. "I'm a Canadian and right now I'm thirsty."

"Shit," he said, "I thought you was the sonofabitch. Sorry. C'mon and join us."

E. K. Bostick had a very large head and biceps, the head wedged into a baseball cap and the biceps straining the fabric of his polo shirt. He was carousing over a few beers after work with two much-muddied gas company roustabouts—Ken Moon and Mike Gardner—both sporting skinny moustaches turned down at the ends like commas. When I joined them at an outside table at the Crossroads Deli, the sun was in free fall, the table crowded with the detritus of fast food, and shadows were crawling up the walls.

E. K. claimed to be an "independent well site consultant," a rawboned Texan who'd been contracted to "supervise completion of a new gas well." *Supervision*, I surmised, accounted for his clean jeans and polo shirt. Ken and Mike did the grunt work—and looked it. Together, they formed a "completion unit" that goes on-site after the drilling has been done and the wellhead cemented over. Each of the three claimed a specialty in "pullin' units," oilman talk for what Mike called "bringin' on the gas."

"We perforate the well and bring it into production," Ken Moon said. "Right now we're flow testing a hole."

E. K. was "testing," too. He spent most of the time trying to persuade an attractive blonde from Nottingham, England, to run off with him to Dallas, his hometown. He vowed to show "Maid Marian," as he called her, "all of the high spots and some of the low."

Over a soft drink, I groused too loudly about Brigham Young, the bone of contention I was picking at that day, having read all about his role in Fort Bridger's history—a controversy that got my dander up. Jack-Mormons, I suspect, Ken Moon and Mike Gardner called me on it. One or the other, I forget which, said, "It's a damn shame you couldn't have met Henderson and put him down too."

"Who's Henderson?"

"My dog."

I deserved that.

. . .

Jim Bridger and his partner, Louis Vasquez, arrived on Black's Fork of the Green River in 1842, Bridger having spent more than twenty years in the West. Louis Vasquez had spent much of his life in the mountains as well, but his reputation as a mountain man was lusterless compared to Jim's. (Popular myth has it that Jim was the first to see the Great Salt Lake.) That summer, the unlikely pair built a rough trading post on prime real estate, hoping to cash in on the migration of Americans to Oregon and California. With its "water very clear" and "timber plenty," as Thomas Bullock sized the place up, the site was an oasis. Both men hoped it would turn out to be their end of the rainbow.

Of the two, Vasquez was better educated, "a Mexican who put on a great deal of style" and who "used to ride around the country in a coach and four." Even in the wild, "bits of aristocratic elegance clung to him . . . like cottonwood fluff," wrote Bernard De Voto. Vain, he proved the easier of the two to manipulate. Bridger was the more savvy but illiterate, signing documents in mountain-man fashion with an "X" followed by the signature of a witness. By mutual consent, Vasquez was officially the "Fort Bridger trader," but he was seldom around, so absent, in fact, that no emigrant "noticed" him "in 1845, 1846, 1849."

• • •

Arrived at "the door of Bridger's" trading post on July 7, 1847, Orson Pratt described the place as the Mormons found it. "The post consists of two adjoining log houses, dirt roofs, and a small picket yard of logs set in the ground, about eight feet high. The number of men, squaws, and half-breed children in these homes and lodges may be about fifty or sixty."

Prices were high at the Bridger-Vasquez trading post, and, having little ready cash, the Mormons didn't loiter but quickly moved on—but not before Brigham had sized up the post's abundant grass, good water, and favorable location.

Although Bridger and Vasquez had chosen the perfect site, by 1847 the fort was already destined to go belly-up as an emigrant trading post. Four circumstances conspired against it: the fur trade was all but gone by 1849; the preferred new route to Oregon and California lay seventy miles to the north of the fort (the Sublette Cutoff); the Donner Party's failed attempt to cross to California by the Salt Lake route in 1846 and its cannibalism in the snows of the High Sierras had spooked other emigrants; and—more to the point—Brigham Young coveted the site.

• • •

Fact is, Jim Bridger was no more delighted to see Brigham move into his back yard than the Mormon leader was to have a much-fabled mountain man squatting on his flank. Jim thought Mormons notoriously cheap, if not an ace or two short of a full deck, so one reason for Jim's "irregular and imperfect" descriptions of the Salt Lake Valley when he had dinner with the Mormons on the Big Sandy is that he deeply mistrusted Brigham Young—not without cause.

General Grenville Dodge, later chief engineer of the Union Pacific Railroad, remembered Jim as "a good judge of human nature," adding, "his comments upon people that he had met were always intelligent and seldom critical." Brigham, on the other hand, was quick to judge, a man not known for his even temper, and Jim Bridger was a Gentile in possession of prime real estate better suited to a Mormon way station on the road to Zion than a private enterprise.

Once settled at Salt Lake, Brigham quickly rousted another unwanted Gentile from the area—Miles Goodyear, a red-headed Connecticut Yankee in King Brigham's Court and Utah's first white settler, a live-and-let-live gent who'd set up a trading post on the Weber River, twenty-five miles above the site of Salt Lake City. "There was a man opened a farm in the Bear River valley," is how Clayton recorded Bridger's first mention of Miles Goodyear at the Little Sandy Crossing. *Farm* is a telling word, implying *crops*. If anyone, Jim Bridger knew corn could be grown in the Salt Lake Valley since Goodyear had been doing it for three years, which makes his thousand-dollar boast to Brigham for a single ear more deliberately off-putting than welcoming. Within a year, Brigham bought out Miles Goodyear—lock, stock, and corn patch—and Utah's first settler, first farmer, and first to make the Great Basin "blossom"—somewhat, at least—"like a rose," moved to California where he died two years later. The Mormons took credit for Goodyear's firsts.

• • •

Brigham Young coveted a lot more than Bridger's trading post on Black's Fork of the Green River. He cast his eye on large chunks of today's Oregon, Idaho, Wyoming, Colorado, New Mexico, Arizona, Nevada, and California, all of which he bundled into an imaginary "State of Deseret." As much a usurper as any American Dreamer of his century, he attempted to stake a Mormon claim to any or all Western lands he could lay hands on and form them into one large Mormon theocracy. After the Treaty of Guadalupe Hildago (1848), when Mexico gave up rights to 1.2 million square miles of the American West, Mormons found themselves back in the arms of the United States whose government they hoped to leave behind. By 1849, with more and more Gentiles swarming through the Salt Lake Valley headed toward the California diggings, the isolation Brigham had counted on for the Saints to get a foothold in their Godly kingdom was fast breaking down. Proposing the widest possible borders for a Mormon "State of Deseret" was Young's last opportunity to put a lock on a large Mormon sphere of influence in the West and warn away intruders.

The "State of Deseret" was another American pipeDream with roots in Manifest Destiny. Having Dreamed it up, Young planned to impose theocratic Mormon authority on everything within its imaginary boundaries, increasing the growing Mormon migraine in Congress. While laying plans for the rule of a "Kingdom of God," he skated on a dangerously thin ice of sedition, further alarming an already concerned federal government. "I say . . . that the constitution and the laws of the United States are just as good as we want them," he thundered from his desert sanctuary, "provided they are honored." "Honored" meant keeping government hands off the Mormons. Rumbled Orson Pratt, "The priesthood upon earth is the only legitimate government of God . . . the only legitimate power that has the right to rule upon the earth." Certain of a Mormon theocracy,

Heber Kimball pulled a rabbit out of his hat: "Christ and brother Brigham will become President of the United States."

A biting editorial in the *New York Times* summed up the feelings of the rest of the country and its government: "Of all the things Mormons least understand, one is political principles. Although they prate on about constitutional rights, very few . . . know anything about the Constitution of the United States. They have shut themselves in a contracted circle of illiberal theological views and outside of that they recognize no point of reason. . . . No political element exists, because Young allows it nothing to feed upon."

By 1850 it was clear that in the Mormons' "contracted circle," Brigham's intention was a territorial takeover in the West. Congress took one look at the proposed Mormon "state" with its outlet to the Pacific at San Diego and saw "nation" written all over it. Alarmed by the size of the proposed state, Congress pared Utah's borders down almost, *but not quite*, to the size it is today. The new "Utah Territory" included southwestern Wyoming, which was snapped up by Brigham as the "Green River Precinct." Like it or not, Jim Bridger and his trading post were now under the prophet's thumb.

Naturally, Jim saw things more to a Virginia-born Missouri Democrat's liking: he resisted any attempted rule by Young or his bogus "State of Deseret" until he found himself firmly under the new U.S. territorial government whose first "Governor and Acting Superintendent of Indian Affairs" was appointed in September 1850.

Guess who?

Immediately, Brigham ordered a census in the Green River Precinct, which turned up "twenty-two males and twenty-four females" living there, roughnecks and noncontributors to Mormon welfare. "There was a trading post," James Linforth observed, "and crowds of traders, gamblers and Indians . . . who live off the emigrants." Dreaming that a chunk of Wyoming was his to do with as he pleased, it pleased Brigham to have Bridger's trading post, unsecured except through squatter's rights. Relations between the two men soured quickly as Brigham leveraged his new federal authority, Mormon-style, over the Green River country.

• • •

At Fort Laramie, in the summer of 1853, Second Lieutenant H. B. Fleming saw signs of smoke and wrote to the U.S. commissioner of Indian Affairs:

> There has been a great deal of trouble between the mountain
> men and the Mormons for some time past. . . . The mountain

men claim the right to the Green River country in virtue of a grant given them by the Indians to whom the country belongs; as no treaty has yet been made to extinguish their title—The Mormons on the other hand claim jurisdiction over the country, paramount to all Indian titles in virtue of it being in Utah territory.

Now, the question . . . is this; since the country lies in the Territory of Utah, have the Mormons or have they not the right to dispose of the country to settlers, to dispose of its resources, revenues, and finally everything in the country . . . before the actual Indian title has been extinguished.

In short order, Brigham closed down ferry operations on Green River, granting new ferry rights to Salt Lake Mormons. Next, he levied a "territorial" tax on the mountain men, which, being good Americans, if few, they raised hell about, demanding "squatter's rights" to the ferries be honored. As for Brigham's "tax," they refused to pay up, arguing it would fall into church coffers.

Eye on the prize, Brigham accused Bridger of turning Indians against Mormons in the Walker War of July 1853, when Utes raided Latter-day Saints settlements whose rapid expansion in the Great Basin had caused game to be driven deeper into the mountains. Never one to find fault with his own, Brigham blamed the "war" not on Mormon land grabs but on Mexican slave traders who, he insisted, stole Ute women and children. Of Bridger, he said, "I believe Old Bridger is death on us, and if he knew 400,000 Indians were coming against us, and any man would let us know, he would cut his throat. Vasqez is a different sort of man." Indeed Vasquez was. An easier target than Jim, he'd been wined and dined or, perhaps, dined-not-wined in Salt Lake City, where he was conveniently allowed to set up a "mercantile" business with Brigham's blessing, no doubt as a further incentive to be "trustworthy."

Although the so-called Walker War (named after a Ute chief, Wakara) was a brush fire in central Utah and a long way from Bridger's trading post on Black's Fork, Jim was accused of selling Utes the powder and lead used in the raids. At best, the evidence was circumstantial. Never one to gather moss, Brigham rolled his stone, revoking all licenses to trade with the Indians—especially Jim's.

U.S. Indian agents on the Green River refuted Brigham's charges against Bridger, claiming blame lay on the head of the Saints for wanting things their way and ignoring the rights of native tribes and the mountain men. One wrote to the commissioner of Indian Affairs in Washington that the Salt Lake Post Office couldn't be trusted with the U.S. mail—not unreasonable since the post office was in Brigham Young's front parlor. (Today's guides at the Beehive House in downtown Salt Lake City—where Brigham franked the daily post, kept a steaming kettle, and wielded his letter opener—still point out the room where neither sleet nor hail stayed the mail's appointed rounds—after a short delay, of course.)

That summer, on August 6, James Linforth visited the Bridger trading post, traveling "over an excellent road" from Green River. His description of the post proves its ownership wasn't yet up for grabs. Noting the "usual form of pickets," he dubbed it "a trading post ... belonging to Major James Bridger, one of the oldest mountaineers in this region." By August 26, when Dr. Thomas Flint paid his visit, the trading post was "in the possession of the Territorial Officers, Mormons, who had, 24 hours before, driven Old Man Bridger out."

Brigham sent 150 armed men to arrest one middle-aged mountain man. He seized the trading post *and* its contents, removing its powder, lead, and cattle to Salt Lake City—a tactic familiar to anyone who recalls the "payment in arrears" taken from the abandoned mission on the Platte River by Brother James Case. In his emperor's new clothes, Brigham ordered the Mormon occupiers to take a "complete" inventory of everything used or sent to Salt Lake—exactly as he'd done with James Case.

Cunning as Brigham was, Jim outsmarted the prophet's emissaries of law and disorder, using decades of knowledge of the Green River country to keep out of sight. The official arrest order stipulated only that the posse "forthwith arrest ... James Bridger and bring him before ... some Justice of the Peace in Great Salt Lake City, to answer the charges aforesaid." No mention is made of Brigham's intention, let alone his legal right, to occupy Bridger's property or confiscate his goods. Yet, by one unverified after-the-fact account, the posse's leader "was instructed to seize any *illegal* goods." True, Brigham had outlawed the "sale" of powder and lead to the Indians, but, technically, none of Bridger's goods were *illegal*; he was free to sell them to anyone but Indians.

Included in the heist were several barrels of "whiskey and rum," which, said Isaac Haight, were "destroyed by doses" over the next three months. Early in November, when the posse "had poured its last drink," it returned to Salt Lake, but not before placing snoops in "secure positions from which strict watch could be kept *on the movements of the fort*" (italics mine). Obviously, the post remained stationary. But Bridger didn't. He showed up with John Hockaday, a surveyor who mapped out "3,898 acres and two roods" of property belonging to the mountain man, a copy of which was duly filed with "the General Land Office, Washington, D.C." Jim posted a sign warning Mormons to keep a mile away, then headed for Washington to defend his claim against the Mormons and the new territorial governor.

• • •

Now the story gets more bizarre. One of the Mormon ledger documents, accounting for "acknowledged debt" for the goods removed—$2,736.21, to the penny—was signed on the dotted line by Bridger himself, suggesting someone had forgotten he was illiterate. "It would appear that Bridger's name was entered on the ledgers to finalize them and close the books since neither Bridger or Vasquez was available at the time," apologists offer, which implies that someone didn't give a damn about Bridger having a say in any Mormon accounting.

In the spring of 1855, after traveling to the nation's capital, "seeking redress through the federal government," Bridger returned. No sooner had he arrived in Utah Territory than he was met by the notorious Mormon enforcer, "Wild Bill" Hickman, cautiously identified in documents as "an agent of the Mormon church." Wild Bill "suggested" that Jim should sell out. Jim waffled. Hickman may have had another persuasive tête-à-tête. Whatever, Jim suggested $8,000, take it or leave it. No sooner did Hickman say "Jack Robinson" than Lewis Robison, a Mormon purchasing agent showed up, papers in hand.

But still Jim wavered, weighing his loyalties to the surviving mountain men on Green River. "Careless and indifferent," was how Robison characterized Jim as he came to grips with his tenuous hold on the post while holding firm to his price. Vasquez was away at the time, "but knowing of the plans to sell the fort," he'd "commissioned H. F. Morrell to be his agent." How Vasquez "knew" the post was for sale isn't clear, but his mercantile connections in Salt Lake City may have played a role in keeping him up to date. With no more blood to be squeezed from a Mormon turnip, Jim finally gave the okay and Robison drew up an $8,000 bill of sale.

But again Jim Bridger waffled. Knowing Brigham too well, he demanded cash up front or no deal. Testy over new terms, Robison offered $4,000 on the barrelhead, the rest in fifteen months. Perhaps another visit from Hickman, the "agent of the Mormon church," persuaded him. He finally agreed. Thus were Bridger and Louis Vasquez's "cattle, horses, goods, flour, sundry articles of personal property and the entire claim, Stand, Trading post, herding ground and all lands" sold into Mormon history. Jim made his "X." Louis Vasquez *per H. F. Morrell*, agent, bargained away his. Almirin Crow signed for the Mormons, along with that gentle voice of persuasion, "Wild Bill" Hickman. Lewis Robison certified the sale and, jig-time, became Brigham's bona fide and newly licensed "trader to the Indians."

On October 18, 1858, the Mormons made the final payment to Louis Vasquez in Salt Lake City, but the question of whether Vasquez the man sold the trading post or was bought and paid for by the Mormons has never been addressed. Through Vasquez, Jim claimed that the Mormon accounting for goods seized in the post's takeover didn't add up, especially since he'd become literate without his knowledge for the first and last time in his life. To avoid this technical difficulty, Brigham paid an extra $1,000 to settle old scores, and Jim eventually made his "X" on the dotted line for $3,763.21.

Even this final restitution turns up another curiosity; built into the document is a full legal disclaimer to cover Brigham's considerable derriere. The final lump sum received on October 18 was agreed to by Vasquez "in full payment according to mutual agreement. . . for all and severally goods, cattle, house rent etc. etc., taken and used by said Lewis Robison, James Ferguson . . . and others (including guns, lead balls, powder, knives, etc. taken by order of Governor Brigham Young, ex-officio superintendent of Indian Affairs of Utah Territory as contraband trade) at Fort Bridger in the year one thousand eight hundred and fifty three."

Three et ceteras cover a lot of . . . well . . . et ceteras from the dealings over the trading post. Nonetheless, this document is the first and only mention that Jim's goods *were taken by order of Governor Brigham Young as contraband trade*. The word "rent"—also a deft touch—is dicey since the period of Mormon occupation isn't stipulated, nor would Brigham have wanted it to be. Signed by Vasquez and witnessed by John Hartnell and James Ferguson, it closed the book on who controlled the trading post. After Brigham paid up (a real steal), he at last gained his wish—Mormon control of the Green River country.

Two questions remain:

First, who occupied the trading post between 1853 when it was seized and 1855 when it was "sold"?

It wasn't Bridger or Vasquez. Brigham Young University professors Fred Gowans and Eugene Campbell claim "mountain men controlled the post until the spring of 1855 when Bridger returned"—a conclusion based on a "previously unknown" letter that turned up in Mormon church archives and that, as they put it, "appears to answer some of the questions concerning the possession of Fort Bridger from the time of Bridger's escape until the purchase of the fort in 1855."

("Appears" is one of those vague words that belies the absence of fact; "escape" implies Jim's guilt.) The letter, "now available to scholars," they write, is "important in clearing up the controversy of the purchase of the fort," and "should put an end to misunderstandings and false accusations against the Mormon Church."

It does nothing of the sort. The four-page letter (Lewis Robison to Daniel Wells) is reproduced on a single page in *Fort Bridger: Island in the Wilderness* (BYU Press, 1975), its text so small that I had to round up a magnifying glass to read it. In it there's only one mention of mountain men, and it isn't in the context of having *occupied* the post: it's in the context of *selling* the post. They suggested to Jim that he keep it: "All was peace with the Mormons," they're reported as saying in the letter, "and he had better keep the place"—meaning the post. Any inference that mountain men occupied Jim's "place" remains unsubstantiated. As for moon-glow scholarship, go figure.

This much isn't in dispute. In 1854, a year *before* Brigham concluded the sale, several emigrant accounts have Mormons on the spot building a "cobblestone wall . . . 16 feet high and five feet thick." (A plaque placed by the Utah Pioneer Trails and Landmarks Association on a fragment of the remaining wall identifies it as having been built in 1855, the year of the sale, but inflates the price paid to $18,000.) In 1975, the 1854 date was also denied by Gowans and Campbell, who cite as evidence emigrants' bad eyesight, passersby too distant from the post to really get a good look, and mistaken identity (some called the wall "adobe").

Second, on what grounds other than suspicion did 150 men ride out to arrest "Bridger and some of his gang," as Mormon Isaac Haight so colorfully put it?

There was no evidence except hearsay, all of it circumstantial. Gowans and Campbell argue, "There appears to be little doubt that Bridger was guilty of disregarding the decree from Governor Young concerning the selling of lead and powder to the Indians." "Appears to be" and "little doubt" muddy the waters in the absence of fact, and smack of untidy revisionist attempts to make the Fort Bridger story come out right—perhaps to fit a "prearranged program," as the Douglas County sheriff's deputy would say. Other than the arrest order, the Mormon record is almost entirely missing—this from a people whose prophet demanded that accurate records be kept of everything taken, but not everything *undertaken*.

The tarnish on the Utah Pioneer Trails and Landmarks Association plaque at Fort Bridger can be read in one missing date: there's no mention of the most hell-raising year in the post's history, 1853, and no mention that Bridger was run off or fled arrest by a Mormon posse. The plaque makes the Mormon era of the post's history sound like a tea party, not a takeover. That the place was purchased "from

Louis Vasquez, partner of James Bridger," as set in bronze, casts Jim as second fiddle to the events and disguises Mormon intentions. I suggest that Vasquez, vain and pretentious, was easily manipulated by Brigham, which helps explain why he was absent much of the time, especially when the Mormon posse rode in. It also suggests a reason—no more than that—for why Vasquez stayed out of sight until the fracas was over and final payment in hand.

At the famous Scopes trial, William Jennings Bryan said, "Professors must have a theory as a dog has fleas"—about the only thing he got right that long, hot Tennessee summer. Professors Gowans and Campbell fit the description. But J. Cecil Alter, Bridger's biographer, has another theory: "The Mormon leaders greatly feared that the image of James Bridger meant as much to the Indians as Brigham Young meant to the Mormons. Such a domination could be dangerous. Thus the Mormons continued their devious efforts to establish themselves as equal or superior to Bridger."

"Devious" sounds right to me.

• • •

At a local motel, I wrangled an uncomfortable bed at an inflated price, saying "ouch" to both. The landlord gave me a disapproving glance and a testy apology. "Peak season for tourists," he crowed. Another "real steal."

48

All through the story of walking, one comes up against mountains.
MORRIS MARPLES, *SHANKS'S PONY*

[We] began to ascend the dividing ridge between the Colorado waters and the great basin. . . . After camping, Mr. Miles Goodyear came into camp . . . the man who is making a farm in the Bear River valley. . . . There are some in camp who are getting discouraged about the looks of the country. WILLIAM CLAYTON,
JULY 10–11, 1847

I took the route around the south end of Bridger Butte, stirring dust underfoot and heading for Muddy Creek ten miles away. Back on the original Mormon

Trail (the Oregon and California Trails went north toward Fort Hall, Idaho), I was walking a corner of southwest Wyoming known to many Utahns as "the Lost County." Originally a piece of Utah Territory (on today's maps it accounts for the notch at the state's northeast corner where Utah and Wyoming meet), it was struck off and given to Wyoming as punishment for the Mormon insurrection of 1857—Washington's way of slapping Brigham upside the head.

It was a very good day, hot but not too hot, dry but not too dry, windy but not too windy; but by nightfall I was off the track, having missed the Muddy Creek turnoff, no sign of the trail. I camped in a ghost town, anxious all night near four abandoned beehive-shaped charcoal kilns, each pointed on top like a Viking's head gear, one collapsed, three intact, and all rank inside with human defecation and urine. Downwind from these impromptu latrines, a breath of sage ruffled into the tent, furling its nylon. Overhead, the evening sky turned dull as steel wool. Low enough to scratch, it intensified a darkness so deep that I felt I could scoop it out in spoonfuls. Up early next morning, ragged from too little sleep, I stared down the empty windows of Piedmont's two remaining derelict buildings, ramshackle and long gray from the weathers. If ghost towns do have ghosts, they lingered that morning.

I struck resolutely southwest toward Horseshoe Bend, a curve on the map where the road passes a jeep track that looked like an access back to the trail. Reaching it, I walked a half mile to the northwest hoping to regain the Mormon track. Instead, I came out atop a steep ridge with a broad, sway-bottomed valley below, clearly the Mormon route since the transcontinental railroad had followed it. The Union Pacific tracks angled in from the northeast, following the grade to Altamont Siding, in plain view to the west, beyond which the railroad traces the original route for three miles until the rails turn north to meet Echo Canyon. The Mormons had hugged an edge of the Oyster Shell Ridge, yawing southwest before cresting a ridge and entering the Great Basin, emerging not far from the site of another long vanished fragment of Dream—the nineteenth-century boom and bust "city" of Beartown. Discouraged and unable to see any easy way down, I hiked back out to the Piedmont Road.

What to do? Retrace my steps to Muddy Creek or move on? At the moment of decision, I felt a chill. Jack Frost (no fooling) pulled up beside me and crunched to a stop. It was sensible Jack Frost who discouraged me from walking a sweltering summer road that was off my chosen path with his offer of a lift around the Sulphur Creek Reservoir to meet the Mormon crossing on the Bear River. Jack was from California's Sacramento Valley, nosing his way through the Cowboy State on a two-week vacation, fresh from a trip to Flaming Gorge and was now squirreling across back roads in a well-used Jeep Cherokee. Fair complected, he'd lost a considerable portion of hair "to early retirement," and his face, like his pate, was a well-done pink. Jack's easy voice carried an undertone of static, as if his personal AM-FM was a hair off the mark, but, unlike his name, he looked considerably melted since his air conditioner had "give out" and he was heading "in a roundabout way," he said, "to Evanston to get it fixed," all four windows on full draft.

"Where are you heading?" he asked.

I answered without hesitation. "To Evanston," I said. "In a roundabout way."

Somewhere between Piedmont and Beartown, I crossed with Jack Frost nipping at my woes into the fabled Great Basin—land of Brigham's desire. Now in a country where all waters flow into desert potholes and none out, I entered the space that perfectly suited the Mormons in 1847—a vast, scoured landscape where "you can hold your breath and hear absolutely nothing, alone with God in that silence," as physicist Freeman Dyson wrote of it. As hellishly hot as it was that afternoon, I imagined God wasn't around, but more likely back in Farson, Wyoming, cooling off with the "World's Largest Ice Cream Cone."

· · ·

The Great Basin was John Charles Frémont's greatest discovery, a land that John McPhee calls "an ocean of loose sediment with mountain ranges (about 150) standing as if they were members of a fleet." Covering portions of five states—California, Idaho, Oregon, Utah, all of Nevada (a finger dips into Mexico), it contains 220,000 square miles with five distinct "basins" and eight rivers that feed into a hundred or more desert "sinks."

The Northwest Lakes Basin covers much of the Oregon Desert, the Lake Lahontan System and the Central Basin traverse most of Nevada, the Death Valley System dips into Mexico, and the Lake Bonneville System covers most of Utah. Lakes Lahontan and Bonneville, both prehistoric inland seas, festered in bowl-like chemical seeps, the largest remaining saline pond of which is Great Salt Lake, fed by the Sevier, the Weber, and the Bear Rivers. As John McPhee says of this seared country in *Basin and Range*: "Most of it is alive. The earth is moving. The faults are moving. There are hot springs all over the province. There are young volcanic rocks. Fault scars are everywhere. The world is splitting open and coming apart." Brigham and the Mormons were the closest of any people on earth to molten magma.

Jack Frost turned out to be good company, a fellow who enjoyed a full measure of history, no matter who it belonged to. He kindly stopped at the Beartown historical marker, "in honor of the pioneers who passed this spot, July 12, 1847," etc., where I gave a colorful lecture on themes Mormon. Still hot under my collar over Brigham's treatment of Jim Bridger, I voiced my suspicions on the matter. With Jack as judge and jury, I prosecuted the case, gave evidence, and summed it up. Jack did everything but take notes, but there was no storm of indignation in his demeanor, and no banging of his gavel when he adjudicated the case as put by a Canadian interloper. He pronounced judgment quietly, as if the hullabaloo was a ripple on a pond.

"No shit," he said.

. . .

Beartown was originally named Gilmer, founded by timber drivers in 1867, many of them Mormon, who cut and hauled logs from lush stands of pine along the Bear River. In October 1868 several Union Pacific Railroad grading crews showed up and promptly raised a ruckus, changing the town's name on a rising tide of American Dreaming to Bear River City. The population swelled to two thousand, but soon, Wyoming style, "desperadoes and roughs took over." The town's citizens and mails were robbed and "people attacked on the street in daylight." As in the standard western sideshow, "Vigilantes acted and three were hanged," which "led to a riot in which 14 men were killed." All this urban growth and calamity took place in *two months,* which later reminded me of a quip by Emo Philips: "When I joined the New York Public Library, the guy told me I'd have to prove I was a citizen of New York, so I stabbed him."

By December the railroad moved on and the "city" downsized to a "town" again, although the Wyoming historical marker is dubious even on this point, dubbing it "a logging *hamlet.*" Stripped of its stands of pines, the settlement soon disappeared. Jack and I looked around for a boot hill, but the hanged, the harried, and all others snatched by the Grim Reaper in Bear City brawls were nowhere to be found.

Another mile brought us to the Bear River, snaking its way toward the Great Salt Lake. At Highway 150 Jack lost his cool for good, punched the Cherokee, and ran for the deep freeze of any hole-in-the-wall bar in Evanston, a scramble of a town where deprived Utahns and Mormon backsliders can bet on the ponies and make whoopee over full-strength Budweiser.

We parted company over the latter, handshakes all round: Jack went scrounging for a dependable mechanic while I went rummaging for a room with a soft

FOLLOWING THE WRONG GOD HOME

mattress and air conditioning on high, where I showered, chilled out naked on a bed with the back support of a concrete block, then ambled out with every intention of chowing down like a pirate in a restaurant called, I think, The Jolly Roger. Sailing in on what I mistook for an appetite, the food was plenty; but spread out, dinner felt less like a treasure than walking the plank. I picked my way hesitantly around the edge of the heaped plate—a pea or two here, a forkful of mashed potato there, and a slice of chicken for good measure—before I put down both sword and skewer to confront a drowned appetite. Eight bucks worth of "home cooking" languished on my plate. This wasn't nouvelle cuisine where there's nothing on your plate but plenty on your bill: I was confronted by a meal that would have made any member of the All-You-Can-Eat Restaurant Association swoon. What it promised in bulk, it lacked in imagination. My appetite had fallen away, I realized, from *grief*.

In three months, I'd crossed an ocean of plain fare and plenty of it from the Cornhusker State to the borders of the Beehive State, every step of it—café to café—wallowing in bland food, in burgs where menus were as predictable as regret on diners' faces—reason enough why Americans are light eaters—"as soon as it's light, they start to eat," says Art Donovan. American Dreams aren't about *good food:* they're about *eating.*

A thousand miles of greasy spoons had moved me to this hour of desperation. I wanted to *taste* something out of the ordinary, perhaps extraordinary—at least something to make me believe it was still possible. However monotonous our daily bread, you'd think purveyors of *grub ordinaire* might try to dress it up with poetic license, give it a hint of taste, even if they use a smoke alarm as a cooking timer.

• • •

In the naming of its on-the-road fare, Americans are woefully unimaginative. For starters, a hamburger contains no ham and a hot dog no dog. Even in a midwestern nightmare so contradictory as "chicken fried steak," a monotony hangs over the American road diet. Across two states, café and restaurant menus were numbed by a victual literalness: "fried chicken," "T-bone steak," "pork chops with applesauce," "tuna sandwich," "bacon and pancakes," "liver and onions," "beans and ham," "roast beef and gravy." What I wanted was a mouth-brothel.

On the other hand, the British—who, until recently, were not known for cuisine at all—have managed to muster a prodigious imagination in defense of their ignoble fare. "Fish and chips" is straightforward enough, but culinary nomenclature in the United Kingdom slides toward figurative tipsiness in dishes like "soused mackerel" and, from there, to even more creative imaginings in "Star Gazey Pie," "Cousin Jim," "Dressmaker Tripe," "Pig's Pettitoes," "Oxford John," "Bedfordshire Clanger," "Toad-in-the-Hole," "Bubble and Squeak," "Bangers and Mash," "Solomon Gundy," and in one very, *very* unfortunately named alcohol-laced beverage derived not from a lisp but a place-name—"Athole Brose." True, many of these dishes taste awful, but at least they taste *different*.

Brose proved confusing to Rupert Croft-Cooke, who had the courage to write a book, straight-faced, called *English Cooking: A New Approach*, which he penned after World War II when food was scarce and what little there was of it in need of a disguise. Of brose-style beverages, he concluded that the Athole variety is made of milky water from steeped oatmeal, drained and mixed with honey and a gill of whiskey. In the United States, the brose (steeped oatmeal broth) is left out entirely and honey as well, except in flu season, so that in Boston the only remaining democratic ingredient is known as the "Irishman's Breakfast," long my father's favorite meal of the day.

Whatever, the British charm of euphemistically naming its cuisine succeeds in disguising "sausage and potatoes" as "bangers and mash." To a footpad yearning to end culinary monotony in America's heartland, a smattering of light-hearted camouflage on the menu could quicken a failing appetite; something, say, like "Drunken Duck," in which a quacker is immersed for six days in port wine, or "Jugged Hare," in which a rabbit is soaked in something of similar proof. In an American café, you never hear a citizen of the contiguous forty-eight mutter, "Yes, I'll start with the cockie leeky (a soup, not a urinary problem), collops for the main course . . . unless you have sheep's trotters . . . with stuffed marrow, scarlet runners and a gooseberry fool for desert and . . . I almost forgot, wouldn't you know . . . a generous measure of Athole Brose."

· · ·

That night, I slept soundly on the downside of two fingers of George Dickle, ate an unimaginative stuffing of "steak and eggs" at another woebegone greasy spoon next morning, then thumbed back to the Bear River crossing. The cowboy who gave me a lift confided that he'd be atoning for his sins for some time to come, either here or shortly in another life. His blurry eyes kept opening and closing with severe uncertainty, as if the distinction between sleep and waking was going to be made by somebody else at any moment. His name was . . . well, skip that . . . and his wife, he said, "is prob'ly waitin' for me with a rifle. She knows I been seein' another woman."

"Working hard at it," I almost ventured (he was dead beat), but settled on, "If she comes out shooting, stay low and roll."

"I dodged my share in Nam," he said. "What she don't know is it's her sister."

. . .

Arrived at Bear River, William Clayton found "a very rapid stream about six rods wide and two feet deep, bottom full of large cobble stones, water clear, banks lined with willows and a little timber, good grass, many strawberry vines." His "cobble stones" were still in evidence ("about as large as a human head," Orson Pratt noted) and the water clear, but the stream was less than two feet deep, and much less than "very rapid." Pratt caught speckled trout in the river for his dinner.

From Bear River, I headed almost west, covering eight or ten miles at a good clip, huffing along at 6,500 feet above sea level, a pale, golden tint to the mid-morning light, suffused with a deeper green that sprung up from patches of grass with an occasional bright stand of wild flowers. By midafternoon, when a formation known as "The Needles" rose from the landscape—much less magisterial than I'd expected—I felt betrayed by my own imagination. An out-cropping of conglomerates composed of small rocks packed together in a clay-based aggregate, it looked like a row of shark's teeth badly in need of caps, its bite worn down by centuries of weather and its parts tumbled along a trail that drops over its southern flank, hugging its way toward Yellow Creek on the Utah border.

Mormons would have ignored The Needles except that in 1847 Brigham Young came down with "mountain fever" nearby and was forced to lay over in its shade—which meant that he reached the Salt Lake Valley both a day late and a dollar short. An advance party rode in on July 23, 1847, and by the time the prophet showed up the next day, they had already dammed a creek and put in a crop of potatoes. Respectful to their prophet, they have ever after celebrated Pioneer Day on July 24, the day Brigham arrived.

Brigham's "mountain sickness"—the same illness that derailed Clayton and others beyond the Little Sandy Crossing —intensified to occasional ravings, although his fever might have been mistaken for normal behavior to folks who knew him best. When he turned "insensible" for part of a day, someone noticed the change and confined the "seer and revelator" to quarters. Heaving to with a bellyache wasn't Brigham's style (he was seldom ill), but I commiserated since I was as anxious and frustrated as he was to get over the last obstacles to Zion. I rested in a wedge of shadow to consider him ranting through the road noise as cattle, oxen, mules, dogs, men, women, children and chickens slipped past him over the ridge. Moments later, leaving Brigham behind as they did, I started downhill. A band of purple crested the horizon as the Wasatch Mountains rose in the distance. Walls of Zion.

• • •

Across Yellow Creek, I stepped into the state of Utah. Beyond Yellow Creek, the Mormon Trail follows a network of dirt roads and ranch tracks. Next evening I almost walked past another Mormon landmark, Cache Cave, before intuition caused me to turn and look again at what appeared an insignificant sandstone formation three-quarters buried in earth and sage. Resembling a skull buried to crown level with a gaping hole in the forehead, it looked the kind of thing that— if it had flesh on it in 1945—Rupert Croft-Cooke (*English Cooking: A New Approach*) would have recommended boiled and served with a zesty lemon-and-pepper sauce.

The cave's interior was shallow, domed, and narrowed toward the rear—easy enough to understand why folks stashed ("cached") goods and supplies there. Pioneer names crowded its walls, most weathered, but "T. Bush" (in tar), "J. R. Hughes," "J. M. Sherwood," "J. Tolman," "E. Saph," "H. W. Woolcott," "J. Campbell," and "P. D. Dodge" decorated its surface on the afternoon I arrived. On July 14, 1847, Thomas Bullock "sat in the Cave all day," faithfully making a copy of "The Word and Will of the Lord" on Brigham's orders, having noted the cave's dimensions—"36 feet by 24 feet & about 4 to 6 feet high." Fifty swallows' nests cluttered its ceiling, but "upon close inspection," Bullock found them "swarming with bed bugs." "Many of the brethren have engraved their names on the sides," he wrote.

Cool under the dome, I took a nap, head on my pack, now and then opening an eye to watch light crawl up its walls as the sun moved ever lower, the cave my last brush with ghosts of the past, since the remainder of the trail ahead proved almost empty of evidence of the Mormons' passing, much of it under tedious asphalt. Cache Cave was a semicolon in the sentence of the Mormon past and, eerily marooned in space, much as it was when Bullock took his leave. I wasn't about to walk any further that day, but I wasn't about to sleep with ghosts either; so I headed for open space where I could watch the sun go down and packed it in. Darkness closed over lands of Zion. All night I heard traffic slurring along Interstate 80, a few miles north. Going under, I wondered if back in Wyoming a crazed wife had shot her husband.

49

If a man walketh in the night, he stumbleth, because there is no light in him. JOHN 11:10

In about one mile turned round a high bold rock, to the right, following the course of the "Weber River" & camped on the East bank. THOMAS BULLOCK, JULY 17, 1847

Echo Canyon is a drop between red conglomerate bastions through which run the lines of communication that carried both Mormon and Gentile contagion in and out of Zion—the Mormon Trail, Pony Express, Union Pacific Railroad, decaying remnants of U.S. Highway 30 (Lincoln Highway), and Interstate 80. The largest steam locomotives in the world were built to haul freight up its grade.

In 1847 the trail ran down a rocky middle where new engines of locomotion smoothly run today, particularly eighteen-wheelers whose whines bounce off the canyon's walls, constantly repeating its name. On its ramparts (alluvial fan gravels from the Cretaceous period), Brigham stationed the Nauvoo Militia to prevent any intrusion by the U.S. Army into Salt Lake City in 1857. Emerging near the spot where Brigham entered Echo Canyon, I stared down the crush of traffic with genuine dread, having entered the twentieth century again, hesitating but an instant before putting out my thumb. The tracks of the pioneers had vanished, overlaid by steel rails and asphalt ribbon.

The young man who picked me up hadn't been to bed in two days and seemed even more likely to fall asleep on short notice than the dedicated working stiff back in Wyoming who was sleeping with his wife's sister. Jeff Fuller, twenty-four, a geology student at the University of Utah, was returning from a hiking trip in Jackson Hole. Jeff had the ragtag, red-eyed look of an insomniac and was anxious to get home to his bunk in Salt Lake City. Our conversation was equally sleepy, since I was lazily watching our deepening fall into Echo Canyon. When Jeff did talk, it was heated, like a blowtorch suddenly sparking and as suddenly shutting off. He fumed over Utah's ecological horror stories, his anger like flammable bursts of gas, each a flame of high-intensity indignation.

"Would you believe it? The government wants to put a nuclear waste dump on BLM land next to a national park! They're out of their minds! Now they want to put a coal-fired power plant near Bryce Canyon! Get this! Get this! They've proposed a railway through the area to dump waste into the Escalante wilderness! Do they think we're all nuts?"

I thought I was almost sane that day, although my mother-in-law once had reservations, but to avoid further outbursts I kept silent, taken in by the scenery. A sentinel of journey's end, the canyon was magnificent; like dying fire, its ferrous "pudding stone" took on a rusty sheen in the morning sun. Aspen and juniper lined the higher slopes. I asked Jeff what he planned to do after college. His answer was unexpected, contradictory.

"If we survive the Reagan administration, I'd like to go to work for the government."

Encouraged that the first person I'd met since crossing the Utah border was a liberal Democrat, I chose not to disillusion a younger man, finding it discouraging myself that Republicans seem a lot like Al Capone but without the charm. In matters of politics that spring, I agreed with Mort Sahl: "Washington couldn't tell a lie, Nixon couldn't tell the truth, and Reagan couldn't tell the difference."

. . .

At the canyon's mouth, the Mormons turned right at "a high bold rock" (Pulpit Rock), now long disappeared to make room for the railway and highway. Brigham Young, Jr., owned a "ranch" on the site, keeping close watch on who or what was headed in or out of Zion. If anything untoward showed up at the mouth of the canyon, a fast horse was dispatched to Salt Lake City with any needed "intelligence." Young Jr. bought the property from a formidable gent named James E. Bromley, the area's first settler, and promptly laid out a town, Echo City. Each of its avenues—eighty feet wide, running east to west—was named after one of his fourteen wives.

Pete Clark, Box 4, Echo, Utah 84024, owns a piece of the ground where Brigham's boy kept watch, a spot that became the site of a Pony Express station. He was out back in a small corral, next to a red, tin-roofed barn when I stopped by to get my bearings. Pete lives in a neatly framed white house with the mouth of Echo Canyon a vast, ruddy yawn behind, interstate traffic whining constantly from its maw. With a face fissured as the bluffs at his back, Pete wore a rolled-brim white straw hat, his eyes set back under the hat's brim in a half-moon of shade.

"Nothing much left of the old ranch," he said. "Just a few foundation rocks."

Todd and Scott Wimmer, identical twins, lined up to listen to our conversation, arms resting on the white rail of the corral. Soon to be teenagers, they would have been identical in dress as well except for different colored T-shirts. I never knew which kid was which, but assumed the T-shirts were used by Pete to keep them straight.

"The boys come down from Portland yesterday," Pete said, unable to hide his pleasure. "Come down to drive me crazy. We was friends until today."

Both boys grinned.

I asked how long he'd owned the place.

"Fifteen years," he answered. "Brigham's kid held the title for many years. Sold out the last twenty-five acres for two hundred dollars."

I lingered long enough to savor a former sentinel outpost of Zion and shake hands. Pete took off one leather glove to do the honors. Nearby were emigrant graves, "with dates wrote on the headstones," Pete said. If there were, I passed them by. I never asked if Pete was Mormon and he never offered—a second good sign.

• • •

Soon after passing Witches Rocks, an eerie stand of hoodoos still true to Frederick Piercy's 1853 drawing of them, I trudged into the town of Henefer heading for a make-do lunch from the shelves of the local store. On the walk in, parts of the Weber River were plastered with Keep Out notices, long stretches of its water fenced off by a privately owned fishing club—a sure sign that the Mormon communal and economic Dream of "one for all, and all for one" had gone under. On the town's shady main drag, a goat was tied on someone's front lawn, mowing away with sharp, efficient teeth. It watched me pass by with the eye of a paid informer. When I looked back, an elderly woman came out of the house and, watching me with unfeigned curiosity, appeared in deep conversation with her satyric lawn mower.

After lunch, I headed toward the mountains and by midafternoon was well into the foothills of the Wasatch. With purple scarps rising on my right and a new strain on my tendons, I trekked past Broad Hollow, a hummocky hillside where the Donner Party labored toward higher ground in their struggle to cross the mountains and reach the Salt Lake Valley. A cairn marked the spot. By nightfall, I'd arrived at East Canyon Dam where the trail disappears under water but where I was welcomed with smiles all round by the staff of a time-share condo development. A friendly lot, they offered me free bed ground next to a creek (accepted) and an invitation to dine (Dutch treat) at the condo's restaurant, which served summer residents and the crush of power-boaters who were zooming up and down the artificial lake with the intensity of maniacs.

When asked, "Would you like something to drink?" and I answered, "Coffee, please," there was silence—momentary, but telling: I'd stumbled into a nest of practicing Mormons. When I acknowledged that I knew that coffee wasn't their "cup of tea," witlessly mixing the metaphor (tea isn't on the Mormon menu either), they looked at each other and chuckled. Good natured and forgiving folk, they pointed out the restaurant where the coffee, as usual, was hot but tasteless. Made by another practicing Mormon (I asked), it recalled a dig by Abe Lincoln: "If this is coffee, bring me tea; if this is tea, please bring me coffee." It being one of those places where you can order "breakfast anytime," I did, but I wasn't as sharp as Steven Wright who once ordered in a similar eatery—so he says—"French toast during the Renaissance."

·   ·   ·

By noon next day I was lost, having followed the original route south from the highway down a meandering gravel ranch road, where I bathed under a rude plank bridge in a cool stream (the one I'd camped next to the night before) and air-dried in its shade. Unable to find even a crude trail over Big Mountain (the trail in Utah was never well marked), I backtracked three miles to the highway and hauled myself up one asphalt switchback after another until I was thoroughly winded. A day away from Promised Land, I put the tent down for the last time a few yards off the road, rummaging in dim light to set it up.

A midsummer storm rumbled in from the west, echoing off the Wasatch and trembling my ease. Tucked up in the tent, I waited out the thunder, peal upon peal, expecting a crush of water. None came. Instead the storm passed to the south, stirring me from time to time until, restless, I got up and watered the nearest tree. Not twenty yards away, Brigham's wagon had labored over a ridge, a trace of road still there, now used by private landowners to reach their holdings. Under galaxies, I started down its slope, trying to get right with Joseph Smith's version of God.

·   ·   ·

"Once you've heard two eyewitness accounts of an accident," Dave Barry says, "it makes you wonder about history." The Greek historian Herodotus understood the problem: "Many things do not happen as they ought. Most things do not happen at all. It's for the conscientious historian to correct these defects." Happening as they ought, or not, most "things" don't happen in the way they come down to us, and as Herodotus suggests, many never happened at all—which is the constant nag about all histories, especially sacred ones. Even Joseph Smith was bewildered by what happened to him, and many "conscientious historians" remind us that he revised his story from time to time, hoping to get it right. Smith could

FOLLOWING THE WRONG GOD HOME

have been talking for Herodotus when he confessed during a funeral sermon, "No man knows my history. If I hadn't experienced what I have, I couldn't have believed it myself."

The question is this: Which part of the history that formed around him did he believe?

While not "rags to riches," Smith's story—true, false, or somewhere in between—is the American Dream fantasy that begins, as does the story of George Washington, Andrew Carnegie, or Babe Ruth, with this line: "From humble beginnings. . . ." In the seconds before a bullet struck the Mormon prophet dead, it must have seemed that things weren't going "as they ought." Perhaps Smith regretted having encountered an angel. One wonders—can't help but wonder—if some of the Herodotean "things" in his life (the golden plates, say, which came and disappeared with the same angel) ever happened at all or, if they did, in the way he claimed they did. That Smith didn't "blame anyone for not believing" his story is less about *blame* or *belief* than about the steadily unfolding myth trailing behind him like a coat of too many odd colors. In Missouri he once cautioned a crowd about his rise from farmboy to prophet: "I cannot tell it . . . shall never undertake it. You don't know me. You never knew my heart."

But why did he not tell his story—shout it from the rooftops—unless there was something in it that he'd rather not mention? Not the least shy when he started out in New York, he was an American original who couldn't contain his enthusiasm for what had happened to him, a lightning-rod prophet who easily made the transition from "author" of *The Book of Mormon* in its first printing to "translator" in its second. Perhaps—just perhaps—Smith's fecund Mormon Dreaming, formed in the collision between the Second Great Awakening and the Enlightenment, had grown larger than even he could explain away, trussed up into an expanding myth, which, like Manifest Destiny or the American Dream, he could neither escape nor fully comprehend. In his accusation that others "never knew" him is an admission that he never really knew *them*. In his accusation that others "never knew" his "heart," there is an admission that he didn't know it himself.

There's pain in Smith's words, and reading them renders him human. Without insecurity over the events of his own journey (why else would he bring up the subject?), Smith's history might never have caught on, might never had sent autocratic Brigham Young along the road I was now walking in the dark, and might never have accounted for missionaries that occasionally affright the Osage, who probably believes, "if you cross a Mormon with an agnostic, you get someone who knocks on your door for no particular reason." The real "thing" is always subtext, and Smith's life, like the unsettling book that gave rise to his shooting star, floats beneath the surface of an aphotic ocean, its deepest secrets hidden. Smith's ultimate talent—and he admitted it—was never to write autobiography.

Fawn Brodie, a direct descendant of Brigham Young, was the first Mormon to go in search of the real Joseph Smith. A proponent of psychobiography, she provides in *No Man Knows My History* the starting point for all serious students of the life and times of Joseph Smith—except for Mormons. For her scholarly "revelations," she was summarily excommunicated—the equivalent to Mormons of a permanent case of the bends—another sure bet that some "things," as Herodotus reminds us, "do not happen as they ought" and "most . . . do not happen at all."

• • •

Back at the tent, still restless, I straddled a nearby log. The storm long since passed and, having peeled the sky to stars, night was too inviting, so I took up stargazing as Joseph Smith and Brigham had done—literally.

Brigham believed that the God of this universe lives on a planet named Kolob—astronomy seldom mentioned by the Saints. Bruce McConkie in *Mormon Doctrine* describes the celestial orb as the "planet nearest . . . the residence of God." In Mormon lore, this means the planet "nearest the residence of the God of All Gods," near which lies planet Kolob, where the God of our Milky Way—one of many Gods—keeps house. (Well, this God probably doesn't "keep house," but a celestial wife surely does—which also posits the possibility of extraterrestrial maid service.)

Uncharted as yet in the heavens (I checked the Peterson field guide to *Stars and Planets*), Kolob is a vestigial and soft-peddled Mormon oddity. I'm not saying Kolob isn't real, only that there's no way yet to prove it isn't. But I am saying that early Mormons, Joseph Smith especially, were *imaginative* and *creative*. Astronomy, McConkie points out "is falsely supposed" to be "a modern science." Copernicus, Galileo, and Kepler, while notable in the field, are all Johnnys-comelately. Abraham, he asserts, stands "pre-eminent as the greatest astronomer of all the ages"—a statement that upsets the folks at Mount Palomar.

Abraham's understanding of time, space, and the heavens is contained in yet another Mormon text, the Book of Abraham—part of yet another Mormon scripture, *The Pearl of Great Price*, in which "movements and relationships of the sun, moon, and stars; and . . . the positions and revolution of the various sidereal heavens" are revealed. "Translated" by Joseph Smith "from a papyrus record taken from the catacombs of Egypt," it contains "priceless information about . . . the creation . . . not otherwise available in any other revelation now extant," McConkie says. As *Mormon* revelations go, that's true. Smith probably thought he was adding to the Pentateuch, but when his lost papyrus turned up in the mid-1960s in a New York museum, it turned out to be a run-of-the-mill Egyptian funeral oration.

However questionable Smith's skill with hieroglyphics (in 1827 the Rosetta stone hadn't yet been deciphered), *The Pearl of Great Price* and the Book of Abraham give insights into deeper Mormon astrophysics. McConkie is vague about the "sidereal heavens" (pronounced *sigh-dir-ee-ul*), except to imply a Mormon affinity with "starry, starry night," although from the density of some of his prose, I suspect that he was struggling with "black holes."

One could say—and I will—that *The Pearl of Great Price* and Book of Abraham are *proven* frauds, an instance in which Smith overstepped himself and that presents Mormons with a heavyweight problem—one they haven't been able to solve. Trading on his reputation begun in *The Book of Mormon* as a "translator" of "reformed Egyptian," Smith invented the story whole cloth, as any reputable Egyptologist with the papyrus in hand would vouch in a second. But here's the rub: if the Book of Abraham was *proven* a fraud, what can be inferred about *The Book of Mormon*? Fawn Brodie called it "the first example of frontier fiction."

For Mormons on the run, the only option is to assert that *The Pearl of Great Price* and the Book of Abraham were divinely inspired and that the text of the funeral papyrus had nothing to do with what came out of the mouth of a prophet. With one foot in Smith's myth and the other in revisionist history, they run but can't hide. It's *faith* that counts, not *fact*. Translated into Mormonspeak, the papyrus was merely the source of Smith's inspiration and the Book of Abraham was divinely "revealed." (The same claim of "divine revelation" is true of the U.S. Constitution, Mormons claim, and must be so for the followers of Brigham or they couldn't swear allegiance to a country they abandoned in the hope of creating a pure "Zionic" theocracy in Spanish territory outside the borders of the United States.) Of the many religious equations for perfection in or under the stars, one answer is: "Go figure." Or, as Daffy Duck once said, "That makes no sense, and so do I."

• • •

Sleep crept over me like a wasting disease. I awoke once in a sweat, fagged and forlorn. Like the lone forty-niner from Maine who was spotted at Fort Laramie walking west with a bulldog in tow and his earthly belongings in a sack over his shoulder, his passing unnoticed except in a shadowy reference in another man's journal, I'd become a mere footnote to history, proving that history hasn't much to do with the anonymous except to give an occasional, unexpected tip of the hat or a Dream of open road.

50

The most obvious and obscure thing in the world, this walking that wanders so readily into religion, philosophy, landscape, urban policy, anatomy and heartbreak. REBECCA SOLNIT,
WANDERLUST

As we near the mouth of the canyon, there is a small grove of elder bushes in bloom and considerable oak shrubbery. . . . It is evident that the emigrants who passed this way last year must have spent a great deal of time cutting a road through the thickly set timber and heavy brush. WILLIAM CLAYTON, JULY 22, 1847

A half mile from the top of Big Mountain, I hefted Roadmaker one last time, tracing a finger around the "Good Red Roads" carved on its haft by the Osage. A resinous scent of pine was in the air that morning and the indolence July carries when mountain coolness salves the skin. Straddling my stargazing log, I ate a tasteless breakfast of leftovers, pine branches moving above me like slowly dipping fans, sunlight flooding through their interstices and splashing the forest floor. A magpie cackled sourly, joined by two sartorially splendid friends, all chattering for the remains.

At nine o'clock, afoot again, Big Mountain topped out. With it came my first look at the Salt Lake Valley—the same spot from which the Mormons viewed it on July 23, 1847, whooping it up with "hallelujahs" and "hosannahs" all around. Wrung out of hallelujahs myself, I couldn't see the valley: a yellow bedsheet of smog hung over the distant city, blocking my view. Power lines sagged overhead and a microwave relay tower crowded out the summit, while the remainder was scabbed off to make a parking lot and overlook. A commemorative cairn built by "Sons of the Utah Pioneers" made me momentarily uneasy that Roy Rogers's cowboy band had converted to Mormonism and had a hand in building it. But I

FOLLOWING THE WRONG GOD HOME

wasn't the only one who didn't toss his hat in the air on his first view of Salt Lake City: William Clayton was "disappointed in the appearance of the valley."

. . .

"Vapor lock," Herb Madsen said.

On a lip of switchback road, Herb and his wife, Nellie, stood beside an over-heated blue Jeep, its hood sprung open, wheezing for air and water. Behind the Jeep was a boat on a trailer. Skeletal in his essentials, Herb gazed into the engine compartment as if into very, very deep water. Nellie, dressed in purple slacks and a blouse flowered in sumptuous orange, red, and blue blossoms, recognized a lost soul and promptly bore her testimony. I'd been expecting something of the sort, since they seemed puzzled by why a "nonmember," as Nellie put it, had an inter-est in walking Mormon history. Yet, in spite of mutual danger, the Madsens and I chatted amicably for fifteen minutes, enough to learn that Nellie was descended from Lavinia Lee Moulton, who "walked every step of the way across the plains," and that her grandfather was a survivor of the Martin Handcart Company's big freeze near Devil's Gate, Wyoming—hefty credentials for Mormon folk.

"I used to sleep with grandmother in a feather tick," Nellie reminisced. "She'd talk me to sleep with tales of crossing the plains." She smiled a smile that must have broken Herb's prop (he worked for Delta Airlines) and added, solemnly, "She endured," which Herb punctuated with an affirmative nod.

"Grandmother married but went ten years without a child," Nellie said. "She went to the church authorities and asked them to let her husband take a second wife . . . because if he did, she believed she would have children. She had faith and God blessed her. She had five children and the second wife had five, but when her husband stayed with the second wife, her pillow was wet with tears."

"Wet with tears," Herb repeated.

It was only speculation on my part, but it sounded as if the second wife had revived a flagging libido, either that or the second missus, overworked and realiz-ing sex wasn't the religious experience it had been cracked up to be, urged him to spread around his newly found energy. Listening to the Jeep wheeze, I suspected Nellie's grandfather had missed something in his first decade of marital bliss, but that's a skeptic for you. That he chose to stay with his second wife also says some-thing about his first: "a homely face and no figure have aided many a woman heavenward."

. . .

Oscar Wilde—who wasn't a woman's man anyway—commented that Salt Lake City interested him because "it was the first city that ever gave me a chance to see ugly women." Mark Twain made a similar comment, but, coming from Missouri, he had nothing in his background from which to make a trustworthy comparison.

Catherine Bates and Mrs. F. D. Bridges wrote that they had never encountered so many homely women than among the Mormons, and the English journalist Henry Lucy saw them as "atrociously dressed" and questioned "whether any master of the art could have greatly improved their appearance." Warming to his subject, Lucy went further: "It was suggested to the profane mind that women so unattractive, having failed to secure monopoly of a husband, had, with the patient resignation of their sex, finally contented themselves with a share." Obviously, these are the denunciations of jealous men and threatened women from another century, but I know for a fact that there are no ugly women in Salt Lake City—at least, not on the day I arrived. Coming off a three-month walk in which celibacy was required before I could leave the house may have played havoc with my eyesight, I admit; there's so many significant details one misses when depraved . . . sorry . . . deprived.

• • •

Herb Madsen's grandfather was likewise a multiplying gent with three wives and thirty—count 'em—children, all helping to create an exponential growth curve in Utah, which explains why so many people in the state have the same last name. "Family reunions in Utah," someone told me, "should be held in convention centers." Good Mormons, Herb and Nellie had faith their vapor lock would pass. I prayed that they were signed up with AAA. As I headed downhill, Nellie took a parting shot. "We wish you well, Scott. Most of all, we hope you read the *Book of Mormon* prayerfully. I know that Joseph Smith is a prophet and the *Book of Mormon* is true."

That anyone had the gumption to talk about *The Book of Mormon* to a man who spent years studying fiction was . . . well . . . charming. Nellie's was a faith not to be quibbled with, and I admired the Madsens for their kindly interest in the soul of a stranger. But whether or not the book was *authentic, genuine, valid, veracious, credible, believable, honest, unadulterated, unexaggerated,* or *unembellished*— all synonyms of *true*—I didn't ask. Nor did I want to. Messing with other people's Dream is bad news, especially in their territory.

As for *testimony,* while Nellie was a gracious *witness* in the Mormon sense, in another sense, I wondered about such "things" as *evidence, corroboration, documentation, proof, substantiation, verification,* and *authentication.* The fact is, *testimony* and *testimonial* are frequently confused. Nellie and Herb gave me the latter—

a *recommendation, reference, referral, voucher, commendation, honorable mention,* a *blurb* or a *plug.* As gullible as the next Canadian, I'm nonetheless partial to *documentation, corroboration, substantiation,* and *verification.* I won't go so far as comedian Rowan Atkinson, who said of another literary effort, "the book is the best work of fiction since fidelity was included in the French marriage vows," but there are those who do believe it. Religion requires the customer to buy a product he can't see while being convinced it has an eternal shelf life—reason enough why it's turned over to trained salespersons and other missionaries.

• • •

On the downside of Big Mountain, as the last of the walk unfolded, even my notes gained momentum: *Collected two butterflies from roadside, one fresh, one crisp. Lean blonde on a racing bike labors up mountain, passes me on the way down. Says, "I just finished a triathlon yesterday. I feel it today." Motorhome labors up mountain towing car. Stops. Overheated. People from Lake of the Ozarks, Missouri. Retired military. Leased the "beast for an RV year," he tells me. "Seeing the country," she says. Both look as if they've seen enough. Sign on back says, "Recycled Teenagers."*

• • •

To get over Little Mountain, the last hump on the trail, an asphalt road forked toward Salt Lake at another stone cairn above Mountain Dell. Whatever message the cairn had to impart was missing, the plaque either stolen or hauled away for revision. The last Mormon campsite before the Mormons arrived in Salt Lake Valley, Mountain Dell has since become a reservoir, another oversized pond to supply a growing thirst and a developer's Dream. On top of Little Mountain, the road switches back on itself, descending into Emigration Canyon where Brigham locked axles to get Mormon wagons down its steep face.

On the last uphill pull over Little Mountain, manic thirst set in. I tried, vainly, to douse it with Adam's ale. About to enter the land of the abstemious, I was beguiled by an overwhelming desire for a cold one—not in moderation, as Christians say of all good things, but in a self-indulgent, line-'em-up, bottom's up, "I'll say when" kind of way. So close and yet so far from the City of the Saints and its handful of licensed watering holes, high-stepping and eyes on the prize, I almost missed a plain white-on-black sign announcing, blandly *CAFÉ.* It slipped in and out of peripheral vision until my stomach, on alert, registered a protest. Housed in an old hip-roofed garage (vintage 1930s) with an addition tacked on back, the café was quietly, tastefully out-of-the-way. A stubby phone booth hung off the side, and a junked blue and rusty pickup, hood raised to signify final agony, was wedged beside it. A plastic sign tacked to the wall next to the entrance announced: "Dinner Hours 4 PM—10 PM."

I swept in on the wings of appetite. Dark-eyed Bobbie Lewis met me at the door, raven haired and welcoming in faded jeans, watermelon blouse, and sandals. "Sit anywhere," she said.

Bobbie was pretty enough to stop a middle-aged stranger in his tracks, but I was more dazzled by the company she kept. Over the counter on a shelf, left to right in order of fancy dress and price, were fourteen different brews, including a South Pacific lager from PNG Brewing, Papua New Guinea. Decked out in exotic fancy dress, its label was an array of tempting colors with palm trees, a smoky lavender island, and a scarlet tropical bird in the foreground spreading brilliant orange wings. On the purlieu of the Big Dry, I ordered the chill with the flaming fowl and the house "Turkey Bird" sandwich. Eating and drinking feathered foodstuffs, I slipped toward comatose.

• • •

"I ran my genealogy a couple of years back," Vance Keele told me, tucking his crutches back into the corner of the dark wooden booth he shared with his wife, Shirley, and his daughter, Kathleen. "Found out we came from Nantucket by way of an Irishman. My Dad said he could'a died happy not knowing that."

A thickset man with a malleable face that changed with his every intention, Vance had broken his Achilles tendon. "A tough one," he called it, wincing.

Kathleen's four stair steps—two, three, five, seven—sat at a second booth, unusually well-behaved. Army brats, they'd been in Japan for six years, three having been born in the Land of the Rising Sun. "We're home between moves," she said. "Looks like we're headed for Mountain Home, Idaho." The name of their destination was fetching, on a par with Home on the Range, Wyoming, before it sold out to the highest bidder.

I'd watched the Keele clan for several minutes, the adults drinking coffee and talking in muted tones. Mormons, I guessed, since nobody else would have two hands around a cup of Joe trying to act invisible. Loosened up on the orange wings of PNG's scarlet macaw, two birds' worth, I voiced my suspicions.

"You're Mormons," I said. "No use denying it."

Vance broke into a broad grin, held up both hands. "We come here once a week," he confessed over Kathleen's onset of sniggering. "Not all of us are perfect, y'know. We drink a couple of cups apiece. We're open about it."

"Breaking the Word of Wisdom?"

"Testing it, you could say."

I bought all three another round of java. As my mother always told me, "Do good while you can."

· · ·

Around 6:00 P.M., near the mouth of Emigration Canyon, I stopped at Ruth's Diner for a pick-me-up. The dive at the last curve before hitting the city limits was flush with smokers and early diners, Ruth herself having set the tone when the place was an out-of-sight hideaway for nicotine freaks and the terminally thirsty. The coffee was hot and tasteless but the atmosphere enthusiastic. In 1847 Mormon wagons rolled along the creek bed behind the place. Forgetful, I left without paying the bill. Two years later, when I offered to pay for my two cups of purloined coffee, a waitress said, "It's still bad, but I drink it. It must have been real bad two years ago."

Beyond Ruth's, I passed the site where the Donner Party had given up, triple teaming their wagons and hauling misery over a forty-degree rise. Frazzled from cutting through brush along Emigration Creek—a scant two hundred yards from open ground—this reckless act later cost them many lives, creating a nightmare that haunts American history to this day. A communication tower rose above me on the site, along with a couple of high-rise apartment buildings. So broken were the Donner animals from the climb that the party was forced to lay over in Salt Lake Valley for two weeks, losing valuable time, which caught up with them in the High Sierra winter of 1846–47. In the mountain snow they lived and died in dugouts, cannibalizing their dead to survive. When the Mormons struggled down the creek on August 23, 1847, using the year-old Donner-Reid "trace" as their guide, it took less than two hours to clear the brush and enter Promised Land.

· · ·

Arrived a day late because of "mountain sickness," Brigham surveyed the Salt Lake Valley from the first high ground beyond the canyon's mouth, known as the "East Bench." Myth has it that he rose up in his wagon and uttered: "This is the place!" If he'd done the same today, he'd likely have framed it as a question. Although an advance party had shown up a day earlier and already planted potatoes, Utah's birthday party is celebrated on July 24, the day when Brigham made his pronouncement. Among Mormons, it wasn't "the place" until God's anointed confirmed it; but he did and all hell has broken loose on every twenty-fourth of July in Utah since then. Think of it like this: if the Fourth of July is a firecracker in Utah, the twenty-fourth is the explosion of an ammunition dump.

Celebrating the centennial of the Mormon trek (1947) and Brigham's confirmation of Holy Land, the state put up a "This Is the Place" monument close to the site of Brigham's approving thunder. Civic pride being as much vice as virtue in most state-sponsored erections, the monument's surfaces are emblazoned with mighty hymns to Utah history, virtue, industry, and vision—sung with conviction, if too loudly.

Atop the monument stand Utah's Trinity—Brigham Young, Heber Kimball, and Wilford Woodruff. Brigham is up front and center in thigh-high boots (an area of the anatomy he knew a good deal about) with his left leg thrust forward and planted on terra sacred, his arm resting on a stout cane. To his left and right stand his two stalwarts. All three gaze across Zion's sulfuric haze toward the largest human-made hole-in-the-ground on earth—the Kennecott copper mine, one of two man-made objects visible from outer space. The other is the Great Wall of China. When I halted at the monument's back gate, the sun was already slipping behind a mountain range. The monument was closed and a sign advised No Trespassing. I scaled the fence, hoping something incendiary would happen—arrest perhaps, which would have made a barbecue of an ending to the book.

But no inflammatory lawmen showed up. I had the place to myself, an eerie sensation, since the monument was surrounded with every ghost of Utah's past—all in bronze. Washakie, the Mormon's Indian friend and occasional enemy, stared from a littering of other rigid notables. Included in the pileup (the monument cries out for a tow truck) are trappers Etienne Provost and Peter Skene Ogden, Catholic fathers Escalante and Jan DeSmet, and John C. Frémont, all five personages in stiff poses against a granite wall, each looking as if he's waiting for a blindfold and a last smoke.

On the east side, I came across something genuinely moving—a bas relief of an emigrant family toiling uphill, assisting a pair of oxen to haul a wagon up a treacherous slope. Five men lean forward on the same taut plane as the oxen, straining against ropes, muscles humped under their labor. Of all the images on the monument, it's the only one with passion and movement. One horn of the nigh ox is rubbed a lustrous gold where the hands of decades of visitors have caressed it. Yet it wasn't a Mormon ox or a Mormon family, but a depiction of the ill-fated Donner Party stuck in the High Sierras. Dream gone sour.

I left the self-congratulatory pile, clambered back over the fence where I was met by a good Mormon friend and colleague—Jerry Jerome. Two days later, I flew back to New York. Linda and Caitlin, both radiant, met me at the airport and took me "home." Even the dogs, six legs between them, recognized me.

. . .

No sooner had I set foot again in the Empire State than I was asked if I didn't think the Mormons were a "cult." Longtime acquaintances who found out where I'd been for three months looked at me as if I'd boldly gone where no man had gone before. Even the Osage seemed temporarily deferential.

Such is the suggestive power of the word *Mormon* that it took me a while to grasp that it wasn't hesitation with which they gazed upon my now lean and leathery middle-aged form, but fear of doorbells ringing. "Assure me," one well-meaning woman said, "that you won't go around knocking on doors and boring people." When I convinced her my intention was prose not proselytizing, she asked, "They are a cult, aren't they?"

. . .

To set things straight, Mormons aren't a "cult." They are, however, a distinct *cult*ure. (I use *cult*, in italic, not in any pejorative sense, but to denote its frequent appearance in words considered less alarming but having the same root.) So far as I can sort things out, it's mainly fundamentalist types who raise the *cult* issue, having nothing better to do on Sundays but *cult*ivate division and promote a limited worldview, although many jack-Mormons and former Mormons—a close friend among them—point out that Mormons, like Moonies, don't let their own go easily. "Up until a few years ago," he pointed out, "the only way to get out was to be excommunicated," something the LDS Church still does with more questioning intellectuals, those openly gay or lesbian, and "uppity" liberal females, as mentioned earlier. So difficult was it to get "disaffiliated" that several would-be dropouts took the LDS Church to court to get their names off the rolls. "Even today," a friend notes, "getting your name struck off opens up a guilt trip. It's never a clean getaway. Mormons track you down," he says. Indeed, any contact with Mormon beliefs or practices can be seductive and contagious—more about a *mindset* than being *mindless*. But that's true of all appealing myths, religious or otherwise.

Mormons do have *cult*ural oddities compared to other religions, but on the whole they're no less dim-witted than Methodists, Catholics, Luddites, or other American Dreamers. As a *cult*ure, mostly-Mormon Utah has many admirable characteristics—the highest literacy rate in the nation, the largest number of bilingual speakers, and the highest percentage of women college graduates, among others. True, it takes an inordinate number of their young men six and a half years to graduate from college, but that's because many spend two years of enforced celibacy on a Mormon mission and six months catching up on homework before they take to the books again. But calling someone else's tapestry a "cult" is short sighted and mean-spirited. To be honest about it, it's usually some other guy's version of Dream that gives us the shakes, and, considering that, Mormons are no different than the rest of us except, like the honey bee they chose as Utah's symbol, they hive together too close for my comfort. I admit I think they're Goofy, but I'm Daffy. *Cult* is a code word for any movement that threatens the dominant Dream-of-the-Month, and, doctrinal oddities aside, Mormons have always run unfairly afoul of it. A scholar of *cult* history, Philip Jenkins, lays the facts out clearly: "Cults differ from churches in no particular aspect of behavior or belief, and the very term . . . is strictly a subjective one; it tells us as much about people applying the label as it does about the groups . . . it describes."

51

As for me, I shall walk in mine integrity; redeem me, and be merciful unto me. My foot standeth in an even place. PSALM 26

President Young then addressed the brethren on the order of building the City. . . . He hoped to live to lead forth the armies of Israel to execute the judgments & justice on the persecuting Gentiles & that no officer of the United States should ever dictate [to] him in this valley, or he would hang them on a gibbet as a warning to others. He showed the spot where the Ensign would be hoisted & never have any commerce with any nation, but be Independent of all. THOMAS BULLOCK, JULY 28, 1847

In September I returned to Salt Lake City to face the heirs of Joseph. "Cities that are dedicated to making money . . . seldom have much energy left for charm," Bill Bryson wrote of Italy's center of commerce, and, like Milan, Salt Lake struck me as charmless. Numbed by an overdose of commercial zeal, it seemed vacuous and sterile; numbed by an overdose of religious zeal, I felt something of the same "queasy guilt" Bryson felt when first sojourning in the villages of rural England— "a terrible suspicion that any pleasure involving more than a cup of milky tea and a chocolate digestive biscuit is somehow irreligiously excessive."

My fear proved groundless, except that to get a gin and tonic at an upscale hotel, I had to buy the Beefeaters in one-ounce bottles, one at a time, from a mini-state liquor store next to the bar. It was an ingenious scheme to mulct the gullible, and Utah should have never gotten rid of it, since I was charged four times—once for the gin, once for the setup (glass and ice), once for the tonic, and last for the tip. If you brought your own wine, the corkage fee was about as pricey as the Château Giscours '82 you bought at the state wine store and carried to dinner in a brown paper bag. Watching the affluent boozing it up from the same brown bag containers as the homeless put a lump in my throat from thinking about the unconscious blow for equality imposed by the Utah State Liquor Commission; but good Mormons have been in charge of the liquor trade since Brigham opened his first brewery.

On close inspection, any Dream of a holy city had vanished, replaced by what Hendrik Hertzberg describes as "a bumpy custard whose ingredients included urban sprawl, the homogenized consumerism of malls, and fast-food restaurants." Except for decorous older homes on the shaded slopes near the University of Utah that reflect a more genteel past and the shady "avenues" near the state capitol, it was like any other urban wasteland. Undistinguished in its civic architecture and redeemed only by the oddity of its famous temple and the plain-style of the Mormon tabernacle, the city was bloated with the architecture of unintended consequences and tedious Mormon wardhouses. A pen-and-ink rendering of the Mormon Mecca in 1854 by Frederick Piercy is one of the few remaining images of its unspoiled beauty, depicting a serenity and emptiness that suited Brigham and his Saints well.

• • •

Temple Square seemed to me the kind of place where breaking wind could be mistaken for blasphemy, although in no way was the atmosphere unfriendly. "Brothers" and "Sisters" abounded, a well-groomed assembly of working faithful crammed into one city block, each so full of good will and sincerity that I was alarmed that a rash of sentimentality might break out and overtake me like the plague of locusts that devastated the Mormons' first crops. The crops were spared by hordes of seagulls from Great Salt Lake who gorged themselves on "Mormon crickets," eating until they regurgitated their dinners before going back for fifths, sixths, and sevenths. Regarded in Mormon myth as divine intervention, the event is commemorated by a monument to the seagull, now the official state bird—appropriate, I think, to a people who scavenged a home as the gulls scavenged grasshoppers.

The art in the visitors center—quite a lot of it—was numbing realism, portraying Old Testament prophets and New Testament disciples with a vigorous sampling of the Tribes of Israel thrown in for good measure. Noah, scorned, was there, ridiculed by his neighbors, the unfinished ark behind him like a rack of barbecued ribs. Abraham and Jacob were illuminated under soft-textured light, and a youthful Daniel interprets Nebuchadnezzar's dream, while, on another panel, enfeebled Isaiah sits at a table, writing of the birth of a messiah with a seventeenth-century inkpot and a quill pen. Nearby, the angel Gabriel explains the Annunciation to Mary.

Merging into New Testament themes, child Jesus appears in the temple astounding priests with his wisdom. Baptized by John the Baptist on another panel, he is soon teaching parables in the hills around Judaea, fishing for men by the Sea of Galilee, riding into Jerusalem on a donkey, soon to be tried before Pilate, scourged, and crucified. In all these tableaus, Jesus appears in dazzling white, not a leftover crumb or a drop of fish oil on him.

In 1985 Joseph Smith was also there, beginning with his vision in the "sacred grove" near Palmyra, New York, an event he was uncertain about himself, having taken the event through several revisions. Heavenly personages float above the boy, bathing him in extraterrestrial light. On another panel, he receives the golden plates from the angel Moroni. Not so much as a lingering doubt or a troubling question shimmers in any of the illuminated tableaus on the walls in the visitors center. Mute certainty hangs over everything, no need for further discussion.

Yet I was moved by a people's faith, and might have been moved even more if Christ in His glory hadn't been Jesus with Nordic features. Still, a potentially blue-eyed Hebrew isn't worth arguing about in a state where Scandinavian names and faces turn up like pennies in pocket change, people from those countries having been one of the more productive fields for early Mormon missionaries. Seven of the fifteen buried at the Willie company gravesite in Wyoming were Scandinavians.

Offered a free copy of *The Book of Mormon* by a volunteer, I declined, having two already in cold storage, although when asked if I'd read it, I admitted I had. Purely as a critic, I also mentioned that evil triumphs over good, which makes for a refreshing change of plot.

• • •

In July 1998—thirteen years later—I went back to Temple Square for another look at the Mormon story, hoping to round out some details for this book. To my astonishment, the Joseph Smith murals had vanished. Gone was the young Mormon prophet blessed by visions. Gone were the golden plates revealed by an angel. Old Testament and New were still on the walls, but the scenes of Joseph Smith's visions, the angel Moroni, and the golden plates had vanished. By 1999, when I returned again, they still hadn't showed up. Nowhere evident on the walls of the visitors center was the unique Mormon Dream that prompted my walk. Like a stone slipping into deep water, it had disappeared, replaced by something nearer to the tepid Protestantism it despised and sought to replace.

"What happened to the murals of Joseph?" I asked my guide, a young woman from Bilbao, Spain, who spoke flawless English.

"They were here when I visited with my family a few years ago," she told me, "but they replaced them."

"They haven't been replaced," I observed. "They're gone. What did they do with them?"

She brushed her already neat hair more neatly, raised her arms in a gesture of ignorance, adjusted the nametag on her blouse, smiled like the gifted and beautiful young woman she was. "I guess they stored them."

Out of sight, out of mind is my guess.

·   ·   ·

No matter what nonbelievers say, I know *The Book of Mormon* was inspired. "Think of the obstacles it faced," I read in a thirty-three-point summary entitled *A Most Convincing Witness.* "Its creator had to be between 23 and 24 years old," not a college graduate (most college graduates can't write, but, fortunately for history, Smith had only three years of formal schooling), and had to complete 239 chapters in eighty days—"54 of them about wars, 21 about history, 55 about prophecy, 71 about doctrines, 17 about missionaries, and 21 about the mission of Christ." By this exceptional account, Joseph Smith added 180 proper nouns to the English language, compared with Shakespeare's 30, and included "the history of two distinct and separate nations . . . covering a period from 600 B.C. to 421 A.D."

None—I repeat—*none* of this convinced me of any *divine* "inspiration"—not even the author's assertion that "thousands of great men, intellectual giants, and scholars" had subscribed their "discipleship to the record and its movement even to the point of laying down their lives"—nothing convinced me, I repeat again, until I came to this: "You must find someone to finance your book with the understanding that he nor you will *ever* receive any monetary remuneration from it. *You must sell the book at cost or less.*" I completely broke down. Only a miracle could account for it. If you don't believe me, ask any publisher.

• • •

Sadly, the visitors center had the aura of a well-appointed mortuary, so I trudged to the famous Mormon Tabernacle. Its pioneer architecture is stunning, beautiful in simplicity and masterful in structural ingenuity. Inside, sans famous choir, I was allowed to hear perfect acoustics as the famous pin dropped, but, more important, I felt the thunder of lost apostolic voices. Here, Brigham castigated Gentiles, stormed the bastions of a conventional Christianity, defended "the principle," and gave the finger to Uncle Sam.

Across West Temple Street, in the Church History Museum, Mormon leaders stared out of publicity stills. These were the "General Authorities." With few exceptions, most were elderly men who looked as if they had vital signs but rather wished they hadn't. They were kindly looking and humble, the type my mother called "gentlemen," obviously well-mannered and obsessively neat atop the Mormon Dream—the Dream that early chose *community* over *individuality*, the heritage that I admired but that seemed to have turned from sounding a golden trumpet to semilabored breathing.

Too much *authority* worries a Canadian, tending to suggest limited points of view and demands for conformity, but a *general authority* is even more alarming. If we must have authorities at all, I'd prefer mine *specific*. I turned to another visitor and whispered, sourly, "Who would want a judge to sentence someone to ten years 'in general'? Or a doctor telling you, 'generally speaking, you've got something bad. Nothing specific, you understand, but I'd count on six months at the outside.'"

She scurried away as if a cat was loose among the canaries, who, as we all know, have but one song and loudly sing it.

• • •

I saved the famous Mormon Temple for next to last, walking around the entire walled city block that encloses it, pacing the final steps around my journey, stopping at last in front of its grand portal. Off limits to Gentiles, it guarded its secrets like a pharaoh's tomb. Out front, a photographer was snapping wedding pictures, two couples having been "sealed" within its walls for "time and eternity," each couple waiting its turn for the shutter to freeze them in yet another Mormon family history. They were beautiful young people, but they seemed to be going Dutch treat. Stepping into eternity with each other, they were no more or less plastic looking than all newlyweds, but an undertone of awful seriousness, like a coat of gray primer, lay behind smiles for the camera.

I wanted to offer a friendly Gentile's advice, tell them everything would turn out all right if only they remembered that marriage is a kind of friendship sanctioned by the police. To Mormon brides I'd offer Kathleen Norris's wisdom: "There are men I could spend eternity with—but not in this life." To grooms a truism from George Coote: "No woman ever shot her husband while he was doing dishes"—or taking out the trash, for that matter. Sadly, no video cameras are allowed inside a Mormon temple, so with no reruns, there's no chance for a Mormon husband (or wife) to play the tape backward and watch himself walk out a free man.

But it was all so *forever*, their leap of faith into marital outer space, everything depending on whether they believed the God of this world lives on a planet called Kolob—well, not really—but that Joseph Smith, among billions of sentient beings across the eons, had alone been handed the keys to the Kingdom of God, his way the path, destination assured, providing you didn't take a road less traveled or, mixing metaphors, rock the boat. Then I remembered Red Martin in the Ponderosa Bar in Elk City, Nebraska, saying, "I'll take a green horse any day over a Mormon. You can't break a Mormon." I was glad for the horses.

Over the great front portal of the Salt Lake temple is carved "Holiness to the Lord," as it was on the Mormon temple at Nauvoo. I sympathized, of course, but didn't waver. The line above the temple door was not the line A. W. Kinglake hoped to see on all churches: "Important if True." It's *ifs* that matter.

. . .

On Second Avenue, a short climb from the main door of the Mormon Temple, the Lion of the Lord lies under a stone slab enclosed by a plain wrought-iron fence in a shady corner of a postage-stamp lot known as the Young Family Cemetery. Next door, crowded against the property line, is a two-story, redbrick apartment house whose occupants look from their back porch over the grave of the second most important man in Mormon history who also happens to be the most important man in the history of the intermountain West. Over the wall in the southeast corner, on the day I visited, one of Utah's homeless had set up camp, ten feet from the remains of the man who saved the Church of Jesus Christ of Latter-day Saints; who organized the settlement of Idaho, Utah, Arizona, and parts of New Mexico; and who wrestled the U.S. government to the mat to preserve his people's right to worship as they wished.

By his choosing, Brigham was buried in a plain pine box, eventually surrounded by a clumping of wives, but how many are buried with him is unclear since several of the graves are unmarked. Nearby is a bust of the prophet, which gives the impression that, in spite of the solemnity of his steady gaze over assorted spouses, he never denied life from the neck down. Unlike the murdered prophet he adored, he was better equipped to be a leader and a tyrant, both necessary qualities to lead a people out of a wilderness. Like Nellie Madsen's grandmother, he "endured," willing his people to do the same.

Although tourists swarm at Temple Square—six million a year—the cemetery was empty. Nor is Brigham's grave much advertised; the Lion of the Lord laid out with wives laid on is perhaps prone to open old wounds or draw unwanted attention. I paid my respects, but couldn't get shuck of my nagging questions.

Whatever happened to the spontaneous, imaginative, and creative juices of Joseph Smith, Jr., a man with huge appetites and astounding Dreams—the genial prophet who loved wrestling with the boys, who cavorted with his maid and other men's wives, who was inspired enough to Dream an evolving, indelible faith out of his New York farmboy's head? What happened to the energy, the inspiration, and the fecundity of his all-American life? What caused so innovative a faith to turn bland, perfectly manicured, so uniform and uniformed? What turned it from a church of prophecy to a church with a prophet?

No ready answers at hand, I sauntered down to the southeast corner of Temple Square to look at something set in concrete—the USGS marker from which the intermountain West was surveyed. Less about ordering of Mormon faith than ordering of Mormon land, it was from that Salt Lake City corner that most of the West's ranches, farms, towns, lots, and back yards were laid out. Set in stone but not in dogma, the marker is the point from which Mormon Dreams were lost or found and are likely to be lost and found again. Around me a city teemed, traffic seething past a statue of Brigham in the intersection, his broad Yankee back to the temple with an arm outstretched as if blessing the commerce that drifted into the distance down Main Street.

Standing at the pumping heart of the Mormon body, I deduced what was missing—the curious absence that H. G. Wells observed in Joseph Conrad: "One could always baffle Conrad by saying 'humour.'" A touch of irreverence was needed to relieve so tedious a sincerity. "Call me old fashioned," Edna Everage once said, tongue in cheek, "but I'm a deeply religious woman. I firmly believe there is something Up There and I'm sure most women do from time to time." "In Utah," Artemus Ward once quipped, "all the pretty girls marry Young."

FOLLOWING THE WRONG GOD HOME

Epilogue

One thing I have learned over the years, is that your impressions
of a place are necessarily, and often unshakably, colored by the
route you take into it.

BILL BRYSON, *NOTES FROM A SMALL ISLAND*

Bill Bryson is right, of course: impressions of place, like intimations of people, politics, or faith are indelibly altered by the route we take toward them. All destinations have roads leading to an interior geography of imagination (poetry), intellect (philosophy), or belief (religion). Whether we stop in our tracks to pray five times each day facing east (Islam), follow the Noble Eightfold Path (Buddhism), trek to the sacred Ganges for a dip (Hinduism), wander yingly and yangly (Confucianism), revere the Exodus out of Egypt (Judaism), or walk in the footsteps of Jesus (Christian), "faith" is always "the substance of things hoped for and the evidence of things not seen." But faith carries no collateral at the local bank, where it's "Dream on" unless you can put up the farm.

If Manifest Destiny eventually became a synonym for American Dreaming, it's also become a synonym for "hit the road, Jack." Mormons were fellow American travelers, no matter what their beliefs, and nothing catches the sense of nineteenth-century movement better than the gold *rush* of 1849. Its themes of restlessness and escapism have been steadfast American favorites from Mark Twain to Jack Kerouac and William Least Heat-Moon. When Americans say "opportunity," they mean, "let's get moving," and Janis Joplin meant to say something like that when she sang, "Freedom's just another word for nothing left to lose." Most Americans riding the tide of Manifest Destiny had "nothing left to lose," Joseph Smith and Brigham Young among them. So they hit the road.

Historically, Americans take to the open road to solve their problems, most often leaving behind one unexamined Dream and taking up another—Mormons and "pioneers" no exception. Both the Smith and Young families skedaddled from Vermont to upstate New York when hardscrabble farming overcame them, and their subsequent moves westward—divinely revealed or not—followed the basic pattern. Whether for *community* or *individual* opportunity, the Dream is three parts "get up and go." Even Henry Thoreau—who seldom left home and never moved from his snug village of Concord, Massachusetts—caught the bug: "Eastward I go only by force, but westward, I go free," he wrote. "The western horizon stretches uninterruptedly toward the setting sun, and there are no towns in it of enough consequence to disturb me."

It's the "me" that's worrisome in Thoreau's manifestly destined words, a one-syllable refrain that's as familiar now as it was then, and which turns up in Broadway musicals—"Don't fence *me* in," for example. Brigham Young wanted to build a boundary around a Mormon kingdom of *us* against all comers—and might have succeeded but for one of his own, James Marshall, who plucked a gold nugget out of the waters at Sutter's Mill near Sacramento.

• • •

Somewhere on my walk, I woke up to the notion that early Mormon genius occurred at junctions—places where their road forked—New York, Ohio, Missouri, Illinois. But American Dreams are born rolling. When Mormonism reached its final destination in Salt Lake City, its arteries began to harden. Following Brigham's lead, it turned defensive and exclusionary, unable to sustain its early creativity, barricading its territory through extensive western settlement, ever wary of "Gentiles" who crossed its real or imaginary borders, and all the while feeding on a psychology of persecution that its most recent prophet is trying to shed. Minus forks in its road or another Joseph Smith to fire its imagination in Utah, its creative juices evaporated like the Great Salt Lake into an all-but-unpalatable brine.

Experimental or *imaginative* aren't words that come to mind when describing contemporary Mormons or their faith. *Pragmatic* does, and a considerate and generous pragmatism is a hallmark of Mormon identity. In that, they are a people set apart. Never a religion of the blind leading the blind (Brigham saw to that), it seems a religion of the bland leading the bland.

• • •

Mormon Dreams strike me as more in keeping with the observations of Reverend Charles Maurice Davies than the sermons of John Donne. In the 1620s,

FOLLOWING THE WRONG GOD HOME

Donne attracted the most common and most noble of people, both types packing London's St. Paul's Cathedral on Sundays to make a full house. Thomas Bacon wrote that Donne's fans "sat, or even stood, undisturbed, except by the murmurs of admiration, sometimes by hardly suppressed tears," and Izaak Walton—who would rather be fishing but couldn't tear himself away on the Lord's Day—described Donne as "a preacher in earnest, carrying some to heaven in holy raptures." Of Donne's sermons, John Russell maintained, "everything about them seems to come from a vanished world—the idiom, the vocabulary . . . the labyrinthine but perfectly balanced phrasing, the gigantic long-echoing metaphors. We shall never [again] hear anything like them."

Which is where, in case you're wondering, the Reverend Charles Maurice Davies comes into the picture. Interested in London's heterodox faiths in the 1870s, Davies made it a point to seek them out and listen to their exponents. This is his account of the Mormons: "Some twelve or fourteen gentlemen were arranged in a semicircle on the stage, sitting in chairs like a troupe of pious Christy Minstrels, and they kept on making speeches, one after the other." Reverend Davies recorded no electric metaphors in use among the dozen or so Mormon elders on the stage, one of whom was Brigham's barber, a fact that the learned divine considered hair-raising. "They spoke of persecutions," Davies said, "and how it was sufficient to say of a man, 'He's a Mormon' to exile him from the pale of respect."

There you have it: John Donne droning on in "perfectly balanced phrasing" and fourteen Mormons merely droning on.

· · ·

Thirteen years after I walked the Mormon Trail, I asked a long-standing and gifted friend, Chris Chester, to define the American Dream. A spare, well-muscled man in his forties, Chester's middle-of-the-back dark hair and Rasputin-like eyes give him a hypnotic, medieval caste. Quirky as the Osage, he's equally adept at literary detail, although less prone to come from shadow into sunlight unless he's dragged.

"It's our individual as well as collective belief that everything will always get better simply because we're Americans," he said without blinking.

Driving east that August across the golden pancake of Kansas, a geography of flat where a driver might swear his axles were up on blocks, so seemingly changeless is the land's surface, he'd transformed himself into Crèvecoeur's "American farmer."

"Repeat that," I demanded.

"About the Dream?"

"Yes."

"It's our individual as well as collective belief that everything will always get better simply because we're Americans."

"Why not *better and better*?"

"I'm not into hyperbole today." He squinted into the Kansas afternoon, Dream's "fruited plains" spread out all around us. "Do you believe it?" he asked, eventually.

"Dream or definition?"

"Take your pick."

"There's no such thing as *collective* belief," I countered, trying to get off the hook. "Belief is a personal thing. What you believe may be similar in ways to what I believe, but it's never the same. You were born here. You're in a better position to define it than I am."

"So you accept my definition."

"Yes. It just isn't mine." Frankly, I didn't know what mine was and I still don't. But I know this: Americans like to think their tunnel vision is the one with the light at the end of it.

Chester grimaced, turned momentarily owly. "Sweet Jesus, is that the best you can do? You've lived here for forty years."

He was right. I considered carefully, then paraphrased—and badly mangled— a line of Margaret Atwood's, a fellow Canadian. This is it corrected: "We are all immigrants to this place even if we were born here: the country is too big for anyone to inhabit completely, and in the parts unknown to us, we move in fear, exiles and invaders."

"You're still avoiding the issue," Chester said.

"I'm sorry."

"Don't apologize," he said. "Canadians apologize for everything . . . even themselves. Just answer the question. What's your definition of American Dream?"

"Canadians have opinions. I have an opinion."

"Which is?"

As Kansas's vast pancake rolled under our wheels, I considered again. "Dream is the myth we invent to keep spooks at bay," I said. "Anybody who claims an American Dream . . . has simply forgotten it was first somebody else's. It came by way of Liverpool, County Cork, the Highlands, Copenhagen, Stuttgart, Dieppe, Hong Kong, Calcutta, Africa . . . everywhere, for Christ's sake. A nation that lays claim to it doesn't own it and never did. It was borrowed from the common well of human *hope*."

"That's better," Chester said, "but not what I had in mind . . . and certainly not *better* and *better* as you seem to think all Americans want it."

"What did you expect?" I asked.

"Some *Canadian* humble pie," he answered.

At that moment, although we'd been friends for thirty years, I began to suspect Chester of American Dreaming. So I shut up and let the matter drop. On the walk to Utah, it was Dream's compulsion that escaped me, not its false promises.

Back home, in the quiet of my study, I discovered something akin to Dream's source in the "great darkness" that Margaret Atwood puts into the mouth of Susanna Moodie (*The Journals of Susanna Moodie*) when Moodie first entered Ontario's nineteenth-century forests, and why I still cling to it like a survivor on a raft.

> It was our own
> ignorance we entered.
> I have not come out yet.

But Robert Penn Warren, an American Dreamer himself, said it best: "The dream is a lie, but the dreaming is true."

American Dreamers [For the Record]

Lewis Archie is still on the "home place" near Glendo. Heber Springs still runs, although Lewis's tank is "leakin' a bit." We had a good conversation a while back, but he was "getting hard of hearing." Turns out Mrs. Archie, who was away the day Lewis and I had dinner on the ranch, is a writer. She has a fine story ("To Leave This Place") in *Leaning into the Wind*, published by Houghton Mifflin. Lewis is seventy-three, "in fine health," and still running cattle. His daughter lives across from him now, but his son has since rented out his log home. They seldom hear from the foster children they raised.

Allen Atkins died in Genoa, Nebraska, possibly the town's best-known and most beloved citizen. A neighbor told me he died "from the complications of old age," but I think he carried a Pawnee's broken heart with him for much of his life. The museum he founded remains in the old bank building (First National Pawnee, I call it) and is actually known as the Genoa Historical Museum. The Indian school (now a national historic site) is being rebuilt as a cultural center to tell the story of what happened there. It's also the site of an annual powwow and reunion in which descendants of its students shake their rattles, dance, and drum. In an act of reconciliation, several hundred boxes of Pawnee bones were retrieved from the State of Nebraska and Smithsonian Institution and were buried at last in Pawnee sacred ground.

Bob and Donna Ballard turned up unexpectedly when I walked across South pass again in June 2002. I thought they'd disappeared into the sagebrush for good. I was signing myself into a Bed and Breakfast in Atlantic City, Wyoming, when the pert woman taking my credti card said, "I know you." Turns out she did indeed, so Bob and Donna and I held a back-slapping reunion in the tidy establishment they now own but are hoping to sell so they can get on with retirement. Bob is as lanky and "western" as the day we met and Donna still turns an eye. One of their boys showed up to say "howdy." Turns out, Bob was a friend of "Wyoming Bob" Lieberenz. An outfielder with a good arm could hit "Wyoming Bob's" cabin from the front yard of the Ballards' snug B & B, although the road to it now sports a gate and a "Keep Out, Private Property" sign.

Wally and "Buzz" Bozak keep a tight grip on the Redwood Motel in Genoa, Nebraska. Neither plan to retire until "the only option is Valley View," Buzz says. She and Wally have several grandkids, including two by Holly, the pretty daughter who delivered my spaghetti dinner during a downpour. Living in a small town, Buzz gets peevish when she gets calls from city slickers asking if the Redwood Motel has "carpeting, television, and showers." She cackled, "I tell 'em we've got dirt floors, an outhouse, and if you need to clean up, there's a hose out back." When I mentioned I was a grandfather, Buzz said, "My god, now you've got to sleep with Grandma!"

"Buddy" and Mary Brisco headed for warmer and drier climes, an acquaintance told me. They now live in New Mexico, but I haven't located them. Since he's moved to the land of the OK Corral, it's a good bet that "Buddy" is still packing a piece.

"Chicago Bob" left the Windy City feet first, I was told. In October 2000, a waitress in the Atlantic City Mercantile in Wyoming remembered him. "His ashes went to the Winds," she said. She meant the Wind River Mountains, and, eating an order of barbecued ribs, it pleased me to think of him, minus metal detector and firearms, blowing across the big land he'd hoped would always "show color."

Bill and Joan Cioni are together but living separately. In 1999, at age sixty, Bill had a massive stroke and is now in a permanent care facility. He found a new job soon after we met outside Fremont, Nebraska, and was at work in Omaha when the stroke paralyzed him. Joan waits tables at a gambling house and eatery. She sometimes takes their two grandchildren fishing at Fremont Lakes. For what it's worth, my short time with Bill and Joan was a treat. Like too many good folks, they were dealt a bad hand.

Pete Clark spends most of his time these days in Arizona and New Mexico. He rents out the house on the property once owned by Brigham Young, Jr. I visited with Pete recently at his daughter's place in Echo, Utah. He still has the look of a horse trader. "Hell, I don't remember you at all," he said, "but then I'm prone these days to forgetful."

Dallas Coder never left Gothenburg, Nebraska. Last I heard, he works for the railroad. I tried calling him three times, but we could never hook up. The last message on his message system was, "I'm sick. I been laid off."

Steven Combs, DDS, still treats poor, wayfaring strangers from the same office in Scottsbluff, Nebraska. As for my dental record, he assured me he'd look it up in his inactive files. An avid pilot, he flies a single-engine plane, treating folks to an occasional flight over parts of the Oregon Trail. His business card no longer uses the image of a molar.

Ellis Countryman, who was "all bunged up," has left his pain behind. What happened to his place near Oshkosh, Nebraska, I haven't found out, but if there's any relatives of his in the great beyond, I hope they take him out to a heavenly chophouse and let loose some fire ants. Of course, Ellis may have gone in another direction and is all fired up about other things. Ellis's name—*Countryman*—resonates what's best about the United States, both promise and hope rolled into one. As he put it, "You think I'm jokin' don't'cha?"

Pauline Cunningham is going strong, but the indomitable *Fern Minnie McManis* is riding further ranges, no doubt checking for errant New Yorkers. Ranching near Broadwater, Nebraska, suits Pauline just fine. The "two Mormons and a pioneer"— perhaps the most revealing statement of the walk—will always have a permanent resting place on the McMannis-Cunningham spread.

The Deputy Sheriff in Douglas County who fretted about "government conspiracies" has moved on. I thought it might have been to somewhere in Idaho, since conspiracy theories run deep in that state. But I was wrong. He's "gone to another county," I was told when I contacted local authorities. I did get his telephone number, but I'm a liberal and frightened to make the call. After all these years, I remain grateful for the lift he gave me and now realize that he wasn't a wing nut short of a firm grip, but just another leftover of the American Dream.

George and Marge Dodds must be on the road again. They aren't listed in the Columbus, Nebraska, phone book. I still have George's manzanita-wood belt buckle and it still shines like polished stone. I keep it on my desk.

Nancy Dunn sold the hog farm after *Richard* died unexpectedly from a heart attack in September 1999. He was fifty. Two years earlier, they tore down their farm buildings and completely rebuilt, expanding their herd to 660 sows. Nancy now lives in Lisco and works as a dental hygienist.

Charlie Evans hung up his guns for good in August 1997. That June, he was still playing Buffalo Bill in the annual Nebraskaland parade, although he "hadn't rode the old horse for several years," his son, Stan, told me. Mrs. Evans died soon after Charlie. Before he took his last ride, Charlie sold his Piper Cub airplane. Stan runs the ranch now, but Charlie's memory, costumes, beaded vests, and black boots are thriving in the Lincoln County Historical Museum.

Kate Freeman, the woman who accosted me on the tracks near North Bend with a milkshake, is no longer listed in the North Bend, Nebraska, phone book. The Chamber of Commerce and the city offices operate from answering machines. I left my number, but nobody called back.

Merlin and Judy Frenzen farmed together until Merlin died in 1992 at the age of fifty-two of "a fast-acting cancer probably caused by too much exposure to pesticides." The boys are grown and have families. As for my erstwhile nocturnal guardians, Chip died of old age, herding strangers to the end. Cujo "went off with one of the boys." Judy has another blue heeler and lives "a half mile south of the farm near Cedar River."

Margaret Garhart closed her café in Fort Laramie, Wyoming, in 1998 and converted it to a home for herself and Harald Peterson. In 1991, Margaret had emergency bypass surgery. A year or so later, a frozen turkey fell on her foot and crippled her for a spell. She lost her husband in 1985, and soon after her oldest son fell off a roof and "was instantly killed." Otherwise, she says, "we're all pretty good." Harald is now fifty-two and "singing in the church choir." A while back, he got the idea to become a Boy Scout, but, as Margaret says, "I had to explain he wasn't a boy." The scouts took him anyway. Margaret has a sign on the front door of the former café that reads, "Old Customers Please Knock."

Ted and Charlotte Gottsch have retired and "are doing some traveling." Their three oldest sons are married and gainfully employed. Cory, the eleven-year-old who brought me the fried mushrooms and invited me to talk at his elementary school, is now twenty-seven, an "over the road truck driver," and a single parent. Ted and Charlotte have ten grandchildren and two great-grandchildren. Charlotte writes, "everytime it's mushroom season or go for a walk, we see you camped down there." I thank them again for the use of their back forty and for one of the most memorable days of the walk.

Mark Hattan disappeared into the sunset heading west from Independence Rock, Wyoming, but he made it to the Hattan family reunion in Oregon—this from a letter I later received from him. I kept looking for Mark in Fruit of the Loom commercials, but he didn't turn up in my least favorite underwear. The afternoon I spent with him on Independence Rock was grand.

Jim and Kathleen Harris have almost remodeled the old farmhouse they moved into outside Genoa, Nebraska, on Saint Patrick's Day in 1975. They now have ten grandchildren. "We feel really blessed," Kathleen says. Knowing Jim and Kathleen, the grandchildren are equally blessed. Jim retired in January 2001. Kathleen left the Genoa Public Library and became the director of a United Way advocacy program for persons with disabilities in Columbus, Nebraska. On the phone, she still has the voice that smiled when she talked.

Ray and Adeline Houdek live on the Nebraska home place where I first discovered Adeline's "help-yourself kitchen," although Adeline writes "our family of 10 (6 girls and 4 boys) have left home." The daughters have scattered, and Ray has retired "but helps his sons farm." They have 31 grandchildren and "2 step great-grandchildren." Adeline enjoys baby-sitting, flowers, and gardening. I'm betting Ray still isn't a fan of Ronald Reagan.

Alice Howell stopped writing for *Buffalo Tales*—the official publication of the Trails and Rails Museum (formerly the Buffalo County Museum) in 1999. "I kind of had to give up," she told me recently from her apartment in Kearney Manor where she was recovering from injuries sustained in "an auto wreck." From 1972 until 1999, she was active in Buffalo County history, and she was as helpful and polite on the telephone in 2000 as she was in 1985. She still thinks some Mormons are "reformed."

Jim and Florence Hughes have passed on, and the home place near Glendo, Wyoming, was sold to their grandson, Ron Lockhart. If Ron is as kind to strangers as his grandparents and he or his wife can cook as well as Florence, there's a bright light at the end of their tunnel.

Clifford Kizzire left first-class for the big mailbox in the sky on March 29, 2000. He died of Parkinson's disease and is buried in Lyman, Wyoming. His wife lives in the old post office (there's now a new one), and the plant jungle is still inside. In October 2000, I visited with her, sitting on the same stool as I had in 1985. Mrs. Kizzire is a kindly woman, as Clifford was a kindly man, and I apologize to both of them for my next comment. Granger, Wyoming, is still the most godawful place I've ever seen, and I'm glad Clifford finally made it out of town.

Wyoming Bob Lieberenz went south permanently three years after we met, still traveling with his buddy, Old Forester. He died in Wamsutter of pneumonia complicated by liver disease, and his ashes were scattered near Atlantic City. Turns out that Bob was a squatter and didn't own the land on which he built his rustic cabin, but he surely loved it—junk and all. A year after his death, I went back to take a look at the place he called home. The gate was locked, the junk still scattered, the cabin forlorn and empty. I miss him.

Ted Long is as productive in the art world as ever, his work in many private collections. "I'm still working on western themes," he recently told me, "a lot of it on Lewis and Clark," having covered "their whole trail except for a little piece in the east." Turns out it was the mouth of the Wood River in Illinois, a place the Osage and I visited one January when the Mississippi had frozen over for the first time in years. His buffalo have passed on. Ted's work is represented in galleries in Tucson and Scottsdale, Arizona; Jackson Hole, Wyoming; and near his summer home in Ennis, Montana.

Herb and Nellie Madsen wrote to me not long after the walk: "that was the highlight of our East Canyon trip to visit with you there at the side of the road. We were able to coast down to the bottom of the mountain where we got the car trouble taken care of." Why didn't I think of that?

"Pepper" and Elfriede Martin have moved to warmer climes, I suspect. I couldn't locate them when I went searching the Broadwater, Nebraska, phone listings. Anyone that does a total stranger's dirty laundry and leaves a basket outside his door full of essentials for soaking sore feet are truly Samaritans. God bless 'em, I say.

Marvin and Irene McGinn haven't slowed down much. Irene says, "we're still working like we're twenty-nine." Mike is running the farm, but Marvin says "the farming is none too good." The McGinns continue to lease land for summer cabins along the Platte River (there's now sixty-one of them), and Marvin tends them in the off-season, drifting across the old Mormon campground as he drifted across the Union Pacific tracks with his wary eye on a stranger with a blue backpack in 1985. Freights still rattle the house as they rumble pass.

Albert and Marjory Nietfeld, on whose property I camped by the Laramie River at Fort Laramie, Wyoming, have gone with the flow. Albert and Marjory's laughter is what I remember most, and I assume some jackasses still think that the oval racetrack Dwight Walker graded with county equipment in 1927 is where the soldiers at Fort Laramie exercised their horses.

Stan Nohre's last known address was Palm Beach Road, Dickinson, North Dakota—the last a state known for its annual winter deep freeze. Palm Beach Road suits Stan's dapper image, but a North Dakota street address where the likelihood of palms is as out of focus as the Dream must be related to a developer who skipped town after leaving his forwarding address on a street sign. If Stan hasn't gone to his final reward, he isn't in Torrington, Wyoming. I hope he's in Las Vegas holding a straight flush.

Susie Oldfather, the extension agent who gave me a tour of the grassland near Fullerton, Nebraska, gave up on bankers, divorced, went to medical school, and is finishing her internship in Omaha. She reclaimed her maiden name, Susan Schuckert.

The Osage remains a Missouri fixture, continuing to weave his own incredible word magic. For a while we had a falling-out, and I once thought I recognized him from a description in a pamphlet from the Wyoming Fish and Game Commission: "Three weasel species occur in Wyoming: long tailed weasel, short tailed weasel (ermine), and least weasel." I was wrong, of course, and we've since made up. I'd like him to know that his spirit did reach Utah before me and that it was an easy thing to let Roadmaker lead the way. Without it—or the Osage's friendship—I might never have made it at all.

Norman Park continues to ride the range on the Dumbbell Ranch near Devil's Gate, Wyoming. Now seventy-three, with his broken hip mended, he's back in the saddle; but his wife advised me I had the story wrong. Norman didn't fall off his horse. "The horse rolled on him," she said. Contrary to my first impression, Norman doesn't like prairie dogs. "The Greenpeace people screwed that for us," he said. "Took all the good poisons away." As for the ranchers who donated the land on the condition that Independence Rock would revert to the original owners if any commercial development took place, the rest stop and interpretive center turned out "kind of agreeable."

Nick and Rose Ponticello are holding their own at the Covered Wagon souvenir shop on the old Lincoln Highway near Kearney, Nebraska. It opens for customers on demand. Nick is still running every day, but when I called, he couldn't remember his age, so he asked Rose. "Eighty-three" she yelled, her voice still alarming. Somebody shot up the place (a drive-by) a year or so ago, but Nick and his neighbors have managed to get things back in shape. He's still the "unofficial basketball coach" at Kearney State. Pootsie, their belly-dragging dachshund, died two years after I came by, and Rose told me they have Pootsie-Two, now thirteen. Nick says I can come stay at his rental apartment anytime.

Glenn and Jean Putnam have disappeared into their anticipated retirement. Everything I know about the oil business (and much of what I've learned about hospitality), I learned under their generous care near Guernsey, Wyoming. I'm sure Atlantic-Ritchfield owes a great deal to Glenn for keeping its crude flowing. Every time I get my oil changed, I think of Glenn and Jean. I hope they've kept on pumping.

Bob Rathburn checked out of the Super 8 in Casper, Wyoming. When I stopped by in 1998, nobody could remember where he and his wife, Bernice, went—although I'm sure Bob took his barbed wire collection. That summer, I also checked for the golf cart I'd dumped under the culvert near Independence Rock. It was still there—along with two drivers, a wedge, and a putter. Just foolin'.

Lewis Ray keeps on stuffing it. His beard has turned white, but his taxidermy shop in Casper, Wyoming, advertises, "Moose or Mouse, Just Drag It to Our House." *Doug Slee* went into the taxidermy business for himself, but closed up shop after four years. Lewis had a run-in with a twelve-foot Burmese python a few years back. "That critter ate twelve pigeons a day. Kept 'im in a big damn cage. One day I went to give 'im water and 'tuk my hand, pulled me into the cage, and wrapped hisself around me." Ray got one hand free and cut "his head off with a huntin' knife." Two customers came in and had to unwind him. "That snake went to the dump," he said.

Charlie Roemer died of cancer in Columbia, Missouri, in the 1990s. A few years after my walk, he ran for Boone County assessor and lost. I keep his election poster on the wall of my study. His hopeful smile and good cheer is what I remember most. On a visit to me, he left a necktie, so after his death I cut out the tie in the photograph and tied the real tie in its place. My favorite photo of Charlie is at a Mormon monument in Garden Grove, Iowa, where he's wearing my pack and leaning on Roadmaker—the day he was driving me to Omaha. Charlie was one of two persons to heft my pack; the Osage was the first. The pack was last used in October 2000, when I walked a section of the trail in Wyoming. Charlie's ghost tagged along.

Joe and Loretta Santin—the generous folks with whom I attended the Palmer, Nebraska, high school play—recently had to put their house up for sale. Both live in a "resthome" in Grand Island, Nebraska. Loretta (77) is in the "advanced stages of Alzheimer's disease" and Joe (80) has Parkinson's disease and suffers occasional dementia, their daughter-in-law told me. The farm is now leased out.

Steve Senteny lives with his folks in Mitchell, Nebraska. "His eyes are real bad and he's hard of hearing now," his mother says. He has a job washing dishes at the Pizza Hut. Fifty-one, he faithfully rides his bike, but his motorcycle license has expired.

Jim and Vera Sillasen built a new home "northwest of the old place" near Keystone, Nebraska, in 1991. The house in which I first tasted the delights of home-canned chicken and beef was bought and moved twenty miles to the shores of Lake McConaughy where it's been refurbished. They "make do" these days with more equipment but less help come haying season, although they still punch cattle on horseback. "You couldn't get Jim off this place with a tractor," Vera says. She continues to "put up" recently deceased critters in quart jars. The fine brass bed I slept in when I walked onto their place never made it to the new house and Vera can't remember what happened to it.

Benny and Helen Stave are keeping the faith in Fremont, Nebraska. They've moved into a new town house for seniors. Benny is eighty and Helen seventy-nine. Helen says they're "older and slower" and have "our share of troubles." They both remember the desperate stranger they picked up before the big storm hit, and Helen saw the hand of God working for my salvation as well as theirs. "The Lord blest us mightily," she says. I believe it.

John and Shiela Syotas sold the Odessa Bar in Odessa, Nebraska. On the day I called to check on the level of rowdiness and hell-raising, the new owner couldn't hear me for the noise in the background. It was 10:30 in the morning. *Todd Gant* has disappeared, he told me, after I yelled my questions into the phone. So has *Nekiia*. When I told him I was writing about his bar, he said, "Are you sure you got all your marbles?" When I replied "No," he said, "Well, then, do you want to buy this place?"

AMERICAN DREAMERS   399

Jack and Carol Wegner are still down on the farm near Palmer, Nebraska. Jack recently resigned after twelve years on the Palmer School Board, much of it as its president. When I talked with him after many years, his first question was, "Are you still eating your asparagus raw?" The B&S Bar in Worms where we raised hell is now called The Night Crawler, but the beer still flows, and Jack still sings for weddings and funerals and is active in the local music scene. Carol still has her grandmother's brass bed that, said Jack, "is yours anytime you come by." I plan to take him up on it.

"Ike" Winkle was not only the most gentle but also the most endearing man I met while walking the Trail. He came as close as anyone to a life well and generously lived. If there's an American Dream, Ike's in it. He weaves in and out memory, especially an image of him seated at a table by the window of his Lingle, Wyoming, home, poring over my trail maps. There's no listing for him in Lingle now, but he's listed in memory and wherever he is, in this world or the next, I hope he's driving "Big Pink," his hand-painted Nash Rambler.

Charles Wood, so far as I know, is still raising Muscovy ducks in Gibbon, Nebraska. So far as I know, he's still eating them.

Nellie Snyder Yost died of pneumonia in January 1992. Her best-known book is *Buffalo Bill: His Life and Times.* Frank Lydie, her husband, fell over dead in the bathroom a year earlier when the big Mississippi riverman's heart gave out. Nellie completed her gruesome story about sadistic Annie Cook, her daughter Clara, and the shameful mistreatment of folks on the country "Poor Farm." *Evil Obsession,* Nellie's last book, was published the year Frank died.

And, finally, *Scott and Linda Chisholm* moved to Paradise, Utah. Both became Catholics and Democrats as a matter of public service.

A Note on Sources

I make no pretense about being a historian, although I am a reader of history. I read widely and compulsively. In creating and constructing *Following the Wrong God Home*, I foraged in many disciplines and genres, including history of the American West, natural history, literature (British and American), ornithology, law, American Indian studies, medicine, politics, and religion. As readers will discover (or have already discovered), I have a connection to the story of the Mormons and their Dream and, as a Canadian, a suspicion of American Dreams in general, including Mormon ones.

Many of the authors I read over the several years it took to write the book are widely known: in several cases, their books are referenced in the text. Where they are not, a well-versed reader will see the shadows (no more than that) of many historians from Leonard Arrington (*Great Basin Kingdom*) to John Keegan (*Fields of Battle*). Arrington's book is, perhaps, the best book ever written about the early Mormon economic experience in the West and describes what amounts to a "third world" view of the Mormon kingdom in the making. But as I began writing with the American Dream in mind, another book of his, written with Feramorz Y. Fox and Dean L. May, *Building the City of God*, provided a source of information on Mormon "community" that helped ferment a raw mash of ideas that later distilled into these pages.

The writings of Francis Parkman, Wallace Stegner, John D. Unruh, Jr., Bernard De Voto, Frederick Merk, Ray Allen Billington, Everett Dick, and Robert Bruce Flanders also temper this book, as well as those of Irene Paden, Fawn Brodie, Juanita Brooks, Linda King Newell, and Valeen Tippetts Avery, among many others. Particularly helpful were Philip Jenkins's *Mystics and Messiahs: Cults and New Religions in American History* (Oxford University Press, 2000), Lawrence Foster's *Religion and Sexuality* (University of Illinois Press, 1984), and Marquardt and Walters's *Inventing Mormonism* (Smith Research Associates, 1994).

Two university presses with indelible interests and publications on the American West, its history, politics, people, and places find a ready expression in the book—the University of Nebraska and the University of Oklahoma. Much of my "general understanding" of the West I learned from the pages of their publications, especially Oklahoma's American Exploration and Travel Series, from which several extracts appear in the text.

My working library (3,500 volumes) for this project on the American West, the Mormons, and natural history was close at hand and widely scoured over the years, as were several volumes of the WPA guides to the states. I have used these materials, not to make a historical monograph that gets Mormon or American history straight, but to write a readable, creative, and hopefully engaging piece of nonfiction rife with personal conjecture, deliberate barbs, and unapologetic inferences. That I'm an expatriate Canadian only increases the excitement of taking potshots at will.

The epigraphs at the beginning of each chapter, as well as those quotations embedded in the text, reflect my association with trail diaries, general literature, travel writing, and nonfiction from Sir Richard Burton and Frederick Piercy to John McPhee and Bill Bryson. The three principal Mormon journals I used were those of William Clayton, Appleton Milo Harmon, and Thomas Bullock.

In 1985, before Signature Press (Salt Lake City) published its unexcelled edition of Clayton's journals, I came across a 1921 copy (obviously expurgated) published by the Clayton Family Association and the Deseret News, the last an arm of the Mormon Church. Clayton's quotations are taken from that copy, which I carried with me to Salt Lake City. In no way is it to be considered the final word. Will Bagley's edition of *Pioneer Camp of the Saints: The 1846 and 1847 Mormon Trail Journals of Thomas Bullock* (Arthur Clark, 1997) was a mainstay, as was a now scarce 1946 publication by the Gillick Press, *Appleton Milo Harmon Goes West*, edited by Maybelle Harmon Anderson. A shelf of overland journals and diaries, Mormon and non-Mormon, helped round out the geography and emotions of overland travel in the two decades before the coming of the railroads.

But the most important source of all was the human voices of American Dreamers I encountered daily. This is their story referenced, more than history footnoted.

Index of Towns, Places, and Landmarks

INDEX OF TOWNS, PLACES, AND LANDMARKS

Winter Quarters, Nebr., 11, 14–15, 37
Winters, Rebecca (gravesite), Neb., 204–206
Witch's Rocks, Utah, 365
Wood River, Nebr. (town of), 110–12

Wood River, Nebr., 112–11
Wurms, Nebr., 101

Yellow Creek, Utah, 362
Young, Brigham (gravesite), Utah, 383–84

INDEX OF TOWNS, PLACES, AND LANDMARKS